9.50 (Title II) ERS 10-66 (Strickland)

THE ARCHAEOLOGY OF CRETE
AN INTRODUCTION

Biblo and Tannen's
ARCHIVES OF CIVILIZATION

Vol. I:
Evans, Sir Arthur, *Palace of Minos at Knossos.* 7 vols.
Vol. II:
Pendlebury, J. D. S., *The Archaeology of Crete*
Vol. III:
Childe, V. Gordon, *The Bronze Age*
Vol. IV:
Sayce, R. U., *Primitive Arts and Crafts*
Vol. V:
Seymour, Thomas Day, *Life in the Homeric Age*

THE ARCHAEOLOGY OF CRETE
An Introduction

by

J. D. S. PENDLEBURY
M.A., F.S.A.

FORMERLY CURATOR AT KNOSSOS
FORMERLY DIRECTOR OF EXCAVATIONS AT TELL EL-AMARNA

With 50 Plates, 53 Text Illustrations and 24 Maps

BIBLO and TANNEN
New York
1963

Reprinted with permission of Methuen and Company

BIBLO and TANNEN
BOOKSELLERS and PUBLISHERS, Inc.
63 Fourth Avenue   New York 3, N.Y.

Library of Congress Catalog Card Number: 63-18049

Printed in U.S.A. by
NOBLE OFFSET PRINTERS, INC.
NEW YORK 3, N. Y.

TO
MY WIFE

Contents

Plates

AT THE END OF THE VOLUME

ix

Unless otherwise stated these plates are from the Author's photographs

Illustrations in the Text

* Drawn by Miss Money-Coutts.
† Drawn by Mr. J. T. Pinion.

Maps

Drawn by Mr. W. H. Bromage

Abbreviations

A.J.A.	*American Journal of Archaeology.*
A.H.N.E.	*The Ancient History of the Near East.* H. R. Hall. 4th edition.
Annuario.	*Annuario della R. Scuola Archaeologica di Atena.*
Arch.	*Archaeologia. Miscellaneous Tracts relating to Antiquity.*
'Aρχ. Δελτ.	*'Aρχαιολογικὸν Δελτίον.*
Arch. Anz.	*Archäologischer Anzeiger.*
Ath. Mitt.	*Athenische Mittheilungen.*
Boll. d'Art.	*Bolletino d'Arte.*
B.M. Cat.	*British Museum Catalogue*
B.S.A.	*Annual of the British School at Athens.*
„ *Sup.*	*Supplementary Papers,* 1, 1923. *Unpublished objects from Palaikastro,* I. R. M. Dawkins and others.
B.C.H.	*Bulletin de Correspondance Hellénique.*
C.A.H.	*Cambridge Ancient History.*
C.G.B.A.	*The Civilization of Greece in the Bronze Age.* H. R. Hall.
C.I.G.	*Corpus Inscriptionum Graecarum.*
C. of A.	*The City of Akhenaten.* Two volumes. Egypt Exploration Society.
C.O.I.	*Communications of the Oriental Institute of Chicago.*
'Eφ. 'Aρχ.	*'Eφημερὶς 'Aρχαιολογική.*
Festos	*Il Palazzo Minoico di Festos.* L. Pernier.
Fimmen.	*Die Kretisch-Mykenische Kultur.* D. Fimmen.
Head.	*Historia Nummorum.* B. V. Head. 2nd ed., 1911.
J.E.A.	*Journal of Egyptian Archaeology.*
J.H.S.	*Journal of Hellenic Studies.*
Liv. Ann.	*Annals of Archaeology and Anthropology in the University of Liverpool.*
Mallia.	*Fouilles de Mallia.*
„ *Ecrit.*	*Ecritures Minoennes.*
Mon. Ac. Linc.	*Monumenti dell' Academia Lincei.*
Mon. Ant.	*Monumenti Antichi.*
Mus. It. Ant. Class.	*Museo Italiano di Antichità Classica.*
Pachyammos.	*The Cemetery of Pachyammos.* R. B. Seager. University of Pennsylvania, the Museum. Anthropological Publications, VII, 1.
P. of M.	*The Palace of Minos.* Sir Arthur Evans. Four volumes and Index.

xxi

Pashley.   *Travels in Crete.* R. Pashley. 1837.

Πρακτικά.   *Πρακτικὰ τῆς Ἀρχαιολογικῆς Ἑταιρείας.*

P.T.K.   *The Prehistoric Tombs of Knossos.* A. J. Evans, from *Archaeologia,* LIX.

Pseira.   *Excavations on the Island of Pseira.* R. B. Seager. *University of Pennsylvania, the Museum. Anthropological Publications,* III, 1.

Rend. Linc.   *Rendiconti dell' Academia Lincei.*

Rev. Arch.   *Revue Archaeologique.*

Rev. Et. Anc.   *Revue des Études Anciennes.*

Sphoungaras.   *Excavations in Eastern Crete, Sphoungaras.* E. H. Hall. *University of Pennsylvania, the Museum. Anthropological Publications,* III, 2.

Spratt.   *Travels and Researches in Crete.* T. A. B. Spratt.

Studies.   *Studies in Early Pottery of the Near East.* H. Frankfort. Royal Anthropological Institute, *Occasional Papers,* 6 and 8.

Svoronos.   *Numismatique de la Crète Ancienne.* J. N. Svoronos. 1890.

T.D.A.   *The Tomb of the Double Axes and Associated Group, etc.* A. J. Evans, from *Archaeologia.* LXV.

Trans. Penn. Univ.   *Transactions of the Department of Archaeology, Free Museum of Science and Art, University of Pennsylvania.*

Τυλ. Μιν.   *Τύλισσος Μινωϊκή.,* from *Ἐφ. Ἀρχ.* 1912.

T.V.M.   *Tylissos, Villas Minoennes.* J. Hazzidakis.

V.T.M.   *The Vaulted Tombs of Mesará.* S. Xanthudides.

Vrokastro.   *Excavations in Eastern Crete, Vrokastro.* E. H. Hall. *University of Pennsylvania, the Museum. Anthropological Publications,* III, 3.

Introduction

I HAVE tried in this book to give some account of the culture of Crete from the earliest times down to the Roman Age. While for the prehistoric period the ground is covered with an infinitely greater wealth of detail in Sir Arthur Evans' *Palace of Minos* yet that work is in the mere nature of the case primarily concerned with Knossos, and where on so vast a site excavation and publication have gone hand in hand it has been impossible for the author to avoid returning to an earlier period when, in the interim between two volumes, fresh evidence has come to light. To treat the subject in historical order is essential. Glotz's method in his *Aegean Civilization* is to take each topic, architecture, pottery, &c., separately and to trace its development right through without reference to anything else. This treatment makes it impossible to obtain a clear view of the culture of any particular period, for we must be able to assess the historical value of such facts as an improvement in architecture coupled with a decline in pottery in the same epoch.

Since this book is concerned with the material aspects of Cretan archaeology, such general topics as the Minoan language and religion are rather summarily treated in a separate chapter which seeks to sum up our knowledge of the civilization of the Bronze Age.

For post-Minoan Crete we are dependent on specialized studies and excavation reports, and it would seem time to try to summarize the results. Since Crete at this period shares the general Hellenic culture, it will be sufficient to point out her local peculiarities.

With regard to the question of the nomenclature to be adopted for the various prehistoric periods there is no question that in the present state of our knowledge it would be absurd to confuse matters by altering the arrangement, originated by Sir Arthur Evans, of nine periods, Early, Middle and Late

Minoan (E.M., M.M. and L.M.) I, II and III[1]. Admittedly recent research seems to show that both M.M.II and L.M.II were practically confined to Knossos and Phaistos and that it might be better to call M.M.1b and L.M.1b M.M.II and L.M.II respectively, but that would merely mean that a mass of important literature already written would be thrown into confusion, and after all the names are mere labels and of no value in themselves. One day perhaps we shall be able to talk in terms of dynasties and regnal years, but until then the present system cannot be bettered. It must, however, be allowed to be elastic. Because L.M.1a begins at Knossos at a particular date, that is not to say that provincial towns, such as the Kastellos above Tzermiadha in Lasithi, discarded all their M.M.IIIb vessels on the same day. So too, while we admit that all over the Near East the Bronze Age falls into three main periods, we must guard against insisting that the Helladic and Cycladic Periods must be exactly parallel to the Minoan. We must allow the possibility that the Neolithic Period in Crete overlaps the Proto-dynastic Period in Egypt and that Early Helladic may overlap into Middle Minoan. Meanwhile, until we have got something better to put in its place the terminology which has acted so well for so long must be kept, and the more subdivisions we can make in it the better.

I have unrepentantly used the term Late Helladic I, II and III for Mycenaean I, II and III. L.H. is more convenient than Myc, it does not attempt to ram the name of a city down the throat of a country, and, as we shall see, we must have some distinction between Crete and the Mainland, so L.M. will not do.[2] As I say these names are only labels they have no intrinsic magic of their own.

[1] Certainly there would be nothing to be gained by adopting the suggestions of M. Franchet in his introduction to Hazzidakis' *Tylissos Minoenne*. He, with insufficient knowledge, acquired on a flying visit to Crete, based an inferior system of chronology for the island apparently on that of prehistoric provincial France. Of his criticisms of the work of every one who had been to Crete before, the less said the better. Nor is Åberg's sweeping division into Prepalatial, Kamarais and Late Minoan anything but a retrogression. See note at the end of the introduction. As Frankfort, *Studies*, II, 125, n., says, none of the alternative schemes alters the sequence of the remains in any way and therefore they do not add to our insight.

[2] We can talk of XVIIIth Dynasty work without implying that the Pharaohs of that Dynasty did it themselves. So too all we imply by L.H. work is work done in Hellas during the Late Bronze Age.

Orthography and the transcription of modern Greek names is a problem. I confess to inconsistency. Ancient names I have transcribed direct in the ordinary way. With modern names it is more difficult. B is pronounced *V*. *Γ* is pronounced right at the back of the throat, like the Arabic *ghain*, so that on the mainland it becomes *y* in front of the thinner vowels. In Crete, however, it is then thickened into a French *j*. *Δ* is pronounced like *th* in then. K in Crete behaves like an Italian *c* and is pronounced like our *ch* in front of the same vowels. X is a guttural *kh*, but in Crete becomes the Italian *sc* in front of the same vowels. The true soft consonants *B*, *G* and *D* are only obtained by placing a nasal in front of the corresponding hard consonants. Thus *μπ*, *γκ* and *ντ*. This nasal is actually heard in many parts of Greece even when it begins a word since the sounds cannot be pronounced without its help, but in Crete—and not only at the beginning of words—there is an adenoidal tendency to drop the nasal sound. Thus you hear Adones for Antones. A*υ* and *ευ* are pronounced *af* and *ef* in front of a hard consonant, *av* and *ev* in front of a soft one or a vowel. The names then will be transcribed as near to this pronunciation as possible, *β* as *v*, *γ* as *g* (a compromise), *δ* as *dh*, *μπ*, *γκ* and *ντ* as *b*, *g* and *d* at the beginning of a word and as they are written in the middle, except in the case of a few foreign names like Mirabello and Frankokastelli ; *αυ* and *ευ* as they are pronounced. *ει*, *ι* and *η* are very nearly interchangeable and I have used the form most commonly met with in the island even where, philologically, it is incorrect, as in Psiloriti and Elaphonisi. The rough breathing is invariably omitted in modern Greek.

But in a few cases a Latinized or other form is universally recognized and it would be pedantry to write Krete or Xanthoudhidhes. Juktas, also, is by now almost always written for Giouktas or Gioukhtas.

With regard to Egyptian names I confess that to me forms like Tuthmosis, Amenophis and Cheops are as bad as the practice of calling Zeus Jupiter. Thothmes, Amenhotep and Khufu are no farther from the contemporary pronunciations and have seen good service. To call Senusert Sesostris is worse, for Sesostris to the Greeks was the conqueror, the hero of the exploits of Rameses II and others.

I have tried hard in the following pages to keep fact and theory apart. A theory, honestly stated as such by its original propounder, is too apt to be used as a fact by his successors until it passes into a basis for fresh theories. Petrie's (in those days) justifiable theory that certain vases found by him at Abydos were of Aegean origin has passed, in archaeological quotation, through the ' Petrie's suggestion that . . .' stage to ' the Early Minoan pottery found by Petrie '. Even now the fallacy lingers on in spite of Frankfort's authoritative denial.[1]

Foreign connexions in particular present problems of especial difficulty. The positive dating of the Bronze Age Periods in the Aegean depends entirely on foreign contacts— mainly with Egypt.[2] Sometimes this is simple, as for example when objects bearing the name of Amenhotep III and Ty are found in L.H.iii deposits at Mycenae and L.H.iii vases are found in the city of their successor, Akhenaten, in Egypt, or when a M.M.ii vase is found in a XIIth Dynasty grave and a XIIth Dynasty statue in a M.M.ii deposit. But in the early periods we have to rely on the evidence of vases of hard stone found in Neolithic or Early Minoan strata or unstratified. These vases may be, and certainly were, kept for years, since they are practically indestructible and always useful. Further-more, we have no proof as to when they were imported into Crete, since they were equally prized in Egypt. If we find a middle predynastic vase still in use at Tell el-Amarna in the XVIIIth Dynasty and in the Royal Tomb at the same place a diorite bowl of Khafra of the IVth Dynasty, it is evidently very dangerous to try and date an E.M. stratum by a proto-dynastic vase found in it.

Local imitations of foreign objects are safer since people do not go on copying something which no longer exists.[3] The clay vase from Agia Triadha, which imitates in shape the baggy alabaster vases of mid-XVIIIth Dynasty and in painted decoration the bands in the stone itself, is better evidence that L.M.i is to be dated to the sixteenth and early fifteenth centuries than are the porphyry vessels that E.M.i is con-temporary with the Late Predynastic Period. But even here we must be careful. At first glance the ivory figurines from E.M. deposits in the Messara are obvious imitations, if not imports, from Upper Egypt of the Middle Predynastic Period.

[1] *Studies*, I, 105 ff.

[2] In the following pages the accepted chronology is used, i.e. Dynasty I, *c.* 3300, but see note to chronological table on p. 300.

[3] This seems to me to disprove Frankfort's theory (*Studies*, II, 140 ff.) that ' Minyan ' ware in Greece is an imitation of the Trojan silver vases which were no longer available.

It is only on the roundabout assumption that they are actually traceable to a backward North African branch of the same race as that which made the predynastic examples that they will make sense.

One would imagine that actual pictures of Minoans bringing objects as ' tribute ' to Pharaoh would be good enough evidence for those objects being contemporary, and so it is at first. Senmut and User-Amen show such pictures in their tombs at Thebes, and very good portraits they are, both of Minoans and of L.M.i objects ; but a generation or less later Rekhmara and Menkheperrasenb also chose to decorate their tombs in the same way and by this time the artists had begun to get certain types for foreigners—one can almost imagine them having wall sheets showing typical men of Crete, Retennu, Naharin, &c. From that it was a short stage to the tomb of Amenemheb, where the artist merely drew ' foreigners ' and gave them names at random.

For comparative dating in Crete itself pottery is of course our chief criterion, and the duration of the periods discussed above is determined by changes of style. Naturally everything is based on Knossos, for not only was that the first and most important site to be excavated but also at Knossos alone is the series complete. But, as has been said, we must always be prepared to accept divergencies from the Knossian series, particularly on the smaller sites. The process of disentangling the various styles and assigning each to its period has been a long one, indeed it is not yet finished. Many people seem to think that over the whole site every period was represented by a neat deposit immediately overlying its predecessor and underlying its successor, separated from each by a nice floor level. This is very far from the case. At a site like Knossos, which was continuously inhabited for millennia, older structures become incorporated into new schemes and absolutely pure strata are rare. In some areas a whole period will be missing and must be filled in from elsewhere. Evidence from stratification and from style must go hand in hand. It is fortunate that Knossos was excavated by two men who realized this.[1]

So, also, it must be recognized that the styles and periods often slide almost imperceptibly one into the next. It was slow progress, not the town crier, that ordained the change from E.M.iii to M.M.i. We must not expect watertight

[1] See note at the end of the Introduction.

compartments nor that objects other than pottery will necessarily conform. Pottery was chosen and rightly chosen as
the criterion because it is by far the most common material.
When broken it is useless. It is not removed to be employed
for something else and the fragments are practically indestructible.

So much for fact.

As to theory, archaeology, as the late Professor T. E. Peet
said, is not an exact science. In the absence of documents
which we can read and believe we are bound to progress by
means of theories. Any theory is justifiable which agrees with
the greatest number of facts known at the time and contradicts
neither a vital fact nor human nature and reason. The most
reasonable theory, which gives a connected history, should
hold the field until a better one is produced or until it is flatly
contradicted by some newly discovered fact. Facts like
words are by themselves useless. They must be combined
as a means to an end. Their duty is at the lowest to provide
the basis of a reasonable theory and at the highest to be the
skeleton supporting the living flesh of history.

Acknowledgements are due to many. The bibliography at
the end gives some of the literature to which I owe a debt.
But first of all comes my duty to Sir Arthur Evans, with whom
I had the pleasure and honour of working at Knossos for five
years and who generously lent me the unpublished diaries
of his early travels and permission to use many illustrations.
His enthusiasm has been an inspiration and I cannot say how
much I owe to him. Hardly less do I owe to the late Dr.
Duncan Mackenzie, my predecessor at Knossos and, together
with Sir Arthur, the founder of Minoan archaeology. It was
my good fortune that I met him in Crete before his retirement.
The cordial assistance of the present energetic ephor, Dr. S.
Marinatos, has always been of the greatest value. It is good
to think that he now has the new museum on which he
set his heart. I must thank Dr. Halbherr and Dr. Pernier
of the Italian Mission, both of them a great loss as
friends and archaeologists, for permission to use much of
their material, some of it as yet unpublished. To Humfry
Payne, late Director of the British School at Athens, whose
tragic death has been such a blow to archaeology, my debt
is great. The loss of our companion on many a journey is still
unbelievable. Of those whose work appears in this book
Miss Money-Coutts drew all the diagrams of patterns and the

seal stones, and Mr. J. T. Pinion the simplified plans. Professors A. B. Cook and A. J. B. Wace have read the manuscript and made many valuable criticisms and suggestions.

Then there is ' Manolaki ', Emmanouel Akoumianakes, foreman of Knossos and the most enthusiastic archaeologist in Crete. The ' Old Wolf's ' eye for a site is unrivalled and no amount of exhaustion on his part or on that of any one else will prevent him from forcing one to search for remains. The work that he has done for Knossos is known to few and I am glad to have the opportunity of mentioning it.

And last but not least come all those companions of our travels and the hospitable Cretans themselves. A journey is a pure joy, whether accompanied by a vigorous young Kourete of Dikte or by an equally vigorous but more reminiscent elderly Idaean Daktyl, whether one's lodging is with the village schoolmaster, in a monastery, or on the bare hillside with the raggle-taggle gypsies. To have stood on Ida, on Dikte and on Aphendes-Kavousi in the clear shrill wind and to have toiled through the hot little valleys with that unforgettable smell of herbs is an experience the memory of which nothing can ever take away from you.

"Αμ' πᾶς στὴν Κρήτην, Κρητικέ, χαιρέττε μου τσὴν Κρήτην,
Χαιρέττε ξέ μου τὸ βουνὸ τὸ γέρο Ψηλορίτι.
    The Exiled Cretan. A Matinadha of Ida.[1]

---

[1] When you go to Crete, Cretan, greet Crete for me,
    Greet from me the mountain, aged Ida.

Note on a Recent Attempt to upset the Accepted Sequence of Periods

ÅBERG IN the fourth volume of his *Bronzezeitliche und Frueisen-zeitliche Chronologie* has made a determined effort to prove that there is little true stratification at Knossos, that the accepted stratification has been invented in accordance with an analysis of the styles of pottery and that this analysis is unsound. From an analysis of his own he maintains that the remains can only be divided with certainty into three periods, Pre-palatial (i.e. E.M.i to M.M.1*a*), Kamarais (i.e. M.M.1*b* to M.M.iii pre-earthquake), and Late Minoan. He dismisses the Egyptian synchronisms for the earlier periods, which have hitherto been accepted as giving some indication of positive dating, and concludes that within his first two periods the various styles of pottery were contemporary. He has been praised by the reviewer in *J.H.S.*, LIV, for pointing out that primitive communities could exist side by side with the advanced civilization of the great palaces. Since, however, every style of pottery is present at Knossos, the result of his argument seems to be that primitive communities were in existence actually *in* the palaces themselves! However pleasant may be the picture of a Sub-Neolithic servant waiting on a M.M.1 lady, the fact remains that Knossos *is* very highly stratified and that a sufficient number of pure strata exist one above the other to disprove Åberg's case, while by no means disallowing the possibility that the provincial towns may lag behind the great centres of civilization to the extent of missing out a period like M.M.ii or L.M.ii.

It is simpler, however, to give a short summary of the evidence which has led us to believe that the various styles of pottery are in sequence and not contemporary. In every case quoted a pure stratum of the period in question lies immediately above a stratum of the previous period.

NEOLITHIC occurs immediately above virgin soil wherever it is found.
E.M.i, deposit on a floor level in the West Court at Knossos (*B.S.A.*, X, 22).
E.M.ii, deposit on a floor level above the preceding (*ibid.*, 20. Cf. *Mochlos*, 42).

E.M.III, deposit on a floor level above the preceding (*ibid.*, 20. Cf. at Vasilike, *Trans. Penn. Univ.*, II, 113, *Gournia*, 50, at Palaikastro, *B.S.A.*, *sup.* 3).

M.M.1*a*, at Knossos no floor of this period immediately overlies an E.M.III level, but cf. transitional types in a pure stratum (*B.S.A.*, XXX, 53). At Vasilike a house was built a little way away from the E.M. site (*loc. cit.*). At Palaikastro a well-stratified deposit was found (*loc. cit.*).

M.M.1*b*, deposit with a small admixture of M.M.II*a* in the West Court at Knossos (*P. of M.*, IV, 97). A pure stratum near by not carried lower (*ibid.*, I, 186).

M.M.II*a*, stratum overlying M.M.1*b* stratum in the Royal Pottery Stores (L., III, ᶜ in the reference museum ; in the North-East Magazines K., I, 2, 4, 6, 7, 8 ; West Court, B., I, 7).

M.M.II*b*, deposit stratified by layers of wood ash above the Royal Pottery Stores (*P. of M.*, I, 240). Åberg's contention that it is all one deposit implies a discrimination of style not usually displayed by catastrophes.

M.M.III*a*, deposit above the Loomweight Area (*ibid.*, fig. 187*b*).

M.M.III*b*, deposit immediately above the preceding (*loc. cit.*) and in the Room of the Stone Pier (*ibid.*, 366).

The above takes no account of the changes in building construction which are associated with the various periods, nor of the development in such arts as seal-engraving and writing which are conclusive.

Chapter I

THE ISLAND

(See Map 2)

Creta Jovis magni medio jacet insula ponto
Mons Idaeus ubi et gentis cunabula nostrae.
Centum urbes habitant magnas, uberrima regna.
AENEID iii, 104–106.

A. PHYSICAL CHARACTERISTICS

THE POSITION of Crete, almost equidistant from Europe, Asia and Africa, marked it out from the earliest times as a stepping stone between the continents. It lies between parallels 23° 30′ and 26° 60′ E. and 34° 50′ and 35° 4′ N.

The landmarks must always have been of assistance to sailors οἷοι ἐν ὄρφνᾳ, and the distinctive shape of its mountains must have enabled them to set their course with ease to its harbours. Juktas, the solitary hill on the low land between Ida and Dikte, its shape like the profile of a bearded god, stands behind the harbour town of Knossos. The mass of Ida and the fantastic peak of Kophinos lead the traveller from Egypt to the anchorage of Fair Havens and the beaches of the Bay of Messara. The chain of islands, Rhodes, Karpathos, Kasos, will shelter a ship coming from Anatolia, Cyprus or Syria, while the triangular hill, Mount Modhi, serves as a guide to the Eastern harbours. The White Mountains, marking the position of Soudha Bay, are visible from Cape Malea. The summits of Dikte come into view soon after a ship leaves the Southern Cyclades for the harbours of Khersonesos or Miletos or the landlocked bay of Spina Longa.

The chief ports to-day are on the North coast, Khania, Rhethymnos and Herakleion, or, as the sailors in the Levant still call them, Canea, Retimo, and Candia. These have been artificially improved, while the other ports of the island have been allowed to fall into decay. Sitia and Hierapetra still have some trade, as has recently Agios Nikolaos, but the

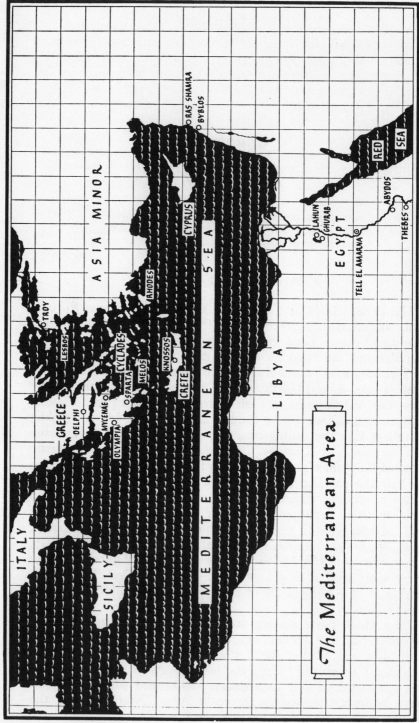

The Mediterranean Area

MAP 1

effects of the jealousy of the three big towns can be seen in the ruinous condition of many ports which were once prosperous.

It is not only jealousy, however, which has in comparatively recent times concentrated the trade on the North coast. Two other factors have combined. First, modern ships must ride at anchor ; they cannot be beached as was the universal custom of antiquity. Secondly, the coastline has changed considerably since Roman times. At some time in the sixth century a great submarine movement took place which tilted the whole island as if on a pivot. As a result the West end was raised in places as much as 26 feet out of the water so that the artificial harbour of Phalasarna on the West coast is now well above sea level and some 150 yards inland, while a corresponding subsidence in the East has caused the disappearance of many of the stretches of sand on to which the ships were hauled, and has swallowed up parts of the ancient towns.[1]

If, however, one takes account of the amount of elevation or subsidence and redraws the coastline to conform with the Admiralty soundings, it will be found that in every case the ancient settlements had either a good beach or the protection of a reef now submerged. Other effects of the earthquakes from which the island has so frequently suffered will be noted later. It is sufficient here to point out how materially one alone has affected the whole physical conformation of the island.[2]

Crete is about 250 kilometres (156 miles) long. Its greatest width is from Cape Stavros, West of Candia to Cape Kephala, the ancient Leon, a distance of 57 kilometres (about 36 miles). The isthmus of Hierapetra, however, is only 12 kilometres

[1] Spratt, II, 230 and *passim*, was the first to recognize this phenomenon. As to its exact date, Professor Newberry tells me that the Arab historian Masaud records that in the year A.D. 535 there was a great earthquake in the Delta as a result of which the land sank and the sea came in, destroying many towns and forming the salt lakes. The elevation of the West end of Crete accounts for the presence to-day of only one of the Mousagorai Islands, Elaphonisi ; the other two were no doubt Palaiokhora Selinou and Trakhila promontories. In the East the island of Mokhlos was once part of the mainland, the isthmus, now sunk, providing it with two harbours.

[2] No doubt the water supply was also altered at various times. Pseira has now no spring. The earliest cisterns are Greco-Roman, yet there was a prosperous settlement here from the earliest Minoan times though it is over 2 miles from the coast and is often stormbound for days at a time.

(about 7½ miles) across, and the isthmus of Rhethymnos is 18 kilometres (11½ miles).

The island is divided up by great blocks of mountains. Perhaps it would be truer to say that a single chain with but two considerable breaks runs the whole length of the island. Along its southern side the mountains come close down to the sea and the various settlements are approached by wild gorges which split the chain. No one who has passed Crete *en route* for Egypt can forget the forbidding appearance of this coast (Pl. I, 2). These mountains throw off spurs to the North which divide up the more habitable parts. In the West are the White Mountains, the Λευκὰ Ὄρη of the ancients (Pl. II, 1). The summits of these, Agios Theodhoros, Soros and Agion Pnevma, run up to 8,000 feet and are among the wildest parts of Europe. The ἀγρίμι, wild goat or Cretan ibex, still survives in some of the practically inaccessible gorges (Pl. I, 1). To these mountains resorted in Turkish times, and I can add of my own knowledge, still resort to-day, those with a price on their head. The men of Sphakia, the champions of the Cretan revolution, are still a race apart. I have met there a white-bearded Καπετάνιος who was at the storming of the fort near the village in 1866.

Connected with the White Mountains by low ranges to the North-West are the two steep promontories of Bousa and Spadha, the Korykos and Tityros of antiquity. To the West broken country descends to the coast and the windswept valleys of Enneakhoria. To the North is the fertile plain of Khania, ' the goodliest plot, the Diamond sparke and the Honny spot of all Crete ', as Lithgow calls it.

East of the White Mountains comparatively low rolling country extends as far as the second great block of mountains. These centre round Mount Ida the modern Psiloriti (ὑψηλὸν ὄρος) (Pl. II, 2). First, near the South coast comes Kedros, an isolated mountain. Between this and Ida lies the fertile Amari valley (Pl. III, 4). Mount Ida itself reaches the height of over 8,000 feet. From its summit a wonderful panorama of the whole island is unfolded. North of Ida is the Mylopotamos valley, separated from the sea by the Kouloukounas range, the ancient Tallaion, which descends steeply to the rocky coast.

East of Ida the country is again low and rolling. The watershed is under 2,000 feet above sea level and the only conspicuous hill is that of Juktas. To the South is the plain

of Messara, well watered and one of the most fertile and productive parts of Crete. This is separated from the Libyan
sea by the Asterousia range—to-day called Kophinos, which
is pierced at intervals by wild gorges which run down to a
precipitous coast.

Next comes the great mass of Dikte—the modern Lasithio-
tika Vouna (Pl. III, 1) centring round a high upland plain which
was thickly inhabited in ancient times. There is a flat strip
along the North coast where carob trees flourish, but except
for the Vianos valley the country is rocky and inhospitable
to the South.

East of Dikte is the narrow isthmus of Hierapetra, flat and
low-lying, bounded to the East by the Thriphte mountains
(Pl. II, 3). It forms a kind of funnel down which pours the
hot sirocco in May (Pl. IV, 3). The mountains between the
isthmus and Sitia extend right across the island, of which this
is one of the wildest parts. Beyond Sitia stretches a high
limestone tableland which reaches as far as the East coast
(Pl. IV, 1 and 2).

A feature of the country, which has not yet been mentioned,
is the number of upland plains. Most of them are completely
surrounded by hills, and the water and snow which collects
there during the winter is carried away by natural swallow-
holes, or χῶνοι as they are called. The higher plains are
used only in the summer by shepherds. In the White Mountains is the plain of Omalós, about 3,500 feet above the sea, too
high for any but summer habitation, which begins when the
shepherds bring up their flocks in April. It is accessible by
the steep gorge of Agia Roumeli, and by easier passes from
Selinos and the North. Next is Anopolis, only 2,000 feet
high with the ancient city of that name on the ridge to the
South (Pl. III, 3). Next comes the plain of Nidha, still preserving the ancient name of Ida (Pl. III, 2). This is nearly 5,000 feet
in height and is covered with cheese dairies to which the
shepherds resort towards the middle of May. Just above it is
the cave of Zeus. Tracks passable by animals lead down to
Anogeia—near the ancient Axos—Krousonas, the gate of Ida
and a city of refuge in Turkish times, Gergeri, Kamarais, by
a track which leads close to the sacred cave, the Amari valley,
and the Mylopotamos valley.

The plain of Lasithi or Psykhro is less than 3,000 feet in
height and is to-day as in ancient times thickly populated
(Pl. III, 1). It is accessible from all directions, with the result

that although it is a self-contained unit it was, as we shall see, by no means cut off from civilization in antiquity, and while in the earliest days it developed a culture of its own it was by no means backward or lacking in contact with the outside world.[1] With Lasithi two smaller plains may be taken, Katharos and Limnarkaros. Both of these lie at a height of about 4,000 feet and are cultivated but not regularly inhabited.

In the mountains of the Sitia Peninsula are many such small plains, most of them at a low enough level to allow of permanent occupation, Zyros, Katalioni, Lamnioni and many others.

The importance of these plains, at any rate in Minoan times, may be judged by the fact that all those East of Ida were carefully guarded by forts.

The main change in the character of Crete since antiquity is the deforestation of the island. The catastrophe in the sixth century A.D. has had no effect on the main features, it has only caused shipping to seek other harbours. But the wanton destruction of the forests has altered the whole aspect. As we shall see, there is a strong probability that in Minoan days at least the whole island West of Ida was a great virgin forest which precluded the advance of civilization except on the coast. Even in Pliny's time Crete was the very home of cypress, and the wood which Thothmes III had received from the ships of Keftiu was still the material for ships all over the Mediterranean. But, beginning probably with the first arrival of man, deforestation has made continual progress, aided not only by a population thoroughly apathetic under Venetian and Turkish rule, but also enthusiastically by the goats, which eat the young shoots, until to-day the cypress is confined to a few trees in the West and to some new plantations in the Lasithi and Vianos districts. As a result the winter torrents have swept away the soil which had been held in position by the trees. In the Lasithi plain, for instance, there is an extraordinary depth of soil due entirely to the fact that the surrounding hills have been denuded. Crete, which was once one of the most fertile and prosperous islands in the Mediterranean, is now one of the rockiest and most barren.

To this cause also must be attributed the lack of water. Few rivers in Crete are more than a trickle in the summer, while

---

[1] The suggestion has been made (e.g. B.S.A., VI, 115) that this plain was until M.M. times a lake, with the Diktaean Cave as a swallow-hole. This is disproved by the fact that the Neolithic settlement at Trapeza is on a lower level than the cave.

most are dry beds only. The Platanias West of Khania, the ancient Iardanos, the Gazanos, West of Candia, the ancient Triton, the Metropolitanos in the Messara, the ancient Lethaios, the Anapodhari flowing from the Messara to the South coast, the ancient Katarrhakhtes, and the Mylopotamos, the ancient Oaxes, are the only rivers which have never been known to dry up completely.

Springs have disappeared and sites such as Omalais to the North of Dikte which evidently supported a considerable population in ancient times are now completely deserted, save for a few *mandras* or shepherds' huts to which water must be brought from a distance.

None of the Cretan rivers, however, can have been navigable even in antiquity and the natural means of communication has always been by mountain paths suitable in many cases only to pedestrians. Such paths frequently begin as mere game tracks. It is not till the coming of wheeled traffic, and swift-wheeled traffic at that, when gradients have to be considered, that artificial roads are cut; the ' kalderims ', or roughly paved roads made by the Romans, Venetians or Turks for military purposes, merely followed the prehistoric paths, and although there are few cases where Minoan banking or Greek bridges survive we are justified in considering that the means of communication between ancient sites was the same as that in use to-day or rather before the network of car roads was begun.

B. ROUTES AND TOPOGRAPHY

It is most important when considering the distribution of sites at certain periods to look at the means of communication each had with its neighbours ; whether easy access from one quarter has caused a site to favour in its style of pottery the technique of another which may lie at a considerable distance from it ; through what sections of the country would pass the traffic from Egypt, influencing perhaps one group of sites while another group is in closer touch with the Cyclades.

Only those who have actually walked the mountains can tell how misleading a map may be, and the maps of Crete are in any case woefully inaccurate. Who would think that from Souia on the South coast to Lakkoi South of Khania is as long a day's journey as from Tsoutsouros, the ancient Priansos, on the South coast to Amnisos on the North coast ? Distances are useless. Times alone matter. The times given here are

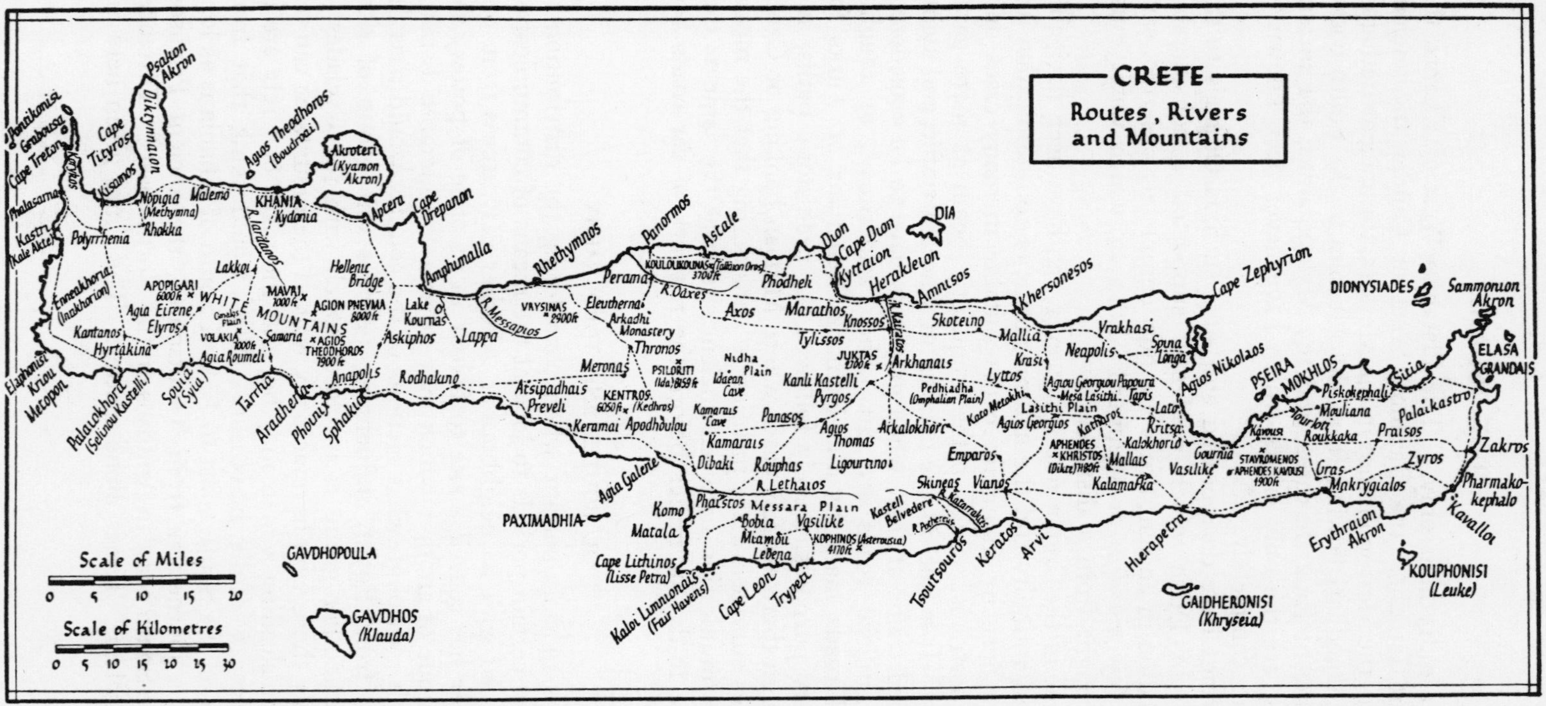
CRETE
Routes, Rivers and Mountains
Scale of Miles
0 5 10 15 20
Scale of Kilometres
0 5 10 15 20 25 30
KHANIA
Kydonia
WHITE MOUNTAINS
Rhethymnos
Herakleion
Knossos
Phaistos
Messara Plain
Lasithi Plain
Hierapetra
Zakros
DIA
PAXIMADHIA
GAVDHOPOULA
GAVDHOS
(Klauda)
GAIDHERONISI
(Khryseia)
KOUPHONISI
(Leuke)
DIONYSIADES
PSEIRA
MOKHLOS
ELASA
GRANDAIS

MAP 2

almost all from personal experience and are probably about half-way between a running messenger and an ordinary party of merchants.[1] They are all walking—not riding—times and do not allow for halts. They vary according to the weather and to how fit the pedestrian was at the time. All that can be said for them is that they have been done.

The routes from the East coast to the isthmus of Hierapetra are three.[2] The northernmost starts at Palaikastro, one of the great centres of Minoan civilization, and after crossing a high limestone plateau descends in rather less than 4 hours to Petras and Sitia. Thence it passes the Middle and Late Minoan settlement at Piskokephali and ascends through wild country to Khamaizi, Mouliana, and Tourloti, whence a steep path leads down to Mokhlos (Pl. V, 3), at that time part of the mainland, in three-quarters of an hour. After leaving Tourloti the path runs high up along the flanks of Thriphte, passes Kavousi (Pl. VI, 1) and reaches Gournia (Pl. V, 4) in about $8\frac{1}{2}$ hours from Sitia. The central route starts from Kato Zakros and ascends sharply (Pl. VI, 2), passing a number of small sites, to Apano Zakros in just over an hour, thence it again rises in a North-Westerly direction, skirts the North side of the hill above Apano Zakros and passing the small settlements and forts near Skallia and Sitanos reaches Praisos (Pl. VII, 3) in $3\frac{1}{2}$ hours from Apano Zakros. West of Praisos there is a choice of roads, one rounding the North side of Romanati via Sykia, the other going round the South side via Adhromyloi and Agios Stephanos (till recently called Gras) and joining the first at Rukkaka ; the former takes about 5 hours, the latter 7. From Rukkaka the road goes on to Avgo and Kavousi, reaching Gournia in rather under 4 hours.

The southern route starts from Pharmakokephalo close to the ancient Ampelos (Pl. VIII, 4), it ascends by Khoumetalo to the Zyros plain in $2\frac{1}{2}$ hours. That this was an important route is shown by the number of guard stations on the way. Thence it turns South-West to Makrygialos and goes along the shore, passes the E.M. site at Agia Photia and reaches Hierapetra in $7\frac{1}{2}$ hours.

[1] A cross-country runner who would undertake to explore the various ancient routes in Greece before the countryside is ruined by car roads would collect a lot of interesting material. The times not from my personal experience are taken from a very useful book, Κρητικά, by N. Kalemenopoulos, 1894.

[2] At every place mentioned on the following routes there exists an ancient site.

North and South run a network of roads, some of them
demonstrably ancient, Palaikastro to Ampelos with its forts at
Kokhlakiais and ' stas Tavernais ',[1] the well-cut and banked
road South of Zakros and the stations at Lidhoriko Skismenes,
Malamourais and Katsounaki, and the route from Lamnoni
via Sitanos and Katsidhoni to Sitia.

The easy road across the Hierapetra isthmus naturally
attracted settlers. Kedhri, Episkope, Vasilike, and Monasteraki are all on the short route of $2\frac{1}{2}$ hours between Hierapetra
and Pakhyammos. But it is somewhat surprising to find that
few of them are of importance and that in none has ever been
found an object of foreign manufacture. Certainly the French
during the Occupation found it advisable to land stores at
Hierapetra and transport them by land rather than face the
dangerous rounding of Cape Sidhero.

From Gournia an easy path leads to Kalokhorio, the ancient
Istron, in just over an hour. At this point the road branches.
One arm turns North to Agios Nikolaos—the ancient Lato
pros Kamara and thence to Neapolis in about $4\frac{1}{2}$ hours, where
it is joined by the road from Olous the modern Spina Longa
which passes Dreros and reaches Neapolis in about the same
time. From Neapolis the road descends by Vrakhasi to Mallia
in 3 hours, whence the coast road via Khersonesos, Nirou
Khani and Amnisos leads to Herakleion in 6 hours or so.

The second arm goes North-West to Kritsa and either
directly up the Minoan road, guarded by the fort known as
the Kitten's Cistern to the Katharos plain, whence it descends
to the plain of Lasithi, again by a guarded Minoan way in about
$8\frac{1}{2}$ hours, or by the magnificent site of Lato ' Etera ' [2] (Pl. VII, 1)
to Tapis and over a high col on the North side of Mount
Aloïdha to Mikro Lasithaki in very much the same time.

The most usual exit westwards from Lasithi is from Kato-
metokhi over to Lyttos in 4 hours and to Knossos in another
5, but two equally serviceable and easier ways exist, one on
each side of the important but as yet unexcavated site of Agiou
Georgiou Papoura. The easternmost descends beside the

[1] It would be more in keeping with the peaceful character of
Minoan civilization and with convivial Cretan habits if we could
take a clue from this name and call all of them taverns rather than
forts.

[2] Lato ' Etera ' was connected with its harbour of Lato pros
Kamara by a road running through the plain of Lakonia, guarded
at its exit by 3 forts at Peponi Khani, Agios Ioannes and Agios
Stavros. This takes $1\frac{1}{2}$ hours.

fortified peaks of Karphi and Koprana to Krasi whence Mallia is reached in about 3½ hours. The western descends a fine gorge to Goniais, Avdhou, and Mokhos, in 2½ hours. From Mokhos to Knossos via the sacred cave at Skoteino and Skalani is about 6½ hours. Karphi and Koprana also guard the route to Omalais, the city of castles, which lies on the now dry northern slopes of Mt. Selena.

Another easy route to the Plain of Pedhiadha is from Plate over the saddle between Mt. Aphendes and Mt. Sarakinos to Geraki in 2¾ hours.

Southwards a road goes from Kaminaki to Erganos and Vianos in 5 hours, where it joins the other main route from the East described below.

The southern route from Hierapetra passes Kalamafka, whence branches go up to the Katharos Plain and to Mallais, and keeping high above the sea reaches Vianos, the ancient Bienos, in some 8 or 9 hours.[1] From Vianos the sacred cleft of Arvi, with its temple of Zeus Arbios, and the twin peaks of Keratos, can be reached in 2½ and 2 hours respectively. Westwards from Vianos are two routes, one reaching Emparos in 2 hours and one entering the Messara Plain near the river Katarrhaktes in 3½ hours.

The Messara plain is naturally too flat and well cultivated to have preserved any trace of ancient routes. The following tracks, however, lead out of it southward through the Asterousia range to the sea. From Kastell Belvedere (Rhizokastro), the ancient Stelai (Pl. VII, 2), a fine track good enough in places for wheeled traffic leads down to Tsoutsouros, the ancient Priansos, in not much more than 1½ hours. From Vasilike two fine gorges lead down to Trypeti in less than 2½ hours, the easternmost, Goulopharango, showing distinct traces of banking and of Minoan guard-houses at Agia Paraskeve and Agios Savas. An easy route also leads from Vasilike via Makry Livadhi to Miamou in 1¼ hours.

Lebena, one of the harbours of Gortyna, is approached most easily from Bobia, the ancient Boibe, via the Monastery of Apezanais. From Bobia also an easy path runs down to Kaloi Limenes—the Fair Havens of St. Paul—in less than 3 hours. Matala or Metallon the other harbour of Gortyna is 2 hours from Phaistos.

The main North and South road of Central Crete, in fact one might almost call it the highway of Minoan civilization,

[1] As to this time I am not certain, as I lost my way.

runs South from Knossos to Phaistos and on to the unexcavated
port of Komo. It was traced by Sir Arthur Evans.[1] The
settlement of Sylamos, and the city of Kanli Kastelli, the
ancient Lykastos, are served. Thence the road runs to the
guard-house at Pyrgos and on to Agios Thomas, perhaps the
ancient Pannona. It turns West to Panasos and can be traced
at intervals to Rouphas near Myrais. It can be picked up
again beyond Phaistos, where it runs down to Sphakoriako and
so to Komo. By this route Phaistos can be reached in about
12 hours. To Komo, via Sphakoriako and Kakodheti, is
somewhat under 2 hours.

Knossos itself was connected with its harbour town East of
the modern Candia by a road which passed close to the cemeteries of Zapher Papoura and Isopata and took just under an
hour. The branches of the road are as follows. From
Sylamos a path ascends to the sanctuary on Mt. Juktas about
2½ hours from Knossos. From the same spot runs a road via
the fort of Karydhaki to Arkhanais in an hour and on via
Vathypetro to Ligourtino and the Messara in another 5 hours.
From Kanli Kastelli a branch of the road runs South-East
towards Arkalokhori, which it reaches in about 3 hours. From
Panasos a branch runs West towards Kamarais, which is somewhat under 4 hours away.

Up to this point most of the sites have been Minoan and
in some cases the actual Minoan-built road has survived.
From here westwards we have no evidence save the occurrence
of sites along natural paths and the occasional survival of a
Hellenic bridge.

Between the Candia and the Rhethymnos district are six
main lines of approach, not counting those which cross the
higher parts of Ida and which are impassable for mules except
in summer.

First comes the North coast route, at first following traces
of a Minoan road,[2] via Palaikastro Rodhias—the ancient
Kyttaion—Agia Pelagia—the ancient Dion, Phodhele the
orange-scented birthplace of El Greco, Bali—the ancient
Astale, Roumeli Kastelli—the ancient Panormos. This route
follows some of the worst tracks in Crete. It joins the next
route just beyond Perama and as far as Rhethymnos takes
just over 18 hours. From Perama a branch leads off to
Eleutherna in 2 hours.

Next comes the route via Marathos and Dhamasta to Perama

[1] *P. of M.*, II, 60 ff.   [2] *P. of M.*, II, 232.

in just under 11 hours and on to Rhethymnos in 4 more. Next the route which passes Tylissos, Goniais and Axos to Perama in 10 hours.

To the South of these routes the great mass of Ida blocks the way, and although the passage to the Nidha plain and beyond is easy enough for a mule, it is unlikely that it would be taken except for a πανήγυρις (religious festival) at the Idaean Cave, which lies some 4½ hours from Anogeia and Krousonas and 2½ from Kamarais.

South of Ida are three main routes, the first two skirting Mt. Kedros to the North, the third to the South. All start at Dibaki which lies 50 minutes West of Phaistos. The first runs up the Amari valley via Apodhoulou, Thronos—the ancient Sybrita (Pl. VII, 4) and the monastery of Arkadhi to Rhethymnos, taking about 13 hours. The next branches off this at Thronos and runs to Meronas, Ellenais, Gerakari and Atsipadhais in 7 hours. Last comes the coast road via Agia Galene, the ancient Soulia, round the North side of Vouvala to Keramai and Agios Ioannes Monastery at Preveli in 10 hours.

The only North–South route I know is from Preveli Monastery via Gerakari, Patsos (Pl. II, 4), Bene, Ornithe and Monopari, which takes by this roundabout way some 17 hours. According to Kalemenopoulos' Κρητικά, the direct route from Rhethymnos to Agia Galene takes about 11 hours and to Preveli 12.

From the Rhethymnos district West the road most in use is that which follows the North coast via Dhramia, the ancient Hydramon, and Georgioupolis, the ancient Amphimalla ; it crosses the Almyros river—the Amphimalla river of Strabo— by a bridge of which the foundations are Hellenic, cuts behind Cape Drepanon, which still preserves its ancient name, and reaches the coast again at Aptera in just over 6 hours. From Aptera to Khania (Kydonia) is 2½ hours.

The southern route continues from Preveli as near the coast as it can, reaching Sphakia in 9 hours and continuing on to Anopolis in another hour and three-quarters. Below Anopolis is the little port of Phoinix, which belonged to the city of Lappa. Strabo implies that a regular route existed from here to Amphimalla, a distance, he says, of 100 stades. This is an accurate measurement of the narrowest part of the island here, from Amphimalla to the South coast at Frankokastelli. To Phoinix, however, it is 120. Presumably the route ran by Kallikrate to Lappa, which I am told takes

7½ hours, and thence by Lake Kournas, the only lake in Crete, called Korion or Koresion in antiquity, to Amphimalla in about 4½ hours more. A more direct route would be through the Askiphos gorge in about 6½ hours.

Westwards from Anopolis the going is hard, but evidently a route existed in antiquity which must have served Araden. Beyond this it descends an almost sheer slide of shale for 2,000 feet to the shore, where there is a spring of water within a few feet of the sea (Pl. I, 2). Agia Aikaterine, where lie the scanty remains of Tarrha, is reached in just over 4 hours. The route North from here to Khania via the magnificent gorge of Agia Roumeli (Pl. I, 1) and the plain of Omalos takes about 13 hours, but the time depends on how much water is flowing in the gorge. Agia Aikaterine to Samaria may take anything from 2 to 3½ hours. West of Agia Aikaterine it is impossible to take pack animals.

From Khania the road runs along the coast to Malemo, crosses the base of cape Spadha, passes Nokhia, perhaps the ancient Pergamos, Nopigia, perhaps Methymna, and reaches Kisamos in about 7 hours. Another branch must have left the main road at Nopigia to serve Rhokka and Polyrrhenia, which it reaches in 3¾ hours, thence to Kisamos in another hour. Polyrrhenia was connected with its port at Phalasarna on the West coast 60 stades away, as Strabo accurately says. From Polyrrhenia to Mesogeia I have not walked, but I am told it is about 1½ hours. From thence to Phalasarna is 1¾ hours.

A rough coast road connects Phalasarna with the south-western cities of Crete. It runs via the watch tower of Kastri, perhaps the ancient Kale Akte, passes the mouth of the Enneakhoria valley, which may preserve the ancient name Inakhorion, and leaving slightly to the West the small site at Khrysoskaletissa monastery, turns up through Sklavopoula (? Douloupolis), thence descending to Palaiokhora or Selinou Kastelli in about 17 hours. Another ancient route to the South must be followed more or less by the modern car road from Kisamos to Palaiokhora. From Palaiokhora the road runs up the Vlythias ravine, passing the site of Kalamyde, to the ancient Kantanos in 2 hours. From there it turns sharply eastwards to Hyrtakina and Elyros 3 hours from Kantanos. From Elyros a well-used track, obviously ancient from the rock-cut tombs and the aqueduct beside it, leads down to Souia—the ancient Syia—in 1½ hours. From this point a scramble of an hour round the cliffs leads westwards to Agios Kirkos (Lissos)

(Pl. VIII, 2), also accessible in about 1½ hours from Elyros. Eastwards, and again accessible by land only by unencumbered pedestrians and goats, lies Voukilasi—the ancient Poikilassos.

From Elyros—though I have only been from Souia, skirting Elyros—a path leads to what seems to be the cemetery of that city at Kampanos and thence via Agia Eirene, near to which village Spratt saw traces of an ancient way up to Omalos, to Khania which is reached in 12 hours or less from Souia.

So much for communications by land, which have changed little save for the gashing of the countryside by car roads. The communications by sea, however, must have played an important part.   Locally, as we have seen above, conditions may have changed since the catastrophe of the sixth century, but things have probably balanced out.   Where one harbour has been rendered useless, another close by has been made accessible.   We can generally judge from the Admiralty Charts what the conditions must have been.

We are fortunately in possession of a most important document, the Stadiasmus.   This is a compilation, parallel to the Admiralty's *Mediterranean Pilot*, of probably the sixth century A.D., but certainly prior to the earthquake.   It gives distances and anchorages as well as the presence of water and facilities for devotion.[1]   Unfortunately the distances have been written in figures, not at full length.   Scribes being notoriously liable to miscopy figures, the document can only be taken to check the relative position of sites.   A further difficulty is created by the fact that, as has been pointed out above, ships in ancient times were beached on stretches of sand or shingle. This means that they would have been able to use certain ports at present inaccessible.   On the other hand, their inability to tack or indeed sail close to the wind must have, even allowing for the use of oars, precluded ships from seeking refuge in what have since become quite safe anchorages.

Another important topographical point is the kind of site preferred for settlement at each period.   So striking are the changes in taste that it would almost be possible, on seeing a photograph of a piece of Cretan landscape and being told that

---

[1] See Appendix A, II, 1, at the end of this chapter.   It is curious that prevailing winds are not mentioned, nor outlying dangers. Several sites which one would have thought to have been of sufficient importance to mention are not named, e.g. Itanos and Ampelos on the East coast, Rhethymnos, Panormos, Amnisos and Miletos on the North coast, Priansos on the South coast.

there was a site there, to give the earliest date of that site.   In Neolithic times we find the inhabitants of Crete dwelling in caves.   Ellenospilo at Potisteria North of Gonia Monastery on Cape Spadha with its settlement 70 metres into the hill-side, Ellenais, Amnisos, Trapeza in Lasithi (Pl. V, 1), Magasa, Skallais and Zakros in the East all show the fear, perhaps of wild beasts, in which Neolithic man went.   On the other hand, the largest settlement, at Knossos, occupies the site of the later Palace.

In Minoan times life was evidently as peaceful as to-day. Unfortified towns were built on low knolls, often near the sea. (Pl. V, 2, 3, 4).   Then, after the break up of the Bronze Age civilization we find the castles of the robber barons on the rocky eyries of Karphi, Kavousi, Vrokastro and the Zakros Gorge.   No consideration of a water supply is shown.   The one concern is inaccessibility (Pl. VI, 1 and 2).   In Archaic times the uncertainty of communal rather than personal safety, inseparable from the petty city politics of Greece, caused the sites chosen to be high flat-topped hills, surrounded if possible by ravines.   Such typical sites are seen at Eleutherna, Polyrrhenia, Prinias, Hyrtakina, Lato, Dreros, and many other places (Pl. VII and VIII, 1).   In Hellenic times and later these sites naturally continued to be occupied, but from the beginning of the fifth century there is a tendency to come down from the city of refuge until in Roman times we see a number of sites occupied which had not been inhabited since Minoan days (Pl. VIII, 2, 3, 4).

C. AUTHORITIES

A word must be said about those who followed the ancient geographers.   They can be easily divided into two classes, the pre- and post-Pashley.

The earliest is the Florentine traveller Buondelmonte in 1422.   His work is included in Cornelius, *Creta Sacra* (1755). Many of the remains which he saw, such as the walls of Kisamos, have now disappeared.

That quaint writer Tournefort makes few excursions into archaeology in his *Voyage au Levant* (Paris, 1717, of journeys in 1700).   Next comes Johann Meursius, who collects all the references from classical authors in his *Creta* (Amsterdam, 1675).   Pococke in the second volume of his *Description of the East* (London, 1745) and Cramer in the third volume of his *Description of Ancient Greece* give a wealth of inaccurate information. Karl Hoeck's *Kreta* (Gottingen, 1823–9) is the first scholarly account of the island. It suffers from the fact that the author never visited it himself, but even Pashley, a most stringent critic, is glad to avail himself of Hoeck's suggestions.

From February to September 1834 Robert Pashley, Fellow of Trinity College, Cambridge, made a prolonged tour of the island during the course of which he identified most of the important sites with an accuracy which had never before been attained and has in few cases since been challenged. His results were published in two volumes, *Travels in Crete*, by John Murray in 1837. They are unfortunately incomplete, private affairs having prevented him from arranging his material from the East end of the island. Pashley's profound knowledge of the language as well as of the antiquities render his work an inexhaustible treasure-house. His scholarship, his humour, and his way with the Cretans have combined to give us a fascinating work. His map was drawn before Spratt's admirable survey and is, in detail, not entirely trustworthy. But it is far in advance of any previous map and clearly marks the position of the sites he determined, though it is not above the suspicion of showing those which in the text he cannot fix.

Captain (later Admiral) T. A. B. Spratt was engaged during the years 1851–3 in surveying the coast of Crete for the Admiralty. The official results obtained by him and his staff are given below in the Appendix as well as in part of the fourth volume of the *Mediterranean Pilot* (last edition 1918 with yearly corrections since). At the same time he made a number of tours in the interior of the island which resulted not only in a quantity of information concerning the natural history and geology of Crete, but also in a critical survey of the archaeological remains in which he was occasionally able to supplement or correct Pashley. He published in 1865 two volumes—*Travels and Researches in Crete* (Van Voorst) illustrated from sketches of his own, the maps being simplifications of the Admiralty charts. His greatest contribution to our knowledge of the island is his demonstration of the convulsion of the earth which tilted the West end of Crete out of the sea and sank the East end.

Neither his scholarship nor his knowledge of the language can compete with Pashley's, but his common sense, enthusiasm and simple directness have produced a most valuable book.

In 1845 Victor Raulin began his work on Crete. His results were first published in ten articles between 1858 and

1869 in the *Actes de la Société Linnéenne de Bordeaux* and were combined in the latter year with a few additions into the two volumes of his *Description Physique de l'Isle de Crète* (Bertrand, Paris). Archaeological topics, except for *obiter dicta* and items in a most useful bibliography, are excluded, and he has not the interest in the problems and life of Crete which Pashley and Spratt display, but his book will remain a permanent and authoritative account of the physical features of the island. His map is based on that of Spratt with a few minor corrections of detail and a different method of orthography.

Captain A. Trevor-Battye was Raulin's only modern successor. His book, *Camping in Crete*, 1913, contains useful information on plants, animals and birds, and its value is increased by Miss Bate's chapter on the remains of early animal life, such as the pygmy hippopotamus found in the caves of the island.

In the year in which Spratt began his work in Crete A. J. Evans was born. After a youth filled with experience enough to last an ordinary man a lifetime he first visited Crete in 1893 in search of sealstones and the prehistoric script which they revealed. His travels in Crete continued at intervals until in 1900 the improvement in political conditions enabled him to begin what has proved to be his life's work—the excavation of Knossos and the revelation of the Minoan civilization. A new world was opened to the archaeologist and historian. His topographical researches which began with the discovery of most of the important sites in East and Central Crete (for which the excavators of these sites have not always given him credit) have continued down to 1924, when, at the age of 72, he traced the course of the Minoan roads from the North to the South coasts. The published results of his work are too numerous to mention here. They are to be found in the Bibliography.

Dr. Federigo Halbherr was also one of the pioneers of archaeology in the island. His many discoveries in Central and Eastern Crete appeared both in the *Antiquary* and in the *American Journal of Archaeology*. The coal-black arab mare on which he would gallop over the mountains has become a legend. His compatriots Mariani, Savignoni and Taramelli also did good topographical work, published in the *Monumenti Antichi*.

The late R. B. Seager, excavator of Mokhlos and Pseira,

made a number of journeys particularly in West Crete. The results of these remained unpublished owing to his untimely death.

Incidental topographical references, subordinated to the main purpose of giving a report of the excavations, are to be found in the early numbers of the *Transactions of the University of Pennsylvania* by Miss Boyd (Mrs. Hawes) and Miss Hall, also by D. G. Hogarth in his account of Zakros in the *Annual of the British School at Athens*, VI, and by R. C. Bosanquet and R. M. Dawkins in their publications of Praisos and Palaikastro in later volumes of the same journal.

The successive ephors of Crete, Joseph Hazzidakis, S. Xanthudides, and S. Marinatos, have actually had little time for anything beyond publishing the results of the numerous excavations they are forced to make owing to chance discoveries by peasants, but a glance at the publications of the Greek Archaeological Society and the Ministry of Education will show what an amount of ground they have covered.

To Joseph Hazzidakis in particular a great debt is due for his foundation of the Syllogos and for his untiring efforts in forwarding archaeological enterprise and in aiding foreign savants during the difficult years of the Turkish domination and the revolts against it.

Svoronos in his *Numismatique de la Crète Ancienne* and Bursian in the second volume of his *Geographie von Griechenland* make a number of apt suggestions but do not know the country personally.

APPENDIX

A. ANCIENT AUTHORITIES ON ROUTES

I. *Land*

8 stades = *c.* 1 mile. 1 Roman mile = *c.* 1½ kilometres. An
asterisk denotes that I have not traversed the whole route or have
not taken the shortest way.

1. **Strabo, X, iv (1st century B.C.).**

Route	Stades	Remarks
Phalasarna–Polyrrhenia .	60	Very nearly correct. Time 3¼ hours.*
Polyrrhenia–sea (Kisamos)	30	Accurate. Time 1 hour.
Kydonia–Aptera . . .	80	Actually about 70. Time 2½ hours.
Kydonia–Knossos . .	800	Actually 600 by the Perama–Marathos route. Time 23½ hours.
Kydonia–Gortyna . .	800	Actually 600 by the Rhethymnos–Thronos–Apodhoulou route. Time 25 hours.
Knossos–Gortyna . .	200	Very nearly accurate by the Minoan road. Time 9½ hours.
Knossos–Lyktos . . .	120	Rather on the low side, nearer 130. Time 5 hours.*
Knossos–sea (Herakleion)	25	Accurate. Time 50 minutes.
Lyktos–Libyan Sea . .	80	This is obviously a mistake for the northern sea and Khersonesos, the Lyktian harbour. Accurate. Time 3½ hours.*
Gortyna–sea (Lebena) .	90	Accurate. Time 4½ hours.*
Gortyna–Metallon . .	130	Actually about 105. Time 4½ hours.
Gortyna–Praisos . . .	180	Priansos is obviously intended. This is usually put at the mouth of the Tsoutsouros, but the next route but one makes it 60 stades from the

Route	Stades	Remarks
		sea, i.e. at Ini, which most scholars agree marks the site of Inatos. In any case the distance is the same and is accurately given. Time from Gortyna to Ini about 7 hours.*
Gortyna–Phaistos. . .	60	Accurate. Time 2½ hours.
Praisos (Priansos)–sea .	60	See above. Ini is evidently intended. Tsoutsouros to Ini is actually nearly 80. Time 3¼ hours.
Amphimalla–Phoinix Lampeon	100	Actually Strabo is giving the width of the island at its narrowest in this part. Thus from sea to sea as the crow flies he is certainly accurate. Phoinix, however, lies some distance to the West of the line and is by the route through the Askyphos gorge about 145 from Amphimalla. Time 7¼ hours.*
Hierapytna–Minoa Lykteon	60	Accurate as to the width of the island at this point as the crow flies. Actually by road it is about 70. Time 2½ hours.
Phaistos–Metallon . .	40	Actually nearer 50. Time just under 2 hours.

2. Peutinger Table, A.D. 350–400.

Route	Roman Miles	Remarks
Kydonia–Kisamos . .	8	This must be the Kisamos mentioned by Strabo as the harbour of Aptera. The table distinguishes 2 Kisamoi. Pashley would put it at Apokoronou Kastelli farther East. If the table is right it must have lain just below Aptera at Fort Izzedin.
Kisamos–Lappa . . .	9	This must be wrong. The distance from Kydonia to

Route	Roman Miles	Remarks
		Lappa is at least 31. Time 11 hours.
Lappa–Eleutherna . .	32	This is an overstatement. The distance is 25 at the outside. Time 9 hours.*
Eleutherna–Sybrita . .	8	Fairly accurate. If anything an understatement. Time 3½ hours.
Sybrita–Gortyna . .	32	Fairly accurate. Time 10½ hours.
Gortyna–Knossos . .	27	Accurate. Time 9½ hours.
Knossos–Khersoneso3 .	16	Accurate. Time 4½ hours.
Khersonesos–Lyttos . .	16	Actually about 11. Time 3½ hours.*
Lyttos–Arkadia . . .	16⎫	Arkadia is one of the most elusive of sites. The two main choices are Melidhokhori, the most probable, and Phrati. These are respectively 20 and 11 from Lyttos and 6 and 20 from Biennos. In point of fact as the figures are given there can be no such place, since Lyttos is less than 14 from Biennos! In any case no site which is as yet unnamed lies at such a distance from either Lyttos or Biennos.
Arkadia–Biennos . . .	30⎭	
Biennos–Hierapytna .	20	An understatement. It is actually about 23. Time 9 or 10 hours.*
Hierapytna–Inatos . .	32	Accurate, assuming that Inatos is at Ini. Time 13–14 hours.*
Inatos–Gortyna . . .	23	Accurate. Time about 7 hours.*
Gortyna–Lebena . . .	12⎫	Lebena and Laseia are wrongly placed on the table, Laseia being shown as lying to the East of Lebena. The distance to Lebena is accurate, however. Time 4½ hours. That to Laseia is overstated, being actually only 13. Time 4½ hours.*
Gortyna–Laseia . . .	16⎭	

Route	Roman Miles	Remarks
Kydonia–Kisamos . .	32	This is the other Kisamos, West of Kydonia. The distance is overstated, being only 25. Time about 7 hours.*
Kisamos–Kantanos . .	24	About right. Time about 8 hours.*
Kantanos–Lissos . . .	16	This is not more than 13, even allowing for going round by Elyros. Time 4¾ hours.*
Lissos–unnamed town .	30	There is no site at this distance East of Lissos. Tarrha is 14. Anopolis 20. 30 miles would bring one to somewhere near Frankokastelli. But in any case the route is for the first 14 miles impassable for pack animals and can never have been of sufficient importance to be shown.

II. *Sea*

1. *STADIASMUS* (*ΑΝΩΝΥΜΟΥ ΣΤΑΔΙΑΣΜΟΣ ΗΤΟΙ ΠΕΡΙΠΛΟΥΣ ΤΗΣ ΜΕΓΑΛΗΣ ΘΑΛΑΣΣΗΣ*) 318.
Byzantine of sixth to eleventh centuries. It must be sixth, for it mentions Phalasarna, which went out of use in the middle of the sixth century.
M.P. = *Mediterranean Pilot*, Vol. IV.
The distances are given in figures and are often corrupt.

Route	Stades Given	Actual Distance	Notes in Text	Remarks
Kasos–Samonion.	500	240	Shelter, water, temple of Athene	Kavo Sidhero (St. Isidore) small harbour by Agios Ioannes church, East of Lighthouse.
Samonion–Hiera Pydna . .	80	420	Anchorage	Ancient moles now ruined.
Hiera Pydna–Bienos. . .	70	130 to Arvi / 140 to Alike below Keratos / 160 to Vianos by land	Small city away from the sea	Vianos is $2\frac{1}{2}$ hours above Arvi and $2\frac{3}{4}$ above Alike (a small M.M.III–L.M.I site).
Bienos–Lebena	70	250	Good water	M.P. 64 says there is anchorage in 10–20 fathoms. But a good beach.
Lebena–Halas	20	30		Lasseia or Thalasseia. Remains of mole connecting Traphos island with shore. Probably sailors also used Fair Havens to West.

Route			Description	Remarks
Halas–Matala	300	100	City and harbour	Subsidence of coast very marked here. Tombs below the sea.
Matala–Soulia	65	Accurate	Harbour and good water	At Agia Galene. Also called Soulena.
Soulia–Psykhion	12	60	Summer harbour and water	The 292 stades of the total is correct. But Psykhion is almost certainly at Kavo Melissa (ﬦ stater of Gortyna in the museum) 60 st. W. of Soulia. The only other site on the coast known to me is below Keramai 35 st. W. of Psykhion. Lamon might conceivably have stood on the site of Frankokastelli, which is about the right distance from Psykhion, and Apollonias might be at Sphakia about 45 st. W. of Frankokastelli and about 35 E. of Phoinix though the only finds near here have been L.M.III.
Hiera Pydna–Psykhion	350	600		
Psykhion–Lamon	150	? correct	City, harbour and water	
Lamon–Apollonias	30	? 45		
Apollonias–Phoinix	100	? 35	City, harbour and island	
Phoinix–Klauda	300	about 200	City and harbour	Spratt saw a Hellenic site on NW. end. M.P. 59 says anchorage in roadstead to E. is 10–20 fathoms.
Phoinix–Tarrha	60	about right	Small town, anchorage	At mouth of Agia Roumeli Gorge. M.P. 57 temporary anchorage for steamers only.

Route	Stades Given	Actual Distance	Notes in Text	Remarks
Tarrha–Poikilassos	60	about right	Anchorage and water	City is in the gorge above Voukilasi.
Poikilassos–Siba	50	45	City and fine harbour	Syia, port of Elyros. M.P. 56 no anchorage now, beach only.
Siba–Lissos	30	20		Agios Kirkos. M.P. 57 calls it a temporary anchorage. There can never have been a good beach.
Lissos–Kalamyde	250	60		Actual city is inland S. of Vlythias. There are traces of a harbour town at Τροχάλοι by Palaiokhora. M.P. 55 good anchorage and beaches.
Kalamyde–Krioumetopon	30	55	High promontory, shelter and water	Traces of buildings and worn columns at Limnaki. M.P. 55 in Port Krio accommodation reduced by rise of land.
Krioumetopon–Bienos	12			Somewhere in bay between Krioumetopon and Elaphonisi.
Bienos–Phalasarna	260	175	Harbour and water	Artificial harbour, now raised above sea level, rings for fastening ships still visible not long ago. M.P. 53 says there is now anchorage within islet and reef of Petalidhos.

Phalasarna–Iousagorai Is.	60	Accurate	Faces East, port and temple of Apollo	This makes the Iousagorai or Mousagorai Pontikonisi. Pliny says they were the three islands round Krioumetopon, i.e. Elaphonisi, and Cape Trakhila and Palaiokhora before the raising of the land. M.P. 23 says there is no change.
Iousagorai–Mese	3	Accurate	Anchorage	The attendant rock S. of Pontikonisi.
Mylai–Treton	50	Accurate	Mylai, 3rd island of Iousagorai. Deep water and Treton, a rocky promontory	Mylai must be part of the mainland now. There are several parts of the site at Phalasarna which must have been islands. Treton is Cape Tigani.
Treton–Agneion	50	Accurate	Temple to Apollo : harbour and an inner bay called Myrtilos. Water	Agios Sostes ? on Cape Bousa. M.P. 26 says the water is too deep for anchoring, stern must be secured to the shore.
Agneion–Kisamos	30	70	A city in the gulf. Harbour and water	Ancient port nearly dry. Remains of massive mole, good beach, no safe anchorage.
Kisamos–Tityros	25	60	High wooded promontory looking N.	? Agios Pavlos on W. side of Cape Spadha.

Route	Stades Given	Actual Distance	Notes in Text	Remarks
Tityros–Diktynnaia	80	Accurate	On the shore	At Meniais or Kantzillieria on E. side of Cape Spadha. Good beach. M.P. 26 coasting vessels can secure under N. cliff. Temple of Britomartis.
Diktynnaia–Koite . .	170	105	Island with anchorage and water on S. side	Must be Agios Theodhoros, one of the Boudroai also called Akoition. M.P. 27 limited anchorage in case of necessity under NE. point in 9–10 fathoms.
Koite–Kydonia	60	45	City and harbour with rocks at entrance	M.P. 29 entrance to harbour impossible with strong N. wind. Scylax says it had a closed port.
Kydonia–Aptera			Minos (? Minoa) is mentioned as if it was identical. But that is opposite, below Sternais on Akroteri.	M.P. 32. Mole was submerged.
(1) sea	150	170		
(2) land	120	75		
Aptera–Amphimatrion . .	150	125	A harbour where vessels can winter	The same as Amphimalla. M.P. 35 says it must have been a good harbour before the land rose and formed a bar only 3 feet below the surface at the mouth.

Route				
Amphimatrion–Hydramon	30	Accurate		
Hydramon–Astale	30	240	Has a beach Harbour to left, with water	At Dhramia. Roman remains. M.P. 37 anchorage for light craft against N. gale. Greco-Roman site. Bali.
Astale–Eleutherna (land)	50	65		The text says Hydramon to Eleutherna but is particularly corrupt at this point. About 4½ hours.*
Astale–Herakleion	100	175	City with harbour and water	Port of Knossos, overbuilt by modern Candia.
Herakleion–Dios Island	40	65		At Agia Pelagia bay and on high ground to North, extensive Roman site. M.P. 41 all three bays have good anchorage.
Herakleion–Knossos (land)	20	Accurate		
Herakleion–Khersonesos	30	130	Winter harbour. Island with tower and harbour	M.P. 43 port too shallow. Ancient moles still show.
Khersonesos–Olous	60	260	Promontory, anchorage, good water. 20 stades away is a small island	The island is the leper island of Spina Longa. M.P. 44 says Poros is a good shelter from N. winds. Ruins of city now partly submerged.
Olous–Kamara	15	35		Lato pros Kamara, at Agios Nikolaos. M.P. 46 says there is good anchorage. Extensive Greco-Roman site.

Route	Stades Given	Actual Distance	Notes in Text	Remarks
Kamara–Istron	25	35		Probably at Kalokhorio and the large site at Nisi and Priniatikos Pyrgos. Area known till recently as Nistrona.
Istron–Ketia	15	215	Shelter but no water	Probably promontory N. of Sitia, where M.P. 47, 48 says there is a good anchorage and shelter from N. wind.
Ketia–Dionysiades Islands . . .	300	85	Two islands, harbour and water	
Dionysiades–Sammonion . . .	120	75		

B. MODERN MAPS AND CHARTS, ETC.

These exclude maps published in books, such as Pashley's, Spratt's or Raulin's.

I. H. Kiepert . . . Creta	last edition 1907	1 : 300,000	This is undoubtedly the best map of Crete available. The method of showing the mountains leaves something to be desired and not enough heights above sea level are given. There are few mistakes in topography or orthography. It is greatly to be hoped that a new edition will be prepared.
II. British War Office . Crete	1905	1 : 300,000	An inferior version of Kiepert's map.
III. Lt. W. D. Downes . The Herakleion District	1907	1 : 100,000	This is a plane table survey covering the eparkhies of Malevizi, Topalti, Temenos, Pyrgiotissa, Kainouriou, Monophatsi and Pedhiadha. It is valuable as being the only

readable contoured survey of any part of the island. It suffers, however, from the surveyor's ignorance of Greek, many of the names being unrecognizable.

IV. Greek General Staff   1 : 20,000 N.D.

V. Capt. (Adm.) T. A. B. Spratt and others .

Herakleion District
Khania
Soudha Bay

1853 onwards

Several sheets of this survey have appeared. It is a pity that such care and trouble as have obviously been given should not have been rewarded by better production.

The Admiralty charts are admirable for the coast, but since Spratt had not adequate facilities for surveying the interior of the island, a number of errors crept in which have been slavishly copied by later maps, including Kiepert. The triumph is Stetkhorio South East of Khania, which perpetuates a marginal note in the proof! The rendering of the mountains is unsatisfactory and again insufficient heights are given.

Admiralty Charts :

2536 A and B show the Western and Eastern parts of the island at 1 : 150,000.
On A also are charts of Matala at 1 : 9000 and Sphakia 1 : 14560.

217 Grabusa 1 : 25,000, Rhethymnos 1 : 9100, Kutri (Phalasarna) 1 : 9100, Port Loutro (Phoinix) 1 : 9100.

1555 Anchorages near Cape Sidero 1 : 40,000.

1658 Khania 1:9900, Suda Bay and Khania 1:36,900.
1904 Megalokastron, Candia or Herak-leion.
2715 Khersonesos Bay 1:9100, Hiera-petra 1:9100, Eremopolis Bay (Itanos) 1:5200.
2724 Sitia Bay 1:14600, Kaloi Limniones 1:14600, Grandes Bay (Palaikas-tro) 1:14600.
2850 Poros Bay, 1:11,600, Spina Longa Harbour 1:19,000. Agios Niko-laos 1:8000.
2982 Standia or Dia Island. Anchorages on South coast.
3691 Suda bay anchorage 1:9970. Mega-lokastro, Candia or Herakleion 1:12,500.

VI. Eleutheroudakis. .   1:300,000   No date   This map is a Greek version of Kiepert. It makes some startling raids into the province of the identification of sites, but it gives the position of more villages than any other map and at least it spells them intelligibly.

VII. A. I. Μπακάκης . .   1:300,000   No date   Printed in Athens in the days of the Autonomy. It may well be the archetype of the above. Few physical features are given.

MEANING OF VARIOUS NAMES

The names of various τοποθεσίαις are often of great value in the discovery of sites. Στὰ Ἑλληνικά naturally raises the expectation of ruins even if not Hellenic. The following is a short list of the modern Cretan place-names most frequently found. All may have the diminutive ' ακι ' attached. Some are of considerable antiquity —the Καλὸς Λάκκος of the Olous-Lato boundary treaty still exists near Ellenika between Spina Longa and Agios Nikolaos.

Ἀμπέλι	Vineyard.
Ἀνάυλοχος	A steep-sided gorge.
Ἄσπα	A steep slope of disturbed earth.
Βίγλα or Βίγλαις (Latin vigil)	A look-out post or Πρόβαρμα (cf. Κορακο-βίγλα = crow's nest) = Ἐδίχτη.
Βόλακας	A boulder.
Γαστριά, Βίσαλα[1] (Central Crete) Κουρούπια (West Crete) Χαλίκια (East Crete)	Sherds. κεραμίδια are tiles only.
Γούρναις or Γουρνιά	A trough.
Δέτης or Δέτι	A steep slope.
Ζάρμας or Ζάρωμας	A connexion. Used like Σελλί for a saddle between peaks in Central Crete. lit. a wrinkle.
Καβόυσι	Hollow in the rock kept filled with water by a spring.
Καμάρα	Arch or bridge.
Καμίνι	Lime pit.
Καμπαθούρα	Shallow pit (Ida district).
Κάστελλος Καστέλλι Κάστρο Καστρί	A fort. The first two may imply Venetian fortifications or even merely a hill strong by nature. The second two almost always imply early remains.
Λαγγός or Λαγγάδα also Λαγκός	An opening out, or small plain, in a gorge.
Λατσίδα . . . . . (East Crete)	A natural basin or hole in the ground = Ταῦκος in Ida district = Λάκκος.

---

[1] Often used as a place-name.

33

Λειβάδι	Meadow or field without stones.
Λογάρι	Treasure = Μάλαμα (West Crete) Μπαρντά (Apodhoulou).
Μάνδρα	Sheepfold (στάνι is unknown in Crete).
Μιτάτο	Cheese Dairy.
Μνῆμα } Μνημεῖον }	Tomb. ἄχλα in Lasithi = τάφος.
Μουρί	Meeting-place.

Νομίσματα
Παράδες
Χρήματα
Φώλαις
  (Latin Follis or Arabic
    Fulus ?)
Μονέτα
  (West Crete)
Κατρίναις
  (East Crete)
	} Coins.

Παιζούλα	A terrace. (? Τραπεζούλα, a little table.) τάφρος or τράφος = a terrace wall.
Παπούρα	A hill or summit, not a peak.
Πλάϊ	Side.
Πόντα	A damp place (ἐπήρε τσὴ πόντα = he caught cold).
Ρουχούνη or Ρούχουνας (W. Crete κάντουνα)	A corner stone (Arabic rukhn).
Στέρνα	Cistern.
Τάπαις or } Τάμπιαις }	Slopes.
Τρόχαλοι } Τροχάλοι }	A mound of stones cleared from the fields— a frequent sign of ancient walls below the surface.
Χαλέπα	A rocky slope.
Χωράφι	Field.
Φαράγγι	A gorge qua gorge.

Chapter II

A. THE NEOLITHIC PERIOD

(*See Map 3*)

THE FULL extent of the Neolithic habitation of Crete is as yet undetermined. Remains [1] have been excavated at Potisteria, Kamarais, Knossos, Phaistos, Mallia, Trapeza and other sites near Tzermiadha in Lasithi, Agia Photia, Magasa near Palaikastro, Skalais near Praisos, Zakros and Sphoungaras near Gournia, as well as elsewhere, but it is certain that further discoveries await the explorer. Individual objects, indeed, such as stone celts, have already been picked up at various sites, mainly in the East end of the island, but these may well belong to the succeeding Sub-Neolithic Chalcolithic Period of E.M. 1. In any case, these sites are widely enough separated to show that the Neolithic inhabitants occupied, however sparsely, as wide an area as came later under the hand of the Bronze Age Minoans. The western settlements at Potisteria and Gavdhos we may perhaps take as unsuccessful exploratory settlements in the West. Probably the country was too wild.

With so few sites upon which to base an argument it would be unsafe to draw definite conclusions as to the places favoured as settlements by the folk of this period. It is, however, remarkable that, with the exception of Potisteria, Gavdhos, Amnisos, Dia, Komo, Mallia, and Sphoungaras, every settlement lies a good hour or more from the sea. The Lasithiote sites, as well as Magasa and Skalais, indeed, may be termed inland sites, while the preference for caves shown at Potisteria, Amnisos, Kamarais, Miamou, Trapeza, Sphoungaras, Magasa, Agia Photia, Zakros, and Skalais proves the uncertainty of life at that time (Pl. V, 1).

At Knossos alone are the earlier stages of Neolithic culture present, and the selection of Knossos in the centre of the

---

[1] References to the publications of the following sites will be found at the end of the chapter.

35

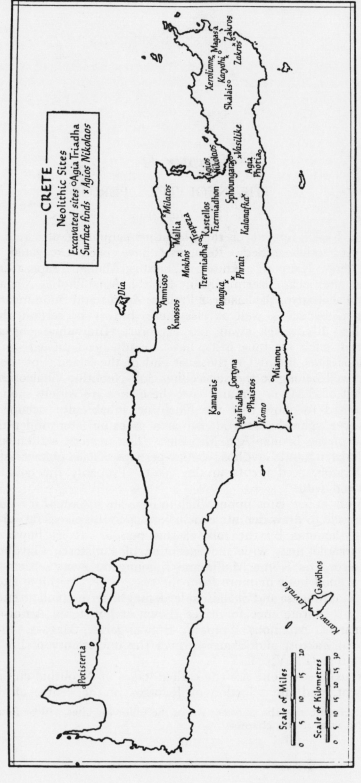

CRETE

Neolithic Sites

Excavated sites o Agia Triadha
Surface finds x Agios Nikolaos

Poristeria o

Pia

Kamarais o

Agia Triadha o Gortyna
Phaistos o
Komo

Amnisos
Knossos

Mokhos x
Tzermiadha x
Panagia x

Miamou

Milatos x
Mallia x
Trapeza o o
Kastellos o o
Tzermiadhon
Sphoungaras o
Kalanafka x

Phrati x

Agios
Nikolaos x

Vasilike x

Agia
Photiao

Xerolimne x Magasà
Karydhi o   Zakros
Skalais o   x Zakros

Kara Lavraka

Gavdhos

Scale of Miles
0   5   10   15   20

Scale of Kilometres
0 5 10 15 20 25 30

MAP 3

North coast as the spot for one of the largest Neolithic settlements in Europe and the Near East is a problem very difficult of solution. As we shall see, although the early connexions here with Anatolia were strong, yet the only evidence we have of direct traffic with the outside world is with Egypt. We must therefore postulate either the indigenous nature of the inhabitants, which is impossible in view of the advanced stage of the earliest strata, or else their immigration or geographical separation from the rest of their kinsfolk at a very early date.

As we have said, at Knossos alone has a large Neolithic site been explored. It extends in fact even beyond the borders of the present Palace area and descends in some places to a depth of over 7 metres. Thus, when men first settled on this spot, they settled on a low knoll, overlooked by the surrounding hills, a knoll on which, so far as we know, there existed no spring, though the Kairatos stream runs close below. Although the coast nearest to them faces directly towards the Mainland of Greece and the Islands of the Aegean, their connexions were with Egypt to the far South and with Asia to the East.

The Neolithic deposit at Knossos can be divided into Lower, Middle and Upper Periods.[1] That some considerable degree of culture had been reached before the settlement was founded is proved by the advanced nature of both pottery and implements even in the lowest strata.

' Lower Neolithic ' occupied the first $2\frac{1}{2}$ metres immediately above virgin soil in the West Court Test Pit. The pottery is hand-made, of coarse brownish clay burnished inside and out, for the most common shapes are open basins and bowls, though the presence of handles and fragments of narrower rims indicates that other shapes were used. No decoration has been found on any of these sherds. The incised ware characteristic of the next phase had evidently not come into use. *Lower Neolithic Pottery*

The transition to ' Middle Neolithic ' is gradual. From $2\frac{1}{2}$ to 4 metres above virgin soil incision gradually makes its appearance and in the fifth metre a new technique appears, the filling of the incisions with a white chalky material.[2] At *Middle Neolithic Pottery*

---

[1] *P. of M.*, I, 35 ; *J.H.S.*, 1903, 158.

[2] Mention is also made, *P. of M.*, I, 36, of a red filling. I can at present only find one example of this. Deep Foundations SE. area of ' Prisons ' (E. III, 6, 7th metre in Palace Museum). It is at any rate admittedly exceedingly rare.

the same time the surface of the unincised vases is sometimes rippled by means of a blunt instrument of bone drawn downwards from the rim.   All the finer vases were carefully burnished.   The clay being better sifted took a brighter polish, which together with the blackish surface distinguishes even the undecorated vases from those of the preceding period. In some cases, notably on one or two sherds from the South Propylaeum, it has a mottled appearance almost like that of the later E.M. Vasilike ware.

The commonest shapes are large open bowls and vases, small jugs, miniature cups, ladles and rectangular trays with partitions and sometimes with short legs.   The wishbone handle was already in use as well as tubular handles, with both

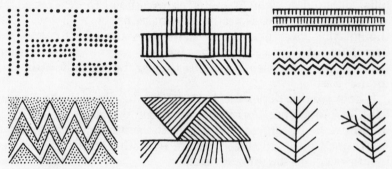

FIG. 1.—Patterns on Neolithic Pottery from Knossos

concave and straight sides, and ordinary strap handles.   Many of the vases were sharply carinated.

As has been said, the decoration consisted of burnishing, rippling and incising.   The chief incised patterns found are hatched triangles and rectangles, straight lines with short dependent lines, zig-zags running round below the rim, chevrons with a dotted field and rough geometric figures made out in dots.   Two sherds, however,[1] seem to show an attempt to represent branches.

Middle Neolithic Figurines, &c.

The same decoration is often applied to the clay spools and whorls which occur frequently,[2] as well as to the rarer representations of birds and animals.[3]   The human figure is found in statuettes, flat fiddle-shaped figures of clay which seem to

[1] *P. of M.*, I, Fig. 9.   [2] Ibid., Fig. 10.
[3] Ibid., Fig. 11.

be peculiar to this period [1] and stumpy steatopygous figures squatting or sitting, which continue into the Upper Neolithic Period.[2]

The stone celts, which are first found in the transitional stage between Lower and Middle Neolithic, continue unchanged into Upper Neolithic. They are of two types, one long and heavy, the other shorter and broader.[3] The stone maces are globular or slightly flattened at both ends. In this period the boring is begun from both ends and in some cases the resulting biconical hole is well marked. Obsidian cores were found in this stratum, showing that that stone was worked on the spot. Its source is uncertain but it is probably Melos or the island of Giale near Nisyros. *Middle Neolithic Stone Celts*

To this period belongs a small deposit discovered at Phaistos.[4] Together with miniature vases of the class mentioned above, too small for use, was a female figure of the second type, a large piece of magnetic iron and a number of sea shells. This association of objects puts one in mind of the later shrines with their figures of the goddess and their votive sea shells. *Middle Neolithic Shrine*

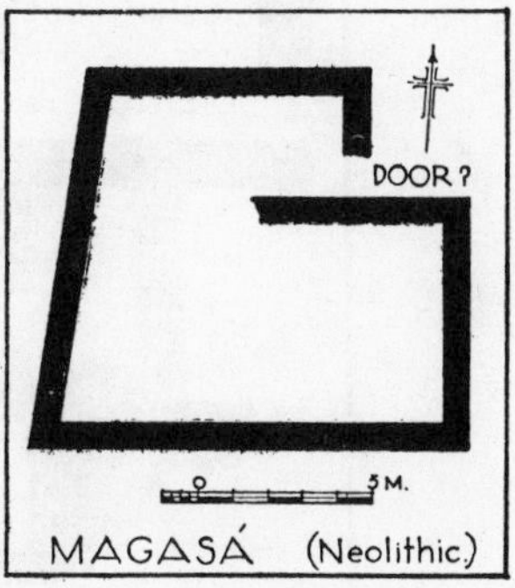

FIG. 2

In the Upper Neolithic Period we are on firmer ground. Two houses at Knossos each showing two layers of occupation, and the rock shelter and house at Magasa, give us some idea of the architecture of the period. *Upper Neolithic Architecture*

The rock shelter is a mere overhanging ledge of rock with the front roughly walled in.[5] The house (Fig. 2) was of the ' but and ben ' type, consisting of entrance room and an inner living room. Only one layer of large undressed blocks of limestone remains. The houses below the central court at Knossos [6] show an elaboration of this primitive system.

[1] *P. of M.*, I, Fig. 12, 1. They are, however, the forerunners of the Cycladic class.

[2] These are eventually no doubt descended from the steatopygous figurines of Upper Palaeolithic Art which had their original home in North Africa.

[3] *P. of M.*, I, Fig. 15*a*.

[4] Mosso, *Mon. Ant.*, XIX, 159 ; Pernier, *Festos*, I, 67, Pl. XI. Some of the sherds have the mottled appearance mentioned above.

[5] *B.S.A.*, XI, 261 ff.   [6] *P. of M.*, II, i, 7 ff.

There is an accretion of small rooms clustering round the main room (Fig. 3).

The clay floors often run under the walls dividing the rooms. These walls were formed of undressed blocks of limestone in a bedding of clay and pebbles. The general absence of openings for doors shows that a raised threshold was as common then as it is now. The upper part of the walls may well have been formed of sundried bricks. A feature of the house is

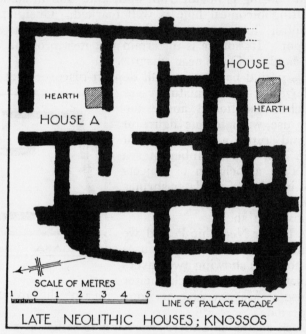

FIG. 3

a fixed hearth of clay and small stones either standing in the middle of a room or up against one of the walls. This type of hearth is well known in Asia Minor and Greece in the early Bronze Age. In Crete, however, save for two examples in M.M.1*a* houses at Mallia,[1] it disappears until the L.M.III*b* Period.

Upper Neolithic Pottery

The Late Neolithic pottery of Crete shows a falling off in technique, though the use of the potter's kiln results in a harder baked reddish surface, occasionally covered with a

[1] Demargne, *B.C.H.*, 1932, 76. He makes a strong plea for the fixed hearth being a regular feature until this latter period.

wash which was afterwards burnished. Incision and filling are dying out and the general appearance of the pottery is dull in the extreme. New shapes, however, appear in the chalice, which is to be so typical of E.M.1,[1] and a sharply carinated bridge-spouted jar[2] which foreshadows a long series of Minoan shapes. The pottery of the two levels in the houses at Knossos was indistinguishable except for a further decline in the art of burnishing, a slightly lighter coloured surface and an almost complete disappearance of incision.

The whole period seems to have been a short, transitional one. The deposit for all its two floor levels was only half a metre deep, and though this might be explained in the present case by the sweeping away of some of it during the formation of the central court, yet a Test Pit in the better-preserved area below the South Propylaeum confirms the shallow depth of the deposit.

The stone implements show no decline in technique, the celts are as fine and varied as ever, the obsidian finely flaked. But copper was coming in, or at any rate imported, for in the lower stratum of one of the houses, in circumstances which precluded it from being an intrusion, was found a copper axe-head.[3]

A remarkable local variation of the Late Neolithic Pottery must here be mentioned, although no more than a preliminary study has been made. In the cave of Trapeza in Lasithi a single pure stratum was discovered which among sherds of a normal Neolithic type produced an individual style. The pottery is of a dark, mottled type, red flecked with black. The sherds seem mainly to belong to cooking-pots, some of them of the two-storied type. But the most peculiar feature lies in the faces which are modelled on the rim and which seem to have their origin in a stylization of the tubular handles, the handle itself becoming a nose, the hollows behind it the eyes, while the mouth is added. Further decoration consists of a vertically applied strip of clay roughly impressed at intervals to form a kind of ' tress ', which is itself later stylized into the well-known rope pattern.

The foreign connexions of the period as a whole seem to *Neolithic* be mainly with Asia Minor, although the presence of fragments *Foreign* *Relations*

---

[1] *P. of M.*, II, i, Figs. 3*m*, 4.   [2] Ibid., II, i, Fig. 3*x*.
[3] Ibid., II, i, Fig. 3*f*.

of Egyptian stone vases, usually too small to identify,[1] an almost carinated mace-head,[2] and the metallic shapes of the chalices mentioned above which can be compared to the miniature copper vases found in the Tomb of Khasekhemui,[3] prove that intercourse with Egypt had already begun. But the figurines have strong Asiatic affinities [4] and the fixed hearth points in the same direction. Of the pottery it is more difficult to say, but striking likenesses have been observed in the early ceramics of Anatolia,[5] while at Megiddo the earliest pottery is indistinguishable from the Middle and Upper Neolithic strata at Knossos, except for the absence of incision, and at Byblos some of the pottery even shows this feature together with white filling. Frankfort,[6] however, would connect the strongly carinated shapes as well as the decoration with Danubian wares.

This, taken in conjunction with the uninterrupted continuation of the culture into the next period when Anatolian influence is more marked, inclines one to the belief in a very early immigration from South-West Anatolia. It is unfortunate that in the graves excavated in Lasithi in 1937, but scanty human remains survived.[7] Anthropology therefore cannot help us.

Neolithic Chronology

As to the dates to be assigned to the period certainty is impossible. There is reason to put the beginning of E.M.1

---

[1] But cf. *P. of M.*, II, 1, Fig. 6, a small limestone vase hollowed out with a tubular drill. A shape characteristic of the protodynastic period, cf. Petrie, *Royal Tombs at Abydos*, II, Pl. LI, 190. Many of the other fragments, however, are of the variegated stones, the use of which tended to die out in the protodynastic period. Professor Wace suggests to me that as in Early Cycladic 1, stone vases are the concomitant of stone axes and stone figurines, so some of these Cretan vessels may be locally made. The stone, however, is Egyptian and we cannot certify any stone vase as being of Minoan fabric until E.M.11.

[2] *P. of M.*, II, 1, Fig. 3k.

[3] Petrie, *Royal Tombs*, II, Pl IXA.

[4] *P. of M.*, I, 49 ff., Fig. 13.   [5] *Liv. Annals*, X, 32 ff.

[6] *Studies*, II, 55. The faces on the pottery from Trapeza described above, discovered, of course, since Frankfort's work, have too obvious an origin on the spot to be related to the Trojan anthropomorphic vases of later date.

[7] That the cave at Trapeza was inhabited in Neolithic times and not used as a burial-place until E.M.1 is clear from the absence of human bones in the one pure stratum and the prevalence of cooking-pots. The burial-places were, as one might expect, small rock shelters.

somewhere about the date of the IInd Dynasty of Egypt, and fragments of what seem to be Late Predynastic vessels have been found in the Upper Neolithic strata of Knossos. But we must remember not only that stone vases are very dangerous evidence, for they may remain in use for centuries after they have been made,[1] but also that with them were found the fragment of a small kohl pot of early dynastic date and the mace-head, which is also protodynastic, and that Egyptian analogies to the chalices are as late as the IInd Dynasty.

It would be dangerous, therefore, to pin our faith to any date much earlier than 3000 B.C. for the end of the Neolithic Period.[2]

For the duration of the Stone Age we have no good evidence. Sir Arthur Evans himself is sceptical as to the value of speculating on the length of time taken for the deposit to form.[3] He has taken the E.M. and M.M. strata as lasting for 1,800 years—from 3400 B.C. to 1600. This occupies below the West Court 2·82 metres of deposit, giving for the 8 metres of Neolithic deposit a space of over 5,100 years. From this he had deducted 10 per cent. for the possibility of the wattle and daub constructions having favoured a higher rate of accumulation and suggested the possibility of the original settlement dating back to about 8000 B.C. As we have seen, however, the end of the period cannot be with safety put earlier than 3000 B.C., and the depth of the stratum seems to be 6·50 metres, which brings it down to about 6700 B.C. In addition, the Neolithic inhabitants, if they resembled their modern descendants, were an untidy race. The rise in floor levels owing to the deposit of filth which accumulates to-day in a peasant's cottage is often as much as a centimetre a year,[4] and while, as Sir Arthur says, speculations can only have a relative value, it is exceedingly doubtful whether we can put back the first arrival of the Neolithic settlers more than a few centuries before 4000 B.C.

[1] Protodynastic vases were found at Mycenae in a L.H.II tomb and at Asine in a tomb of L.H.III date. A Middle Predynastic vase was found in use in a house at Tell el-Amarna.

[2] In these pages the generally accepted dates for the early dynasties are employed, but see note on the chronological table, p. 300.

[3] P. of M., I, 34.

[4] We have seen how little difference in culture there was between the deposits on the upper and lower floors of the late Neolithic houses at Knossos, and these were 25 cm. apart.

SITES WHERE NEOLITHIC REMAINS HAVE BEEN FOUND

(a) Excavated Settlements

AGIA PHOTIA . . Rock shelter — One vase. Hawes. *Gournia*, 56. Site is 35 m. W. of village near hamlet of Pherma. 2½ hr. E. of Hierapetra.

AGIA TRIADHA . Unpublished — Sherds. Unpublished.

AMNISOS . . Cave of Eileithyia — Sherds. Marinatos, Πραχτιχά, 1929, 95. Site is on the hill above the coast, W. of Karteros village.

GORTYNA . . Deposits . — Sherds from the Acropolis and from Volakais near by. Pace, *Annuario*, I, 372.

KAMARAIS . . Cave . . — Two sherds from the original find. Dawkins, *B.S.A.*, XIX, 12. Site lies nearly 2 hr. above Kamarais village on Mavrokorphe.

KASTELLOS TZER-MIADHON — Rock shelters — Burials excavated 1937 by the writer.

KNOSSOS . . Houses . — Architectural and domestic finds. Evans, *P. of M.*, I, 32 ; II, i, 1. Pottery : Mackenzie, *J.H.S.*, 1903, 158. Stratum extends all over the palace area. Houses excavated below the Central Court.

MAGASA . . Rock shelter and house — Architectural and domestic finds. Dawkins, *B.S.A.*, XI, 260. Site lies 1½ hr. SW. of Palaikastro.

MALLIA . . . Stratum. . — Sherds. Chapoutier-Charbonneau. *Mallia*, I, 18–20, 47. Stratum below Quarter V of the Palace. *B.C.H.*, 1928, 363.

MIAMOU . . . Cave . . — Vases, sherds, &c., from lowest level with fireplaces. Taramelli, *Mon. Ant.*, IX, 303. *A.J.A.*, 1897, 287. The cave is below a house in the village.

PHAISTOS . . Settlement . — House and sherds, &c., below Western section of the palace. Pernier, *Mon. Ant.*, XII, 22. Mosso, *Mon. Ant.*, XIX, 159. Pernier, *Festos*, 67.

POTISTERIA . . Cave of Ellenospilo — Vases and sherds 100 m. in from the mouth. Marinatos, *Mitt. über Höhlen und Karstforschung*, 1928, Fig. 3. The cave is ½ hour's sail N. of Gonia Monastery on the E. side of the Diktynnaian promontory.

SKALAIS . . Cave . . Sherds. Bosanquet, *B.S.A.*, VIII, 235. Cave lies on N. side of Praisos plateau.

SPHOUNGARAS . Rock shelter Sherds. Hawes, *Sphoungaras*, 46, and *Gournia*, 56. Deposit cleared out of the cave which lies between Gournia and the sea.

TRAPEZA . . Cave . . Vases and sherds. Excavated by writer in 1936. Cave lies 10 min. above Tzermiadha. *A.J.A.*, XL, 371 ; *Arch. Anz.*, 1936, 162. Deposit near by excavated in 1937.

TZERMIADHA . Cave burial At Skaphidhia, excavated by the writer, 1937.

ZAKROS . . Cave . . Two sherds. Hogarth, *B.S.A.*, VII, 142. Cave is in gorge above Kato Zakros.

(*b*) *Surface Finds*

(Note : the axes may belong to the succeeding E.M.1 period).

AGIOS NIKOLAOS Stone axe in the Candia Museum.

DIA . . . Sherd from walled field above and NE. of Agia Pelagia bay. Found by writer 1935.

GAVDHOS . . Sherds and obsidian from Karavi bay and Lavraka. Levi, *Art and Archaeology*, 1927, 176 ff.

KALAMAFKA . Stone axe in the Candia Museum.

KARYDHI . . Stone axe in the Candia Museum.

KOMO . . . Sherds picked up by R. W. Hutchinson, 1937.

MILATOS . . Stone axes in the Candia Museum from spots called Dhrakona and Kountouro. Xanthoudides, 'Aϱχ. Δελτ., IV, Παϱ. 10.

MOKHOS . . Vase in peasants' hands. From Edhikte or Anemoskia, a summit ½ hr. E. of village or from Mouri by the lake below the latter.

PANAGIA . . Stone axe from Kophina. Levi, *Annvario*, X–XII, 26.

PHRATI . . Stone axe from Prophetes Elias. Ibid., 40.

VASILIKE . . Vase in the Candia Museum and sherd picked up by writer from the Kephala.

XEROLIMNE . Stone axe in the Candia Museum. This may come from Magasa, q.v., which is not far away.

ZAKROS . . Stone axe from Skourokephalo by the new church in Apano Zakros. Bought by R. W. Hutchinson, 1936, for the Candia Museum.

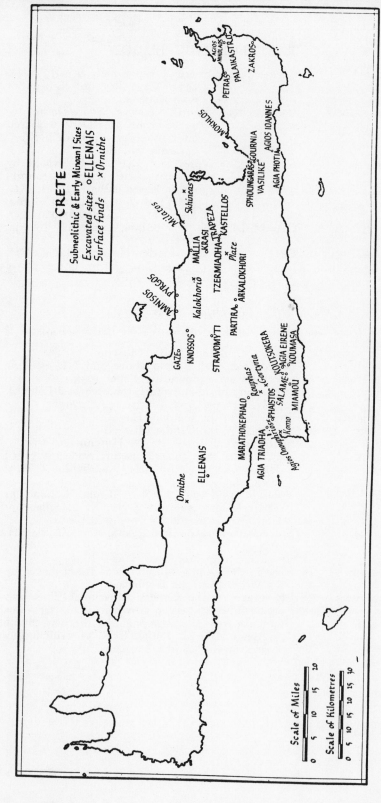

CRETE
Subneolithic & Early Minoan I Sites
Excavated sites ○ ELLENAIS
Surface finds × Ornithe

MORICHLOS

Milatos
Skinaes ×

AGIOS
NIKOLAS
PETRAS
PALAIKASTRO
ZAKROS
AGIOS IOANNES
AGIA PHOTIA
VASILIKE
SPHOUNGARAS○GOURNIA

MALLIA ×
×KRASI
TZERMIADHA-TRAPEZA
KASTELLOS
Plate ×
ARKALOKHORI
PARTIRA ○

Amnisos
PYRGOS
Kalokhorio ×
KNOSSOS ○
GAZE ○
STRAVOMYTI
×Gortyna
Rouphas
KOUTSOKERA ○
SALAME ○ AGIA EIRENE
KOUMASA
MIAMOU
PHAISTOS ×
Komo
Agios Onouphrios

MARATHOKEPHALO
AGIA TRIADHA

ELLENAIS ○

Ornithe ×

Scale of Miles
0   5   10   15   20

Scale of Kilometres
0 5 10 15 20 25 30

MAP 4

B. THE EARLY MINOAN PERIOD

I. EARLY MINOAN I (E.M.I)

(See Map 4)

The First Early Minoan Period is in the nature of a transition from the Neolithic to the full Copper Age of Early Minoan II.   The earlier stages, indeed, are rather to be styled Sub-Neolithic, a stage which seems to have lasted for a considerable period in the centre of the island.

The balance of power and the progressive force of culture has swung away to the East and it did not return to the centre for many years.

Ten sites in the East have been at least partially excavated, while from two more come chance finds.   Eight excavated sites lie in the South, while four more await the excavator.   In the centre of the island are twelve excavated sites and chance finds from four more.   One excavated and one unexcavated site lie to the West of Ida.   In contrast to the Neolithic Age the settlements seem to be chosen for their accessibility from the sea.   The exceptions are either sacred or sepulchral caves such as Arkalokhori and Stravomyti, or where a flourishing population has expanded along an easy route as in the Messara, and in Lasithi.

Of the architecture of the period we know practically nothing. *E.M.I Architecture* At Knossos the houses were swept away to make room for the Central Court of the first Palace.   No walls survived in conjunction with the earliest deposit at Vasilike.   The scantiness of the E.M.I deposits in the Messara forbids us to attribute to this period the building of any of the circular tombs.   At Mokhlos alone were found traces of rectangular stone houses which seemed to be connected with the small E.M.I deposit in the town.

To compensate for this, however, a greater number of *E.M.I Graves* graves are found.   These occur in rock shelters and caves at Miamou, Trapeza, Zakros, Sphoungaras, Agia Photia, and Agios Nikolaos near Palaikastro.   At the last-named site an examination of the human remains was possible, resulting in the discovery that the skulls were all of a pronounced dolichocephalic type, with long narrow faces, and that the average height for a man was 5 feet 2 inches, for a woman 4 feet 11 inches.[1]

The pottery is still hand-made and begins to show a reddish core, perhaps due to increasing skill or to the use of the potter's oven. The main general difference between it and the pottery of the preceding period is that the burnishing

FIG. 4.—Patterns on Early Minoan 1 Pottery

of the whole surface of the vase dies out, its place sometimes being taken by a lustrous black slip.[2] Incision is revived, but the filling of the pattern with white is never found.

The pottery varies considerably in different areas.

1. *Central Crete.*—In this part of the island the old Neolithic tradition dies hard. Indeed, true E.M.1 as opposed

[1] *B.S.A.*, IX, 347.   [2] *J.H.S.*, 1903, 165.

to Sub-Neolithic must have been a very short period. At Knossos the most common Sub-Neolithic shapes seem to be open bowls, ladles, handleless cups, hemispherical or with a base, and pedestalled bowls. Slightly later come a few fragments of the burnish technique described below, and with them several fragments which have stripes in chalky white paint or more rarely in crimson. This perhaps was a revival of Neolithic tradition. Still fewer have a dark on light technique, and it is perhaps permissible to regard these as imports from the East.[1]

At Pyrgos and Arkalokhori the material is richer. Unfortunately neither site is stratified and both contain later pottery. It is therefore on stylistic grounds that the attributions must be made. We see here an advance on the Sub-Neolithic shapes of Knossos in the tall grey chalices with a burnished decoration perhaps representing grained wood (Pl. IX, 1, c).[2] One of these has a crinkly rim suggesting a metallic origin, or more probably the irregular rim of Cretan gourds. This shape and fabric are peculiar to the centre of the island, though burnish decoration has been found in a settlement at Ellenais near Amari West of Ida.[3]

Suspension pots come in with a high neck imitating gourds and with their handles pierced vertically as opposed to the horizontal piercing of the Neolithic Age. These, too, have a grey surface and are frequently decorated with incised patterns (Pl. IX, 1, a and b).

In this part of the island the incision, while more elaborate and covering more of the vase than in Neolithic times, is careless and consists mainly of thin chevrons divided by vertical lines or of rough wedge-shaped dots. Often the vase looks as if it had been merely scratched by a child, so random and irresponsible is the decoration.

The painted ware from Pyrgos (Pl. IX, 2, a) is entirely dark on light. It seems to correspond more to the painted ware of

---

[1] The paint approximates more to the reddish-brown lustre of the East than to the clear matt red of the South. Evans, *P. of M.*, I, 63, quotes Mackenzie as to its being the first appearance of true glazed technique in the Aegean.

[2] *P. of M.*, I, 69, where the shape is eventually derived from a wooden bowl with withy handles set on a stand. Hazzidakis, *B.S.A.*, XIX, 39, thought the decoration was an irregular spiral. Frankfort, *Studies*, II, 88, sees in it a rough geometric design, but it seems too irregular for that.

[3] *J.H.S.*, 1932, 255.

the South next to be described than to that of the East.   The
shapes, however, betray some connexion with the East in the
beaked jugs and the comparatively elaborate variations of them.
The paint itself, too, corresponds more in tone to that of Eastern
Crete—though the bad condition of many of the vases may
be responsible for the darkening of the clear red in use in the
South.

2. *Southern Crete.*—The grotto at Miamou [1] seems to provide us with the only definitely Sub-Neolithic pottery in this
part of the island.   The most interesting shapes are a two-
handled carinated bowl and a square-mouthed two-storied
jar, while an incised suspension pot shows the transition to
E.M.1 proper.

The E.M.1 pottery is still mainly of grey clay, but the
shapes are distinctly in advance of those found in the North
and centre of the island.   Suspension pots are common but
with a short collar, not with the long bottle neck of the North.
Some are placed on a tall base and in one case from Koumasa
are actually nested together to form a kind of kernos.[2]   One
from Agios Onouphrios is fitted with a small cap.[3]

Pots with the burnish decoration of Central Crete are very
rare and are probably imported.[4]   Incised decoration is
confined to dots covering the whole body of the vessel, diagonal
lines in bands round the body and occasionally roughly cut
concentric semicircles resting on a line encircling the body,
the spaces filled with dots (Pl. IX, 1, *h-j*).

The painted decoration is best seen on the well-known
jug from Agios Onouphrios [5] (Pl. IX, 2, *b*).   The deposit
here was unstratified, but the date of this vase is clearly
shown by its round bottom, a convenient mark of distinction between E.M.1 and E.M.11 jugs.   The matt paint of
a clear red runs in thin vertical and diagonal stripes over
the body.   The stripes narrow down at the end, giving a
rather scrappy appearance to the vase.   This feature is also
seen on sherds from Phaistos, where the ends of the lines
have almost the appearance of bunches of grass.[6]   Little
effort seems to have been made to evolve a definite pattern.

---

[1] *A.J.A.*, I, 287.
[2] *V.T.M.*, Pl. XXV, 4194, but Evans, *P. of M.*, I, Fig. 43*c*, considers it E.M.11–111 ; it is, however, indistinguishable in fabric from
the rest.
[3] *P. of M.*, I, Fig. 23.   [4] Kutsokera, *V.T.M.*, 75.
[5] *P. of M.*, I, Fig. 25.   [6] Pernier, *Festos*, I, 115 ff, Pl. XII.

Such cross-hatching as occurs seems to be quite accidental. This painted decoration in the South in fact gives much the same impression of irresponsibility as the contemporary incised decoration of Central Crete.

3. *Eastern Crete.*—In this part of the island also we seem to leap almost direct into the E.M.1 Period. The only pottery which can be called Sub-Neolithic for certain is that found at Agios Nikolaos, near Palaikastro, in a rock shelter containing many burials.[1] The most typical shape was a two-storied suspension pot with a tall horned cap which could be tied on to it (Pl. IX, 1. *f*). This shape recalls the Sub-Neolithic deposit at Miamou.

Another deposit, however, which must be placed at the very beginning of E.M.1 proper, if indeed it is not actually Sub-Neolithic, occurred below Tomb V at Mokhlos.[2] Here rough clay ladles continue the Neolithic tradition. There are hemispherical cups and ringstands. No decoration was found, the vases being of coarse red clay sometimes covered with a red wash and sometimes pared into shape with an instrument which has dragged open the clay, leaving irregular holes on the surface. This feature occurs also on several sherds from the gulf of Mirabello now in the British Museum.[3] The particular interest which attaches to this group, however, is due to the presence of what appears to be a very primitive form in clay of the ' Horns of Consecration ', which play so large a part in later Minoan worship. The whole group indeed may well be votive.

Other sites, however, show no Sub-Neolithic characteristics. At Gournia, Vasilike, Zakros, Palaikastro, Mallia and Krasi the E.M.1 Period springs into full flower. Round-bottomed jugs are found frequently painted (Pl. IX, 2, *e*). The decoration is more carefully done than in the centre or South, the semi-lustrous reddish-brown paint being laid on to form ' double axe ' or ' butterfly ' patterns.[4] Carefully hatched triangles are found on pedestalled suspension pots which are also ornamented with bands of paint round neck and foot (P. IX, 2, *c* and *d*). These suspension pots, like those in the South, have a short neat neck. They are frequently decorated with incised patterns which show that the makers

---

[1] *B.S.A.*, IX, 340. [2] *Mochlos*, 92.
[3] *B.M. Cat.*, 410. In return we get an imitation of Southern painted patterns in burnish at Arkalokhori. *B.S.A.*, XIX, Fig. 6*b*.
[4] e.g. *Gournia*, Pl. A, 3.

had a better eye for design than those in the centre or South
(Pl. IX, 1, *d*, *e* and *g*).   Neat concentric semicircles appear,
the background filled with dots.   Even bands of herring-
bone, chevrons or cross-hatching run round the body of the
vase.[1]

The impression we get is that the makers of these vases
were working on an old tradition to which they had been
trained.   Since the Neolithic ware of the district is scanty
and undecorated at that, and since we can hardly assume that
the technique is copied from the centre or South of the island,
from which the East differs so much and which it outstrips
in every way, we must look abroad for these new influences.

E.M.1
Tools

A fragment of copper occurred in one of the vases from the
votive deposit at Mokhlos.   This, however, is not enough to
prove more than an acquaintance with metal, since, as we
have seen, a complete axe-head of copper was found in a pure
stratum in one of the Upper Neolithic houses at Knossos, an
obvious import.   True the forms of some of the daggers in
the earlier part of the succeeding period point back to a more
primitive ancestry, but we have no proof that that ancestry
is Cretan.   Copper tools or weapons have yet to be found
in an E.M.1 stratum.   Meanwhile, we may take it that the
ordinary implements, whether tools or weapons, continue to
be of the stone and obsidian types which are found in such
quantities in the Sub-Neolithic strata at Knossos and which
differ in no way from those in use during the Later Neolithic
Period.[2]

E.M.1
Figurines

The human figurines differ little from those of the Neolithic Period.   Stone, however, tends to become the more
usual material.[3]   One class adheres to the more upright
steatopygous type already described, while another approximates to the stylized Cycladic figurines.   As Sir Arthur Evans
has pointed out, more interest seems to be taken in the face,
which in one case from Central Crete is carefully rendered.[4]

[1] An obvious imitation of this type of decoration was found at
Knossos in the 1st metre of a test pit on the E. side of the NE. hall
(K., II, 5, in the Palace Museum).   This had bands of concentric
semicircles both standing on and depending from a central line.
They are placed so as to overlap each other and give the impression
of a rough spiral.   The technique is too rude to suppose it was
imported.
[2] As said above, p. 35, all the stone celts from these sites may
be E.M.1.
[3] *P. of M.*, I, 64.   [4] Ibid., I, Fig. 13, 20.

It is noteworthy that every example which can be assigned to E.M.1 comes from the centre of Crete, with one exception, which is said to have been found at Gortyna.[1]

As for seal stones, we are unfortunately compelled to rely on stylistic evidence alone. Such seals as are attributed to this period are large, conical or three-sided and made of steatite. Their decoration is very primitive and consists of roughly drawn pictographs in which distorted human figures predominate.[2] On one example we seem even to have a proto-Minotaur.[3]

*E.M.1.
Seals*

The foreign relations may be divided into two classes, direct and indirect. Of the direct influences Anatolia plays the most important part. The beaked jug points in that direction, but more significant is the fact that the handle is thrust through the wall of the vase and emerges on the inside not only in Anatolia but also in E.M.1 Crete and indeed all over the Aegean.[4] The low-collared suspension pot may also have a similar origin.[5] The most important sites of pure E.M.1 as opposed to Sub-Neolithic, as we have seen, lie in the East of the island, where in contrast to the Neolithic remains the settlements are usually chosen for their harbours, or at any rate for their accessibility to the sea. We have seen that the eastern end of the island steps almost without a break into the E.M.1 Period, and it is difficult to account for these phenomena in any other way than by assuming an actual wave of immigrants from South-Western Asia Minor.

*E.M.1
Foreign
Relations*

Now, as we have seen, the centre of Crete remained some considerable time in a Sub-Neolithic stage, while the East had progressed to true E.M.1. It is therefore not remarkable that at the same time as Anatolian influences begin to come in from the East, the centre should also betray connexions with the same culture but at second hand—through the Cyclades which it faces. The bottle-necked suspension pots found at Pyrgos and Knossos are closely paralleled even in their incised decoration by bottles from Antiparos and elsewhere.[6] Perhaps it is in the Cyclades also that the origin of the circular incised vase in grey clay from Patema near Palaikastro must

---

[1] Ibid., I, Fig. 13, 8.   [2] Ibid., I, 68.
[3] *Scripta Minoa*, I, 118.
[4] See Frankfort, *Studies*, II, 86, for references.
[5] *Studies*, II, 87
[6] Cf. *B.M. Cat.*, 309.

be sought.[1] Cycladic influence, however, is slight. It is not until E.M.III that it becomes really strong.[2]

Since it is on the Egyptian evidence that we rely for positive dating, it is particularly important that it should be scrutinized thoroughly. As is to be expected, such evidence as we may allow comes from the South and centre of the island. In Neolithic times Knossos, as we have seen, had some connexion with Egypt, and in the South the harbour town of Komo, through which undoubtedly the later trade passed, was already in existence in E.M.I.[3] It is therefore disappointing in the extreme that no E.M.I stratum yet excavated has produced any datable Egyptian object. A syenite vessel of the type common in the first two dynasties was found on the borders of the Neolithic and Sub-Neolithic clay deposit in the South Propylaeum.[4] But it was not in that deposit.[5] Similarly other stone vessels have been found dumped in the unstratified deposit North and North-West of the Palace. These presumably came from the E.M. strata swept away to form the Central Court in M.M.I, but to which E.M. period they belong it is impossible to say. They include fragments of two hornblende porphyry bowls of Middle Predynastic type and another of a Ist or IInd Dynasty type.[6] Similarly unstratified was the half of a diorite mace-head of Late Predynastic date.[7] We cannot allow these as evidence. Hard stone vases are used for hundreds of years after their manufacture, as we may see from the occurrence of Predynastic vases in late tombs at Mycenae and Asine, at Tell el-Amarna in use in a house of the XVIIIth Dynasty and at Venice to-day in St. Mark's.[8] Although, then, the Minoan was by E.M.II a maker of stone vases of a very high order and was therefore less likely to treasure foreign imports, no E.M.I stone vases have come to light, and in many of the cases above mentioned

[1] B.S.A., Sup., Fig. 2.

[2] Aberg, op. cit., 242, would make Pyrgos and Krasi practically Cycladic colonies, but it seems more probable that they are examples of branches from a parent stock common to Crete and the Cyclades which happen to have developed in the same way. Ellenais, where similar pottery exists, is away to the West of Ida, and close to Arkalokhori where ' Pyrgos ware ' is found lies Partira with its tall-capped suspension pots like those of Agios Nikolaos.

[3] P. of M., II, 88.

[4] Ibid., I, 65 ; B.S.A., IX, 98 ; cf. Petrie, Meydum and Memphis, III, Pl. XIX, 7. It is certainly not Predynastic.

[5] P. of M., II, 30, 31.   [6] Ibid., I, 65.

[7] Pendlebury, Aegyptiaca, No. 24.   [8] Ibid., 3.

these vases may have been imported in Neolithic times. They would have given us a *terminus ad quem* if only they had been stratified, but that is all.

This being so, we have still the possibilities of the artistic influence exercised by Egypt on Crete. But in this respect we flounder deeper into the morass both in this and the next period when such influence as is recognizable on seals from Central Crete and figurines from the Messara seems to be purely predynastic. In E.M.i the seal stones seem to show the influence of a class of late predynastic cylinder and prism seals in the representation of men and monsters. These types in Egypt, however, go back to Mesopotamian origins, and it is possible that in this case the tradition came direct from Asia with no Egyptian transmission.[1]

We are therefore unable to date with certainty the Sub-Neolithic and E.M.i Periods. Fortunately, as we have seen, the end of the true Neolithic Period comes some time in the Ist or IInd Dynasty,[2] and, as we shall see, there is some evidence to make E.M.ii contemporary with the IVth–VIth Dynasties. Further than that we cannot go.

E.M.i Chronology

SITES WHERE SUB-NEOLITHIC AND EARLY MINOAN I REMAINS HAVE BEEN FOUND

WEST CRETE

(a) *Excavated Site*

ELLENAIS AMARIOU House . . Vases. Marinatos, *J.H.S.*, 1932, 255. The excavation has been filled in again. It lies N. of the village.

Cave . . Sherds probably from burials. Marinatos, *Arch. Anz.*, 1932, 77 ; 1933, 295. Cave lies NE. of the village.

(b) *Surface Finds*

ORNITHE . . . Stone axes in the Rhethymnos museum from the site at Tabiais, E. of the village. Ornithe is on the S. slopes of Mt. Vrysinas, S. of Rhethymnos.

[1] *P. of M.*, I, 68.

[2] Is it possible that the Egyptian influences which have been seen in the Messara (Frankfort, *Studies*, II, 96 ; *P. of M.*, II, 22 ff.) are the result of refugees not from Menes' conquest of the Saite kingdom in the North-Western Delta but from that of Khasekhemui.

CENTRAL CRETE
(a) Excavated Sites

AMNISOS . . .	Cave . .	Vases, &c., from burials in Eileithyia cave. Marinatos, *Πρακτικά*, 1929, 95 ; 1930, 91.
ARKALOKHORI . .	Cave . .	Vases, &c., probably from burials. Hazzidakis, *B.S.A.*, XIX, 35. Cave lies under summit of Prophetes Elias Hill.
GAZE	Pit . . .	Sherds. Hazzidakis, *'Αρχ. Δελτ.*, II, *Παρ.* 23.
KASTELLOS TZERMI-ADHON . . .	Settlement .	Traces on the summit. Excavated by the writer, 1937.
KNOSSOS . . .	Stratum. .	Vases, &c. Evans, *P. of M.*, I, 56. Remains of settlement exist all over the Neolithic stratum, particularly in the West Court and round the South Propylaeum.
KRASI	Deposit .	Vases from earliest deposit by built tomb. Marinatos, *'Αρχ. Δελτ.*, 12, 102. The tomb is above the village to the SE.
MALLIA	Deposit .	A few sherds. Chapoutier, *Mallia*, I, 48 ; *B.C.H.*, 1928, 367.
PARTIRA. . . .	Tomb . .	Vases from fissure in rock. Marinatos, *B.C.H.*, 1931, 517.
PYRGOS	Cave . .	Vases from burials. Xanthoudides, *'Αρχ. Δελτ.*, 1918, 136. Cave lies on a headland E. of Nirou Khani.
STRAVOMYTI . .	Cave . .	Sherds from excavations of 1898. Evans, *P. of M.*, II, i, 68.
TRAPEZA . . .	Cave . .	Vases, &c., from burials. *A.J.A.*, XL, 371. *Arch. Anz.*, 1936, 162.
TZERMIADHA . .	Cave . .	One suspension vase in the Skaphidhia Cave. Excavated 1937.

(b) Surface Finds

KALOKHORIO PEDHI-ADHOS	Three-sided seal. Evans, *P. of M.*, I, Fig. 37.
MILATOS . . .	Suspension pot in the Candia Museum. No. 15.
PLATE	Jug, axes and stone bead from spot called Katsoukheiroi, seen in peasants' hands by the writer, 1935 and 1936.
SKHINEAS . . .	Sherds seen on Koprana by the writer, 1937.
UNKNOWN PROVEN-ANCE	Calcite figurine. Evans, *P. of M.*, I, 64, Fig. 13, No. 20.

SOUTH CRETE

(a) Excavated Sites

AGIA EIRENE . .	Deposit .	Vase near circular tomb. Xanthoudides, *V.T.M.*, 52. The site is hard to find, about 1 hour NE. of Vasilike in the Messara.
AGIA TRIADHA .	Deposit .	2 vases, probably of this date, from Tholos. A. Banti, *Annuario*, XIII, XIV, 164 ff.
KOUMASA . . .	Deposit .	Sherds and vases by circular tomb. *Ibid.*, 9, 34.
KOUTSOKERA . .	Deposit .	Sherds and vases by circular tomb. *Ibid.*, 74. The site is half an hour N. of Vasilike in the Messara.
MARATHOKEPHALO .	Deposit .	Earliest deposit by tomb. Xanthoudides, 'Αϱχ. Δελτ., 1918, Παϱ. I, 14 ff.
MIAMOU . . .	Cave . .	Vases, &c. Taramelli, *A.J.A.*, I, 287 ; *Mon. Ant.*, IX, 300.
PHAISTOS . . .	Deposit .	Mainly below W. end of the Palace. Mosso, *Mon. Ant.*, XIX, 199. Pernier, *Festos*, 115.
SALAME	Deposit .	Sherds near circular tomb. Xanthoudides, *V.T.M.*, 73. The site is 100 yd. from Koutsokera.

(b) Surface Finds

AGIOS ONOUPHRIOS	Vases, &c., in the Candia Museum, perhaps from deposit near a circular tomb. Evans, *Cretan Pictographs*, Supp., 105. The site is on the low hill above the inn where you turn off the main road to Phaistos.
GORTYNA . . .	Stone figurine. Evans, *P. of M.*, I, 64, Fig. 13, No. 8.
KOMO	Sherds from southern headland. Evans, *P. of M.*, II, i, 88. The site is just north of Matala in the bay of Messara.
ROUPHAS . . .	Sherds from the settlement on the line of the N.-S. road from Knossos. Evans, *P. of M.*, II, i, 80.

EAST CRETE

(a) Excavated Sites

AGIA PHOTIA . .	Rock shelter	Vases, &c. Hawes, *Gournia*, 56.
AGIOS IOANNES .	Cave . .	Sherds from burials. Hawes, *Trans. Penn. Univ.*, I, 214.

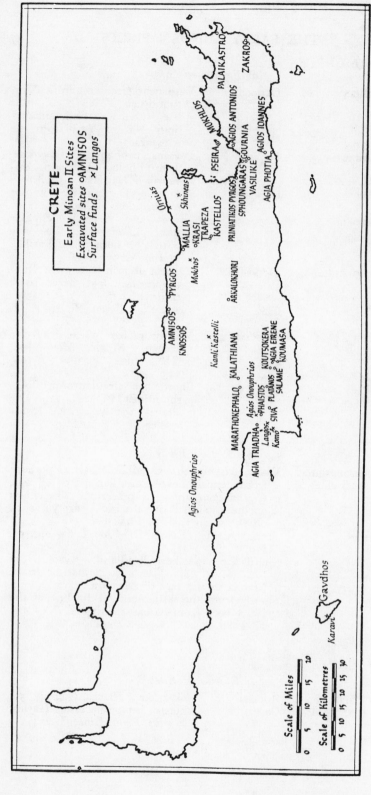

CRETE

Early Minoan II Sites
Excavated sites ○AMNISOS
Surface finds ×Langos

PALAIKASTRO
ZAKROS
NIROKHLOS
AGIOS ANTONIOS
PSEIRA○ ○GOURNIA
Ortias AGIA PHOTIA○ AGIOS IOANNES
Skhineas× VASILIKE
KRASI TRAPEZA PRINIATIKOS PYRGOS○
MALLIA○ KASTELLOS SPHOUNGARAS○
Mokhos× PYRGOS○
AMNISOS○ ARKALOKHORI
KNOSSOS○
Kianli Kastelli×
MARATHOKEPHALO○ KALATHIANA○
Agios Onouphrios KOUTSOKERA○
AGIA TRIADHA○ ×PHAISTOS○ AGIA EIRENE○
Langos× PLATANOS○ SALAME○ KOUMASA○
Komo× SIVA○

Agios Onouphrios
×

Gavdhos
Karavi×

Scale of Miles
0   5   10   15   20

Scale of Kilometres
0 5 10 15 20 30

MAP 5

AGIOS NIKOLAOS . Rock shelter Vases from burials. Tod, *B.S.A.*, IX, 340. Human remains. Duckworth, ibid., 344. The site is 1 hr. SW. of Palaikastro.

GOURNIA . . . Deposit . Sherds. Hawes, *Gournia*, 37.

MOKHLOS . . . Deposits . Vases from votive (?) deposit below tomb V and earliest deposit in town. Seager, *Mochlos*, 92, Fig. 48. *A.J.A.*, XIII, 279.

PALAIKASTRO . . Cemetery . Vases from N. cemetery. Bosanquet, *B.S.A.*, VIII, 290. One vase from Patema at the S. end of the site. *B.S.A.*, Supp., 5.

Deposit . Deposit in town. *B.S.A.*, X, 200, Supp. 4.

PETRAS . . . . ? . . . Six sherds. Forsdyke, *B.M. Cat.*, I, 412, 413. Not published in report *B.S.A.*, VIII, 282.

SPHOUNGARAS . . Rock shelter Vases, &c. Hawes, *Gournia*, 56.

VASILIKE . . . Deposit . Vase and sherds from lowest level below houses. Seager, *Gournia*, 49 ; *Trans. Penn. Univ.*, I, 207.

ZAKROS . . . Rock shelter Vases from burials. Hogarth, *B.S.A.*, VII, 142. The site is a little above Kato Zakros.

(b) Surface Finds

HIERAPETRA ISTHMUS Incised sherd. *B.M. Cat.*, I, 414.

MIRABELLO GULF . Sherds. Ibid., 407–11.

2. EARLY MINOAN II (E.M.II)

(See Map 5)

The second Early Minoan Period is the climax of the so-called Early Bronze Age in the Aegean.[1] The use of metal is now general and we are justified in speaking of a real civilization whose arts and crafts have reached a considerable stage of culture.

The East end of the island is still ahead of the rest culturally ; but in density of population the South is making rapid

---

[1] Analyses of daggers show that true bronze is not yet in use. Such alloy as appears is still fortuitous. *B.S.A.*, XIX, 47 ; *V.T.M.*, 26, and see below.

strides, due apparently to some external impulse.   The centre
and North of the island alone lag somewhat behind.   For the
first time, however, there seems to be a common civilization
extending over all the populated districts and the differences
observable between district and district are no more than are
natural when communications by land are difficult and by sea
are directed to that point of the outside world which lies nearest
to the particular area.

In Central Crete the caves of Arkalokhori and Pyrgos are
still in use, the one as a sacred place the other as a place of
burial.   At Knossos a few house floors appear below the
southern terraces.   How much more material of this period
once existed can be guessed from the frequent occurrence of
E.M.ii sherds which had been swept away with the earth when
the central Court was levelled and the debris therefrom used to
bank up the NW. quarter of the first Palace.   Another large
site lay at Kanli Kastelli, SW. of Juktas, where on the spot
called *Visala* (pot sherds) a certain amount of pottery has been
picked up on the surface.

In South Crete, particularly in and round the Messara, sites
lie thick.   The circular tombs which now appear for the first
time are dotted all over the plain and up into the foot-hills of
Ida, while traces of what may have been one are observable at
the great port of Komo to the South.   No settlement unfortunately has yet been excavated.   It has been considered
remarkable that no settlements are known which correspond in
date to the E.M. elements in the tombs, whereas in several
cases settlements have been excavated which seem to begin
with the latest, M.M.i, elements in the same tombs.   Åberg
has used this fact to prove his thesis that the contents of the
tombs, E.M. and M.M., are all contemporary, without apparently considering it strange that no E.M. stone vases or seals
are ever found in the *ex hypothesi* contemporary settlements.[1]
There is, however, a perfectly rational answer.   The M.M.i
settlements are few enough and can easily be explained by a
change of site, as at Vasilike in East Crete, which took place
for some reason we can no longer see.   As for the E.M. settlements they remain undiscovered because Xanthoudides mainly
concerned himself with tombs, only excavating such settlements as lay in the immediate neighbourhood.   It is extremely
improbable that houses would be built in great proximity to

[1] Åberg, loc. cit., 250 ff.

tombs still in use,[1] and in the case of a fertile area such as the Messara the sites of villages change very little in the course of ages. It is extremely probable that we should look for the settlements under the modern villages, for that of the tomb at Marathokephalo below Moroni, of Dhrakonais below Phournopharango, of Khristos, Koutsokera, Salame and Agia Eirene below Vasilike, where a chance cutting for a road has already shown M.M.I sherds.

In East Crete the finds centre round the old ports of Palaikastro, Mokhlos, Pseira, Gournia and Zakros, with only two inland sites, Vasilike and Agios Antonios, both of which are within striking distance of the sea.

Again, it is the easterners who are the sailors pure and simple, probably relying on the fertile Hierapetra Isthmus and the few rich valleys running up from the East coast for necessaries of life but mainly engaged in sea traffic. The southerners, naturally enough, on entering the Messara plain, were converted to an agricultural and pastoral life almost at once—though still keeping open the old trade with Africa through the port of Komo. The men of Central Crete are consolidating themselves, taking what they can from their more progressive neighbours but content to wait.

From the anthropological point of view we have at last more to go on, though it must be added that some of the bodies examined may belong to the succeeding periods. Skulls from Agia Triada,[2] Agia Eirene,[3] Koumasa,[4] Palaikastro,[5] Platanos,[6] Porti,[7] and Zakros,[8] have been measured, and all show a pronounced dolichocephaly. This feature is so continuous throughout the Minoan Period that we may take it that from an anthropological point of view there is no evidence from E.M.I to L.M.III that any change of racial type took place.[9]

The architecture, both domestic and funerary, is much better known than that of previous periods. The houses at Vasilike are the best example of the one, the circular tombs in the Messara of the other.

E.M.II: Architecture

---

[1] It is of interest to note that such M.M. settlements as have been found near tombs are situated in one case (Koumasa) close to a tomb where the M.M. deposit is very insignificant, and in the rest where it is totally lacking. In any case, I believe the M.M. deposit to have been votive and not funerary.

[2] Sergi, *Mem Ist Lomb.*, XXI, 252.   [3] *V.T.M.*, 126.   [4] Ibid.
[5] *B.S.A.*, IX, 344.   [6] *V.T.M.*, loc. cit.   [7] Ibid.
[8] *B.S.A.*, VII, 150.
[9] Mackenzie, *B.S.A.*, XII, 230 ff. ; Evans, *P. of M.*, 1, 8.

Two large houses were excavated at Vasilike (Fig. 5, and Pl. XV, 1). They consisted of a number of rectangular rooms

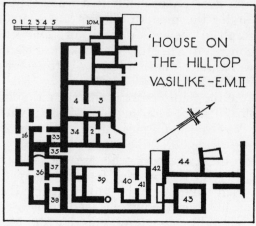

FIG. 5

of fair size whose complexity at first seems bewildering. Many of the rooms, being surrounded by other compartments, have

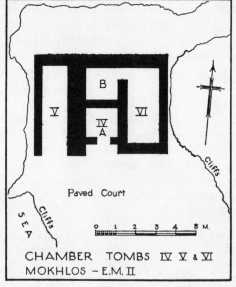

FIG. 6

no outside walls, and the probability is that we must look for a light-well even at this early stage. The lower part of the

walls is of stone, while above were sun-dried bricks tied by
wooden beams vertical and horizontal.   The wall surface was
covered with a rough stucco with a fine red finish as hard
as Roman cement, which has to a large extent preserved the
walls.

In tomb architecture we find the survival of an earlier type *E.M.II*
of building.   The old ' but-and-ben ' house-form of Neolithic *Tombs*
days continues in the built tombs, the roofs of which may have
been of reeds and clay (Fig. 6).   They were built of roughly
squared stones and consist of an outer and inner chamber, the
latter to one side of the former.   The elaboration of this plan
occurs at Palaikastro [1] (Fig. 7), where more chambers are added

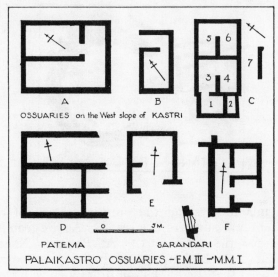

OSSUARIES on the West slope of KASTRI

PATEMA   SARANDARI

PALAIKASTRO OSSUARIES – E.M. III – M.M. I

FIG. 7

to the ossuaries.   The houses of the dead, in fact, were the
traditional houses of the living of a bygone era.[2]

But at the same time a new type appears in the Messara.
Here we find circular tombs used for generations by the family
or community (Fig. 8 and Pl. V, 2).   The interior diameter
varies from about 13 metres to just over 4 metres.   The thickness of the walls is usually between 1.50 and 2.50 metres, and
the greatest height to which any have been preserved is 2.70
metres.   They are built of roughly dressed stones with smaller
stones in the interstices set in clay mortar.   Most of the

[1] *B.S.A.*, XI, 270.   [2] Cf. Mackenzie, *B.S.A.*, XIV, 365.

examples are built up from a flat floor of virgin rock and stood completely free. At Agia Triadha and Kalathiana, however, they back up against the sloping hillside. In no case, however, are they comparable to the rectangular lined chamber tombs of Knossos or to the tholoi at Mycenae, which depend for their preservation on the pressure of earth from without.

The problem of their roofing is complicated. If one takes the inward lean of the walls to indicate that they were vaulted over and were primitive tholoi, one would obtain a rough estimate of the height by assuming that it equalled the diameter, as in the case of the tholoi of Mycenae. Now such a structure, with a height of 13 metres and a wall thickness of $2\frac{1}{2}$ metres,

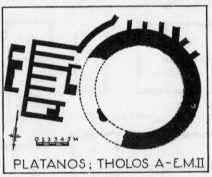

PLATANOS; THOLOS A-E.M.II

FIG. 8

would be unable to stand the outward thrust of the upper parts without pressure from outside. As we can see, they stood free for the most part.[1] At Platanos Xanthoudides found about 25 cubic metres of building stone which he thought proved that the tombs ran up to a considerable height and were domed. This amount of stone, however, would only suffice for an additional 80 centimetres of height. The walls survived in one place to 1.10 metres, and making a very generous allowance for small stones and bonding clay, we cannot admit that any greater height than $2\frac{1}{2}$ metres is proved. It seems best to assume, therefore, either that they were covered with a flat roof resting on beams or else that the dome was continued in thatch.[2] As against this, Xanthoudides noticed in many of

[1] In Tomb A at Platanos, however, there are six narrow walls abutting on to the South side which might be buttresses.

[2] Mr. Heurtley, indeed, has shown me a photograph of a round hut in West Macedonia. The stone walls run up about 2 metres and the hut has a conical thatching, at the top of which rests a circular

them traces of burning as if a huge pyre had been lit. There was no evidence for the cremation of the dead ; it appears more probable that the fires were lit for purificatory purposes, or that if they were thatched the roofs had accidentally caught fire.

The entrance to the tombs faces East and consists of a low door not more than a metre high formed of monolithic jambs and a heavy lintel. Outside this is a shallow stone-lined pit acting as a vestibule. This feature is elaborated in Tomb A at Platanos, where a whole series of chambers occur, and a similar annexe is seen at Agia Triadha.

The number of burials runs into hundreds, and these tombs were evidently the receptacles of the dead of a family or clan for many generations. Their use continues on into the beginning of M.M.i, though most of them, if not all, were built in E.M.ii.

While these circular tombs have their home in the Messara,[1] caves and rock shelters continue to provide a burial-place in the North and centre of the island, while at the same time cist graves and fragments of larnakes make their first appearance at Sphoungaras.

The pottery is a direct development of the style of the previous period and is more or less uniform throughout the island. *E.M.ii Pottery*

First comes the monochrome grey ware, descended directly from the Sub-Neolithic wares. A fine example from Mokhlos is shown in Pl. X, 1, *f*, where not only the fabric but also the shape betrays its pedigree. With this must be taken the dark, burnished lids (Pl. X, 1, *a*). These. are common in the Messara and at Arkalokhori, extremely common at Trapeza, while only three or four examples are known from East Crete except at Mokhlos.[2] They have been taken for pedestalled

stone to prevent the rain coming in through the orifice. Such a stone was found by Xanthoudides at Platanos and taken for a cap stone, and one unexcavated noticed by myself and our foreman at the Monastery of Kalergi, N. of Kastelli Pedhiadha. *V.T.M.*, 91, cf. Marinatos, *Arch. Anz.*, 1930, 103. The analogy drawn in *V.T.M.* with the cheese dairies on Mount Ida is not a fair one. They are all fairly small and the rough vaulting is made possible by the use of the great flat slabs of limestone which are common there. The tombs, on the other hand, are built of smallish rough stones. Seager, *Trans. Penn. Univ.*, II, 131, doubted whether they were roofed at all.

[1] There is one at Krasi and suspected ones at Kalergi and Pedhino near Adhromyloi (see Map 13).

[2] *Mochlos*, 20, 71 ; *Sphoungaras*, 49. The latter is oval in shape.

fruitstands or offering tables,[1] but the fact that the decoration is confined to what would in that case be the under surface, combined with the fact that in a number of cases the base of the ' pedestal ' is too convex to allow it to stand, makes it clear

FIG. 9.—Patterns on Early Minoan II Pottery

that they were intended for covers, though the vessels corresponding to them are uncertain.[2]

Other monochrome vessels are of rough red clay or of buff clay, more finely levigated and covered with a thick slip which

[1] *P. of M.*, I, 75.
[2] Xanthoudides, *V.T.M.*, 10, believes they covered the coarsely made cooking tripods. But they may equally well have been used with vessels of perishable materials such as wood or gourds.

took a good polish. The handleless cups have usually a low base (Pl. X, 1, *c*) and some show signs of paring which becomes so common in the succeeding periods. On a house floor at Knossos [1] was found a cup with a high swung handle which has since been paralleled by one from Vasilike and a great number of examples from the unstratified deposit in the cave at Trapeza. Open bowls are common. The jugs have a flat bottom and their spouts are higher than in the preceding period, though not of so exaggerated a type as appears at Vasilike during the latter part of E.M.II.

A great advance in painted decoration is shown (Fig. 9). The surface of the vase is more carefully prepared than in E.M.I and the rather dull red or brown varnish stands out more effectively. Lattice work and hatched triangles are common, particularly on small spouted jars (Pl. X, 1, *b*).[2] On jugs two hatched triangles are frequently joined at the apex to form a kind of butterfly or double axe pattern (Pl. X, 2, *f*). Such cups as are decorated are content with a narrow band of colour just below the rim. Dishes and bowls also show a band round the rim or, as in a few cases from Knossos,[3] a broad band of lattice work runs right across the inside. But one example from Mokhlos exhibits the most elaborate and successful decoration to be found in the whole period (Pl. X, 1, *e*). So unusual is it that Frankfort [4] has seen in it an importation whether direct from Syria or via Cyprus. His arguments are based on the colour and consistency of the paint and on the concentric circles which form part of the decoration. I have, however, examined the vase very closely, and in my opinion the unusual appearance of the paint is due to the fact that the slip was more than usually thick, which accounts for the paint standing out, while the colour is merely a different tone, not a different medium. The concentric circles are admittedly a Cypriote and Palestinian feature, but they form a very small element in the design, which in every other respect consists of typically E.M.II motives, however elaborately and unusually arranged. Concentric circles also are a motive which might occur to anyone who had a space to fill, though it is curious that they do not appear elsewhere in Crete until the Proto-

---

[1] *P. of M.*, I, Fig. 40, top right, and from Vasilike, *Gournia*, Pl. XII, 17.

[2] Cf. *V.T.M.*, Pl. XXVI, *b*.

[3] e.g. *P. of M.*, I, Fig. 40, bottom row.

[4] *Studies*, II, 122.

geometric period.[1]   So, while we may admit the possibility of
the artist having seen such foreign wares, we may still regard
this bowl as a good example of E.M.II pottery.   Mention must
also be made of the anthropomorphic vase from Koumasa
(Pl. XII, 3), which is the earliest of its kind.

At Vasilike in East Crete the period was one of great
prosperity and activity.   Two distinct phases could be distinguished,[2] and during the second of these a local style of pottery,
of which a few examples occur in the earlier level, finally ousts
the ordinary dark-on-light ware.   This local pottery, frequently known as ' Vasilike ware ', is so excellently made that
the discoverers imagined that the potter's wheel must already
have been introduced.   The most, however, that can be allowed
is a very primitive form of ' tournette '.   In shapes it is inclined
to fantastically long spouts on jugs and jars (Pl. X, 2), although
the ordinary forms survive.   The influence of metal vases is
often shown in the angular shapes, frequently accompanied by
imitation riveting (Pl. X, 2, a).[3]

The individuality of the style, however, lies in its mottled
surface.   This mottling was obtained by means of uneven
firing.   Frankfort [4] describes how the coals in the oven are
allowed actually to touch the pot at intervals giving a yellow
centre surrounded by a black ring of irregular form caused
by the smoke while the background remains brown or red.
Innumerable variations are found, though the difficulty of
ensuring the position of the coals meant that formal designs were
out of the question.   Pl. X, 2, d, however, seems too regular
to be the result of chance.   The great spouted jar, c, on the
same plate, also seems to have some method, but as Frankfort
points out, the effect is less rich in colour and gives the impression of having perhaps been executed with a burning branch.

Before the end of E.M.II, vases of this style had been exported to other parts of Crete [5] to be imitated locally, some-

[1] Except two examples from Kamarais, Pl. XXII, 3, b.
[2] *Trans. Penn. Univ.*, II, 114.   It must be remembered that Period 1
has since been attributed with certainty to E.M.I, leaving Periods 2
and 3 for E.M.II.
[3] A few examples, however, where the dots run down the side of
the vase, may indicate the stitches of a leather original.   The double
handle occasionally found may be derived from the folding in of
leather or metal.   [4] Op cit., 90.
[5] e.g. Knossos, E., III, 18, in Palace Museum ; Mallia, *Mallia*, I,
14 ;   Trapeza, Gournia, *Trans. Penn. Univ.*, I, 186 ; Priniatikos
Pyrgos, *Vrokastro*, 84.

times in the true technique as at Palaikastro,[1] sometimes with the mottling copied in paint as at Trapeza and in the Messara.[2] Both the original style and the imitations of it continue into the following period with various modifications which will be mentioned in their place.

E.M.II sees both the beginning and the culmination of the manufacture of stone vases (Pl. X, 3 ; XI, 1 and 2). Those found in the tombs at Mokhlos admit of the most accurate dating and are indeed the only ones which can be dated with certainty to this period.[3] They are carved in green, black and grey steatite, breccia, marble, alabaster and limestone, all of them stones to be found in Crete even if not in the immediate neighbourhood. Their colouring is brilliant and the veins in the stones are utilized very skilfully for effect. The workmanship is excellent, particularly in view of the fact that it is a new industry. The vases seem to have been roughly blocked out first and finished by careful hand-grinding, the interior being hollowed by means of a tubular drill, probably a reed worked with sand and water. It is certainly an extraordinary phenomenon that vases of such distinction should be turned out with no previous experience. It has been suggested, and with reason, that the impetus was given by direct contact with Egypt, where the art of fashioning vases of the hardest stone had been known from the earliest times, and certainly the shapes of many of them lend colour to this (see the end of the section). The lack of poor specimens may be accounted for by the fact that the best only were buried with the dead, while those of the softer stone with which the first experiments were no doubt made were in daily use, more liable to be broken at the time and more perishable in the course of centuries.[4]

E.M.II Stone Vases

Besides vases with Egyptian affinities are many which are purely Minoan in character and which show how soon the new art was nationalized. Nothing could well be more typically Minoan than the vases shown in Pl. X, 3, *g* and *m*, which are translations into stone of clay vases of the period. In addition are simple bowls, open spouted bowls, vases with pedestals and small jugs, while in one tomb occurs a breccia lid which reminds one of the tall caps of E.M.I.

In the Messara it is dangerous to attribute any of the stone vessels to this period with the possible exception of some of

[1] *B.S.A., Sup.*, 5. [2] *Annuario*, XIII–XIV, 236.
[3] *Mochlos*, 99. [4] Ibid.

the rectangular ' pepper and salt ' vases (e.g. Pl. X, 3, b). Even of these the majority seem to belong to E.M.iii, and their Egyptian connexions will be discussed there. The rest, whether from their uninspired technique or from their likeness to datable vases from Mokhlos, must certainly be put to the later date.

At Trapeza, however, where the cave was evidently a fashionable burial-place in E.Mii, there do occur vases, though unstratified, which are undoubtedly of that period. Pl. XI, 1, shows some of the examples, usually of green steatite, which most nearly resemble the types of Mokhlos.[1] The pedestalled cup also is obviously early. Indeed, it may well be one of the links for which we have been looking, for it is of the soft speckled grey steatite which rots so easily, and with its ringed stem it seems to link on even to the previous period.[2]

Though by no means typical of the period, the lid shown in Pl. XI, 2, must be mentioned to show the approach to naturalism already achieved.[3] The handle of the lid is in the form of a half-starved village hunting-dog, with ears, though curiously not tail, cropped, of the kind which to-day accompanies you on your walks, stealing and poaching without shame.

E.M.ii
Metalwork

The use of copper is now widespread (Pl. XI, 3). Two types of dagger occur, the earlier triangular form which frequently appears alone [4] and the later long form with a medial rib which seems to supersede the other in the Messara at any rate, before the end of the period. At Mokhlos the triangular dagger seems to persist to the end of E.M.iii.[5] In no case is the handle, which must have been of wood or bone, preserved.

The triangular type is shown by two examples, one from Koumasa with a straight top, one from Platanos with the top scalloped (Pl. XI, 3, e and g). Transitional types from Kou-

[1] e.g. *Mochlos*, Fig. 7, 2h.
[2] Cf. a goblet on a shorter unringed stem, *Mochlos*, 77, XXI, 7.
[3] Ibid., 20, another from Tylissos is published à propos of a lid from Byblos on which is a squatting bull, by Miss Money-Coutts. *Berytus*, III, 129. Though it does not go so far as to say so, this article has almost convinced me that the lids are not Minoan at all but Syrian.
[4] e.g. at Platanos, *V.T.M.*, 107.
[5] *Mochlos*, 107, but a long dagger was found in an E.M.iii ossuary at Palaikastro, *B.S.A.*, *Sup.*, 116, and another in an ossuary where a large number of E.M.ii vases were found. So East Crete was not backward.

masa are *i* and *f*, the latter of silver and showing a medial
rib. The long type is shown in *b*, also of silver ; it corresponds
to shapes found at Salame in a pure E.M.II context, though
itself it is not stratified. The socketed arrow-head from Tomb
XIX at Mokhlos must surely be intrusive.

Another object of copper which is common at this period
is a small blade rather like an axe with a convex edge and
two holes at the end of the tang. Examples were found at
Mokhlos,[1] Koumasa and Platanos,[2] while an unstratified
example from Trapeza still preserves a small ivory handle
which prolongs the line of the blade. This, together with a
distinct wearing at one end of the edge, shows that the original
excavator's theory is correct and that they were not merely
votive models but objects for use probably connected with the
toilet. Tweezers, too, are found both at Mokhlos and in the
Messara. They are of a simple type with the two ends
widened. At the top the arms are sometimes pinched in to
form a loop at the end. A tool somewhat resembling the
toilet knives but much larger is shown in Pl. XI, 3, *a*. It was
probably used for wood-cutting. In the same tomb at Koumasa was found a fine-toothed saw. In Tomb II at Mokhlos
appeared a double axe of copper and two smaller ones of lead.[3]
Their stratification is certain and they are the first examples
of an object which, as a religious symbol, is typical of the
Minoan Age.[4]

It is unfortunate that only one of the figurines which have
been attributed to E.M.II was found in a stratified deposit.
This is an unpainted clay figurine from Palaikastro.[5] The
body is a mere column, the arms are short stumps on a level
with the face, on which eyes and nose alone are marked. The
neck, waist and legs are not indicated. For the rest we must
go on style alone. Signorina Banti has made a most careful
analysis of the various types of figurines from the larger
tomb at Agia Triadha,[6] and has come to the conclusion
that it would be dangerous to date any but the most primitive
to this period. Her conclusions will fit very well with the
rest of the Messara and also with the finds at Trapeza, the
only other site where E.M. figurines have been found in any

*E M.II
Figurines*

[1] *Mochlos*, 107.   [2] *V.T.M.*, 28.   [3] *Mochlos*, 34, 107.
[4] Whence came the shape ? Hall, *Essays presented to Sir Arthur
Evans*, 42, publishes a flint example of very early date from Egypt.
[5] *B.S.A.*, XI, 273, *Sup.*, 131.
[6] *Annuario*, XIII–XIV, 243.

numbers.[1] In Pl. XII, 1, the middle row shows typical examples of this type, with a triangular pointed body, a triangular
or rhomboidal head, and in one case rudimentary arm stumps,
these are from Trapeza, while the top and bottom figures on
the right in Pl. XII, 2, are from Platanos.   The materials are
exclusively limestone and crystal.   Their foreign affinities we
shall discuss later, but I think we are already justified in
considering them as original products of the Messara whence
they were exported or, in the case of Trapeza, imitated.

*E.M.*II
Seals

The seals of the period are also a difficulty.   There are only
three well-stratified examples, all from Mokhlos [2] (Fig. 10),
while one more from Mokhlos and one from Sphoungaras are
of the same style although E.M.III pottery as well as E.M.II
was present.[3]   They are of ivory or steatite—easy materials to

FIG. 10.—Early Minoan II Seals

cut.   Three from Mokhlos are cylinders pierced both vertically
and horizontally, one is a signet, while that from Sphoungaras
has a bird's head.

Two of the designs shown in the figure are of a distinctly
Egyptian type, the other has a simple lattice pattern at one
end and at the other conventional scrolls.   In any case, they
must belong to the end of the period, and we may well agree
with Frankfort [4] that it is really with E.M.III that Minoan
glyptic art begins.

*E.M.*II
Jewellery

One of the most surprising results of the work at Mokhlos
was the extraordinary amount of gold which was found and
the skill shown in fashioning it.   Pl. XIII, 1, shows a typical
group of objects, all well stratified to this period except the

[1] The only other examples are Knossos, *P. of M.*, II, 31 ; Mokhlos,
Mochlos, Fig. 47, 5 ; Palaikastro, *B.S.A.*, *Sup.*, 149 ; two bought and
one a surface find.   The other figurines from Trapeza which we at
first attributed to E.M.II are, we are now convinced, E.M.III.

[2] *Mochlos*, 34, 54, 108.

[3] Ibid., 70, and *Sphoungaras*, 52.   [4] *Studies*, II, 123.

pendant at the bottom on the right of the centre. It may be chance that has preserved so much at Mokhlos whereas the Messara is singularly poor. But since such gold work as remains at Koumasa and Platanos is almost certainly E.M.III, and one can hardly believe that tomb robbers will confine themselves to digging for objects of the earliest date while ignoring the upper levels, it seems as if this contrast reflects the comparative wealth of the East and the South pretty fairly.[1]

The most advanced work is seen in the fine chains from which depend leaves or pendants,[2] and in the representations of flowers and sprays. The gold is thin leaf and the designs on it are either *répoussé* work or pricked. In the case of bracelets the edges seem to have been turned over to grip a core of leather.[3] Headbands occur with designs pricked out on them. That shown in Plate XIII has two dogs on each side facing the centre. At each end are holes for the strings which tied the tiara on, but in some cases it seems as if pins, such as that shown with a daisy head, were used instead. Another [4] has two eyes upon it, which has led to the suggestion that we have here a fore-runner of the gold masks of Mycenae.[5] This, however, was the thickest gold of all and seemed to the excavator to have been clearly intended to be worn during the lifetime of the owner. Holes occur along the top of many of these diadems, and it is possible that some of the pendants may have been attached to them as a fringe, though from their position at the top it rather suggests that a net cap was worn over the head. Perhaps to this period belongs a tiny gold mask intended to cover a core of some other material.[6] In gold long tubular beads occur and small flat ones,[7] as well as simple forms which will be elaborated in E.M.III. Rock crystal, limestone, corne-lian, shell, and faience were also used, the shapes being flat, short tubular, or flattened spherical or pear-shaped.

[1] But cf. *V.T.M.*, 110, where it is explained by the theory that the plundering of previous interments was a regular feature so that only the last burial escaped intact. This, if true, makes the contrast between East and South one of morals rather than wealth.

[2] Exactly paralleled by one from the lower stratum in Tomb A at Platanos. *V.T.M.*, 111. Cf. the group of jewellery, probably contemporary from Thyreatis, now in Berlin. Karo, *Schachtgraber von Mykenae*, 188, 300, 350.

[3] *Mochlos*, 68.

[4] Ibid., 27.

[5] *P. of M.*, I, 97.

[6] *Mochlos*, 78.

[7] Ibid., 55, 78.

No actual imports from abroad have yet been found in E.M.ii strata, but imitations and resemblances are just as important.[1]

The most frequently quoted examples of Egyptian or rather Libyan influence are the primitive statuettes from the Messara. Signorina Banti[2] disclaims any possibility of direct influence from Predynastic Upper Egypt.[3] But it must be remembered that it is the Libyan element in that Predynastic civilization with which we are dealing, an element which seems to have continued strongly as far East as the Western Delta until dynastic times.[4] This may be somewhat roundabout, but it seems the only theory which will explain certain factors in the Messara, the apparently bearded figurines, their cloaks, and the sudden appearance of a circular type of tomb, perhaps thatched but almost certainly connected with the ' *mapalia* ' of Libya.[5] These features were practically confined to the Messara, where they shortly died out. Other traits, however, found more favour and spread all over the island. Evans has pointed out and illustrated [6] the Libyan affinities of the Minoan side lock, the codpiece, and the plain bow with a broad-edged flint tip to the arrow, all of which persisted into later times. The ' pepper and salt ' pots (Pl. X, 3, *b*) spread elsewhere during E.M.iii but then die out.

Just as for Libya, the most natural approach to Crete was directly across to the South Coast, where the Messara bay offers the safest haven, so the natural line of traffic with Egypt led along the East Coast and round to Mokhlos. It is here, therefore, as we should expect, that direct Egyptian influence is most felt.[7]

On Pl. X, 3, *f*, *h*, *k*, and *n*, are examples clearly copied from Egyptian originals. The most common type is the ointment pot, *f* and *k*, which attained considerable popularity in the

[1] I purposely omit the diorite bowl (*P. of M.*, I, 86) and moustache cup (*P. of M.*, II, 57), both of the IVth Dynasty, because neither was stratified.

[2] Op. cit., 92.   [3] Hierakonpolis and Nagada. Petrie, *Nagada*, 45.

[4] *Studies*, II, 97, and references there given.

[5] *P. of M.*, II, 31 ff. The round building at Tiryns, *Tiryns*, III, 80 and 203, seems to be of transitional E.H.–M.H. date, i.e. contemporary with M.M.i.

[6] Ibid., 34 ff.

[7] Why Palaikastro should be so barren of Egyptian contacts it is hard to see. But it is clear that the site was comparatively unimportant in Early Minoan times.

Messara. This shape exists in Egypt from the Ist to the VIth Dynasty, but in its more refined form, as shown in *k* only from the IVth to the VIth. The tall vase, *h*, resembles the Egyptian ' *hes* '-vase, which with a simple rim like this ranges from the Ist to the IVth Dynasty.[1] The vase, *n*, with two vertically pierced handles, resembles Ist-Dynasty examples, though in Egypt the handles are pierced horizontally.[2]

Evans[3] has seen in the exaggerated spouts of Vasilike a reflection of Early Dynastic copper vessels, where the prominent spout connects with the interior by a very small hole, a feature of the Cretan vases also. This, taken in conjunction with the indications of metal originals to be seen in a number of shapes in Vasilike ware, is a strong argument in favour of considerable Egyptian influence.

It is noteworthy also that two of the seals shown in Fig. 10*a* and *b* have both distinctly Egyptian designs. Both, unfortunately, seem very sophisticated for so early a period in Egypt; the design on *b* looks almost Middle Kingdom, but there is no question of their stratification.

Of direct Anatolian influence it is more difficult to find a trace. That E.M.I owed much to that region we have already seen, but E.M.II seems to be a natural development along the same lines, and though no doubt connexions were maintained, there is no new element coming in at that period which must be explained by a fresh wave of immigrants.

The pottery, peculiar to Vasilike, is a highly specialized form of ' Urfirnis ' ware—the pottery covered with a lustrous black or brown wash—which develops in Greece and the Islands, no doubt with an ultimate Anatolian origin between Early Helladic–Early Cycladic 1 and 2, and it seems most probable, considering the position of Vasilike, that it is a few settlers from the North rather than from the East who introduced it.

Our positive chronology, then, is still dependent on Egypt. *E.M.II Chronology* We have seen that the stone vases from which the Minoan examples were copied range from the Ist Dynasty until the VIth, with the majority in the IVth to the VIth, and it seems safest to retain the old dating of E.M.II from 2800 to 2500 B.C.

---

[1] Reisner, *Antiquity*, V, 200 ff., has made a careful study based on his work at Giza (*Mycerinus*), but he refuses to recognize any vases found in Crete as Predynastic in spite of the almost conclusive argument of material, for variegated stones begin to drop out before the end of the IInd Dynasty.

[2] *Mycerinus*, Pl. 70, *b*.   [3] *P. of M.*, I, 80.

SITES WHERE EARLY MINOAN II REMAINS HAVE BEEN FOUND

WEST CRETE

(b) Surface Finds

AGIOS ONOUPHRIOS		Hard plaster like that of Vasilike, indeterminate sherds, found by writer, 1935. Also story of stone axes found near the church. Site above Mesonisi in Amari.
GAVDHOS . . .		Sherds at Karavi. Levi, *Art and Archaeology*, 1927, 176 ff.

CENTRAL CRETE

(a) Excavated Sites

AMNISOS . . .	Cave . .	Vases from Eilythyia cave. Marinatos, Πρακτικά, 1929, 95 ; 1930, 91.
ARKALOKHORI .	Cave . .	Covers and daggers. Hazzidakis, *B.S.A.*, XIX, Fig. 4f.
KASTELLOS TZERMI-ADHON	Settlement	Traces on the summit. Excavated, 1937, by the writer.
KNOSSOS . . .	Houses .	Vases, &c., from floors on S. slope. Evans, *P. of M.*, I, 71.
KRASI	Tomb .	Vases and implements as well as building of the circular tomb. Marinatos, 'Αρχ. Δελτ., 12, 102.
MALLIA . . .	Stratum .	Vases, &c., immediately underlying first palace in Quarters III–VI. Chapoutier, *Mallia*, I, 13–20. *B.C.H.*, 1928, 367.
PYRGOS . . .	Cave . .	Vases and daggers from burials. Xanthoudides, 'Αρχ. Δελτ., 1918, 136.
TRAPEZA . . .	Cave . .	Vases, daggers, and figurines from burials. Excavated 1936. *A.J.A.*, XL, 371. *Arch. Anz.*, 1936, 162.

(b) Surface Finds

KANLI KASTELLI .	Sherds picked up from settlement at Visala. Evans, *P. of M.*, II, 71.
MOKHOS . . .	Sherds and plaster on Edhikte, a summit ½ hr. E. of the village ; also a stone vase in a peasant's hands. Found by writer, 1935.
ORNIAS . . .	Traces of rock shelters found by the writer, 1937.
SKHINEAS . . .	Sherds on Koprana seen by the writer, 1937.

SOUTH CRETE

(a) Excavated Sites

AGIA EIRENE . .	Tombs .	Vases from in and round the circular tombs. Xanthoudides, *V.T.M.*, 52.

AGIA TRIADHA   .   Tombs   .   Large circular tomb and contents.
                                Mem. Ist Lomb., XXI, 248.
                                Banti, *Annuario*, XIII–XIV, 164
                                ff. *Mon. Ant.*, XIV, 679. Smaller
                                tomb, *Rend. Linc.*, 1905, 392.

KALATHIANA .   .   Tomb   .   Daggers, &c., from circular tomb.
                                Xanthoudides, *V.T.M.*, 76, 82.

KOUMASA .   .   .   Tombs   .   Main contents of circular tombs.
                                Ibid., 8.

KOUTSOKERA .   .   Tomb   .   Sherds from circular tomb. Ibid.,
                                74.

MARATHOKEPHALO Tomb   .   Vases, &c., from the circular tomb.
                                Xanthoudides, *'Αρχ. Δελτ.*, IV,
                                Παρ. 21.

PHAISTOS .   .   .   Deposit .   Sherds, &c. Mosso, *Mon. Ant.*,
                                XIX, 204. Pernier, *Festos*, 115 ff.

PLATANOS .   .   .   Tombs   .   Vases and daggers from the circular
                                tombs. Xanthoudides, *V.T.M.*,
                                88.

SALAME   .   .   .   Tomb   .   Sherds and daggers from the circular
                                tomb. Xanthoudides, *V.T.M.*,
                                74.

SIVA   .   .   .   .   Tombs   .   Two circular tombs, earliest con-
                                tents. *Ausonia*, VIII, *Sup.*, 13 ff.

(b) Surface Finds

AGIOS ONOUPHRIOS Vases, &c., probably from a circular tomb.
                                Evans, *Pictographs, Sup.*, 105.

KOMO .   .   .   .   Sherds and possible remains of circular tomb.
                                Evans, *P. of M.*, II, 88.

LANGOS   .   .   .   Sherd picked up and walls seen in gorge between
                                Kamilari and Komo by writer, 1934. *B.S.A.*,
                                XXXIII, 89.

EAST CRETE
(a) Excavated Sites

AGIA PHOTIA .   .   Cave .   .   Vases from burial. Boyd-Hawes,
                                Trans. Penn. Univ., I, 183.
                                Gournia, 56, 60.

AGIOS ANTONIOS .   Cave .   .   Vases from burial. Hall, *Vrokastro*,
                                183, by church near Kavousi.

AGIOS IOANNES .   Cave .   .   Vases from burials. Boyd, *Trans.
                                Penn. Univ.*, I, 214.

GOURNIA .   .   .   Deposit .   Sherds and vases from the town.
                                Hawes, *Gournia*, 37. Also cf.
                                Mosso, *Dawn of Mediterranean
                                Civilization*, 289, for traces of a
                                copper mine of this date at
                                Khrysokamino.

MOKHLOS .   .   .   Tombs   .   Vases, seals, daggers, &c. Seager,
                                Mochlos, passim.

                    S ettlement Houses and contents. Seager,
                                A.J.A., XIII, 274.

PALAIKASTRO . .	Stratum .	Deposit in lowest strata of δ 32 and block X. *B.S.A., Sup.*, 5.
	Ossuaries.	Vases, &c., from Kastri and Ellenika. *B.S.A., Sup.*, 6 and 7. *B.S.A.,* X, 196.
PRINIATIKOS PYRGOS	Settlement	Earliest deposit. Hall, *Vrokastro,* 84.
PSEIRA . . .	Stratum .	Deposit below floor of Room 4, House A. Also stray finds. Seager, *Pseira,* 17.
SPHOUNGARAS .	Cave . .	Vases from burial. Hawes, *Gournia,* 56.
	Tombs .	Cist and larnax. Hall, *Sphoungaras,* 49.
VASILIKE . . .	Settlement	Houses and contents. Seager, *Trans. Penn. Univ.*, I, 213; II, 115. Hawes, *Gournia,* 49.
ZAKROS . . .	Cave .	Vases from burial. Hogarth, *B.S.A.,* 142.

(b) Surface Finds

| HIERAPETRA ISTHMUS | Spouted jars and sherds. Forsdyke, *Brit. Mus. Cat.*, I, 424, 425, 429. |
| MIRABELLO GULF | Bowl, cup, and jug. Ibid., 416, 423, 426. |

2. EARLY MINOAN III (E.M. III).

(See Map 6)

The Early Minoan III Period is a curious and difficult one to define, for, as we shall see, it can in some ways be called transitional between the Early and Middle Bronze Age in Crete, yet at the same time it has features of its own in the East and South which mark it off as a new epoch, while in the centre and North it is very clearly the end of the archaic Minoan Period.

The map shows a few more sites in the North, a concentration on the main sites in the East and the old sites in the Messara continuing. One point to be noticed is the comparative scarcity of unexcavated sites where surface finds have been made. This is not necessarily due to the fact that there are very few such sites, but to the fact that so much of the less highly decorated pottery is indistinguishable when in fragments from that of the previous period. Thus it is inconceivable that the great site of Komo was abandoned in E.M.III, it merely happens that no typical sherd has been picked up.[1]

[1] I would also draw attention to the list of sites where E.M. pottery has been found which cannot be more closely dated. P. 289 following and Map 13.

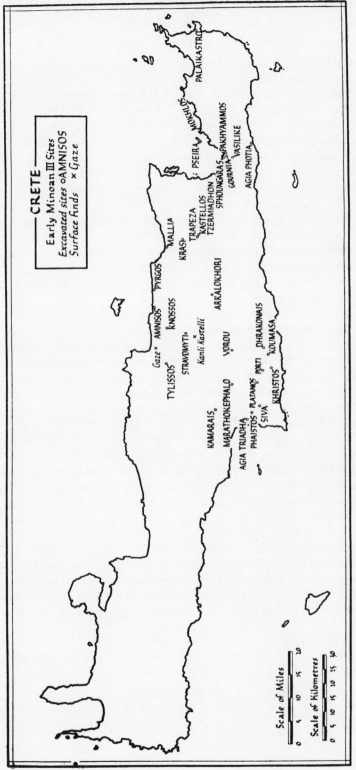

CRETE
Early Minoan III Sites
Excavated sites ○ AMNISOS
Surface Finds × Gaze

PALAIKASTRO

: PSEIRA ● MOKHLOS
PAKHYAMMOS
GOURNIA ○ ●
SPHOUNGARAS
VASILIKE
AGIA PHOTIA ○

TRAPEZA
KASTELLOS
TZERMIADHON
MALLIA
KRASI ○

PYRGOS
AMNISOS ○
Gaze ×
KNOSSOS ○
STRAVOMYTI ○
× Kanli Kastelli
VOROU ○
ARKALOKHORI
DHRAKONAIS
KOUMASA
PORTI
KHRISTOS ○

TYLISSOS ○
MARATHOKEPHALO ○
KAMARAIS ○
AGIA TRIADHA ○
PHAISTOS ○ PLATANOS
SIVA ○

Scale of Miles
0   5   10   15   20

Scale of Kilometres
0   5 10 15   20

MAP 6

E.M.III
Architecture

Architecturally the period is poor. At Vasilike the big E.M.II house had fallen into ruin and the hovels of the new period built of smaller stones huddle against one of the surviving walls.[1] No other buildings which can be definitely assigned to E.M.III are known, though some of the M.M.I houses at Pseira, Mokhlos, Palaikastro, Agia Triadha, and Tylissos may well have been built on earlier foundations or been adaptations of the earlier houses.[2] The great Hypogaeum at Knossos has been attributed to E.M.III.[3] But the contents were almost exclusively M.M.I, and the number of E.M. fragments, which is expressly stated to be a vanishing quantity, do not seem sufficient to date it back to that time, for they may well have fallen in like the accompanying Neolithic from the surrounding earth. But the most important structures of this time which must have been on the summit of the mound were swept away when the Central Court was made.[4]

E.M.III
Tombs

The architecture of the built tombs both at Mokhlos and in the Messara is indistinguishable from that of the preceding period. In the East and centre of the island rock shelters are still in use and larnax and pot burials are coming into fashion. That there was no break between E.M.II and III is shown by the consistent re-use of tombs whether caves or built ones. Indeed, in the Messara, Porti, Khristos, and Vorou are the only ones hitherto excavated which seem to have been built in E.M.III.

E.M.III
Pottery

The great difference between the pottery and that which has gone before is the substitution of light-on-dark for dark-on-light decoration. (See Fig. 11, where for convenience the patterns are done in dark on light.) Now this reversal seems to require some explanation, and having regard to the tremendous quantity of E.M.III pottery found in the East of the island, we have one ready to hand. The mottled ware of Vasilike had during the latter part of the E.M.II practically driven out the dark-on-light geometric decoration, or had at any rate become the fashionable style. Now undecorated monochrome or comparatively monochrome pottery never seems to have appealed to the Cretans. The mottled decoration was a chancy business in any case and

[1] *Trans. Penn. Univ.*, I, 218 ; II, 113, 118.
[2] *Pseira*, 9 ; *A.J.A.*, XIII, 274 ; *B.S.A.*, IX, 300 ; *J.H.S.*, XXXIII, 365 ; *T.V.M.*, 79.
[3] *P. of M.*, I, 104.
[4] This evidently happened at Gournia also, accounting for the mass of E.M.III pottery found to the North of the site. *Trans. Penn. Univ.*, I, 191.

practically impossible to regulate. Some decoration was essential, and one finds mottled ware of E.M.III incised and punctuated.[1] But even that somewhat primitive method of decoration was not particularly effective, and since the dark varnish of E.M.II would not show up on the dark background of the mottled ware, the designs were drawn in matt white.[2] It is evident from the few examples of this technique which exist that it was soon realized that the mottled background added nothing to the effect and the white designs appear almost at once on the background of a black varnish.[3]

The new style soon spread to Central and Southern Crete and in the Messara seems to have lasted as long as in the East of the island. In the North and centre, however, we shall find reason to believe that it was fairly short-lived.

The long-spouted jar still occurs (e.g. Pl. XIII, 3, d), but there is a tendency even in the east to curtail the spouts after the Messara fashion (e.g. Pl. XIII, 4, b) and to adopt the squatter form which was popular in the south.[4] Before the end of E.M.III the ordinary ' hole-mouthed' jar has appeared (Pl. XIII, 3, h) with its horizontal handles, which imply the existence of larger varieties than the one shown.[5] The jugs, too, have lost their exaggerated spouts (Pl. XIII, 4, a, c, e) and have a tendency to a broad flat base, sometimes with a slight foot but always giving a somewhat squatter appearance than E.M.II examples. Note that the rivet is still shown at the base of the spout, though the shapes are no longer metallic. A two-handled vessel is shown in Pl. XIII, 4, d. But most typical of the period are the cups. The pedestalled cups of E.M.II have disappeared, at any rate from among the decorated fabrics, and the most common shape is the rounded tea-cup, usually without a handle (Pl. XIII, 3, e and f) but occasionally found with small horizontal handles up to four in number slightly below the middle. Pl. XIII, 3, g, shows a shape which has survived from the

[1] e.g. *Mochlos*, 97, and several examples from Trapeza. We have already noted in the previous section that imitations both in the true technique and in paint last on in other parts of the island into E.M.III. Cf. *Pseira*, 17.

[2] *Trans. Penn. Univ.*, II, 119 ; *Studies*, II, 93.

[3] A similar explanation probably accounts for the identical change from dark-on-light to light-on-dark decoration in Early Helladic times.

[4] *Mochlos*, Fig. 50, 92, in shape like our Pl. X, 1, b.

[5] *P. of M.*, I, Fig. 76, shows a jug with a vertical handle, a rounded body and a hole mouth, which is clearly the forerunner of those of M.M.I at Vasilike and Palaikastro. It is from Mokhlos.

previous period, a cup with a small open spout. A number of
cups without this spout are known, some of them with a slightly
flaring foot and with or without a vertical handle.[1] A more
elaborate shape is shown in Pl. XIII, 4, *f*, which is to have a
long history. It is to be noted that the handles are always
either round or only slightly flattened in section. The strap
handle has not yet appeared. Many of these cups are of very
fine fabric, some of them almost meriting the term ' eggshell '.

An oval boat-shaped dish is occasionally found with an open
spout at one end and a knob or a horizontal handle at the other.[2]
An askos appears at Vasilike,[3] and anthropomorphic vases of the
same type as the E.M.II vase described above (Pl. XII, 3) at
Mokhlos and Koumasa.[4] Anthropomorphic and theriomorphic
vases seem to be favourites in the Messara at this time. Xanthoudides figures [5] bulls grappled by acrobats, small jugs
similarly grappled at the neck, a delightful fledgeling with its
beak open and a series of askoi in the shape of birds which bear
an astonishing resemblance to a middle Predynastic class in
Egypt.[6] From the Messara also comes a queer type of vase
exactly like a pair of trousers with very thin legs, which re-
appears again in M.M.I.[7]

For the best examples of the new white on black decoration
we must look to the East (Fig. 11). No type of design which
appears in any other part of the island is here unrepresented.
Seager [8] would see two periods, examples from the second of
which only have been found in an unmixed stratum and that
in only one spot—the well at Vasilike. Typical of the first he
makes the cross-hatched lozenges and circles, of the second
the more conventional designs on the ' eggshell ' cups. But
although the fact that two subdivisions can be made out is of
great importance for the internal chronology of Crete in this
and the next period, it is safer first to view the designs as a
whole before drawing conclusions.

The great advance in design is the introduction of the
curvilinear and spiraliform motives. The rectilinear patterns
are merely an elaboration of those of E.M.II. The commonest

[1] *Trans. Penn. Univ.*, I, 194.   [2] Ibid., II, 122.   [3] Ibid., II, 120.
[4] *Mochlos*, 64 ; *V.T.M.*, 2.
[5] *V.T.M.*, all from Koumasa on Pl. XXVIII.
[6] *J.E.A.*, XII, 52. Cf. *Studies*, II, 103, note and references.
[7] *V.T.M.*, Pl. XXVIII, but cf. *Studies*, II, 44, for analogies from
Thessaly
[8] *Trans. Penn. Univ.*, II, 122.

is a zigzag between lines running round the body of the vase, the resulting triangles being alternately hatched and left plain. Fig. 11, 1, shows the commonest scheme which occurs below the rims of cups. Pl. XIII, 3, *g*, shows it spread over the whole

FIG. 11.—Patterns on Early Minoan III Pottery

vase. Most of the decoration, in fact, is confined by bordering lines which sometimes run up at a slant as in Pl. XIII, 4, *c* and *e*, or depend in loops as in Pl. XIII, 3, *d*. The general rule is horizontal designs, never the vertical ones which appear in M.M.1.

The introduction of curvilinear motives, however, is more important. The simple semicircle either above or below the line (Fig. 11 ; 3, 4, 11, 12) might be accounted for by supposing a revival of the incised designs of E.M.1, but when we come to the interlocked curves and the running spirals we must certainly look elsewhere, and certainly towards the Cyclades, where the spiral motive was already well known. In Crete, nearly every variation appears in this period, spirals with thick centres, simple forms of running or rather connected spirals, joined by one or more lines or by triangles (Pl. XIII, 4, a), and even an elaborate design taken from contemporary seal stones.[1]

But in this new passion for linking the designs the earlier free standing motive was not forgotten, and we find in the circles, decorated inside with hatched segments, squares or crosses, the true forerunners of the rosettes which are to be such a feature of later Minoan pottery. Sometimes, admittedly, the painter fell between two stools. He had a good single piece of decoration, but he felt he must keep up with the times, and what might well have been an effective design, if unconnected with its fellow on the other side of the vase, is spoiled by meaningless lines between the two, which only serve to exaggerate the intervening space by dividing it up in an ugly way.[2]

For the first time animal figures make their appearance. It is easy to see how they began. An adaptation of the old ' double axe ' motive such as Fig. 11, 19, gave the idea of the body of an animal, and it is a small step to add the head of a goat at one end. Sometimes a hatched oval gave the potter the same idea and legs and ears are added.[3] Eventually animals designed as animals from the first appear.[4]

Before the end of the period polychromy is found, red paint as well as white being used on the black background. This may well be the result of a scheme of decoration not yet mentioned in which a part only of the vase was covered by white

[1] *P. of M.*, I, Fig. 77, from the Kamarais cave. It is the only good specimen of E.M.III pottery from the whole of the Messara district.

[2] e.g. Palaikastro, *B.S.A., Sup.*, Fig. 5c.

[3] *Trans. Penn. Univ.*, I, Pl. XXVIII, 28.

[4] *B.S.A., Sup.* Pl. III, 1. This sequence of events has already been seen in the faces on the Neolithic pottery at Trapeza, p. 41, above. Naturalistic forms result from chance resemblances in geometric patterns just as often as geometric patterns are the outcome of stylizing naturalistic forms.

designs on black, the rest being left its natural reddish colour.[1]
The red is a deep Indian red, easily distinguishable from the
lighter orange which comes in in M.M.i.   It is used sparingly
and the examples known are few.   At Palaikastro a cup has
alternate festoons of white and red and a small red circle
surrounded by white dots; from Knossos comes a short-spouted
jar with red lines bordered with white radiating up from the
base.[2]

On the North coast, at Pyrgos, appeared a number of vessels
of dark brown burnished pottery, often incised (Pl. XIII, 3,
a–c).   Though the cave is unstratified, vessels of this fabric
are quite distinct from the earlier Sub-Neolithic, E.M.i, incised
wares.   Whether they are of local fabric, as Evans thinks, or
actual imports from the Cyclades, it is hard to say.   Personally,
I am inclined to think they are the latter, but at all events there
are among them the first examples of cylindrical pyxides which
begin to appear in Crete at this point.

The burial larnakes, of which examples are found at Pakhyammos and Pyrgos, are of plain clay, oval, with a pair of
vertical handles on each side near each end.   The lids are
flat.   In the case of a smaller burial chest from Pakhyammos,
which was decorated with a white trickle pattern on the buff
ground, the lid was slightly vaulted and had a handle on each
side at the top.[3]

The E.M.iii stone vases at Mokhlos show a distinct decline. *E.M.iii*
They are smaller and soft black steatite begins to be used to *Stone Vases*
the exclusion of the harder variegated stones.[4]   A fine exception,
however, is a spouted cylindrical vase of breccia from Tomb
XXIII.[5]   The shapes, as in the succeeding period, are mainly
confined to small bowls with lugs, and a higher shape of bowl
with a hook handle,[6] the former shape occurring at Trapeza in
some numbers.

It is probable that the bulk of the stone vases from the

[1] *B.S.A.*, *Sup.*, Fig. 5a, and several examples in the plates, *Trans.
Penn. Univ.*, I.   In a very few cases at Palaikastro dark-on-light
patterns exist, but it is possible that they may belong to vases which
have also light-on-dark.   *B.S.A.*, *Sup.*, Pl. III.

[2] *B.S.A.*, *Sup.*, Fig. 5d; *P. of M.i*, Fig. 78.

[3] *Pachyammos*, Pl. XII.

[4] *Mochlos*, 101.   Cf. the disuse of variegated stones in Egypt after
the IInd Dynasty.

[5] Ibid., 80, and Pl. III, called in one place E.M.ii but presumably
finally dated by the tiny marble pyxis from the same tomb.

[6] Ibid., Fig. 37, XVI, 5.

Messara is to be dated to this period. Some of them are in variegated stones (e.g. Pl. X, 3, *d* and *e*) but the whole impression is drab in the extreme. The bowl with a hook handle appears in some quantity, but the favourite shape is the ' bird's nest ' vase decorated with incised patterns (Pl. X, 3, *c*) and frequently having one or more minor depressions round the main cavity, and the small bowl with marked rim and foot (Pl. X, 3, *e*). The first continues into the next period both here and elsewhere, but the second seems to be exclusively a product of the Messara and of this period. Slightly less common is the type shown in Pl. X, 3, *d*, with a marked rim and a body swelling out below. This shape is almost invariably incised, whether as in the present case by mere ribbing below the rim or by hatched triangles rising from the widest point of the body. The ' pepper and salt ' vases continue, as can be seen by the way in which the patterns incised on them keep pace with those on the ' birds' nests '. Another shape, rather uninspired, which probably appears at this date, is a verticalsided cup.[1]

The oblong stone palette on four stumpy legs or with a convex underside has interesting Egyptian parallels.[2]

E.M.iii
Metalwork

The metalwork is indistinguishable from that of E.M.ii. Bronze is still unknown. The long daggers are firmly established, though the triangular form seems still to be used.[3]

E.M.iii
Figurines

The figurines are now much more highly developed. This is no doubt due to the importation of marble examples from the Cyclades (Pl. XII, 2) and it is easy to see their influence on those made locally. The most direct copies are those of bone, which seem to be a local product of Lasithi (Pl. XII, 1, top row), since only one example has hitherto come to light at any site other than Trapeza.[4] Unlike their Cycladic prototypes, some of them at least have a split apron and seem distinctly male, but their origin is obvious.[5] Whether the two small gypsum objects at the bottom of the same plate are to be considered as in any way connected with the fiddle-shaped ' idol ' of Cycladic origin (Pl. XII, 2, top centre), or whether they are merely very

[1] *V.T.M.*, Pl. XXXIX, *a*, 1062, also an example from Trapeza.
[2] Ibid., 36.
[3] *Mochlos*, 107, and Porti, where the absence of a single E.M.ii sherd makes it improbable that the tomb was built before E.M.iii.
[4] Agia Triadha. Banti, *Annuario*, XIII–XIV, 191, No. 134, *a*.
[5] Very few of the Cycladic figurines are male, but in such cases they always seem to be shown performing some action like playing on a harp or a flute.

primitive local products, it is hard to say. In the Messara Cycladic figurines appear in considerable numbers and seem to have been greatly prized, since in many cases they were mended in antiquity.[1] Yet it is curious that, unless we take some of the examples in stone other than marble as slavish local copies, they do not seem to have affected the local type to anything like the extent one would expect. Indeed, the figurines which we might reasonably assign to this period seem rather to be descendants of the primitive ones of E.M.II,[2] although they widen at the base, as if to represent a skirt. Their hands are clasped over their chests instead of hugging their stomachs, and if we are to look outside Crete for their forbears, we shall have to go to Mesopotamia, to the statues of the Sumerian Ur-nina of Lagash.[3]

Hand in hand with the figurines go the seals, since we begin *E.M.III Seals* to find at this period the handle of the seal frequently carved to represent a bird or animal. The most delicate of these, which from the pattern on its base is clearly E.M.III, was found at Trapeza (Pl. XIII, 2). It is of ivory, a very favourite material at this time, and represents a monkey. Others show a dove with its young, a boar's head, a lion crouching over its prey, an ape and a two-headed bird (Pl. XIV, 1). Conical and pyramidal tops are also known as well as three-sided seals, cylinders with engraving at either end, flat two-sided seals, button seals and signets. After ivory, steatite of various colours is the commonest material.

The East of Crete is remarkably barren of seals. The centre of the island is represented by a few examples bought from villagers and some from Trapeza. The tombs of the Messara therefore give us practically our only criteria, and though the argument *e silentio* is always dangerous, we are, I think, justified in this case in believing that the centre of the art was here in the South and that thence it spread, but very slowly, to other parts of the island. Owing to lack of stratification, the attribution of seals to this period must be on stylistic grounds, but it is comparatively safe, for, as we have seen, E.M.II need hardly be considered, while M.M.I will provide enough stratified examples to distinguish its own types quite clearly.

The richness and variety of the patterns is extraordinary,

---

[1] *V.T.M.*, 21 ; *P. of M.*, I, 115.
[2] Banti, op. cit., 246, but see below.
[3] Hall, *Ancient History of the Near East*, Pl. XII, and see below.

particularly when one considers that this is a new art.   Some
external influence must have come in.

The spiral in different arrangements is a frequent design
(Fig. 12, 3).   A looser variety becomes the curvilinear meander,
and it has been suggested that the rectangular meander (Fig. 12,
1) is a derivation of this form under the influence of textiles.[1]
At all events this pattern, its simpler form (Fig. 12, 5), and its
complicated descendant the labyrinth, all make their appearance
at this period.   Rosettes occur as one would expect.

But the most important feature is the regular introduction
of animals and of human figures.   A number of seals from
Platanos, of the cylindrical type, bear such representations.
Best of all is one which shows a procession of lions round the
circumference and of spiders round the centre of one end,
while the other has three scorpions.[2]   Apes and wild goats are
found.[3]   Human figures of a rough kind appear,[4] as well as

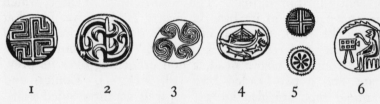

1   2   3   4   5   6

FIG. 12.—Early Minoan III Seals

boats and fishes (Fig. 12, 4), the prototypes of the marine
subjects which form so large a part of the later Minoan repertoire.[5]   A useful design from a dating point of view is, as we shall
see, the ' double sickle ' motive (e.g. Fig. 12, 2), which appears
on button and bead seals.

In almost every case the grouping is extremely effective and
the field is filled admirably in a way which for a new art is most
surprising.   The cases in which an effective design has not
been attained seem to be rather the fault of the particular artist
than evidence that the principle was not understood.[6]

E.M.III
Jewellery
The jewellery is hard to distinguish from that of E.M.II,
and the only objects which we can with comparative safety

[1] *P. of M.*, I, 121.   Cf. the figure on the sword-hilt from Mallia.
B.C.H., LX, Pl. XXXVIII, 2, of L.M.I date.
[2] *V.T.M.*, Pl. XIII, 1039.   Note that the scorpions are headless
as in Egypt.   Cf. Gardiner, *Egyptian Grammar*, 468.
[3] Ibid., 1044, 1103.
[4] *P. of M.*, I, Fig. 87, 6, and Fig. 93.   [5] Ibid., Fig. 89b.
[6] e.g. *V.T.M.*, Pl. IV, 516 ; Banti, op. cit., Figs. 88, 100.

attribute to this period are the cylindrical pendants decorated with applied spirals in gold wire or with simple leaf patterns in *répoussé* work.[1] The slight collars at each end are noteworthy. Beads of steatite, rock crystal, sard, and cornelian occur. The shapes are spherical, tubular, flattened discs, and, for the first time, amygdaloid.[2]

Stratified imports are again lacking for this period, although certain scarabs and seals from Agia Triadha, Aspre Petra, Platanos and Marathokephalo must almost certainly belong to the E.M.III deposit in the tombs [3] But more important are the cases where designs on seal stones find their obvious counterparts in Egypt. Whether or not such seals as the scaraboid with the top in the form of a weasel from Porti [4] is an import or a local imitation is of little consequence, for a glance at a representative collection of Egyptian seals well dated to the First Intermediate Period (i.e. VIIth–Xth Dynasties) shows that practically every single linear design found in Crete as well as the shapes of the back of the seals are closely paralleled.[5] The button seal is typical of the period, as is also the introduction of the scarab and the animal figure on the back. The human figures reversed so that the head of each is by his neighbour's foot occur in Egypt, and Evans has made out a ' family tree ' beginning with the two reversed lions and leading to the double sickle pattern (Fig. 12, 2).[6]

E.M.III Foreign Relations

Many of the parallels are too close, especially when taken together with the actual imports, to be anything but proof of direct contact between Egypt and the Messara at this period. Frankfort has, however, given reason to believe that many of these features are themselves introduced into Egypt at this time from Syria and that many of the animal-shaped seals from Crete are nearer to the parent Syrian stock.[7]

However that may be, it seems safer to assume contact between the Messara and a strongly Syrianized state in the Delta of Egypt than, in the absence of any evidence in East Crete, to allow direct contact with Syria itself.

[1] e.g. *V.T.M.*, Pl. XV, 455, &c., and LVII, top row.
[2] e.g. Ibid., Pl. LVIII.
[3] *Aegyptiaca*, 9, 29 and 35.   [4] *V.T.M.*, 68.
[5] Cf. *V.T.M.*, Pls. VIII, XIV, XV, with Brunton, *Qau and Badari*, I, Pls. XXXIII and XXXIV.
[6] *P. of M.*, I, 123, Fig. 92.
[7] *J.E.A.*, XII, 90 and 94 ; *Studies*, I, 132 ; II, 122. As for the ivory, elephants were found in Syria as late as the fifteenth century B.C., so that both areas had an equal opportunity of acquiring it.

Against this must be put the evidence of the figurines. The draped type with its hands folded over its chest is much closer to Mesopotamia than to anything else, and if the unstratified ivory head with traces of shell inlay in the eyes from Trapeza shown in Pl. XIII, 2, is not an import it was certainly made by a craftsman who had studied the art on the spot.[1] The extremely high dates to which the nearest parallel must be put, i.e. before the time of Sargon, means either such figures continued to be made in Syria for some hundreds of years after they disappear in Mesopotamia or else that we must push back the Messara figurines to E.M.II—a not impossible conclusion, but one which leaves a gap in the series which is hardly filled by the Cycladic figurines. This conclusion is more difficult when we think of the great strides made in engraving as shown on the seals.

The stone palettes have already been mentioned. The Egyptian parallels are of much earlier date, being predynastic and protodynastic, though they may well have survived, for an example was found in use at Tell el-Amarna.[2] The Egyptian examples, however, are flat on both sides, whereas the Minoan examples are either convex below or have four short legs. In any case it is not so much the object itself as the proof of a similarity of customs in regarding paint as an article of toilet which is important.

A good parallel to the anthropomorphic vases is found in an XIth Dynasty deposit at Rifeh.[3]

The pyxides and figurines from the Cyclades have already been mentioned. In addition to these, a number of vessels of island marble and Cycladic shape appeared at Mokhlos.[4] All of these imports date to Early Cycladic II and III, by which time the spiral had made its appearance.[5] The great increase in the number of obsidian blades wherever E.M.III objects occur is further proof of close contact with the islands.

E.M.III Chronology   Leaving aside the doubtful evidence of the figurines and palettes, we find that the seals, which are the most typical pro-

[1] Cf. this head with one found in the Second Oval Temple at Khafaje (*c.* 2800 B.C.–2600). *O.I.C.*, 19, Fig. 75 and p. 85. Dr. Frankfort, however, would prefer to attribute our head to the Syrian civilization of which we are only now beginning to learn.

[2] References *V.T.M.*, 129 ; *City of Akhenaten*, II, 43.

[3] *P. of M.*, II, 258.

[4] e.g. *Mochlos*, Pl. III, XXI, 10, Fig. 46, VII, *a*.

[5] Cf. *B.M. Cat.*, I, 1, XXVIII f., and group given in Child's *Dawn of European Civilization*, Fig. 22.

duct of the period in the Messara, show a strong resemblance to types which are datable with certainty in Egypt to the First Intermediate Period, that is to say, from the end of the VIth Dynasty to the beginning of the XIth, from about 2500 to about 2200 B.C.

SITES WHERE EARLY MINOAN III REMAINS HAVE BEEN FOUND

CENTRAL CRETE

(a) *Excavated Sites*

AMNISOS . . .	Cave . .	Vases from cave of Eileithyia. Marinatos, Πρακτικά, 1929, 95 ; 1930, 91.
ARKALOKHORI .	Cave . .	Many sherds from outside the entrance. Hazzidakis, *B.S.A.*, XIX, 35.
KASTELLOS TZERMIADHON	Settlement	Traces on the summit. Excavated in 1937 by the writer.
KNOSSOS . . .	Buildings	Hypogaeum ; latest deposit on the house floors S. of the Palace. *P. of M.*, I, 103 ff. Cycladic figurines and copper daggers found at the Teke on the Candia road. *Arch. Anz.*, 1933, 298.
KRASI	Tomb .	Some of contents of circular tomb. Marinatos, ’Αρχ. Δελτ., XII, 102.
MALLIA . . .	Deposit .	Sherds. Chapoutier, *Mallia*, I, 13 ; II, 27. *B.C.H.*, 1928, 368.
	Cemetery	Rock shelters on the coast. *B.C.H.*, 1929, 527.
PYRGOS . . .	Cave . .	Burials in larnakes. Xanthoudides, ’Αρχ. Δελτ., 1918, 136.
STRAVOMYTI . .	Cave . .	Sherds from excavations of 1898. Evans, *P. of M.*, II, 68.
TRAPEZA . . .	Cave . .	Vases, &c., from excavations of 1936. *A.J.A.*, XL, 371. *Arch. Anz.*, 1936, 162.
TYLISSOS . . .	Settlement	Earliest sherds from first period of occupation. Hazzidakis, *Tylissos Villas Minoennes*, 79. *Ausonia*, VIII, 76 ff., Fig. 12.

(b) *Surface Finds*

GAZE	One sherd found in the cutting of the road by Miss Money-Coutts and Miss Eccles, 1934. *B.S.A.*, XXXIII, 92.
KANLI KASTELLI .	Sherds from Visala E. of the village. Evans, *P. of M.*, II, 71.

SOUTH CRETE

(a) Excavated Sites

AGIA TRIADHA . . Tomb . Some of contents of circular tomb. A. Banti, *Annuario*, XIII–XIV, 164 ff. *Mon. Ant.*, XIV, 677.

Houses . Contents of some houses below main court of palace. *J.H.S.*, XXXIII, 365.

DHRAKONAIS . . Tombs . Some sherds from the circular tombs. Xanthoudides, *V.T.M.*, 76.

KAMARAIS . . . Cave . One vase and a few sherds. Dawkins, *B.S.A.*, XIX, 1.

KHRISTOS . . . Tomb . Vases, &c., from circular tomb. Xanthoudides, *V.T.M.*, 70.

KOUMASA . . . Tomb . Some of contents of circular tomb B. Ibid., 3.

MARATHOKEPHALO Tomb . Some of contents of circular tomb. Xanthoudides,' Ἀϱχ. Δελτ., 1918. Παϱ. 1, 14 ff.

PHAISTOS . . . Deposit . Sherds and Vases. Mosso, *Mon. Ant.*, XIX, 204. Pernier, *Festos*, 115.

PLATANOS . . . Tombs . Earliest contents of circular tomb B and smaller interments. *V.T.M.*, 88.

PORTI . . . Tomb . Earliest contents. Ibid., 57.

SIVA . . . . Tombs . Latest deposit in the circular tombs. *Ausonia*, VIII, *Sup.*, 13 ff.

VOROU . . . Tombs . Earliest deposit from circular tombs. Marinatos, 'Ἀϱχ. Δελτ., 13, 155.

EAST CRETE

(a) Excavated Sites

AGIA PHOTIA . . Cave . . Sherds from burials. Boyd-Hawes, *Trans. Penn. Univ.*, I, 183. *Gournia*, 56, 60.

GOURNIA . . . Deposit . Large deposit of sherds from a trench to the N. *Trans. Penn. Univ.*, I, 191. *Gournia*, 57.

MOKHLOS . . . Tombs . Contents. Seager, *Mochlos, passim*.
Settlement · Deposits below later houses. Seager, *A.J.A.*, XIII, 274.

PAKHYAMMOS . . Tombs . Child burials in pots. Larnax burials. Seager, *Pachyammos*, 9.

PALAIKASTRO . . Bone enclosures Bosanquet, *B.S.A.*, VIII, 292. At Ellenika, Ibid., X, 196. At Kastri, Ibid., XI, 268.

Deposits In the town site. Ibid., IX, 300. *Sup.*, 7.

PSEIRA . . . Settlement Deposits in houses of first period. Seager, *Pseira*, 17.

Chapter III

THE MIDDLE MINOAN PERIOD

I. MIDDLE MINOAN I (M.M.I)

(See Map 7)

IN M.M.I the swing of power has gone to the North and centre of Crete, and the first elements of the great palaces appear. When the pottery is discussed reasons will be given for believing that in this part of the island the period overlapped E.M.III elsewhere [1] and that the earliest style of vase painting, M.M.Ia, was almost confined to Knossos. It is symptomatic of this centralization that M.M.II never reaches most sites which continue with a local form of the M.M.Ib style until M.M.III. M.M.II will be treated in a separate chapter, but it must not be forgotten that it is a local development of M.M.I, nor that the earliest protopalatial remains at Knossos and Mallia are contemporary with the latter half of E.M.III in the Messara and in the East. [2]

To some time early in the period must be attributed the regularization of the great route across the island from Komo in the South to Knossos, for not only does the fort at Anagyroi [3] guard the road but it is clear that the monumental entrance to the Palace at Knossos was also founded. [4] Another route to the coast from the Messara was considered worth guarding and remains of a small station are visible at Agia Paraskeve at the top of the Goulopharango Gorge which leads down from

[1] *P. of M.*, I, 108.

[2] Very good evidence for this was found in June 1937 on the Kastellos Tzermiadhon in Lasithi. Here a house was excavated which had clearly been continuously occupied. Below the floors and in the interstices of the walls was M.M.I. pottery. The deposit *on* the floors was uniformly M.M.III, and outside, round about the base of the walls, was a mixed dump of M.M.I and M.M.III. Not a single M.M.II sherd was found.

[3] Is this a local contraction for Agioi Anargyroi?

[4] Ibid., II, 146. In its final form it no doubt dates from M.M.III.

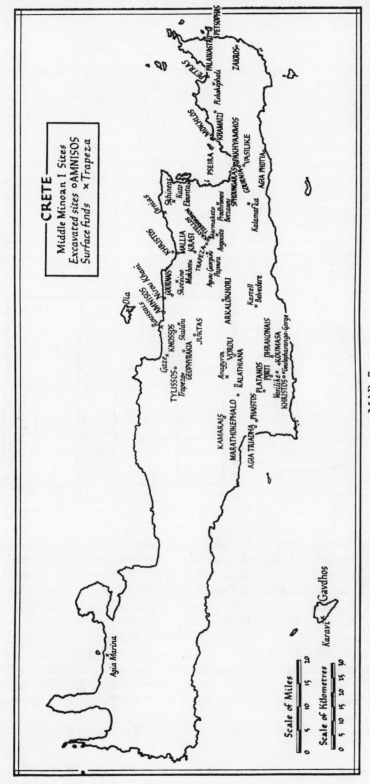

CRETE

Middle Minoan I Sites
Excavated sites ○ AMNISOS
Surface finds × Trapeza

Agia Marina

Dia

Karoussa
Iouktas
AMNISOS
Nirou Khani
KNOSSOS
Gaze × Skalani
GEOPHYRAKIA
Trapeza
TYLISSOS
JUKTAS
Anagyroi ×
VOROU
KALATHIANA

KAMARAIS
MARATHOKEPHALO ○ PHAISTOS
AGIA TRIADHA
PLATANOS
PYRTI
Vasiliki × ○ KOUMASA
KHRISTOS × Goulipharango-Gorge
DHRAKONAIS

ARKALŌKHORI

Kastell
× Belvedere

Ornas
Skhineas
Kato × Ekantaas
MALLIA
GOUNNAIS
KRASI
Skoteino
Malchos
TRAPEZA ○ Marmaketo
Agiou Georgiu Angoisis
Papoura
Prathromos
Baraboun
SPHOUNGARA
GOURNIA
KHRISTOS
Kalamafka
KATO ○ SPAKHYAMMOS
VASILIKE
AGIA PHOTIA

PSEIRA
MOKHLOS
KHAMAITZI ○
Psilakphali
ZAKROS
PETRAS
PALAIKASTRO ○
PETSOPHAS
SYNCLOS

Scale of Miles
0   5   10   15   20

Scale of Kilometres
0 5 10 15 20   30

Karavi
Gavdhos

MAP 7

the M.M.1 site at Vasilike to Trypeti, though at the latter point no surface traces of this date remain.

The foundation of the Palace of Knossos must be put at the very beginning of M.M.1.   Such structures as had stood on the top of the mound were swept away, mainly to the North-West corner, where they served to level up yet more of the area, and a great central court was formed.   Round this court were grouped isolated blocks of buildings—' insulae ' many of them with rounded corners.   To the North was a long paved court, the remains of which extend at either end

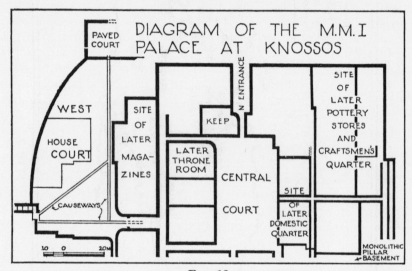

Fig. 13

from below the later ' Theatral Area '.   To the West was another court bounded by a heavy enceinte wall and approached from the West by means of a ramp.   Immediately within the wall lay a number of houses whose cellars descended below the level of the court.[1]   Across the court ran slightly raised causeways.   In the South-East corner lay two entrances to the Palace.   One ran straight through eastwards to the Central Court past a number of magazines, the other ran South, through some prototype of the later West Porch, and no doubt followed very much the same line as the Corridor of the Procession, to be joined at some point by the stepped approach

[1] *B.S.A.*, XXX, 53. *P. of M.*, IV, 50 ff.

from the South mentioned above. A broad entrance led from the northern court guarded by a strongly walled ' keep ', the main lines of which were preserved till the end of Minoan times. The West wing of the Palace was split in two by the long North–South corridor which later served the magazines. West of this the remodelling has been too complete to allow of reconstruction, but between the long corridor and the Central Court the blocks of buildings into which the later palace falls clearly mark the site of the various insulae. Clearest of all is the block occupied during the latest palace period by the Throne Room system. Here the rounded corner still survives. East of the Central Court the Palace sloped down in a series of narrow terraces to the great east wall which is still visible.

It is extremely probable, in view of the continuity of the Palace's history, that many of the later passages and corridors mark the position of open lanes between the isolated blocks.

To these earliest elements in the Palace belongs the Monolithic Pillar Basement, a well-preserved structure which may have formed part of a more elaborate building. The two rectangular piers are the first examples of the pillars which are to be so common later (Pl. XV, 2).

The Palace at Mallia also dates from the beginning of M.M.1 and presents many of the same features, though the most recent research tends to stress the amount of remodelling carried out in M.M.III. The original elements, however, the Central Court, courts to West and North with direct access to it, and the way in which even in its present state it seems to split up automatically into semi-independent blocks, go to show that in essentials it remained the same (Pl. XV, 3).

In M.M.1b the western façade of Knossos was remodelled. The earlier rounded corners were abolished and the entrance direct to the Central Court was blocked. The main features of the present façade with its gypsum orthostates belong to this period, as does much of the terracing to the South.

At Phaistos it would seem that the Palace was founded in M.M.1b, for the pottery of deposits immediately prior to its foundation are of a type which we shall see is transitional between E.M.III and the M.M.1 of the South and East.[1] Here the conformation of the site, placed as it is on the brow of a steep hill which descends rapidly on three sides, precluded the adoption of the rectangular plan of Knossos and Mallia.[2] To the West lay (Pl. XV, 4) a paved court, crossed like that

[1] *Festos*, I, 135, Fig. 59. [2] Ibid., Pl. II.

at Knossos by causeways which led to an entrance in the middle of the West façade.[1] At a higher level to the North is another court, which however occupies only a small area.[2] The Central Court is bordered by buildings only on the West, North and northern part of the East sides, the remainder running up to the edge of the plateau. A series of heavy walls to the North by the later entrance passage implies perhaps that originally a broad entrance comparable to that of the same period at Knossos led into the court at this point. Of the internal arrangements no more can be made out than at Knossos, for the great rebuilding in M.M.iii seems to have been even more thorough.

Except for the facing of ashlar in limestone or of gypsum slabs bound by wooden bars dovetailed into mortices which front walls of rubble in the great buildings, the masonry is usually of small stones roughly dressed, sometimes very neatly and carefully laid.[3] The foundation blocks were often of great size, as in the case of the old West façade at Knossos, but the actual walls seldom show a block more than 35–40 centimetres in length. The stones are invariably hammer-dressed, the saw not yet being used for masonry.

The rounded corners seem to be peculiar to Knossos, and since there is no topographical reason for them as there is in the house at Khamaizi (see below), we must look elsewhere for the explanation. They are not a natural construction in either brick or stone, although examples in the former occur in Meso-potamia in the Larsa Period.[4] What they are typical of is a wooden or reed palisade, and it is just conceivable that at Knossos we have in these ' block houses ' the survival of a tradition which is very old indeed.

Another feature which is common to the West façades of the three early palaces is the base slab or podium, which projects

[1] It is not made clear in the text but it seems most likely that the addition of steps at the North end of the court and the construction of a single-columned propylaeum corresponding to the Theatral Area and the West Propylaeum at Knossos are the work of M.M.ii.

[2] Right up against the West wall of this court is a row of holes, obviously for columns of wood. They are too close to the wall to be part of a verandah and it is clear that the wall is contemporary with the paving. They may have been merely a decoration.

[3] e.g. *P. of M.*, I, Fig. 109, and to a less extent *Festos*, I, Fig. 54.

[4] e.g. at Tell-Asmar and a doubtful earlier example (Early Dynastic) at Khafaje. *O.I.C.*, 17, p. 70, Fig. 60. They were always at street corners where baggage animals might knock against a sharp corner. Perhaps the Knossian examples were rounded for the same reason.

in some cases nearly half a metre beyond the orthostates and is often as much as 40 centimetres high. No explanation of this has been given and in succeeding periods it either disappears or is reduced to a matter of a centimetre or two.[1]

The slight set-backs or recesses in the walls of the façade also are puzzling. At Mallia, both in the West Court and on the South side of the Central Court, they are regular; at Phaistos they occur, but the façades are too ruined for us to say more than that; and at Knossos they are quite irregular. They never seem to bear any relation to a room behind.

They have been explained as survivals of the bays between the square projecting towers on an outer wall.[2] But in such a case one would expect them, however irregularly the towers had been spaced, to assume some sort of symmetry once their origin had been forgotten. Again it has been suggested that they are devices for breaking the monotony of a wall by a play of light and shade.[3] But to this also it can be objected that symmetry would be at least a certain consideration, while at Mallia, where the recesses are symmetrical, the South façade of the Central Court would receive no sun to cast a shadow, while most of the West façade would itself be shadowed until late evening by the projection of buildings farther South. An explanation is the more desirable because several of the angles come immediately in the middle of the only possible position for windows in the upper story at Knossos if such existed.[4]

To the very beginning of M.M.$1a$ must be put the houses inside the western enceinte wall at Knossos.[5] Only the basements remain, but in one case there are two floor levels separated by 50 centimetres of filling. On both floors the deposit was pure M.M.$1a$. In the other house a flight of red plaster steps led down to a room also paved and lined with red plaster, which contained in one corner a shallow oblong receptacle formed by ridges of plaster, and in the centre of the room a shallow sunken circle with a deeper depression in the middle (Pl. XVI, 1). It is possible that this bowl was intended to receive offerings—indeed, the room as a whole rather reminds one of the later sunken lustral areas—or it may have had a brazier standing over it and have been for convenience in

---

[1] Professor A. B. Cook suggests to me that it may be a survival of the stone base of a crude brick wall.

[2] *P. of M.*, I, 269. [3] *Mallia*, II, 10.

[4] See Fig. 31 below, and p. 186.

[5] *P. of M.*, IV, 66; *B.S.A.*, XXX, 53.

brushing up fallen ashes. Demargne [1] inclines strongly to this
view and compares it to the fixed hearths found in some of the
M.M.1a houses at Mallia. A big tray in thick red clay with
horizontal handles and distinct traces of carbonization was
found in the house and the diameter exactly fits the hollow.

Owing to the fact that both the houses were razed to the
ground and had their cellars filled in when the West Court was
extended in M.M.II, the plans are not very helpful, but a magazine with deep bays like the Monolithic Pillar basement and a
possible light well between the westernmost house and the
enceinte wall can be distinguished.

The construction throughout is of small rough stones bonded
by clay. Traces of bricks, originally unbaked but burnt red

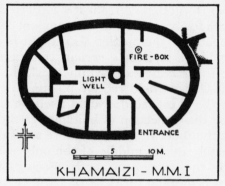

FIG. 14

by some fire, were discovered, as in the South-East quarter of
the Palace at Mallia. The good red plaster reminds one somewhat of the early Vasilike houses, and traces of the same plaster,
evidently from an upper floor, were found at various levels
above the magazine.

Slightly later in M.M.1 comes the unique oval house at
Khamaizi (Fig. 14). Mackenzie has clearly demonstrated that
its shape is fortuitous, determined by the lie of the ground,
rather than a regular form or an introduction from elsewhere.[2]
He has pointed out that it is in essentials a rectangular plan
modified to fit an oval perimeter.[3] Its plan is interesting in
that it is built, like the palaces, round a central open court or
light well. In this it contrasts not only with the houses of

[1] *B.C.H.*, XXXII, 87, but at Khamaizi there was a movable one.
[2] *B.S.A.*, XIV, 415 ff.   [3] Ibid., Figs. 20 and 21.

earlier periods but also with the only other M.M.1 houses of which we have a comparatively complete plan : House A at Vasilike (Fig. 15), where a number of rectangular rooms are thrown together with little attempt at organized planning, and a few houses at Kalathiana which are square in plan. One of them, House H, has a well-squared stone facing and the set-backs we have noticed in the palaces. In the other settlements of the period, as at Pseira, Mokhlos, and Palaikastro, later building has effectively prevented the recovery of the plans. It is fairly certain, however, that except for Khamaizi the private houses show no more regularity of plan than did those of E.M. times.

In connexion with the architecture mention must be made

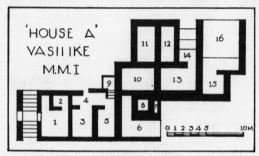

FIG. 15

of the earliest traces of the elaborate system of drainage and arrangement for water supply at Knossos.[1] Good examples of the clay pipes were discovered below the South Porch and below the Corridor of the Draughtboard. They are about three-quarters of a metre long and taper sharply, so that the resulting head of water drives out any obstruction. They have narrow collars which fit neatly into the next pipe where they are cemented. It is possible that the Minoan engineers had already discovered the principle that water finds its own level, for under the South Porch the pipe-line shows an upward slant of more than one in twenty. At this point, however, they are laid on the earth which filled the Hypogeum and may therefore have sunk. So certainty is impossible.

In the Messara a number of the circular tombs are still in use. *M.M.1* At Vorou and Dhrakonais the main deposit belongs to this *Tombs* period, while at Agia Triadha the deposit is so rich that special annexes seem to have been built to contain the offerings. This

[1] *P. of. M.*, I, 141.

leads one to believe that in many cases the deposits are of a votive rather than of a funerary nature.

It has been noted above, when the tombs were first described,[1] that the site of one or two of the settlements was changed. Where this is so and a new settlement was founded close to the E.M. tomb, that tomb is no longer used.[2]

In East Crete the rectangular ossuaries of Palaikastro and the built tombs of Mokhlos are still in use and indeed still being built. Larnax and pithos burials are becoming more common, as at Pakhyammos and Sphoungaras. In one case, at Agia Photia, sherds were found in a rock shelter.

In North and Central Crete the rock shelter still seems popular as a burial-place. The rectangular ossuary, however, has come in at Gournais and has reached its most elaborate form at Mallia. Here, between the Palace and the sea lies the spot known for generations as Khrysolakkos, the Pit of Gold, from the quantity of gold ornaments discovered by the peasants digging at random. Excavation brought to light a magnificent ossuary surrounded by a wall of well-dressed stones, outside which was a paved area. Within the boundary wall were innumerable chambers of varying size, all built of small stones, in which were heaped the bones of the dead with their funeral furniture around them. One of the chambers, however, was in the nature of a place of offerings, for to one side stood a low fluted base of stucco, which was at first believed to be part of the shaft of a column, but which later investigation proved to be hollow and probably intended to receive libations.[3]

M.M.1
Sanctuaries

In M.M.1 we find a new type of building, the sanctuary on a peak. Juktas South of Knossos, Prophetes Elias above Mallia, and Petsophas above Palaikastro are good examples ; Zakros, Khristos and Piskokephali seem also to be of the same nature, while the structure on the top of Edhikte near Mokhos is more likely to be a sanctuary than a fort guarding a non-existent road.[4]

Juktas, though we do not know its ancient name, was the legendary burial-place of Zeus, and the origins of its sanctity

[1] See above, p. 60.
[2] Koumasa alone is the exception and there the M.M. sherds were not associated with burials, but were outside as if they were offerings at shrines.
[3] *B.C.H.*, 1933, 74.
[4] It does, however, look out over the Gulf of Mallia, and could be a ' Βίγλα ', or look-out post, as opposed to a ' Φρούριον ', or fort.

are lost in the mists of time.[1] Surrounding the northern peak
is a massive temenos wall, which, together with the fragments
of large pithoi, denotes the possibility of the summit having
been a city of refuge, a Kresphygeton, in times of trouble.
The sanctuary itself almost overhangs the steep western face
of the mountain. The actual building seems to date from
L.M.I, but the plan is so primitive that we may be almost
certain that some structure, perhaps of more perishable
materials, stood here from M.M.I. It consisted of an outer
room, approached by an ascending entrance passage and
flanked by a store-room. Behind this was a rectangular inner
chamber, some 5 by 8 metres, floored, in later times at least,
with white plaster. Votive offerings in the shape of vases and
figurines dating from the very beginning of M.M.I until M.M.II
were found in a stratum of grey ash immediately overlying the
rock. Above this was a stratum of burnt earth containing
M.M.III sherds which extended beyond the limit of the building.

No plan of the sanctuary at Mallia has been published. At
Petsophas the history of the sanctuary is similar to that of
Juktas. A lower layer of black earth and ash containing the
M.M.I figurines, above this a disturbed layer, also M.M.I,
and finally a building of almost exactly the same type as the
L.M.I building on Juktas, even to the white plaster floor. An
additional feature, however, is a plaster bench surrounding the
inner room on three sides. In this case there was some
evidence for believing that the walls of the later building
corresponded in part at least to those of the earlier.

The sanctuary at Khristos is a rectangular building with
a square projection in the middle of its East side. Below the
main chamber runs a great cleft in the rock, now choked with
fallen stones, which may have been the entrance to a cave.

It is possibly at this period that caves ceased to be places of
burial and became places of worship. At Trapeza no burial
could be assigned to M.M.I, which was in any case a scanty
deposit. Nor do any of the other caves, Eileithyia, Arkalokhori, Agia Marina, Skoteino, the second Trapeza near Tylissos,
or Kamarais, which contain M.M.I deposits, seem to have any
human bones associated with them.

The earliest phase of M.M.I pottery is excellently represented *M.M.I*
at Knossos, less well at Mallia, where the action of the soil has *Pottery*

<hr>

[1] *P. of M.*, I, 153. Professor A. B. Cook would derive the word
from Διώκτας—the Pursuer from the legend of Minos' pursuit of
Britomartis. *Zeus*, II, 939, n. 1.

destroyed the paint, and hardly at all elsewhere, save for a few poor examples from Tylissos and Giophyrakia. This, coupled with the fact that there is a very small quantity of E.M.III found at these Northern sites compared with the richness of that period in East and South, is good evidence for M.M.I being well under way in this part of the island while E.M.III was still generally in vogue at the other sites.

The slow wheel has already come in and many of the vases show parallel striations on the base where they were cut off by means of a string. Much, however, is still done by hand, as witness the pinching in by the fingers of the stems of cups and the paring of jugs, jars, and cups.

Two very early pure deposits have come to light which really represent a period transitional between E.M.III and M.M.1a. One was below the floor of the Vat Room,[1] the other was the deposit on the earliest floor in the house inside the West wall.[2] In both deposits were vases which can be described as ' border-line cases ', e.g. Pl. XIV, 2, 1 (with a band of Indian red and incisions), 4, 12 and 18 and *P. of M.*, I, Fig. 118a, 1 and 2 (where the patterns are in the new M.M.1 chalky white paint). In the Vat Room deposit also are several incised Cycladic pyxides, such as we have seen appear at Pyrgos in E.M.III. The rest of both deposits, however, is typical of very early M.M.1a, while the upper levels of the house, together with all the contents of the other house, contain an almost complete corpus of mature M.M.1a pottery, including the polychrome style.

As further proof of the closeness in date of M.M.1a to E.M.II at Knossos the common short-spouted jug in buff clay with the butterfly or double axe pattern in front in red paint may be mentioned [3] as well as the persistence of other dark-on-light designs which elsewhere had died out (Fig. 16, 2 and 3, and a number of examples on Pl. XIV, 2). Dark on light and light on dark, in fact, go hand in hand. The creamy white has given way to a more flaky, chalky white, the Indian red has become orange and the black background of E.M.III now varies from lavender grey to purplish-brown.

The most typical vases of the period, which are invaluable for dating purposes, are the small jugs with a short cut-away neck decorated usually with a broad leaf-like slash of paint

---

[1] *P. of M.*, I, 165.   [2] *B.S.A.*, XXX, 60.
[3] e.g. *P. of M.*, I, Fig. 118a, 9 and 21.

drawn diagonally across each shoulder, two white lines to mark the centre of the leaf and bands round the neck and body (e.g. Pl. XIV, 2, 13).

Even commoner are the handleless cups with or without pedestal which were decorated below the rim with a band either

FIG. 16.—Patterns on Middle Minoan 1a Pottery from Knossos

of red or black paint on buff or of white on black. A more elaborate pattern and one curiously anticipating L.M.1a is shown on Pl. XIV, 2, 8, where the red spikes are picked out with a central rib of white. A type with a comparatively high pedestal and a more spreading body was ornamented with bands of red and white on black, above which diagonal lines reached the rim.[1] Tumblers occur, sometimes in the finest eggshell ware. These are frequently mottled in a way recalling the Vasilike style, and are occasionally decorated with circles surrounded by dots.[2] A variety of handled cups is found. Some recall E.M.II shapes with a broad band of dark paint at the foot and a segment of a circle on each side below the lip (Pl. XIV, 2, 6).[3] More finely shaped examples with a carinated shoulder, a low foot, and a high swung handle have a design of white dots (cf. Fig. 16, 14) on a polished background of mottled red (cf. example lacking handle, Pl. XIV, 2, 11). Larger straight-sided cups are often polychrome with a design of roundels, sometimes joined by diagonal lines (Fig. 16, 13 and 15).

The jugs are usually more graceful than those of E.M.III, the spouts being narrower. A splendid example is shown in Pl. XIV, 2, 2, with a background merging from red to black and a decoration of orange circles surrounded by white dots with a white cross in the centre (Fig. 16, 18).[4] The imitation rivets on the spouts still appear on some of the coarser examples (e.g. Pl. XIV, 2, 14). Some of these have three handles between which radiate patterns of the type shown in Fig. 16, 4. Others have a band of clay round the neck with diagonal cuts.

Spouted jars with a carinated or curved body and horizontal handles provided a variety of forms of decoration varying between the simple white lines on Pl. XIV, 2, 18, to the elaborate patterns shown in Fig. 16, 6, 9, 12, and 16.[5]

Open bowls were often elaborately decorated inside. One particularly fine example[6] has a red-brown background with a big central ring of orange-red surrounded by two white lines. Round these are five lozenges in white with white dots and orange bends within (Fig. 16, 10).

The pithoi have thin walls and seldom stand much more than a metre in height. Four vertical handles are the rule. Rope patterns in horizontal and diagonal bands occur.[7] Other store jars have a high rounded shoulder, a tapering body, and a short flared neck. The handles when horizontal are placed somewhat low down and are tilted up ; when vertical they meet the lip of the vase. These vases are decorated with red bands

---

[1] B.S.A., XXX, Pl. XIV, gives a good idea of the range of colours.
[2] Ibid., No. 17.   [3] Cf. Mochlos, Fig. 22, VI, 6.
[4] B.S.A., XXX, Pl. XIII, in colour.
[5] Cf. also ibid., XXX, 64, and Pl. XIV.
[6] Ibid., XIV, 12.   [7] Ibid., Fig. 6.

and arcs or with white bands. One example is incised with the design on Fig. 16, 19. Large jugs are found as well as bridge-spouted and round-spouted jars. These are usually mono-chrome, but occasionally the upper part is decorated with a dark brown wash which is sometimes allowed to trickle down the side of the vase. A unique jar, shaped like a bucket with two horizontal handles, had a wide ledge pierced with holes running all round the interior near the mouth and a small spout pulled out from the rim. This was no doubt for straining.[1]

Typical of this early period of M.M.1 are the so-called ' sheep bells ' (Pl. XIV, 2, 16 and 24) with diagonal and hori-zontal lines of red, horns and a loop handle. The small per-forations on top or in front may possibly have been for a string to support the clapper.[2] It is conceivable, however, that they are lids, descended from the horned caps of E.M.1.

Another pure deposit below the West Court gives a few additions.[3] Here was found an early form of fruit-stand or pedestalled bowl with a simple brown or buff decoration of lines and dots and a magnificent polychrome jug, which to judge by the deep red employed must belong to the very beginning of M.M.1a; it is painted round the shoulder with a series of double axes outlined in red bordered with white and filled with white dots (Pl. XVII, 1, a).

The vase in the form of a dove painted in orange-red and white on a black ground which was found in the Monolithic Pillar Basement may have had a ritual use.[4]

The beginnings of ' barbotine ' are seen in a kind of ' barnacle work ' in relief and a modification of it consisting of narrow diagonal ridges. At this stage the work is usually applied to cups and bowls only.[5] Many of the chevron and dotted patterns associated with very early polychromy seem to go back to Neolithic prototypes, and it is possible that such designs had been kept alive in other materials such as wood, while the influence of the incised and filled Cycladic pyxides must not be forgotten.[6] This is perhaps the explanation of so peculiar a cup as Pl. XIV, 2, 10, which shows a white-filled herring-bone incision on a dark polished ground.

In the Messara the style of pottery which most nearly corresponds to that just described is shown in the stratum

---

[1] All these types are illustrated in *P. of M.*, I, Fig. 118a, or *B.S.A.*, XXX, 67, Fig. 7.
[2] *P. of M.*, I, 175.   [3] *B.S.A.*, XI, 16.
[4] *P. of M.*, I, 146.   [5] Ibid., IV, 87.   [6] Ibid., 89.

immediately underlying the magazines of the first palace at Phaistos.[1] Most typical are the squat bowls with a short spout,

FIG. 17.—Patterns on Middle Minoan 1b Pottery from Knossos and the Kamarais Cave

which might be mistaken for E.M.III examples were it not for the difference in the white paint. A group which must also be

[1] *Festos*, I, 135.

assigned to this date appeared at Porti, and a few vases from Agia Triadha, Platanos, Dhrakonais and Kalathiana,[1] but the extremely small quantity of pottery which can be ascribed to this transitional period is proof of its short duration.

In the East of Crete E.M.iii seems to persist right through, and there is no group we can definitely assign to even a transitional period, much less to M.M.1a in the Knossian sense.

For the second phase of M.M.1 pottery, M.M.1b at Knossos, we are fortunate in having a pure deposit on a house floor again below the West Court.[2] It is perhaps significant that the houses immediately within the West enceinte wall were razed to the ground at the end of M.M.1a and the M.M.1b deposits are all of them further back from the wall. Is it possible that a sudden attack or the threat of it was the cause of this? That, as so often in ancient warfare, the houses huddling up against the wall were deliberately destroyed in order that they should not be fired by lighted arrows? Or were they actually so fired, for we must remember the traces of burnt bricks, and as a result was a space afterwards left within the wall?[3]

A selection of the vases is shown on Pl. XVII, 2–4, and the principal patterns in Fig. 17. The most typical shape for this period is the low cup with straight or slightly outcurving sides and a ribbon handle (Pl. XVII, 3). The decoration is frequently polychrome, the red which is now somewhat more approaching crimson being almost always bordered with white. The patterns on the cups are still purely geometrical and consist of vertical and horizontal bands, loops and saltires. This practice of bordering red with white may have given rise to the deliberate imitations of breccia which are first found at this time.[4] In the same way the linked disks, of which one variety is shown in Fig. 16, 15, seem to have been naturalized by M.M.1b into a rather stiff pattern of berries on stalks,[5] and the

---

[1] V.T.M., 58 ff., with Pl. VI (except 5067), Pl. XXXVI, a, top row, LI, b; Annuario, XIII–XIV, 172 ff.

[2] P. of M., I, 186; B.S.A., X, 14.

[3] Cf. the houses at Mycenae and in Greek times regulations as to the distance which must be left between house and wall. Ditt., Syll., 308–9 (Athens and Nisyros); Jahreshefte, 1899, Sup., 33, on Philon, Τειχοποιικῶν, § II.

[4] Cf. P. of M., I, 177.

[5] Ibid., I, Fig. 133b; IV, Fig. 66e. All these examples are good illustrations of a formal pattern giving rise to naturalistic designs.

three stiff spikes of Pl. XIV, 2, 8, become the crocuses on the fine cup shown in *P. of M.*, IV, Pl. XXVIII. More natural forms are coming in, the plant forms (e.g. Fig. 17, 11–14, 21) are still stiff but they are recognizably intended for plants. The design in Fig. 17, 24, is from a squat bridge-spouted bowl found in the Kamarais cave (Pl. XVIII, 3, *a*) and has been recognized as a whorl shell. But a simpler form which may have no connexion originally is found on a fruit-stand at Knossos.[1]

The decoration tends to become closer and more of the vase to be covered by it (Pl. XVII, 2, *c*, and the pattern Fig. 17, 10, from another fragmentary example). The fabric is usually finer and the cups shown in Pl. XVII, 4, *a* and *b*, are as thin as any M.M.II eggshell. The shapes are more sophisticated and the flaring rim is becoming common for cups. Barbotine has begun to be used in conjunction with painting. In moderation this is passable, but the clumsy jug (Pl. XVII, 1, *b*) from a house south of the Palace is a diastrous achievement both in shape and design. It is, however, fortunately unique at Knossos and is either an import or a copy of the vulgar Messara style described below.

In the South the prevailing decoration is barbotine, which seems to have run riot on the jugs (Pl. XVIII, 1 and 2). These jugs, which are particularly common in the annexe to the tomb at Agia Triadha, seem to be typical of the district. They are comparatively squat with a low, almost horizontal spout and usually three handles. Two or three specimens, like the jug from Knossos, have a white wash over the barbotine which is bordered with red or white lines. Otherwise the decoration is simple, consisting merely of bands of plain colour and an occasional spiral (Pl. XVIII, 2, *a*).[2] Many are monochrome and the sea of prickles is relieved only by an occasional round flat surface or indentation [3] (Pl. XVIII, 1, *d*, and 2, *c*). A less violent form of barbotine is shown on Pl. XVIII, 1, *c*. This is the first appearance of the four-handled jar with a rounded rim which has a long history in front of it. Another variation is shown on Plate XVIII, 2, *b*, where bosses take the place of prickles and where the diagonal ridged strips recall a form of decoration in M.M.1*a* at Knossos. More pleasant are the tumblers (Pl. XVIII, 2, *e*) with a decoration of white and red

[1] Cf. *P. of M.*, IV, 114.   [2] *V.T.M.*, Plate V, 4973.
[3] Ibid., 4971.

on buff,[1] the carinated cups (ibid., 3) and the open bowls with simple patterns inside.[2]

The vases from the Kamarais cave fall into rather a different category (Pl. XVIII, 3 ; XXII, 3, *b* and *k*). A very high proportion are open spouted bowls of a squatter type than is found elsewhere. The decoration is brilliant in the extreme and it is evident that the finest wares were bought here for the making of offerings. The phrase ' Kamarais style ' was originally used to denote all polychrome pottery, a terminology which not all archaeologists have yet grown out of. Later it came to mean particularly the M.M.II, palace style. Yet by far the greater proportion of the painted vases here belongs to M.M.1*b*. Barbotine is found, but infrequently except as a small element in the decoration. A number of vases with a comparatively simple geometric pattern (e.g. Pl. XVIII, 3, *e* and *g*) are probably contemporary with the end of M.M.1*a* at Knossos. Others, such as *a*, *b*, and *c*, are of the finest type of M.M.1*b*, while others again are clearly M.M.II and will be treated in their place. Besides the whorl-shell noticed above, other natural forms occur, e.g. the fish on *b* and a rude figure of a man.[3] The cup, *c*, is typical in shape though the effective decoration is better than any examples from elsewhere.

Clay lamps were found at Porti.[4] They consist of an open flat-bottomed bowl with a cut in the side for the wick and a stick-handle. Another type has a projecting spout for the wick and a loop handle, while a third is on a short thick pedestal.

The pottery of East Crete is difficult to subdivide. As we have seen, E.M.III seems here to have overlapped M.M.1*a* at Knossos, and tne latter must have been nearly over when what we can safely call M.M.1 begins in this part of the island. The dark-on-light wares we should naturally expect to be the earliest, but they occur throughout with the most advanced shapes and forms of decoration, some of which must be contemporary with M.M.II at Knossos. There is perhaps, however, a greater proportion of them in House B at Vasilike, which Seager[5] was inclined to believe earlier than the other M.M.1 House A. But the low cups are of the shape typical of M.M.1*b*

[1] Ibid., Pl. IX, 6862, and cf. *P. of M.*, IV, Fig. 64, from Knossos.
[2] *V.T.M.*, Pl. IX, 6859 ; VI, 5054. In spite of the simplicity of their pattern, it seems impossible to include them among the earliest M.M.1 elements owing to the shade of red which is (not in the plate) much less orange.
[3] *Mon. Ant.*, VI, Pl. IX, 10.   [4] *V.T.M.*, 63.
[5] *Trans. Penn. Univ.*, II, 114 and 126.

at Knossos, and it would be most unsafe to take the dark-on-light decoration as a criterion of date.

Cups, tumblers, and jugs in dark-on-light show a very

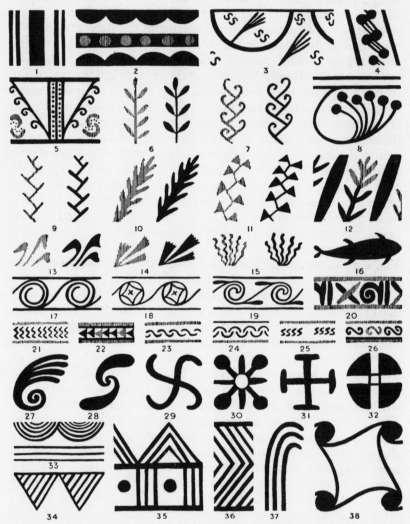

FIG. 18.—Patterns on Middle Minoan 1 Pottery from East Crete

limited range of patterns.   Pl. XIX, 3, *b* and *d*, and 4, *b* and *d*, nearly exhausts them.   Tumblers and low-footed tea-cups are also found, however, with the herring-bone pattern of Fig. 18, 36, and with the hatched triangles of 34.   The plume design of

Pl. XIX, 4, *b*, is as characteristic of East Crete as the slashes over the shoulders of small jugs are of M.M.1*a* at Knossos. The linked disks of Pl. XIX, 4, *d*, appear in various forms on jugs and pithoi [1] (Pl. XXVII, 2, *b*). A more regular form is shown in Fig. 18, 38. This is common on jugs, pithoi and larnakes and no doubt influenced the adoption in M.M.III of the elaborate linked spiral.[2] A more architectonic motive appears on a large pithos with two rows of handles from the cemetery at Pakhyammos (Fig. 18, 35).[3]

The light on dark provides a much richer series. The cups in Pl. XIX, 2, *a*, *c*, *e*, are very close to E.M.III and their decoration consists of simple designs in white on black, the white as elsewhere being more chalky and volatile than in the previous period. The pattern on *e* and Fig. 18, 28, is typical of East Crete from now onwards, and so is Fig. 18, 27. Feathery designs as in *c* and Pl. XIX, 1, *c* and *d*, become common and are often combined with S's of greater or less intricacy. Linked disks, either singly or in pairs, run diagonally up the vase (Pl. XIX, 1, *e*), where the white has vanished but preserved the background, and 4, *c*.[4]

Some of the polychrome cups appear, from the orange paint, to have come early in the period (e.g. Pl. XIX, 2, *d*, Fig. 18, 5). One of the two fine cups which came from House B at Vasilike has a distinctly metallic shape with a crinkly rim which we more naturally associate with M.M.II.[5] It has, however, a distinctly early feature in the hatched triangles within the rim.

Leaf patterns are common, particularly on jars large and small of the type of Pl. XIX, 1, *f*.[6] Typical of East Cretan work is the alternation of white and red in the vertical patterns. Other varieties are seen in Fig. 18. A highly schematized form is Pl. XVIII, 4, *a* (Fig. 18, 11), which comes from a spouted jug from Agia Photia.[7] These jugs (cf. Pl. XIX, 2, *b* and *f*, and 3, *a*) are characteristic of East Crete at this time, though they are popular on a larger scale in L.M.1 elsewhere. Fifteen

---

[1] Cf. *Pachyammos*, Pl. XX, and p. 29, where some are of M.M.III date, another argument against using dark on light as a criterion of early M.M.1.

[2] *Sphoungaras*, Figs. 30–2 ; *Pachyammos*, Pls. XI and XX, p. 28.

[3] Ibid., 24, and Pl. XVII. [4] *Mochlos*, Pl. VIII.

[5] *Trans. Penn. Univ.*, II, 128, 1, Pl. XXXI.

[6] Ibid., Pl. XXXII. [7] *Gournia*, Plate A, 1.

of them were found in one room in House A at Vasilike.[1]
Some, as in the Palaikastro examples (Pl. XIX, 2, b and f),
have white paint only on the black background, others, as
Pl. XIX, 3, a, have red lines as well. The decoration consists of a frieze of fishes in white paint.[2] At Palaikastro the
patterns are more varied, for sprays and crosses occur (Fig. 18,
14 and 31).[3]

A curious series of bowls come from the ossuaries on the
same site.[4] These are polychrome and in the middle have a
figure, a bird or an ox. In one case there are over 150 sheep
with their herdsman, the outside of the bowl being decorated
with a simple rectilinear pattern perhaps to represent the fence
of the sheepfold.

Lastly we come to a group which I suggest is probably contemporary with M.M.II in the great centres though naturally
stratigraphic evidence is lacking.[5] This is the series of two-
handled cups, specimens of which are shown in Pl. XVIII, 4.
Their metallic origin is obvious (c, actually of silver, from
Gournia, is shown for comparison). Together with a curious
bowl from Pseira with a crinkly rim, a spout and imitation
rivets where the handles join, which is painted half black
and half white, they give evidence of considerable skill in
metal-work.[6] Another group, the surface of which had an
iridescent effect, clearly imitated copper.[7] The two-handled
cup from Palaikastro (Pl. XIX, 1, a) cannot be separated from
the Gournia examples. Its pattern alternates red and white
like so much of the mature M.M.I of the East. A few bridge-
spouted jars from the same site may also well be contemporary
with M.M.II.[8] The presence of elaborate rosettes rather points
to that conclusion. The cup from Gournia (Pl. XVIII, 4, e,
Fig. 18, 17) with its running spirals must be on the borders of
M.M.III.

Some sites in the eastern half of Central Crete, such as
Gournais and Mallia, seem to link on to the eastern group at
this time. The linked disks of Fig. 18, 38, are found at
Mallia.[9] The curved swastika of Fig. 18, 29, is found at

[1] Trans. Penn. Univ., II, 125.
[2] Cf. a bowl from Knossos. P. of M., I, 182.
[3] B.S.A., Sup., Pl. IX.   [4] Ibid., XII.
[5] Palaikastro has a few imported M.M.II vases which will be
described in the next chapter.
[6] Gournia, Pl. C. Pseira, 20.   [7] Trans. Penn. Univ., II, 125.
[8] B.S.A., Sup., Pl. XI, b and d.   [9] Mallia, II, Pl. XI.

Palaikastro and Mallia, at the latter on a miniature jug of the
same shape as that from Gournia shown in Pl. XVIII, 4, d.
There is one example there, wrongly restored with a foot, of
the spouted jugs already mentioned as typical of East Crete.
At Gournais the jug shown in Pl. XIX, 3, g, has a pattern of
sprays not unlike examples from Palaikastro. A miniature
monochrome jug with a circular rim, a round body, a small
handle and criss-cross incisions round the neck, which was
found in quantities at Khamaizi and Palaikastro, also appears
in large numbers at Trapeza and Mallia as well as at Krasi
and Nirou Khani.[1]

The stone vases show a distinct falling off, though at Mokhlos *M.M.1*
such charming vases as Pl. X, 3, i, in brilliant red and blue *Stone Vases,*
breccia, are still produced.[2] Otherwise apart from an occasional *&c.*
bowl of veined marble (Pl. X, 3, l) black steatite seems to be
the only material. The shapes are mainly small lugged bowls,
though larger ones with a slightly carinated profile and a distinct
lip occur,[3] and for the first time we find a ' blossom vase ',
that is to say, a vase of the shape of the ' Birds' nests ' but
slightly taller and with a vertical decoration which begins with
plain fluting but which comes in time to imitate petals.[4]
Another, more advanced example, was found at Koumasa in
Tomb E,[5] and it is possible that certain bridge-spouted types
which resemble pottery may belong to M.M.1.[6] But it is
dangerous to claim any of these for the period although it
is clear that the industry continued without a break. The
safest thing to say is that in all probability the same shapes
continued more or less unchanged.

Seager mentions five stone lamps which were found in
House A at Vasilike. They were of the pedestalled variety.
Unfortunately no illustration is given and I have been unable to
find them in the Museum.[7]

The making of figurines in stone seems to have died out. *M.M.1*
One example from Porti (Pl. XIV, 1) separates itself off, *Figurines*
however, so distinctly from the others in the Messara that I
am inclined to believe that it might have been made at this date,

---

[1] *B.S.A.*, IX, 323.
[2] From Tomb III, which was practically pure M.M.1. It may, of
course, be an heirloom.
[3] *Mochlos*, Fig. 28, XI, 7 and 15.   [4] Ibid., XI, 12.
[5] *V.T.M.*, Pl. XXXI, 687.   [6] Ibid., III, 718 ; XI, 1910.
[7] *Trans. Penn. Univ.*, II 126. He says that only two could be
moved. Probably these also eventually disintegrated.

while another in ivory from Platanos (Pl. XII, 2, middle right) may conceivably have been so also.[1]   No doubt the decay of stone-working was due to the strides made in ceramics and the realization that clay was a far easier medium than stone.   At all events M.M.1 is richer in clay figurines than any other period.   Most of them were no doubt intended for votive offerings, as the innumerable figures of men and animals from Juktas and Petsophas, as well as those from the ossuary at Gournais, show.   But the rhytons in the shape of bulls from Koumasa and Mokhlos, though some may have had a ritual purpose, were no doubt used in daily life.[2]

Earliest of the human figurines is a head from the West Court at Knossos.[3]   The features except the prominent nose are barely indicated.   The low fez is striped red and black and the short hair is indicated in brown.   Next come the figurines found close to the oval house at Khamaizi (Pl. XX, 1).   Traces of red paint remain on the bodies.   The features are clearly, if roughly, marked.   The men are naked, unless the codpiece was indicated in colour, which looks possible in the case of the right-hand figure.   Again, the hair is cropped and a mere scalp lock left on top of the head.   The woman wears a bell-shaped skirt ; above the waist she is bare, but on her head is a low caul or turban.   Although there is an air of stiffness about them, it is noteworthy that the arms are free and indeed in a somewhat truculent attitude.   Such freedom could only come when clay was the normal material and there is no real tradition in stone behind.

The Petsophas group is much larger and probably covers practically the whole of the M.M.1 Period in East Crete, whereas the Khamaizi figurines are in the earlier half.   The two best-preserved figurines are shown in Pl. XX, 2.   In modelling they are somewhat inferior to those from Khamaizi but the use of polychrome decoration and the greater details of garb which are shown make them livelier and certainly more interesting.[4]   The flesh of the women is painted dull white, that of the men red or dark brown, after the Egyptian conven-

---

[1] *V.T.M.*, 67, No. 171, and 121, No. 229.   The holes may well have been intended to have movable arms and legs fitted into them and possibly a phallos.

[2] Ibid., 40, No. 4126.   The paint is distinctly M.M.1.   *Mochlos*, 60.

[3] *B.S.A.*, XXX, 70.

[4] For a detailed description of the dress, *B.S.A.*, IX, 361 ff.

tion. The women wear a bell skirt sometimes with a girdle and bodice with a high peaked collar open to the waist. The hats are not unlike the bag hat of Henry V's reign, but some are of a flatter variety and resemble the picture hats of the 1900's. Most of the men wear nothing but a codpiece and belt. The latter is drawn very tight to accentuate the naturally slim waist of the Minoans, and it is possible that the thick padded codpiece was necessary as a kind of primitive truss, for violent effort with an artificially constricted waist is very productive of rupture. It is the simplest possible form of dress, which later had more elaborate developments without losing the two main elements, the tight girdle and the codpiece. Across the front is slung a dagger. It is remarkable that it still seems to be of the triangular shape which even in East Crete ought to have died out in E.M.III. One or two of the figures show a pair of tight shorts and one has a plaid slung over his shoulders. On a few figures necklaces, bracelets and leggings are indicated in white. While the features of the women are indicated in black paint, those of the men are hardly shown at all. One fragment, however, of a much larger figure shows a lifelike and well-modelled face with the nose, nostrils, and eyes carefully marked.[1]

By far the larger proportion of figures are standing, but a small group is seated, one in a high-backed chair, the rest on camp stools, which are made separately as in the case of a seated figure of this period from Trapeza.

Separate limbs, arms, legs and torsos are found, often with holes for suspension. Miniature animals are common, goats, ibex, dogs, stoats, and tortoises. Miniature cups, trays and loaves of bread may have been attached to some of the figures or offered separately.

An interesting object is a low cart on four wheels from Palaikastro, the first wheeled vehicle in the Aegean.[2]

The tall objects which Xanthoudides regards as phalloi may be mentioned here.[3] Their date is uncertain, but since a very similar object was found in the M.M. shrine at Koumasa, the examples from the tomb area probably belong to M.M.1. The phallos is so seldom represented in Crete that one is inclined to compare these objects with the Egyptian funerary cones.[4]

---

[1] Ibid., Pl. XII, 34.   [2] B.S.A., Sup., 17.   [3] V.T.M., 41.

[4] Mr. N. de Garis Davies kindly sends me a note that these cones are mainly Theban. They begin in the XIth Dynasty and are undecorated before the XVIIIth. They were originally a decorative feature

The metalwork is considerably advanced. Tin is at last found in sufficient quantities to justify in some cases the use of the term bronze.[1] The dagger still retains its lengthened form. Perhaps the medial rib is usually more pronounced, though many examples lack it. The new feature which we are entitled to associate with M.M.1, however, since it never occurs except in conjunction with M.M.1 pottery, is the tang projecting up into the hilt from the top of the blade (Pl. XI, 3, *d*, from Platanos). This is usual in the Messara, but again the East seems somewhat backward, and there is only one example at Mokhlos,[2] while at Palaikastro there is none. At Khamaizi a long chisel, a spearhead, two rather square double axes and an adze were found.[3] A number of very small single axes were found at Palaikastro.[4] At Platanos two large double axes were found which from their extreme thinness must be votive offerings.[5] Unlike those intended for use, the cutting edges are flared. There is no certain evidence of their date, but they were found in a deposit where the majority of pottery was M.M.1, and it is hardly likely that votive offerings would be made before the objects which they copied were in common use.

But the crowning achievement of the metal-worker was the great bronze sword of Mallia with its hilt of gold-plated ivory and its pommel of crystal. It is nearly a metre long with a thick flat medial rib to strengthen it. With it was found a dagger, also originally hilted with gold and with a flat medial rib. Neither sword nor dagger have the tang which we have suggested came in at this period. A third object from the group must be mentioned, though it is of stone. It is an axe-head of brown schist, the butt carved to represent a springing leopard on a leash. The blade is covered with a design of running spirals. This group may almost be taken as part of the regalia of the king of Mallia.[6]

That some regular form of pictographic writing was in use can be seen from the signs on the base blocks of the earliest parts of the palaces at Knossos and Phaistos, which correspond in form with signs in the developed linear script.[7] The double axe occurs both in its square and ' butterfly ' form, a trident,

of tomb façades. In some cases, however, they may represent conical loaves of bread.

[1] *P. of M.*, I, 195, and references.   [2] *Mochlos*, Fig. 45, XI, 22.
[3] *P. of M.*, I, 194.   [4] *B.S.A., Sup.*, 118.   [5] *V.T.M.*, 109.
[6] *Monuments Piot*, 1926, 1 ; *P. of M.*, II, 271 ff.
[7] *P. of M.*, I, Fig. 99.

a conventional tree, broad arrows, crosses and stars, ' dumb-
bells ' and other simple signs.   These were masons' marks
perhaps signifying what place they were to occupy or perhaps
denoting the gang of workmen.[1]   Together with these must be
taken various incised inscriptions on vases.   A pithos from
Khamaizi is incised with a sign resembling the Egyptian pavilion, a miniature jug with incised decoration round the neck
of the type described above, from Prodhromos Botzanou near
Kritsa, has a double axe, a cross and a version of the Egyptian
negation sign,[2] a similar jug from Trapeza has a dog and a libation
vase, and examples from Mallia, Nirou Khani and Krasi are

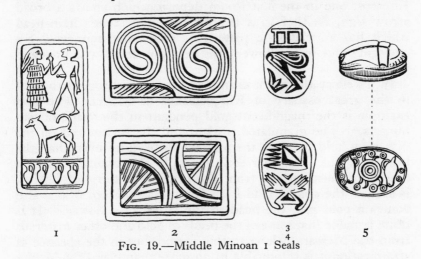

FIG. 19.—Middle Minoan i Seals

also inscribed.   But while by themselves these marks might
merely denote personal badges, the seal stones confirm that
hieroglyphs were now in comparatively common use.

Most usually the hieroglyphs appear on three- and four-sided
seals of a rather longer shape than those of E.M.III.

*M.M.1
Seals*

The general effect is not so pleasing as in the case of mere
designs, for calligraphy was in its infancy and the primary object
was to get the signs in somehow.   But when the object is
pure decoration the advance over the previous period is obvious.
Fig. 19, 1, shows one side of an ivory half-cylinder found somewhere near Knossos.   It shows a man of the Petsophas type

[1] This latter is the case at Tell el-Amarna (see forthcoming *City of
Akhenaten*, III).   It is not evidence of piece-work but a check to see
that each gang did its quota.

[2] *P. of M.*, I, 639.

with a dagger making advances to a long-haired woman clad
in a flounced robe falling from her shoulders, a strange contrast
to the modish dresses of Petsophas and possibly showing
Asiatic connexions.   Below is a fine hound, and in the exergue
are four beaked ewers, probably of metal, for the type is
unknown in clay.

The other side shows an archer and his dog pursuing an
ibex.   The chisel-edged arrow he is using and the composite
bow appear again as a hieroglyph on a steatite bead seal from
Mallia.[1]   Another shape which now comes in is the flat bead-
seal (Fig. 19, 2).   Several impressions on clay were found at
Knossos, one in the Vat Room deposit which shows a broad
arrow sign, another in a deposit near the stone drain-head
which has an elaborate pattern of diagonally connected S's
enclosing four-leafed flowers, the field powdered with dots and
palmettes.[2]

M.M.1
Jewellery

In jewellery the finest examples have been brought to light
in the great ossuary of Khrysolakkos at Mallia.   The first
example is the magnificent gold pendant in the shape of two
hornets.[3]   The granulated work round the bodies and on the
disk they hold between them is exquisite, finer even than the
best in Egypt.   Another early example of granulation, which
may have been derived from the pricked patterns of E.M.II,
is seen in the golden toad from Koumasa.[4]   From Mallia also
comes a gold pin, the head in the shape of a flower.[5]   It is
quite possible that some of the beads of gold and other materials
from the Messara belong to this period, but in the absence of
stratification it is impossible to do more than claim for M.M.1
such objects as resemble most closely those which were found
safely stratified.

In the Vat Room at Knossos a number of green and blue
faience beads both disk-shaped and globular were found.
Inlays of shell and of the same faience appeared which had
surrounded quatrefoils of some other substance.

M.M.1
Foreign
Relations

The only Egyptian objects which have been found in a pure
deposit of this date are from Gournais.[6]   In one of the ossuaries
here were found beads and a scarab of the XIIth Dynasty and a
scarab which is of the date of the First Intermediate Period,
though it may be a local copy.   There are, however, other
Egyptian objects which, though strictly unstratified, cannot be

[1] *P. of M.*, II, 50.   [2] Ibid., I, Fig. 119a and 151.
[3] Ibid., IV, 75.   [4] *V.T.M.*, Pl. IV, 386.
[5] *P. of M.*, loc. cit.   [6] *Aegyptiaca*, 15.

dissociated from the latest deposit where they were found.[1]
From Tomb B at Platanos come two XIIth-Dynasty scarabs,
one having on it a figure of the goddess Taurt. From the
annexe to the large tomb at Agia Triadha comes an ivory ape
amulet. From the cave at Trapeza came a very fine glazed
steatite scarab of a pattern which begins in the XIth Dynasty.

Evans has pointed out the way in which Egyptian patterns
of the XIIth Dynasty were copied and adapted on M.M.1
seals,[2] and several signs which must owe their origin to Egypt
have been pointed out above. In addition, Fig. 19, 4, shows a
Minoan version of an Egyptian hieroglyph for palace or tower.

It is probably chance or rather artistic convention which is
responsible for the lack of examples of Minoan dress before
this period, and the Libyan influence which may be inferred
from the codpiece must have dated back many centuries.[3]

At Platanos, in a deposit of M.M.1 polychrome vases, was
found a haematite cylinder of Babylonian origin, the date of
which can be reasonably fixed to the period of Hammurabi,
i.e. about 2100 B.C.[4] A cylinder of similar date was found to
the West of Candia.[5] The flounced Babylonian skirt may be
compared with the garment of the woman in the seal above
mentioned. Another object which is clearly imported is the
limestone head shown in Pl. XX, 3. It was found in the top
stratum above a group of burials in a rock shelter on the
acropolis, West of the palace at Knossos.[6] It bears a striking
resemblance to a figure from the second temple of Sin at Khafaje,
though the date of the latter cannot be later than about 2550 B.C.[7]

[1] *Aegyptiaca*, 35, 9. The seal from Agia Triadha which I called
(ibid., 9) XIIth Dynasty has an even better parallel in the First
Intermediate Period. *Qau and Badari*, I, Pl. XXXIII, 190.

[2] *P. of M.*, I, 201.

[3] Ibid., II, 34. It is rather significant that even now the Libyan
long locks are not shown. It looks as if it was a much later fashion
in Crete.

[4] *V.T.M.*, 117; *P. of M.*, I, 197.

[5] Ibid., II, 266, Fig. 158.

[6] This stratum contained many M.M.III sherds from the superimposed
pithos burials. I am indebted to Messrs. R. W. Hutchinson and
R. J. H. Jenkins for permission to publish this.

[7] *O.I.C.*, 19, Fig. 84. It is interesting to note that the latest
Mesopotamian parallels to the bull rhytons of this period cannot be
brought down later. Dr. Frankfort, *from photographs only*, thinks it
might conceivably go down to Ur III with 2186 as the lowest possible
limit. *P. of M.*, II, 259. The grappling of the bulls which is seen
on the Messara rhyton has a Cappadocian parallel of about 2400.
Ibid., 259, n. 4.

Asiatic or Anatolian influence may perhaps be seen in the general layout of the palaces, but such evidence as has been offered is of a considerably later date.[1] Admittedly the principle of a central court or light area surrounded by buildings is new, but it is a form which would naturally occur to any one who wished to set up a monumental structure more than two rooms deep and more than one storey high.

We have already seen the pyxides imported from the Cyclades at the very beginning of M.M.1, which may well have been part of the same consignment as were found at Pyrgos, though that site had not yet reached the M.M.1 stage. On the other side a little M.M.1a and much M.M.1b pottery of Knossian fabric was imported into Phylakope in Melos during the first period of the second city in Middle Cycladic 1.[2] That Minoan influence reached even further is shown by the jug of local fabric from Dhrakhmani with the butterfly or double axe pattern in a Middle Helladic tomb and a two-handled, bridge-spouted bowl of M.M.1a date found in an Early Cypriote III tomb at Lapithos.[3]

For the origin of the metal prototypes of the fluted cups with two handles from East Crete we most probably look to the second city of Troy, while a striking parallel in clay to the silver vase was found at Alişar and is of approximately contemporary date.[4] Hittite examples and cups from Alaca Hüyük are datable to shortly after 2100.

M.M.1
Chronology

Taking the evidence of foreign connexions, then we may say that M.M.1 begins in the centre of the island about the end of the First Intermediate Period, in the rest of the island somewhere in the XIth Dynasty, a good date for the early part of it being given by the Babylonian cylinders. At Knossos and Phaistos it comes to an end early in the XIIth Dynasty. In the rest of Crete a development of it runs parallel with M.M.II, the lower limits of which will be discussed in the next chapter. For Knossos 2200 to soon after 2000 B.C. are the most probable dates.

[1] *O.I.C.*, 269.
[2] *Phylakopi*, Fig. 127; Åberg, IV, Figs. 326, 328. It is maintained by the latter that it is East Cretan. In the example he gives the nearest parallels are to be found in Figs. 17, 10 and 23, both from pure deposits at Knossos.
[3] *Prehistoric Thessaly*, 204. The so-called ' Kamares ware ' from Orkhomenos is light-on-dark Early Helladic ware. Ibid., 194. I am indebted to Miss V. Grace for permission to refer to the Cypriote vessel.
[4] Cf. *Studies*, II, 142; Schmidt, *Anatolia*, Fig. 109.

SITES WHERE MIDDLE MINOAN I REMAINS HAVE BEEN FOUND

WEST CRETE

(b) Surface Finds

AGIA MARINA . . Double stone vase from Gerospilio cave. Marinatos, *Mitt. über Höhlen und Karstforschung*, 1928, Fig. 4.

GAVDHOS . . . Sherds from Karavi. Levi, *Art and Archaeology*, 1927, 176 ff.

CENTRAL CRETE

(a) Excavated Sites

AMNISOS . . . Cave and Settlement — Vases, &c. Marinatos, Πρακτικά, 1929, 95 ; 1933, 93.

ARKALOKHORI . . Cave . . Few sherds outside the entrance. Hazzidakis, *B.S.A.*, XIX, 35.

GIOPHYRAKIA . . Settlement . Vases. Marinatos. Unpublished. Candia Museum. *Catalogue*, 8433 ff.

GOURNAIS . . Ossuary. . Vases, &c. Hazzidakis, ᾿Αρχ. Δελτ., I, 59.

JUKTAS. . . . Sanctuary . Vases, &c. Evans, *P. of M.*, I, 151.

KASTELLOS TZERMIADHON — Settlement . Extensive remains, excavated by the writer, 1937.

KHRISTOS ISLAND — Cemetery and Settlement — *B.C.H.*, 1925, 473 ; 1928, 502. *J.H.S.*, 1926, 240.

KNOSSOS . . . Palace . . First foundations. *P. of M.*, I, 127. Viaduct, II, 93, 146. Enceinte wall, IV, 50.

Town . . *P. of M.*, IV, 66. *B.S.A.*, XXX, 53. *J.H.S.*, 1901, 78.

Cemetery . Rock shelter on the Acropolis to the W. *J.H.S.*, LV, 168.

KRASI . . . . Tomb . . Latest deposit in circular tomb. Marinatos, ᾿Αρχ., Δελτ., 12, 102.

MALLIA . . . Palace . . Many deposits and architectural features. Chapoutier, *Mallia*, I, II, 27. *B.C.H.*, 1928, 368 ; 1929, 521 ; 1930, 517 ; 1931, 515.

Town . . Houses, *B.C.H.*, 1924, 496 ; 1925, 473 ; 1928, 502, 504 ; 1929, 527 ; 1931, 513 ; 1933, 296.

Cemeteries . Shelters on coast. *B.C.H.*, 1929, 527. Khrysolakkos, 1930, 424, 521 ; 1931, 512 ; 1934, 268.

Sanctuary . On Mt. Prophetes Elias. *B.C.H.*, 1928, 505.

TRAPEZA . . .	Cave . .	Latest deposit of any size found in excavations of 1936. *A.J.A.*, XL, 371. *Arch. Anz.*, 1936, 162.
TYLISSOS . . .	Settlement .	Earlier occupation of site. Hazzidakis, *'Εφ. 'Αρχ.*, 1912 ; and *Tylissos Villas Minoennes*, 79.

(b) Surface Finds

AGIOU GEORGIOU PAPOURA	Vase from a cave here, seen by writer, 1936.
ANAGYROI . . .	Sherds from what appears to be a guard-house on the Minoan road. Evans. *P. of M.*, II, 77.
AVGOUSTE . . .	Traces of burials, seen by the writer, 1937.
DIA ISLAND . .	One sherd from Agia Pelagia bay. Found by the writer, 1935.
ELOUNTA . . .	Vases from a well at Kato Elounta, seen by the writer, 1937.
GAZE	Sherds from the side of the car road, found by Miss Money-Coutts and Miss Eccles, 1934. *B.S.A.*, XXXIII, 92.
MARMAKETO . .	Sherds and a seal from Phakidhia above the village, seen by the writer, 1935–6. Cf. Dawkins, *B.S.A.*, XX, 4.
MOKHOS . . .	Stone vase and sherds from summit of Edikhte, E. of village. Seen by the writer, 1935.
NIROU KHANI .	Miniature jugs with inscriptions, *'Εφ. 'Αρχ.*, 1906. Plate 9, 1–3.
ORNIAS . . .	Traces of settlement, seen by the writer, 1937.
ROUSSAIS . . .	Traces of Ossuary. Franchet, *J.H.S.*, 1918, 204
SKALANI . . .	Signs on blocks of big building at *Στὰ Σεραϊα*. Evans, *P. of M.*, II, 62.
SKHINEAS . . .	Sherds on Koprana, seen by the writer, 1937.
SKOTEINO . . .	Sherds from large cave. Evans, *P. of M.*, I, 163.
TRAPEZA . . .	Sherds from a cave 1½ hr. SW. of Tylissos. Hazzidakis, *Tylissos Villas Minoennes*, 75.

SOUTH CRETE

(a) Excavated Sites

AGIA TRIADHA . .	Tomb . .	Latest deposit in Tholos A. Banti, *Annuario*, XIII–XIV, 164 ff. *Mon. Ant.*, XIV, 677.
	Houses . .	Below court .*J.H.S.*, XXXIII, 365.
DHRAKONAIS . .	Tombs . .	Main deposits in circular tombs. Xanthoudides, *V.T.M.*, 76.
KALATHIANA . .	Settlement .	Architectural and other finds. Ibid., 84.
KAMARAIS . . .	Cave . .	Vases, &c. Dawkins, *B.S.A.*, XIX, 1.
KHRISTOS . . .	Tomb . .	Later contents of circular tomb. Xanthoudides, *V.T.M.*, 70.
	Sanctuary .	On peak above the tomb. *P. of M.*, II, 81.

KOUMASA . . .	Deposit .	Sherds near rectangular tomb. Γ., *V.T.M.*, 42.
MARATHOKEPHALO	Tomb . .	Latest deposit in circular tomb. Xanthoudides, *Ἀρχ. Δελτ.*, 1918, Παρ, 1, 14 ff.
PHAISTOS . . .	Palace . .	Sherds found below floors. Pernier, *Festos*, 130 ff. *Mon. Ant.*, XIV, 313.
PLATANOS . . .	Tombs . .	Latest deposit in circular tombs. *V.T.M.*, 88.
PORTI	Tombs . .	Latest deposit in circular tomb and scattered burials. Ibid., 55 ff.
VOROU . . .	Tombs . .	Main deposit in circular tombs. Larnax burials. Marinatos, *Ἀρχ. Δελτ.*, 13, 137, and undug settlement.

(b) Surface Finds

GOULOPHARANGO GORGE	Sherds from what seems to be a fort at the top of the gorge at Agia Paraskeve. Found by writer, 1934. *B.S.A.*, XXXIII, 87.
KASTELL BELVEDERE	Sherds from summit. Seen by writer, 1936.
VASILIKE . . .	Sherds from the side of the road by the school. Found by writer, 1934. *B.S.A.*, XXXIII, 86.

EAST CRETE

(a) Excavated Sites

AGIA PHOTIA . .	Cave . .	2 sherds. Hawes, *Trans. Penn. Univ.*, I, 185.
GOURNIA . . .	Settlement .	Early buildings and deposits. *Gournia*, 38.
	Burials . .	Ossuaries, *Trans. Penn. Univ.*, I, 186. *Gournia*, 56.
KHAMAIZI . . .	House . .	Vases and figurines from oval house. Xanthoudides, *Ἐφ.᾿Ἀρχ.*, 1906, 117. Mackenzie, *B.S.A.*, XIV, 414.
MOKHLOS . . .	Tombs and Settlement	Latest deposits in built tombs. Seager, *Mochlos, passim*. Latest deposits in first town. Seager, *A.J.A.*, XIII, 274.
PAKHYAMMOS . .	Burials . .	Pithos burials. Seager, *Pachyammos, passim*.
PALAIKASTRO . .	Ossuaries .	At Kastri, Dawkins, *B.S.A.*, X, 202 ; at Ellenika, *B.S.A.*, X, 196 ; at Patema, *B.S.A.*, IX, 306 ; and by the town site, *B.S.A.*, VIII, 292.
	Deposit .	In the town. *B.S.A.*, *Sup.*, 9.

PETRAS . . .	Deposit	Vase from below later house. Bosanquet, *B.S.A.*, VIII, 282. Other vases. *B.M. Cat.*, I, A. 507–9.
PETSOPHAS . .	Sanctuary .	Vases and figurines. Myres, *B.S.A.*, IX, 356.
PSEIRA . . .	Settlement .	Houses and contents of first town. Seager, *Pseira*, 9, 18.
SPHOUNGARAS	Burials . .	Larnax and pithos burials. Hall, *Sphoungaras*, 56.
VASILIKE . .	Settlement .	Houses, &c. Seager, *Trans. Penn. Univ.*, II, 113.
ZAKROS . . .	Sanctuary .	Votive figurines from overhanging rock at Apano Zakros. *P. of M.*, I, 151.

(b) Surface Finds

KALAMAFKA . .	Sherd from Kephalovrysis at the top of the village, seen by the writer, 1935.
PISKOKEPHALI .	Walls and sherds seen by Evans. *Diary*, 12/4/94. Figurines. Marinatos, *J.H.S.*, 1932, 255.
PRODHROMOS BOTZANOU	Libation vase found here. Evans, *J.H.S.*, 1894, 279.

2. MIDDLE MINOAN II (M.M.II)

(See Map 8)

This period, as has already been said, is a purely Knossian and Phaistian one.[1] When the Minoan chronology was first drawn up, M.M.II included much of what we now call M.M.1*b*, and as a result the list of sites where it has been discovered must be treated with caution. Naturally, provincial sites imported vases of the latest fashion from the great centres whenever they could, but it was only the most important which could afford to do so, and these imports are found either in a stratum with M.M.1 vases or sometimes in a little deposit by themselves as if they were special treasures. Sacred caves such as Kamarais, the Diktaian cave, and Trapeza, naturally were given the best. The seal stones from Sto Dhaso and Kedhri in East Crete need not surprise us, for they are easily transported ; nor need the inscriptions at Mallia, for the importance of writing was greater than mere objects. The deposit at Kouphonisi where quantities of murex shells were found may well be the relics of a royal industry, for the towering importance

---

[1] Cf. page 94, n. 2, above for the evidence that elsewhere the M.M.1 style of pottery continued down to M.M.III.

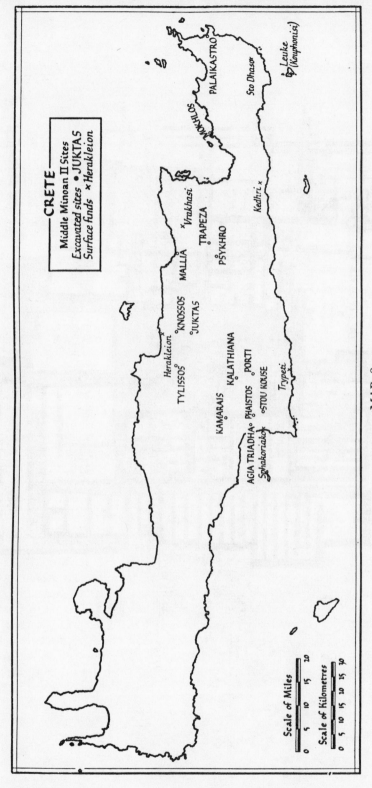

CRETE

Middle Minoan II Sites
Excavated sites • JUKTAS
Surface finds × Herakleion

MALLIA
TRAPEZA
PSYKHRO
×Vrakhasi
MOKHLOS
PALAIKASTRO
Sta Dhasa
Leuke
(Kouphonisi)
Kedhri ×

°KNOSSOS
JUKTAS
Herakleion ×
TYLISSOS °
KALATHIANA
PORTI
KAMARAIS
AGIA TRIADHA° PHAISTOS °
Sphakoriakos °STOU KOUSE
Trypeti

Scale of Miles
0   5   10   15   20

Scale of Kilometres
0   5   10   15   20   30

MAP 8

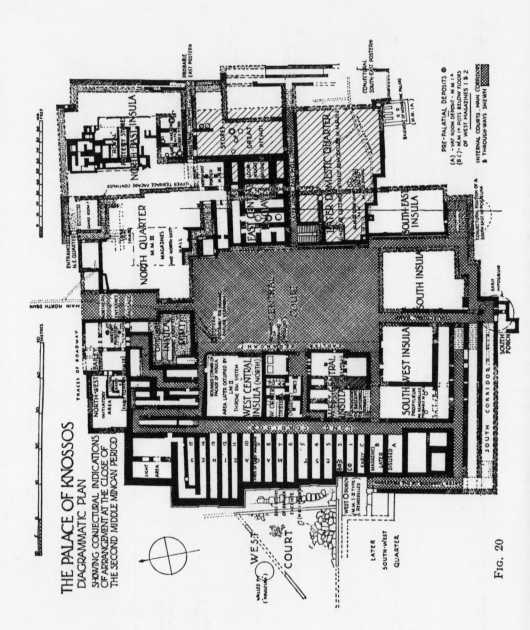

THE PALACE OF KNOSSOS
DIAGRAMMATIC PLAN

SHOWING CONJECTURAL INDICATIONS
OF ARRANGEMENT AT THE CLOSE OF
THE SECOND MIDDLE MINOAN PERIOD

FIG. 20

128

of Knossos and Phaistos at this period must surely mean that
between them they shared the lordship of the whole island.

At Knossos the breaking down of the barriers between the
block-houses of M.M.1 was completed and the broad lines of
the Palace as it is to-day were laid out. The old Keep with
its walled cells was floored over and transformed. The West
Porch with its single column was built. The West Magazines
in their present form were constructed. A subsidiary entrance
to the West of the old North entrance was laid out and with it
some form of a ' Lustral Area ' where the visitor descended a
flight of steps to purify himself before entering the palace.

M.M.11 Architecture : I. Palaces

The M.M.1 houses in the West Court were pulled down and
the paved court allowed to run right over them (Pl. XVI, 3).
Three circular walled pits, or ' koulouras ', were sunk in the
paving to receive the broken pottery from the rubbish-heaps.[1]
The early court to the North was raised considerably in level
and a broad flight of steps was constructed running South to
the West Court.

But the crowning architectural achievement of the period
was on the East slope. The earlier narrow terraces by no means
suited grandiose ideas and a great cutting was made deep down
into the neolithic strata below. This occupied practically the
whole East side of the Central Court. The supporting walls
of this cutting are part of the original construction, although
the internal arrangements apart from the drainage system were
largely remodelled in M.M.111. It seems to have been divided
into two halves, a southern, which was, at any rate later, occupied by the Domestic Quarter, and a northern, which consisted
of deep heavily walled basements perhaps designed to support
a predecessor of the great East Hall. East and North of this
were the pottery stores and craftsmen's quarters. Descending
to it must have been some ancestor of the Grand Staircase.

The buildings at Phaistos which belong to M.M.11 afford
interesting parallels with Knossos. The West porch, with
column and guard-room, the sunken area near by, corresponding to the early lustration area by the North-West entrance at

[1] The absolute lack of stratification in the contents shows how the
pottery was thrown in as each rubbish-heap got too big. The fragments were clearly tipped in, quantities at a time, from the North-
East corner. Thus M.M.1*b*, which no doubt came from a little-used
rubbish-heap, was found quite high up, while a piece of M.M.111,
thrown away just before the koulouras were covered, was found at the
bottom of a slide.

Knossos, the West Court with its ' kouloura ', as well as many details of construction, all show great resemblances.

In the nature of a shrine are the two pillar rooms in the West Wing at Knossos (Pl. XVI, 2), which are probably to be referred to this date.   Each of these rooms has its roof supported on a square pier built up of four blocks of gypsum, which are liberally incised with the double axe sign.   Beside one of them is a sunken stone vat to receive liquid offerings.

In the north-eastern corner of the West Court at Phaistos is a M.M.II shrine, with three cells built out beyond the façade and a rectangular chapel behind surrounded by benches on three sides.   In the latter was found a table of offerings of clay with a stamped design of oxen and S's round the rim and a conch shell used as a trumpet.[1]

An interesting parallel was found in the loomweight area at Knossos in a stratum dating, like the contents of the shrine at Phaistos, to the latter half of the period.[2]   Here occurred a model of a pillar shrine, the masonry shown in chequers as in the later Miniature Frescoes and the ends of beams represented as disks.   With it were the remains of miniature altars, surmounted by the sacred horns, a model palanquin in clay, fragments of clay conch shells, and a group of three round pillars surmounted by square capitals each of which bears two round beams on which perch doves.   A charming vase of pale blue faience, with a neck and foot of gold and a gold spray of leaves resting on a pan containing some carbonized substance, was also found.[3]

There are a number of features which are typical of the palace architecture of M.M.II.   The well-squared limestone blocks have a clay bedding about a centimetre thick between each course.   Instead of wooden door-posts or gypsum bases, the framework of the door is often cut in the blocks of the façade.   Both in open courts and indoors the paving often consists of thick irregular slabs of limestone, known to the workmen as ' Kalderim ', from a resemblance to the paved roads of Turkish times.   In the latter half of M.M.II it is replaced by smooth slabs of close-grained limestone, known locally as

---

[1] *Festos*, I, 195, 229.

[2] The building of the shrine may well have been in the first half or even in M.M.i*b*.   As there was no catastrophic break between the periods to seal in a deposit, the contents naturally represent the latest phase.

[3] *P. of M.*, I, 221, 252.

' almond stone '. The interstices were filled with red or white plaster which has given it the name ' Mosaiko '.

The column bases are high in proportion to their diameter and a great use is made of variegated stones such as breccia, conglomerate, serpentine and porphyry. The beauty and hardness of these stones often caused the bases to be reused in later times. The shafts of the columns must have been now, as later, of wood.

The drainage system of the Domestic Quarter also belongs to this period.[1] The main conduit, lined with stone, cemented and big enough for the passage of a man, ran in a circle with its watershed in the South-East corner of the later Hall of Colonnades and its effluent on the East slope. Shafts for the drainage of the roofs lead down into it. An elaborate latrine may have been a later addition. The gypsum lining to the wall has a groove for the supports of a wooden seat rather over half a metre high. In front is a sloping slab leading to a sink connecting with the main drain. The aperture itself is masked by a projection which may have been intended to prevent an escape of sewer gas. Similar drains and conduits occur in other parts of the palace, and a very fine example runs down the North entrance.

As to the internal decoration of the Palace, naturally very little has survived. A fragment of painted plaster, which may belong to the previous period, has an Egyptianizing ' *waz* ' motive.[2] But the first real piece of mural decoration must be the so-called ' Saffron Gatherer '.[3] This panel, of painted plaster, represents a greyish-blue figure plucking crocuses and putting them into vases. The rocky setting is conventionally indicated by wavy lines of white and black on the general red background. The flesh colour of the ' boy ' is most peculiar and seems more suitable to an underworld god of Egypt. But is it a boy? He is naked but for two red strings round his waist, and what is more, one can make out (in the original, not in the reproduction) a tail waving above him ! Surely he is a monkey like the blue monkeys who pick flowers on a scene in the later House of the

*M.M.*II
Frescoes

---

[1] Ibid., 224. [2] Ibid., 201.
[3] Ibid., 265 and III, 22, for the stratification. Snijder, *Kretische Kunst*, 28, doubts the stratification, and certainly the artistic arguments he puts forward are very strongly in favour of a M.M.III date, which would bring it into closer connexion with the Blue Monkeys and would save it from being by a long way the first representation of a figure human or animal.

Frescoes. His attitude is simian enough. As the head of the 'Saffron Gatherer' is missing, we cannot tell for certain, but when we consider that the conventional red for male, white for female figures is already fixed at Petsophas and that the monkeys who appear in the House of the Frescoes are also painted blue, it seems a strong argument [1] (Pl. XXV, 1).

A more conventional form of wall decoration was found in the North-West Portico, where fragments of stucco showed that the black background had been 'printed' with a sponge dipped in yellow paint and pressed lightly on the wall.[2] This printed decoration appears also on the pottery.

M.M.II
Architecture :
II. Private

The only private house which may date from this period, since M.M.II pottery is the earliest found in it, is that at Stou Kouse, South of Phaistos. It is square in shape, about 11 metres each way. It consists of one large room into which the front door opens direct, two smaller rooms to the North and two to the East. The outer walls are roughly dressed on the outside and consist of fairly large stones on a foundation of small ones. These large stones vary in length from 80 centimetres to a metre and are all headers. The interior walls are of small stones laid in a clay mortar.

The Town Mosaic (Pl. XXI, 1) gives us a good idea of the appearance of the ordinary house of M.M.II.[3] These faience plaques, which may have served as inlays to decorate a wooden chest, were found in a M.M.IIIa filling close to the Loomweight Basement, but from their style it is clear that they must be taken with the terra-cotta shrine described above. They represent the houses of a town. Other fragments show trees, soldiers, animals, and the prow of a ship. Water is also indicated by plaques with a wavy blue line in the Egyptian style. It has been suggested that the whole may have represented the siege of a town by the sea, like the rhyton from Mycenae.

The houses are two and more stories high and the construction seems to be of masonry tied in with great wooden beams. Sometimes, as is usual in the palace, the window-sills and lintels are continuous with the beams, at others the windows are set isolated in the masonry. Some of the window-panes are painted scarlet, which seems to imply the use of oiled parchment or some such anticipation of glass.

In the case of the right-hand plaques in the two top rows of the plate a thick bedding of clay mortar is seen between the

[1] I believe Professor Pernier first put this theory forward.
[2] Ibid., III, 362.   [3] *P. of M.*, I, 301.

blocks, further evidence for their M.M.II date. The roofs are
flat, and though the slope of some of them has been taken to
represent an incline for drainage purposes, it is unlikely that such
a refinement would be shown on such small objects. The
towers are interesting. Is it possible that we have here some
indication of clerestory lighting for inner rooms?

Few tombs of this period have been discovered. It is *M.M.II Tombs*
probable that some of the tombs in the Mavrospelio cemetery
originally date from M.M.II, but most of them were cleared
out for subsequent burials. At all events it is clear that
the old rock shelters were now beginning to be improved by

deeper cutting into the
hillside and are fore-
shadowing the later
chamber tombs [1] (Fig. 21).
They are mainly of irregular shape and very probably
a new niche was cut for
each interment, or a
shallow pit was sunk in
the floor of the tomb.

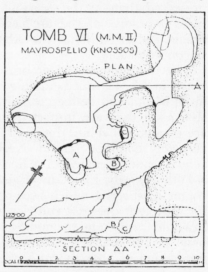

Two vases were found
in the large tomb at Agia
Triadha, and it is clear that
the circular tombs were
still in use. Unfortunately
Xanthoudides does not ex-
plain the type of tomb in
which the vases in Pl.
XXII, 1, were found.

FIG. 21

The first phase of M.M.II pottery was well illustrated in the *M.M.II Pottery*
Royal Pottery Stores in the North-East Quarter of the Palace
of Knossos, and in the Magazines which lie near them, corresponding to the early magazines bordering on the West Court
at Phaistos. In the latter was found the knobbed pithos shown
in Pl. XXII, 4, with rows of handles to facilitate transport.
It is decorated also with knobs and ropes as well as with a trickle
ornament imitating the stains caused by an overflow of the
contents. Gigantic examples standing well over 6 feet high
were found at Knossos of a similar but more elongated shape
and having an elaborate rope pattern imitating the rope cradle
in which they must have been moved.[2]

[1] Cf. *Archaeologia*, LXXXII, 125.   [2] *P. of M.*, I, Fig. 175.

A typical shape is the pedestalled cup, usually with a band of white paint on a black background below the rim. These cups are very similar to those of M.M.1a, but the body is more rounded and the stem slopes gradually down to the pedestal without leaving a depression in the latter.[1] Another type which is also invaluable for dating is shown in Pl. XXII, 1, b, a comparatively straight-sided cup with a small handle. The small size of the strap handles is also an indication of date. The white is rather more creamy than in M.M.1, though more fugitive than E.M.III, and the black glaze of the background has taken on an almost metallic lustre and is usually less well preserved than in the previous period. In the polychrome vases two sorts of red are used. One approximates to the orange red of M.M.1a, the other is a deep crimson, but both are unmistakable.

The outlining of red or brown paint with white which we noted in M.M.1 as resembling veined stone is carried further in M.M.IIa, and deliberate imitations of breccia such as that shown on the vase imported to Palaikastro (Pl. XXII, 1, e) are common. White dots, imitating the flecks on liparite, are also very common (cf. Pl. XXII, 1, b), and in one case the actual shape is copied of a liparite bowl which itself imitates a IVth-Dynasty Egyptian original.[2] Barbotine, dated by the colour of the red which accompanies it, is still used, though fortunately it does not run riot as in the Messara. It is seen in a mild form round the middle of the beautiful crinkly rimmed bowl in Pl. XXII, 3, l, where it is employed to give the impression of rose thorns.[3]

We have already seen that eggshell ware was made as early as M.M.1a, but in the present period it reaches its acme. Examples from the House of the Fallen Blocks and from the Royal Pottery stores are shown in Pl. XXII, 3, g and h. The former is one of those airy bubbles which seem to float in the hand.[4] Another example has the calyx of a water lily in relief rising from below as if to increase the illusion. The latter is equally finely made, though the shape is not so beautiful. It shows well the typical rosette of M.M.IIa, with rounded tips

---

[1] *P. of M.*, I, Fig. 177. A curious parallel is the disappearance of the ' water-holding ' base of the Gothic pillar about A.D. 1220.

[2] Ibid., I, Figs. 127f and e and 55.

[3] Ibid., Supplementary Pl. III, a.

[4] For the pattern cf. Ibid., II, Pl. IX, a, in colour.

to the petals (cf. Fig. 22, 13).[1] The shapes are largely metallic and fluting both real and imitated in paint occur (Fig. 22, 6). Stamped patterns on the metallic sheen are found.[2] Pl. XXII, 3, *j* (Fig. 22, 5) is a fine example of double arcading imitating an original in repoussé work and inlay.

FIG. 22.—Patterns on Middle Minoan IIa Pottery

Another typical vase is shown on the same plate *i* (Fig. 22, 1). It is of a shape which continues for a long time and is found in the Vapheio gold cups. The printed decoration occurs in

[1] Ibid., I, Pl. II, *c*. It is for that reason that I would attribute the Abydos Vase (ibid., Fig. 199*a*) to transitional M.M.IIa–*b*.

[2] Ibid., Fig. 182.

dark on light and light on dark, the sides of the cup being the one and the base the other. White blobs dabbed on with a sponge are found on vases of the same shape and recall the printed sponge pattern of the frescoes. Light on dark and dark on light is also well illustrated in the bowl *l*, where the outside is painted in red and white on black and the buff ground of the interior is flecked with brown.

A magnificent bridge-spouted bowl was found in a deposit in the North-West Treasure House.[1] Back and front are decorated with an elaborate scroll-work surrounding a kind of Tudor rose, while below the handles on each side rises a fleur-de-lis. A flattened jug, much resembling a pilgrim bottle, had each side divided into four by a swastika in red. In each of the quarters was a plume in white (Fig. 22, 14).[2] These plumes must, I think, be connected with the ' tangential loop ' typical of East Cretan decoration from M.M.1 onwards.

Another class, which has only recently been distinguished, has been called ' Creamy-bordered '. A number of examples were found in the excavations of 1930 in the West Court. Beaked jugs with a black background surrounded by white bands and a red-centred spiral frieze (Fig. 22, 10) have a red collar and a white neck and spout in front of which is a tall formal plant decoration in red. Equally typical are fruit-stands, the main part of the bowl painted with a kind of primitive tortoiseshell pattern radiating from the centre and the rim painted a creamy colour and decorated with an embossed pattern of spirals.[3]

Embossing, in imitation of metal, is frequently found. A good example from Phaistos is shown in Pl. XXII, 3, *d*, where cockle-shells appear in relief on the outside and corresponding marks of fingers inside show where the clay was pressed into the mould.[4] The popularity of this technique is seen by comparing the bridge-spouted bowl, *f*, also from Phaistos, which but for the pattern on the rim might have been an intruder into the M.M.11*b* stratum in which it was found.

Another pattern, which has considerable importance owing to its occurrence on sherds found in Egypt, is the racquet and ball. A bowl with this design was found in the Royal Pottery stores and fragments of a very fine pithos with a similar

---

[1] For the pattern, cf. Ibid., 247.   [2] Ibid., II, 215.
[3] Ibid., IV, Colour Pl. XXIX.
[4] *Festos*, I, Pl. XXX, *b* ; *P. of M.*, IV, 117, for this and examples from Knossos.

decoration were discovered by the House of the Fallen Blocks.[1]

Although Knossos has provided us so far with most of the examples, it must not be supposed that the potters of Phaistos were inferior. It merely happens that, while at Knossos, a number of structural alterations seem to have taken place before the end of M.M.11a, which sealed in the deposits, at Phaistos, in most cases the same floor levels were in use throughout, so that only the pottery of M.M.11b has been left. A number of vases, however, have survived, among which is the fruit-stand (Pl. XXII, 2) with radiating petals in the bowl and formal friezes of petals and lozenges on the stem.[2] Eggshell cups appear surrounded by wavy lines between which are small rosettes with a red centre (cf. Fig. 22, 3).[3] Another example has the appearance of being built up of blocks of stone with mortar between.[4]

The bowl from the Kamarais Cave (Pl. XXII, 3, a) has a typical M.M.11a rosette, and a finer example shows a highly stylized octopus. Its body is cross-hatched, each tentacle holds a disk surrounded by dots and the two lower ones have petals depending from them.[5]

Even though not wealthy enough to train her potters in the Knossian school, Palaikastro was able to import some of the finest specimens of M.M.11a. Besides the cup shown in Pl. XXII, 1, e, there is a graceful eggshell cup with white wavy lines running round it and circles of dots (Fig. 22, 4). Examples in the same ware of impressed shells were also found.[6]

It was the invention of the quick wheel which evidently caused these great strides in ceramics. On the bases of many vases can be seen the concentric semicircles where a string cut the pot away from the wheel while it was still revolving. The quick wheel meant the possibility of eggshell vases becoming common, and fortunately it meant the end of barbotine.

For the second pottery phase of M.M.11 the Loomweight Area afforded the best stratified deposit.[7] Here came to light a great squat jar over half a metre high. Its lustrous black background was painted with a group of three palm trees in dull white

[1] Festos, II, Colour Pl. IX.   [2] Ibid., I, Pl. XXII.
[3] Ibid., XXI, a.   [4] Ibid., XXVII, a.
[5] B.S.A., XIX, Pl. X, a.   [6] Ibid., Sup., 15.
[7] P. of M., I, 248 ff. So-called owing to the discovery of over 400 pear-shaped clay loomweights of this date.

with details in red.[1] Polychromy, however, is tending to die
out in the smaller vases. This is shown particularly well in the
group found with the shrine described above where the small
jugs and cups have designs such as those shown in Fig. 23,
4 and 5, while a large bridge-spouted jar has the design 2
between a row of white disks with red centres. This spiky

FIG. 23.—Patterns on Middle Minoan IIb Pottery

foliate band is typical of M.M.IIb, and with it goes the sharper
pointing of the petals in the rosettes (Fig. 23, 10). Large spirals
are common (Fig. 23, 9) and the stiff crescents of Pl. XXII,
3, c, and Fig. 23, 3, appear for the first time. Decoration
tends to run in bands round the vase instead of being spread
over it. But though the large loose spirals are apt to look

[1] P. of M., Fig. 190. The palm still grows wild at Vagi on the
East coast, North of Palaikastro.

rather coarse, one large jar at least which is decorated in the
grand manner is most effective.   This is a tall jar with a
narrow neck and rather low horizontal handles, from Phaistos.[1]
The decoration consists of four linked scrolls, rather like the
linked disks of East Cretan M.M.1.   These are surrounded by
a circle which frames the whole pattern.   The outer angle
where the connecting tangent leaves each scroll is painted red
and from it project spiky leaves.   A diagonal line runs across
the centre from left to right and on either side of it are small
objects like caltrops in red and white which may be meant to
represent sharp-petalled flowers.

Another large jar with a pinched-in mouth, from Phaistos,
from the Sanctuary,[2] had broad vertical stripes of alternate
buff and brown, separated by white lines.   On the buff stripes
is the design in brown with a white centre shown in Fig. 23, 6 ;
on the brown stripes is a rather sprawling pattern of connected
loops with scarlet flowers between.

Of humbler vases good examples were found in a pit in
Tomb XVII of the Mavrospelio cemetery at Knossos.[3]   There
were conical cups with a rough decoration of brown paint,
cups similarly decorated with a short broad foot and a slight
outward curve near the rim, flat saucers with a very low foot
and rather taller ones sloping out to the rim.   Round-mouthed
jugs were found either with a red wash or with vertical lines
of white on black.   Coarse sherds from burial pithoi with
trickle pattern or bands in black and red were found at the top
of the pit.

A version of the tortoiseshell ware survives to tide over
the gap into M.M.III, but the imitation of stone ceases with
the remarkable bridge-spouted jar painted to look like conglomerate and a fruit-stand similarly painted from the Kamarais
Cave.[4]   Beetles and cockle-shells appear in relief on several
vases and the beginnings of a close imitation of nature are
shown in the representation of flowers and plants, particularly
on another vase from the Kamarais cave which shows crocuses
in white with red pistils and stamens sprouting from an undulat-
ing band which represents rocky country.   The Minoan artist
had, in fact, already started to show the setting of the objects he
draws, a naturalistic impulse which no other ancient people
attempted to follow until after the downfall of Crete.

[1] P. of M., I, 257 ; Festos, I, Pl. XXXII.
[2] Ibid., I, 260 ; Festos I, Pl. XXV.
[3] B.S.A., XXVIII, 279.   [4] P. of M., XIX, Pls. XIX and IX.

M.M.II
Metalwork

It is curious that no objects of bronze, whether swords or daggers, have as yet come to light in deposits of this period. No doubt the long dagger of M.M.I continued in use until M.M.III. A corroded cube of iron was found at Mavrospelio but does not imply any knowledge of the use of the metal. It may have been magnetic.

M.M.II
Figurines

Figurines also are lacking except for the foot of a painted terra-cotta figurine from Knossos,[1] and so for the most part is jewellery, for valuables would be searched for after the earthquake which seems to have brought M.M.II to a close. A few beads occurred in the M.M.II*b* deposit at Mavrospelio. They included a cylindrical example in white faience with zigzag fluting, beads in white, blue and brown faience, globular, semiglobular and fluted, cylindrical, oval and pointed oval. Globular beads in amethyst and crystal occur. The only stone vase to be found in an M.M.II deposit also came from this pit. It is a squat jug in steatite with a wide circular mouth.

M.M.II
Script and
Seals

The seals of M.M.II show a great advance over those of M.M.I, which was after all in the nature of a transitional period when the hieroglyphic script was coming in and when human and animal figures were first being introduced as the centre of the composition, not as mere subordinates to a geometric pattern. Now in M.M.II these figures are adapted to the shape of the seal, attention is paid to grouping and composition and the inscriptions are well arranged with an eye to calligraphy.

A new type of hieroglyphs, or rather an improvement on the old type, was now in use. This did not survive the end of M.M.II and is therefore an admirable criterion of date. These signs were impressed or inscribed on bars, fiddle-shaped labels, and flat tablets. A hoard of these, together with clay seal impressions, was found in a deposit just East of the North end of the Long Corridor which served the West Magazines. This deposit had been sealed in at the close of M.M.II. A very similar group came to light in the North-West Quarter of the Palace at Mallia, which contained also elements of the M.M.I script. The signs on the tablets and bars are naturally more cursive than those engraved with care on a seal stone, but their recurrence on both is conclusive.

Already a numerical system has been worked out, very much on Egyptian lines. A stroke, straight or slightly curved for the unit, a dot for ten, a longer slanting stroke for a hundred, a lozenge for a thousand and a V for a fraction, probably ¼.

[1] *P. of M.*, III, 453. But it certainly looks of Hellenic date.

The inscriptions seem to read mainly from left to right, though sometimes there is a *boustrophedon* arrangement. This is in contrast to the Egyptian system, where right to left was the rule, except where one inscription balanced another on the opposite side of a door or niche. Furthermore, no clue is given, as in Egypt, to the direction in which the inscription is to be read by always making a human or animal figure face towards

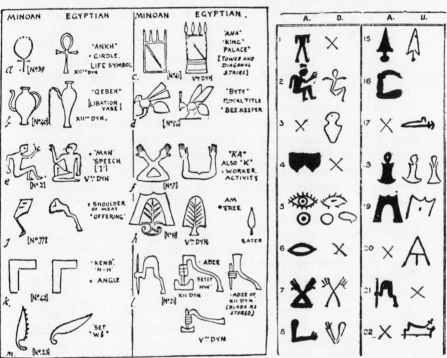

FIG. 24.—Middle Minoan II Hieroglyphic Script

the beginning. The individual groups of signs are sometimes, however, marked by a cross.

A few of the signs are so close to the Egyptian that they must almost certainly have been borrowed, though on the whole the Minoan syllabary is remarkably independent. Fig. 24a gives a number of parallel signs, while 24b shows how closely the cursive script on the tablets keeps to the more formal hieroglyphs engraved on the seals and how often the same groups of signs are repeated.

These pictographs are of the greatest interest in showing us the forms of domestic and agricultural implements. We see jugs, adzes, carpenters' right angles, saws, plumb-bobs, ploughs, lyres, and sistra. We see olive sprays, and those often in company with a ship as if to prove the export of olive oil. Wheat, saffron, perhaps silphium are there. Ships with a central mast, high prow and stern and oars, both galleys and ' busses ' seem to be there. The domestic animals are shown, dogs, horned sheep, goats, short-horned and long-horned cattle and a quantity of other objects of whose existence we know but whose shape we could not tell but for the script.[1]

The clay seal impressions which were found are roughly three-sided. They have been pinched round the string with which the object to be sealed was bound, and often more than one face is stamped.

Two impressions are of particular interest, for they seem to represent the first attempt at portraiture. One shows a man with a big aquiline nose and either a crown or an elaborate arrangement of hair, the other a boy with a sharp straight nose and close-cropped curly hair just like the intelligent small boys you meet in any Greek village.[2] It has been suggested that we have here portraits of a reigning king of Knossos and of his son. On the same lump of clay which bears the man's head is another impression consisting of three hieroglyphs, a five-barred gate, a leg and a sign which may represent the silphium plant. Very likely this is his name, and it is noteworthy that a magnificent three-sided bead seal of carnelian bears the same signs, with the addition of a snake, surrounding a cat *sejant gardant*[3] (Fig. 25b). Other impressions show a hind beside a stream, a wild goat, a fish and an octopus stranded in a pool and a small boy attending a ram by a manger.[4]

The seals themselves are cut in harder stones than those of M.M.I. Carnelian, agate, rock crystal, chalcedony, and jasper are common. Favourite shapes are the signet (Fig. 25a), three- and four-sided bead seals, lentoids, and circular seals with two sides or with one side only, the back being carved to

---

[1] *P. of M.*, I, Fig. 214. [2] Ibid., Fig. 201.
[3] Ibid., Fig. 204a. The other sides also show hieroglyphs, in one case a very similar group occupying the centre of the field between palmettes. Is it possible that we have here a trace of the different official names of the king? Pharaoh often showed his ' Son of Ra ' name, his King of Upper and Lower Egypt name and his Golden Horus name on one object.
[4] Ibid., Fig. 202.

give a grip. The beauty of some of the designs is great.
Nothing could be more graceful than the ibex shown in Fig. 25c,
from a lentoid gem of agate, and there are others as good. Most
curious of all, shown in Fig. 25d, is a four-sided prism, the
winged head on which has an astonishing resemblance to
Jacobean cherubs.

In our dating of the period we are extremely lucky. In a *M.M.II Foreign Relations*
pure M.M.IIb deposit below the North-West corner of the
Central Court was found the lower part of a diorite statue.[1]
It represents a figure seated on a square throne which is inscribed on three sides. His name is given as Ab-nub-mes-
wazet-user, true of voice (i.e. justified or deceased). It is
possible, however, that his name is simply User and that the

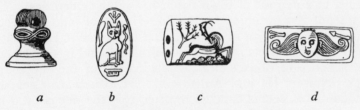

| *a* | *b* | *c* | *d* |

FIG. 25.—Middle Minoan II Seals

rest of the signs are epithets, a title, or his father's name. If
the compound name is really correct it is more in keeping with
XIIIth-Dynasty nomenclature, but it has been conclusively
shown that the details of style are typical of the very early part
of the XIIth Dynasty and never occur later.[2] This monument
is exceptional in that it is the only Egyptian object found in the
Aegean which must have a personal connexion. Vases can be
the result of trade, scarabs may be souvenirs but a personal
non-utilitarian monument such as this can only imply the presence of the man himself. It may be that User was the Egyptian ambassador to the court of Minos or that he was the agent
of some temple sent to buy wood as in later days Wenamen
journeyed to Syria. In either case the statue was no doubt
dedicated in one of the Palace shrines, for wherever he went

[1] Though at this point the paving of the Court had disappeared and
M.M.III was found near by, the statue itself was found with typical
M.M.IIb sherds, and such sherds underlay the undisturbed paving
immediately adjoining. *P. of M.*, I, 268.

[2] Evers, *Staat aus dem Stein*, II, 96, in his very careful analysis
confidently ascribed it to the time of Amenemhat I, c. 2000–1970 B.C.

the Egyptian courteously paid his respects to the local gods [1] (Pl. XX, 4).

In the Diktaian Cave above Psykhro was found the amethyst scarab shown in Fig. 19, 5. It was found before excavations began, but it must be connected with the earliest deposit in that cave, which is M.M.11b. Both the material and the cutting of the scarab point to a XIIth-Dynasty date. The obverse, however, has been engraved by a Minoan artist. In the centre is a rayed sun, a common hieroglyph, between beaked vases. These vases seem rather earlier than M.M.11, though vases very like them occur in the script.[2] In the field are concentric circles.

In Egypt the parallel dating is even more conclusive.[3] M.M.11a sherds, displaying typical patterns, were found at Haraga in a deposit of town rubbish, by the cemeteries. The town itself was occupied by the better class of men connected with the construction of the Pyramid of Senusert II ($c.$ 1906–1888 B.C.), and a stela of this Pharaoh was found in the deposit. The absence of objects bearing the names of the succeeding kings Senusert III and Amenemhat III, which are elsewhere very common, seems conclusive proof that the deposit did not extend into their reigns.[4]

In a tomb at Abydos, which, besides objects of typical XIIth-Dynasty fabric, contained glazed steatite cylinders bearing the names of Senusert III (1888–1849 B.C.) and Amenemhat III (1849–1801 B.C.), was found a fine example of the bridge-spouted bowls.[5] This is dated by Evans to M.M.11b, but it is possibly a transitional type between M.M.11a and b owing to

[1] *P. of M.*, II, 220. This accounts for its discovery in so late a stratum of M.M.11. Offerings might remain in a shrine for a long time.

[2] *P. of M.*, Fig. 214, 47–49.

[3] I am informed that the harbour works at Alexandria tentatively claimed as Minoan in *P. of M.*, I, 292 ff., are now considered definitely Hellenistic.

[4] Ibid., II, 212 ; Engelbach, *Harageh*, 10 f. Åberg, loc. cit., rejects such evidence.

[5] *P. of M.*, I, 267. The chronology of this tomb also has been disputed by those who would accept it at once were it not that it provides such good parallel dating. ‘ The cylinders must have been copies, or heirlooms must have been put into a later interment.’ But the fact remains that no single object from this tomb *need* be later than the XIIth Dynasty, and the only two closely datable objects are of that Dynasty. Such objections have been made to practically every synchronism. But where M.M.11 vases are found in XIIth-Dynasty deposits and a XIIth-Dynasty object in a M.M.11 deposit there is nothing more to be said.

the rounded ends of the petals, and a very similar vase from Knossos shows the racquet pattern which is typical of M.M.11a [1] (Pl. XXI, 2).

The rubbish-heaps of the town of Lahun, built for the workmen engaged on the Pyramid of Senusert II, produce many sherds of M.M.11b date. The town was largely deserted after the Pyramid was finished and the rubbish of the small population which continued to reside there was dumped in the empty rooms. All the M.M.11 sherds were found at the bottom of the rubbish-heaps outside the town and clearly belong to the period when the town was fully inhabited. No object later than the XIIth Dynasty was discovered in conjunction with them.[2] Together with these sherds were found numerous imitations in local clay.

By this time the Minoan craftsman was standing on his own feet and was working out his own salvation without the direct influence from abroad. Certain motives, naturally, were borrowed, but they were always given a Minoan turn. The slavish copying of the previous periods has gone. Among the motives which came from Egypt the most important is the lotus, which was in Crete at once adapted and formalized. The palmette also must have a Nilotic origin. The various forms of scroll-work are by now so elaborated that to talk of Crete borrowing from Egypt or vice versa is impossible. The original idea may have been Egyptian but no doubt each country worked it out in its own way.

On the other hand, the use of amethyst and other hard stones, so popular in Middle Kingdom Egypt, as well as the skill to cut them, cannot be native.

At Ras Shamra in Syria an M.M.11a sherd has been found.[3]

Pottery of both M.M.11a and b was imported into Phylakope in the Second City [4] into Aigina in Middle Helladic times.[5] A sherd was found in a later tomb in Cyprus.[6]

---

[1] P. of M., IV, 137.

[2] Ibid., I, 266 ; II, 210 ; B.M. Cat., I, 91.

[3] J.H.S., 1936, 133 ; Syria, 1937, 151. The tomb was in use from the nineteenth till the fourteenth century. The ' Hyksos ' pottery found in such tombs does not necessarily imply a later date than the XIIth Dynasty. The Hyksos were in Syria long before they arrived in Egypt.

[4] P. of M., I, Fig. 186b–e (M.M.11a) ; Phylakope, 149, Fig. 126 (M.M.11b).

[5] P. of M., II, 211 ; Gnomon, I, H.i. 47. The so-called Middle-Helladic sherds which were found at Lahun are Syrian. Aegyptiaca, 112.   [6] J.H.S., 1911, 111.

We see then the great intimacy of the relations between the great centres of Knossos and Phaistos and the XIIth Dynasty in Egypt. If we take M.M.II*a* to begin about 2000 B.C. and to end somewhere in the reign of Senusert II, say about 1875, and M.M.II*b* to run down to the end of the XIIth or beginning of the XIIIth Dynasty, between 1800 and 1750 B.C., we shall not be far wrong.

The end of M.M.II seems to have been marked by a severe earthquake which sealed in a number of deposits both at Knossos and Phaistos, leaving them in a pure unmixed state.[1] At Pseira, Mallia, Mokhlos, Gournia, and Palaikastro a similar disaster seems to have brought an end to their corresponding period (M.M.I). At all these sites the succeeding M.M.III Period seems to have begun immediately, though at Vasilike the disaster may have wiped out or disheartened the whole population, for it was not reoccupied. It is only on the assumption of some catastrophe such as an earthquake that we can account for the complete break which occurs between obviously consecutive periods. That it was not a disaster brought about by enemies seems clear from the absence of burning which one associates with a sack and also from the way in which M.M.III follows on with no lack of continuity.

SITES WHERE MIDDLE MINOAN II REMAINS HAVE BEEN FOUND

CENTRAL CRETE

(a) Excavated Sites

JUKTAS. . . .	Sanctuary .	A few sherds in the sanctuary proper. Evans, *P. of M.*, I, 151.
KNOSSOS . . .	Palace . .	Consolidation of the building. *P. of M.*, I, 203 ; III, 356. Koulouras, IV, 61.
	Cemetery .	Chamber tombs at Mavrospelio. Forsdyke, *B.S.A.*, XXVIII, 295.
MALLIA . . .	Deposit .	A few sherds which may belong to this period. Imported. *Mallia*, I, 51, and many of the inscriptions. *Ecritures Minoennes*.
PSYKHRO . . .	Cave . .	Earliest deposit in the upper part of the Diktaian Cave. Hogarth, *B.S.A.*, VI, 101, Fig. 27.

---

[1] *P. of M.*, I, 299.

TRAPEZA . . . Cave . . A few sherds from excavations of 1936. *A.J.A.*, XL, 371. *Arch. Anz.*, 1936, 162.

TYLISSOS . . . Houses . . Earlier houses in settlement. Hazzidakis, *'Εφ. 'Αρχ.*, 1912.

(b) Surface Finds

HERAKLEION . . Sherds from the harbour town E. of Trypeti. Evans, *P. of M.*, II, 229.

SOUTH CRETE

(a) Excavated Sites

AGIA TRIADHA. . Tomb . . Possibly two vases from ' Tholos ' A. Banti, *Annuario*, XIII–XIV, 240.

KALATHIANA . . Settlement . Vases, &c., from houses. Xanthoudides, *V.T.M.*, 81.

KAMARAIS . . . Cave . . Vases, &c. Mariani, *Mon. Ant.*, VI, 333. Dawkins, *B.S.A.*, XIX, 1.

STOU KOUSE . . House . . Earliest deposit at τοῦ Βραχνοῦ ὁ Λάκκος. Marinatos, *'Αρχ. Δελτ.*, 1922–5, 53.

PHAISTOS . . . Palace . . Architectural and other features. Pernier, *Festos*, 146.

PORTI . . . . Tombs . . Latest finds in the cemetery. *V.T.M.*, 61.

(b) Surface Finds

SPHAKORIAKO . . Sherds from Minoan station N. of Komo. Evans, *P. of M.*, II, 90.

TRYPETI . . . Sherds from above path to Khristos. Ibid., 82.

EAST CRETE

(a) Excavated Sites

MOKHLOS . . . Object . . Seal from Tomb III. *Mochlos*, 39, Fig. 14.

PALAIKASTRO . . Deposits . In town site. *B.S.A.*, X, 211, *Sup.*, 15.

(b) Surface Finds

STO DHASO . . Seal. Evans, *J.H.S.*, XVII, 343. *P. of M.*, I, 275, Fig. 204*e* (between Zyros and Ampelos).

KEDHRI . . . Evans, Ibid., publishes seal (Fig. 204*k*).

LEUKE ISLAND . Sherds, seen by Bosanquet. *B.S.A.*, IX, 276. (KOUPHONISI) Jug, possibly of this date, in the Candia Museum. *Cat.*, 3361.

VRAKHASI . . . A few sherds by the side of the road at ἡ ὀπίσω βρύσις. Seen by writer, 1935.

3. MIDDLE MINOAN III (M.M.III)

(See Map 9)

The Third Middle Minoar. Period was in the nature of the beginning of a new era, as Evans has called it. It marks the rise of the great palaces as we see them to-day, for, in spite of considerable alterations in detail, the plans of Knossos and Phaistos are essentially those of M.M.IIIa. The present section will take the story down from the severe earthquake at the end of M.M.IIb to the equally severe one towards, but not quite at, the end of M.M.IIIb.

The map shows how quickly the island recovered from the disaster and how much more thickly populated it had become before the end of the period. There is one point in particular worth noticing, and that is that in the East and South of the island the settlements seem to be concentrating on the big cities, while in the North and centre villages and towns are springing up all round. The balance of power has come to stay there, and although the power of Phaistos is shown by the magnificence of its palace, yet it ruled over few towns.

The wild country West of Ida is being penetrated, and seeing that remains have been found at Apodhoulou and Pistagi, it would not be at all surprising to find that a settlement existed at Rhethymnos, for the two former sites are on the direct route between Phaistos and the North coast. Furthermore, whether the site at Khalara near Patsos is a cave, as it certainly seemed from a superficial investigation, or merely a rock shelter for burials, it implies something of a population in the district.

The old sacred caves seem to be losing their popularity. Except for a few sherds Trapeza has nothing to show and the cult has evidently been transferred to Psykhro. The Kamarais cave, too, is falling into disuse. Other caves, however, at Keratos and Spiliaridhia near Avdhou have acquired sanctity and serve the spiritual needs of the newly grown population. Skoteino and the cave of Eileithyia seem to keep their hold. The only peak sanctuary that keeps its position is that on Juktas, and, as we have seen, that hill had also the character of a city of refuge.

M.M.III
Architecture
In architecture the disaster which had just occurred gave the builders of the palaces a comparatively free hand. They kept

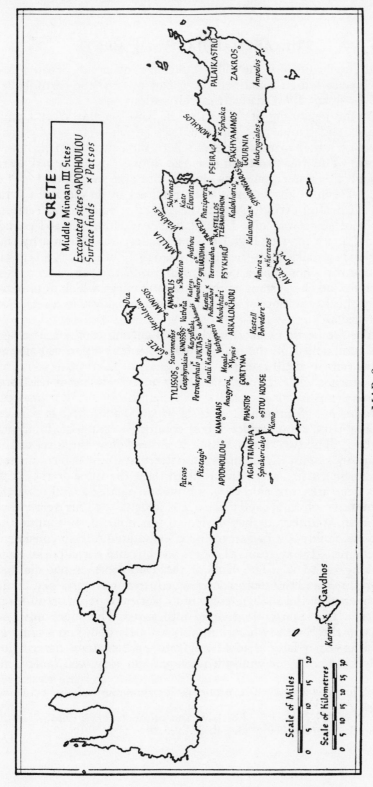

CRETE

Middle Minoan III Sites
Excavated sites ○ APODHOULOU
Surface finds × Patsos

PALAIKASTRO
ZAKROS
Ampelos

Sphaka
MOKHLOS
PSEIRA × Sphaka
PAKHYAMMOS
GOURNIA
Makrygialos

Skhines
Kato
Elounta
Phaziperra
SPILIARIDHIA Andhou
Anthonis Monastery
Termiadha KASTELLI PRAFEZA
Kastelli TZERMIADHON
Pedhiadhos Kaloklorio
PSYKHRO Kalamafka × SPHOUNGARAS
Amira × × Keratos
Alike × Alike

VRAKHASI
MALLIA
AMNISOS
Dia
Herakleion
GAZE
ANAPOLIS × Skoteino
Stavromenos × Skoteino
TYLISSOS ○ Vathria Kalergi
Geophyrakia × KNOSSOS ○ Karydhaki ×
Petrokephalo JUKTAS ○ Arkhanais
Karsli Kastellir Vathypetri ×
Megale Moukhtari
Anagyroi ○ × Nypsis ARKALOKHORI
KAMARAIS GORTYNA Kastell
STOU KOUSE Belvedere ×
Patsos AGIA TRIADHA ○ PHAISTOS ○
× Pistagi × Sphakoria ○ Koma
APODHOULOU ×

Dia

Scale of Miles
0   5   10   15   20

Scale of Kilometres
0 5 10 15 20 30

Karavi × Gavdhos

MAP 9

to the main lines of the older buildings, no doubt because the thick walls which contained them had resisted the earthquake, but in detail they made great alterations.

At the beginning of M.M.IIIa at Knossos the West Court was extended over the older houses which were now pulled down or rather razed to a level where the court could run over them. The two westernmost ' koulouras ' were paved over though the eastern one was cleaned out and kept open.[1] The West Porch seems to have been retained in its old form. In the ' Theatral Area ', North-West of the palace, the eastern flight of steps was added about half-way along the old paved court, and a kind of Royal box or bastion was inserted by the angle they make with the steps running South (Pl. XXIII, 1). Beside the steps runs a gutter to drain off the rainwater ; this gutter is on the system of the parabolic curve which automatically checks the flow of water by leading it down in a series of waterfalls.[2]

The Domestic Quarter in the great cutting on the East slope was remodelled on the plan, which, with few superficial alterations, remained till the end. The Grand Staircase, descending two stories below the Central Court and ascending at least one above it, was constructed. It remains one of the greatest monuments of antiquity, with its broad shallow treads flanked by low parapets on which stood columns to support the upper flights. The two stories which it serves below the level of the court are practically identical in pattern and are also connected by smaller staircases. In order to light the interior rooms of this large area, one side of which was up against a wall of earth, a number of light-wells were constructed. This feature of Minoan architecture has already been noticed, but until the present building it had never been elaborated into so consistent a scheme. Every group of rooms had one and a small colonnade looking on to it. The Hall of the Double Axes had no less than three, and the room round which they were grouped could be opened to the air by a continuous series of doors on all three sides. The quarter is divided into two. The more intimate part to the South, which contains a toilet-room and latrine as well as—at a later date at any rate—a bathroom, is reached only by a series of winding passages and may well have been

[1] This seems the most probable interpretation of the evidence. *P. of M.*, IV, 64.
[2] *P. of M.*, III, 247. For later and more elaborate example at the East Bastion see below and ibid., 240 ff.

the harem quarters of the Palace.[1] To the North of this, over the Loomweight Area, presumably lay a large hall, the water from the roof of which was collected in a store tank in the court below whence an open conduit led it to a blind well.[2] To warm the draughty rooms low tripod hearths of stucco, decorated with paint, were used.[3]

At the North end of the Palace, the old wide entrance was narrowed down all along to the width of the upper section (i.e. about 2 metres) by means of throwing out a line of bastions on each side. The blocks of these bastions are marked with signs typical of the period among which is repeatedly found at this point a trident as if to signify the sea-gate. At the lower end was a square pillared hall out of which a gateway led westwards, and joined the road leading away from the 'Theatral Area'.[4] On top of the bastions, at a level with the Central Court, were colonnades, the eastern one of which led on to the upper story of the pillared hall. These colonnades were later decorated with painted plaster reliefs of bulls, which will be described below (Pl. XXIV, 2).[5]

The Lustral Basin by the North-West Portico belongs to M.M.iiia in its present form with the gypsum lining to the basin proper and the stepped balustrade though the backing of small blocks laid in thick beds of mortar is earlier (Pl. XXIV, 1).[6] In the West Wing a door was placed at each end of the central section of the Long Corridor of Magazines, and in the area so enclosed cists were sunk both below the floor of the corridor and of the Magazines (Pl. XXIV, 3). Some were lined with masonry faced with lead and seem to have contained treasure, the rest were deeper and were lined only with hard plaster as if they were oil vats.[7]

The South Propylaeum was built, a very broad structure entered from the South by five passages, between tall door jambs and consisting of two unequal parts each fronted by two columns. In the southern part is a cist.[8]

In the latter half of the period, after an earthquake, it seems, had done a certain amount of damage, a few minor alterations took place. The most important of these consist of the 'Temple Repositories'. These are large stone-lined cists

[1] *P. of M.*, I, 325.
[2] Ibid., 378 ff. The arrangement of the walls below shows the plan, Fig. 278.
[3] Ibid., 390. [4] Ibid., 393. [5] Ibid., III, 159 ff.
[6] Ibid., I, 405. [7] Ibid., 448. [8] Ibid., II, 692.

which contained the offerings and decoration of some shrine close by, perhaps the predecessor illustrated in the Miniature Frescoes of that which was built in L.M.I, on the Central Court façade. Other alterations and repairs it is difficult to assign, and it seems safer to leave a discussion of the Palace in its final state until the great rebuilding towards the end of M.M.IIIb.[1]

At Phaistos the steps leading up North from the West Court were remodelled and a wall built behind them. The old shrine was filled in and, behind where it had been, a flight of steps led up eastwards into a propylaeum with a central column behind which three columns gave on to a light-well. North of this is a peristyle from which in some way no longer clear access was obtained to what seems to have corresponded on a smaller scale to the Domestic Quarters of Knossos. South of the Propylaeum lies a short corridor with magazines opening off it on either side. This is approached direct from the Central Court through a propylaeum which is peculiar in being divided longitudinally by two columns with a third on the façade of the court itself. The court is surrounded by a veranda, the roof supported on square piers. East of this are further structures which are much denuded and traces of a second peristyle and an eastern court.[2] It may be noted here that Phaistos seems hardly to have suffered at all either from the slight earthquake which necessitated repairs at Knossos at the end of M.M.IIIa nor from the very severe shock near the end of M.M.IIIb which did great damage to the latter. As the floor deposits show, the palace remained till the final disaster, practically as it was rebuilt at the beginning of M.M.IIIa.

It is probable that the small palace at Agia Triadha was first built early in M.M.III, the lack of floor deposits of the period being accounted for by the fact that the floors themselves were in continual use until the end. Here as at Phaistos we find the Peristyle, which seems to be a feature of South Cretan architecture. At all events at Knossos, it occurs but once and then on only three sides in the South-East house.

At Mallia the reconstructed palace seems to have retained more of the features of the original M.M.I structure than did the others. It appears that the upper stories had not been as extensive as elsewhere, or so one is led to believe by the absence of stairways, and therefore the destruction was not so great. The most noteworthy feature is the row of columns alternating with square piers, each connected by a grille with its

[1] *P. of M.*, I, 462.   [2] *Festos*, I, Pl. II, and the forthcoming *Festos*, II.

neighbour, which borders the Central Court on North and East. This palace also seems not to have been altered before its destruction.

The following are various points of construction which are good criteria of date. The column bases are now of gypsum or limestone instead of the variegated stones of M.M.II. They are also appreciably lower in proportion to their diameter. The older style, however, was conventionalized in a curious way. We see in the frescoes that many of the wooden columns had a dark band, varying in height, immediately above the base. In some cases this is painted to represent breccia. For the columns themselves we now have the evidence of the wall paintings. They were of wood plastered and painted and two types can be distinguished. The first and most common has a round shaft increasing in diameter towards the top, the capital consisting of a cushion between two mouldings and a square abacus above. The shape of the columns, which reverse the usual taper, is known in the rough stone pillars of Minorca and Malta, and is also seen in the stone supporting pillar built into the foundations of the stepped portico at Knossos.[1] But for wood there was a traditional and a practical reason for placing the tree trunks upside down.[2] In primitive times there must always have been a danger of unseasoned timber sprouting, which would be obviated by planting it upside down. But no doubt the main reason was to allow the wide capital to throw drips of water clear of the base which would otherwise rot. Usually the shaft of the column was plain, but concave fluting is found quite early and convex fluting in the next period, while spiral fluting is not unknown.[3] The usual colour of the columns was red or black with counterchanged capital picked out in white or yellow. The proportion of height to diameter at base seems from the indication of the levels of different stories to have been 5 : 1, though those which have less structural importance vary considerably. The other type is seen in the Miniature Frescoes and on the Boxer vase from Agia Triadha. It tapers upwards and is surmounted by an oblong block decorated with disks.[4]

[1] *P. of M.*, III, 322.
[2] Cf. wooden telegraph poles planted upside down to-day.
[3] *P. of M.*, I, 344 f. Ibid., II, 522.
[4] Ibid., III, 63. They may well be supports for an awning as there suggested, but one would prefer to suppose that they are intended to show one pillar behind another, in the Egyptian convention, not one on top of another.

It is no longer only rubble masonry which is tied in with balks of timber. This construction was by now evidently considered an aesthetic feature and good cut blocks appear between the wooden ties. These blocks are now carefully fitted together and no longer show the deep clay mortar bed of M.M.II. For the most part the flooring consists of slabs of gypsum in place of the older ' mosaiko ', and a dado of gypsum slabs is often found covering the lower part of the walls. The door jambs are of wood with gypsum bases. These features, together with the floor cists or ' Kasellas ', are typical of M.M.III architecture.

A fine example of a private house of the period was found below the South-East angle of the Palace.[1] The lower story only remains and it is probable that the main entrance led into the floor above from the higher level to the West. From this a flight of stairs led down to the ground floor. This was divided into two parts, the southern corresponding to the Domestic Quarter with, as has been noticed, a small peristyle, the northern being mainly occupied by a pillar crypt. The top block of the pillar was incised with a double axe and beside it was a truncated pyramid of gypsum with a socket in the top which we know was the base of a double axe.

Fig. 26 shows two houses also below the South-East angle of the Palace which were destroyed by the earthquake in M.M.IIIb, when great blocks were hurled into them from the Palace façade. The ' House of the Fallen Blocks ' consisted of a large L-shaped room, well lighted by a window in the West wall, and smaller rooms to North and South. It seems to have been the dwelling of a craftsman, for a number of stone lamps was found, including one unfinished example. Separated by a narrow paved lane, down one side of which ran a stone drain, lay the ' House of the Sacrificed Oxen '. This house is slightly larger and contains four medium-sized rooms. In the North-West and South-East corners of the southernmost of these were discovered the heads of two large oxen with the great horns of the *urus*. In front of these were the remains of painted terra-cotta altars with three stumpy legs. The decoration of the larger was in simple bands, but the smaller had sprays of grasses painted on the legs and a black band round the body dotted with white to imitate stone.

The plan of neither of these houses shows an outside door and the probability is that access was obtained from an upper floor by means of a trap-door and a ladder.

[1] *B.S.A.*, IX, 4 ff., and *P. of M.*, I, 425.

Burial customs seem hardly to have changed at all in this period. Pithos burials are somewhat commoner and rock shelters seem to have been abandoned or rather improved so that at Knossos they can now be termed chamber tombs. At Isopata only an isolated deposit indicated that the cemetery went back as far as M.M.III, but many of the tombs at Mavro-spelio were in use by the earlier part of the period. This practice must be a purely local one, for elsewhere, even at the immediately neighbouring sites, pithos burials were found, several indeed round about Knossos itself.

In the East a few of the earlier built tombs showed later

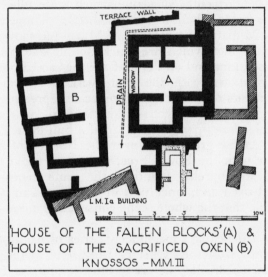

'HOUSE OF THE FALLEN BLOCKS' (A) &
'HOUSE OF THE SACRIFICED OXEN (B)
KNOSSOS – M.M.III

Fɪɢ. 26

deposits, though whether these are burials or votive offerings it is impossible to say. In the South the circular tombs were completely abandoned, but tombs of the new period have still to be found.

The mason's marks visible on the walls of the Palace tend to be less deeply cut. In M.M.IIIa they are still easily visible, but in M.M.IIIb they need the light at the right angle to be seen at all. The trident, the double axe, the star, and, in the Domestic Quarter, the distaff, are all typical of the period.

The wall-paintings are more advanced.[1] In M.M.IIIa we

[1] For the possibility that the 'Saffron Gatherer' belongs to this date see above, p. 131, n. 3.

find in the lower East-West Corridor a dado with imitation marbling, above which was a labyrinth pattern in dark brown on a yellow ground. This imitation of stone painted as a dado below the main scene remained popular down to the end of the Palace. In the Loomweight Area, fallen from the hall above, were fragments of an elaborate spiral design apparently forming a square frame with two diagonals, a pattern recalling an M.M.iii*b* painting of lattice-work at Phaistos. The background is a deep red and the spirals are blue, picked out with black and white. Similar designs were found elsewhere in the Palace. More ambitious are the fragments from one of the cists in the Thirteenth Magazine which were filled in at the time of the great rebuilding in M.M.iii*b*. These are in the style of the Miniature Frescoes of M.M.iii*b* and show a building with columns into which are stuck double axe blades. Between the columns and on the roof are the sacred horns. The masonry is shown with the framework of wooden beams. Other fragments on a corresponding scale represent crowds of spectators roughly but effectively sketched in. A fragment on a larger scale shows part of the head of a bull in very much the same style as the great relief over the North Entrance.[1]

Together with the Spiral Fresco must be taken the pieces of painted stucco relief found in the same deposit. These represented oxen and, since part of a human arm was found, it is probable that the whole scene consisted of a bull-grappling contest.[2]

To M.M.iii*b* belong a magnificent series of paintings. Over one of the doors of the ' Queen's Megaron ' in the Domestic Quarter was a charming picture of blue dolphins and fish of all colours. A border of coral or sponge is added on the light blue background and the bubbles flying off the fins are shown also (Pl. XXV, 2). From the East Hall come the fragments of the fresco known as the ' Ladies in Blue '. This showed a group of ladies in elaborately decorated garments toying with necklaces. From some room over the old ' Keep ' at the North end of the Palace come the Miniature Frescoes.[3] The first panel centres round a shrine, consisting of a central portion

---

[1] *P. of M.*, I, 356, 370, 443, 527. [2] Ibid., 375.
[3] I think they must be placed before and not after the earthquake at the end of M.M.iii*b*. The test described *P. of M.*, III, 33, seems conclusive, and they are of quite a different style from those we know were executed during the restoration and at the same time have such close resemblances to the M.M.iii*a* class described above.

with two columns standing on a raised block of masonry flanked
by side chambers on a lower level with one column apiece.
On either side and below are grouped the spectators.   On a
level with the shrine are seated groups of women in flounced
skirts, bare breasts and sleeves to the elbow.   They have long
hair elaborately coiffeured, headbands and necklaces.   They
are engaged in the most lively conversation, the gestures so
vividly shown that one can almost hear the shrill chatter.   As
a general background are shown the heads of the rest of the
crowd outlined in black with white eyes and necklaces, in the
case of the men on a red wash, and in the case of the women on
a white wash.   The whole is an extremely successful shorthand
for a mixed mob (Pl. XXV, 3).

In the only other panel which could be restored we see a
group of girls performing a dance in an area bounded either by
low walls or by such causeways as ran across the Western
Court.   It is hard to say which.   Two or three olive trees,
painted in blue, shade some of the spectators, among whom the
feminine element is not only larger than in the other panel but
keeps more to itself.   The same shorthand convention for men
and women is used, but an element of individuality is introduced by the more excitable male members of the crowd waving
their hands in the air.   It gives the impression of a football
match on a Saturday afternoon.   Other fragments show a
group of unarmoured warriors hurling spears.

The practice of painted reliefs in plaster reaches its height
in M.M.III*b*.   The ' Jewel Fresco ',[1] of which nothing remained
but the fingers of a hand holding a necklace from which hang
pendants in the shape of negroid heads, is life-size.   But the
scheme of decorations in the colonnades above the North
Entrance is gigantic.   Large fragments of a colossal relief of
a charging bull have been found fallen from the western
colonnade, together with smaller fragments of human figures.
Clearly there was a scene from the bull-ring or perhaps from
the rounding up of wild bulls from a ' farm ', since conventional
rockwork is shown in the foreground.   Somewhere in the scene
occurred the relief of an olive tree with red, black and green
foliage carefully shown.   A similar painted relief seems to have
stood on the back wall of the eastern colonnade, though as this
had been deliberately pulled down in L.M.III the fragments
were scanty.   A very good comparison has been made between
this scene and that on the cups from the tomb at Vapheio,

[1] Since destroyed by an earthquake.

which cannot be earlier than the fifteenth century.[1] These
scenes, or at least the charging bull, seem to have stood long
after the Palace was destroyed.   The fragments were found on
a level with Geometric pottery, and it may well be that these
fierce guardians had something to do with the avoidance by
the Greeks of the Palace site as uncanny and haunted, and who
shall say how much colour they gave to the legend of the
Minotaur ?

Elsewhere in Crete the same style of decoration was in
vogue.   Curiously enough, Phaistos has produced only the most
meagre examples.   At Tylissos, however, a few pieces of the
miniature class came to light which showed boxers advancing
much in the style of the steatite rhyton from Agia Triadha,[2]
while at Pseira part of a scene in relief resembling the ' Ladies
in Blue ' was found.[3]

These paintings were true fresco work.   Everything goes to
show that the colours were applied when the stucco was still
moist, for they have often run quite a depth below the surface.
Sometimes the outline was rapidly sketched in with a blunt
point.   In architectural pieces horizontal lines were made at
close intervals with a taut string.   In cases where an elaborate
pattern was to be shown the surface involved, but no more, was
divided up into small squares.   It is possible even that more
complicated designs were produced by some stencilling process.
According to analyses the stucco was of lime-plaster, the white
paint hydrate of lime, the black carbonaceous shale or slate,
the yellow an ochre which on calcination produces light red,
the deep red some form of haematite, the blue silicate of
copper.   The green was obtained by mixing blue and yellow.[4]

M.M.III
Pottery

The pottery of M.M.III*a* shows a distinct falling off from the
standard even of M.M.II*b*.   Evidently the art had received a
severe set-back.   This must have been due either to the earthquake at the end of M.M.II or to some great advance or popularity in the making of vessels in other materials.   The latter
is most probable.   One cannot believe that an art such as the
potter's declined in that short period ; but if the finest craftsmen
were to devote their energies elsewhere, then the decline is to
be expected.

The continuity of various forms of decoration proves that
the break was not complete.   Variegated and inlaid stone is

[1] *P. of M.*, I, 542, and III, 377 ; I, 544 ; III, 46, 81 ; I, 525 ; III, 167.
[2] '*Εφ. 'Αρχ.*, 1912, Pl. XIX.
[3] *Pseira*, Pl. V.   [4] *P. of M.*, I, 532.

still imitated in pottery,[1] but the metallic glazed black paint
has gone and red paint is sparingly used.[2] Owing to the fact
that Knossos alone seems to have suffered at the end of M.M.IIIa
from an earthquake severe enough to seal in various deposits,
the description of shapes and decoration which follows is
almost confined to that site.

The quick wheel has come to stay and a number of plain
vessels, cups, and saucers show a spiral fluting made by the
finger of the potter as the wheel stopped [3] (Pl. XXVI, 3). The
most typical vases are, as usual, cups. Those with handles
have nearly the same shape as M.M.II examples, but the rim
is apt to spread and the handles are larger, some of them
approximating to the type on the gold cups of Vapheio.[4] The
handleless cups have a flaring rim and swell out in the body
above a sharp base.[5] With these, as good evidence for dating,
may be taken the elongated shape of the small store jars
(Pl. XXVI, 2, c), which are sometimes combined with a ring-
stand at the bottom, moulded in clay and imitating the Egyptian
practice where the pointed base was inserted into a stand.[6]
Many of these have ledge handles slightly below the greatest
diameter of the vase, others have horizontal handles tilted
vertically and overtopping the mouth. Others again, usually
those with beak spouts, have three handles meeting the rim.
In some cases the mouth is oval and two handles run from
shoulder to rim (Pl. XXVI, 2, b). This latter class is somewhat squatter. Tall jars with a wide mouth and a tubular
spout are found, sometimes decorated with a trickle pattern
in red paint (Pl. XXVI, 1, b). Two kinds of tripods are
common, both undecorated. One has a bucket-shaped body
and short vertical legs, the other has a more rounded body, two
handles, and the legs splayed out.

The use of red paint is dying out and the decoration is mainly
white on black. A fine exception was found in the South-East
rubbish-heap.[7] It is a globular rhyton decorated with palm
trees and sprays, the former much resembling the palms already
described on an M.M.IIb jar. Other fragments were found on
Gypsadhais hill South of the Palace. These display lace-like
designs and are of rather a precious and decadent character.[8]

It has been said that variegated and inlaid stone is still
imitated in pottery (Pl. XXVIII, 1). At Knossos this form of

[1] Ibid., 413.
[2] Ibid., 552.
[3] Ibid., 589.
[4] Ibid., 245.
[5] Ibid., 588.
[6] Ibid., 415.
[7] Ibid., 594.
[8] Ibid., 593.

decoration was usually confined to white dots, copying the shell inlays in stone vases (see below), but in East Crete conglomerate is indicated (Fig. 27, 4 and 8), as also on a basin from North of the Palace at Knossos.   The tortoiseshell ripple is still found.[1]

Flowers and leaves are shown in white on black.   Fig. 27, 1,

FIG. 27.—Patterns on Middle Minoan III Pottery

shows a group of tulips from a vase which, though it was found in an M.M.IIIb Magazine, is, on analogy with similar designs from elsewhere, almost certainly M.M.IIIa.[2]   The spiral, however, is still the most common form of decoration (Fig. 27, 5).   The rosettes also survive but the petals are separated from the

[1] P. of M., I, 598.   [2] Ibid., 606.

central disk.[1] A stellar design similar to the later example in Fig. 27, 10, was found on a burial jar from Gaze.

From East Crete came a number of interesting vases. A pattern which is typical of this part of the island from now onwards makes its first appearance at Gournia. This is of the shape shown in Fig. 27, 9 (M.M.IIIb), and consists of three loops leaving the central disk at a tangent.

From Pakhyammos comes a very fine burial jar with a design of dolphins and sea foam, very reminiscent of the Dolphin Fresco at Knossos. It seems to be transitional between M.M.IIIa and M.M.IIIb.[2] At the same site the linked disks of M.M.I persisted in dark on light and another most effectively decorated jar shows a frieze of broad leaves in white on black.[3] Palaikastro produces a few examples of the naturalistic plant designs already mentioned. From Zakros comes a cup with the tendril pattern of Fig. 27, 7, and from Mokhlos come two of the most beautifully if formally decorated vases which can be assigned to the period. One of these is a burial jar with two rows of false spirals, linked and extended into an ogival shape, while between the handles are incised double axes picked out with white dots. The other is a cup with a high-swung handle, a vertical rim and a swelling body coming sharply in to the base. This is decorated with a meander pattern again in white on black.[4]

The barbotine tradition has unfortunately not yet died out at Knossos and a number of vases are decorated with applied sprays of barley and moulded reliefs of crabs, shells, and barnacles.[5]

The few larnakes which have been found are undecorated. They differ from those of the previous periods by being rectangular with a square rim and two rows of handles.[6]

The second half of the period, M.M.IIIb, sees the dark-on-light decoration becoming more popular at the expense of the light-on-dark. Before the close of this phase, indeed, there occur several vases which might well be of L.M.I date were it not for the absence of the bright red paint and for a rougher, duller surface.

For dating purposes the undecorated cups are as usual the

[1] Ibid., II, 369.
[2] *Pachyammos*, Pl. XIV.
[3] Ibid., XX, XXI.
[4] *Mochlos*, Figs. 51 and 31.
[5] *P. of M.*, I, 415, 522.
[6] *Pachyammos*, Pl. XII, X, *a*, but the evidence of Trapeza may put them earlier.

most useful. The finer examples are shallower than in the previous period and have a low pedestal. They resemble squat goblets. The rougher examples flare slightly at the base and are distinguishable from those of L.M.1 by the rounded edge of the base.

Two deposits at Knossos provide a wealth of material for the domestic pottery : the Royal Magazines and the House of the Sacrificed Oxen.[1] In the former small jugs with a high neck, at the base of which is a collar, and projecting knobs, are common. There are three-legged pipkins with perforated conical covers. Double vases shaped like cups joined by strips of clay at the rim and the base are also provided with the same covers as are fire-boxes with a double interior, the inner skin being perforated. Most of these vases show traces of the poor purplish brown paint with which they had been covered. In the house the poverty of the pottery is shown by the number of hand-made jugs and pitchers. Some are covered with the dull wash already mentioned, though a few are decorated with bands of the same paint on the buff ground, and one has a number of large S scrolls, the ends splitting into sprays. The jugs and handled cups are identical with those of M.M.IIIa, but new shapes occur in the shallow bowls with curved bases, and in the straight-sided handleless cups with a flaring rim of the same type as those found joined together in the Royal Magazines. A number of unusual shapes was also found. The most curious are perhaps the round vases with a flat base and a ring at the top for suspension. The only opening is a large round hole in the side. Evans suggests that they may have been hung up for the swallows to nest in. They cannot be shelters, lanthorns, for lamps since the latter are always too big for them and there is no trace of burning. These lamps have a recurved rim and a projecting stick-handle.[2] Another interesting object was a low flat-topped tripod with a number of holes in the top as if to hold eggs, and yet another was a tubular object, open at one end with a slot at the other, which has been interpreted as a container for a ball or roll of thread or wool.

The Temple Repositories contained a great quantity of jars,

[1] *P. of M.*, I, 565 ; II, 305.
[2] In connexion with these lamps the pottery braziers from the Mavrospelio cemetery should be mentioned. The handle is the same but the rim is flat, except above the handle, where it curves up into a screen. *B.S.A.*, XXVIII, 251.

mostly low-spouted pitchers.[1]   The oval mouth is frequently
found.   One example of this shape has half the vase covered
with a dull lilac brown paint on which sprays of white grasses
are painted.   Another shows both light-on-dark and dark-on-
light technique, a big frieze of connected disks in brown being
bordered by running spirals in white on brown, with a clumsy
form of tortoiseshell decoration above and below.   A third
example has the very effective design in yellow and white on
brown shown in Fig. 27, 3.   Tall ewers with a small collared
neck and rather a narrow mouth are also found, frequently
decorated with broad false spirals in white.   The first, however,
shows a survival of polychromy and of the imitation of variegated stone, though much formalized.[2]

In a small magazine just south of the Domestic Quarter was
found a charming group of small jars (Pl. XXVI, 1, *a* and *c*,
and Fig. 27, 2).[3]   These had a dull lilac brown glaze ground
on which lilies were painted in white in a style which recalls
the frescoes.   With these was found a large full-bellied pot
with two small handles at the rim which was decorated on each
side with white spirals (Fig. 27, 5).   Cups also appeared with
a dull brown running spiral and with a rough tortoiseshell
pattern.   More interesting was a candlestick of a shape which
traces its origin to Egypt of the IVth Dynasty.   The under
surface of this was decorated with a chain of false spirals in
white.

Adjoining this magazine was a bathroom containing a very
graceful bath-tub with horizontal handles.   This is low at the
foot and curves up to the head with a notch on the rim half-way
along each side which looks like the position of a sponge rack.
The decoration consists of sprays of grass in dull brown or buff
arranged in panels bordered by a raised rim.

Behind the Magazine of the Lily Vases was another room
in which were found several jars of pithoid shape; like their
smaller relatives, they were provided with projecting spouts,
but since they were too large ever to be tilted when full the
spouts are not pierced right through and in some cases form a
mere knob.   The finest of these was decorated with the cross-
pattern seen in Fig. 27, 6 (Pl. XXVII, 1).

True pithoi are well represented at Knossos.[4]   In shape
they are elongated.   The handles are arranged in rows dividing
up the body of the vase.   The rope pattern with which they

[1] *P. of M.*, I, 556.   [2] Ibid., Pl. VII.
[3] Ibid., 576, 603.   [4] Ibid., II, 418 ; IV, 634.

are decorated differs from that of previous periods not only in being somewhat conventionalized but also in having the markings on the clay strips done with a tool and not by hand. A trickle pattern in dark paint is common and examples occur with bands of impressed circles and medallions surrounded by rope-work.

The true 'Medallion Pithoi' have been the subject of much dispute, for the dating of them contributes arguments to the controversy over the dating of the Tholos tombs at Mycenae. The arguments for assigning their first appearance to the transitional M.M.III–L.M.I Period immediately after the earthquake which destroyed Knossos towards the end of M.M.IIIb will be given later.

M.M.III Metalwork

The bronze weapons show a distinct advance on those of M.M.I. The great sword of Mallia must certainly be regarded as an exception at that date and we are justified in saying that the sword as such is first found in M.M.III. Well-stratified examples come from a deposit at Isopata and others from a votive pit in the cave at Arkalokhori.[1] These swords are of the rapier type, some of them as much as a metre long with a well-marked central rib. The shoulder is rounded and a short flat tang projects from it. The daggers are merely smaller versions of the swords and often lack the tang. A very fine example came from the M.M.III deposit in Tomb II at Mokhlos. It has a pronounced central rib accentuated by raised bands and a kind of triple axe design at the top. In Tomb XX was found a shorter, blunter example as well as three spearheads, the long split sockets of which are bound with a ring at the end. These latter are in shape like socketed daggers. The deposit in the North-West House at Knossos containing double axes of the M.M.I shape, flared chisels and thin adzes probably belongs to this date, together with a whetstone not unlike an early Egyptian stone palette in shape.[2] With these was a straight-sided, long-legged cauldron of bronze, and it is clear that the use of bronze for vessels was now common, for the 'Vapheio Cup' shape is not only found copied in clay but is illustrated by a very fine bronze example from Tomb XII at Mokhlos with a beaten design of ivy leaves.

M.M.III Stone Vases, &c.

The stone vases have a greater variety of shapes than in M.M.I and II and the miniature vase has died out. Many of the shapes are those of pottery, for the better class of which indeed they now provided a substitute. Spouts, handles, and some-

[1] *P. of M.*, IV, 845. *T.D.A.*, 3.   [2] *P. of M.*, II, 628.

times necks were made separately. A favourite material in
M.M.IIIa was brown limestone, in which was found a fine ewer
with a graceful high-swung handle and a plait-work decoration
on the body as well as a number of bridge-spouted jars, the
bodies of which were drilled with holes to receive inlays of
shell [1] (Pl. XXVII, 3). The 'blossom bowl' is becoming
more common, though it does not reach the height of its
popularity until the transitional M.M.III–L.M.I period. The
'bird's nest' bowls are still found but they are higher in the
shoulder.[2] These vases are made in steatite and marble. The
lamp on a pedestal begins at this period, two plain examples
being found stratified in the Palace at Knossos,[3] while the owner
of the House of the Fallen Blocks was evidently a manufacturer
of them, eight lamps being found in a single room. One shows
a curious stem swelling out five times. The decoration is
confined to a zigzag pattern round the rim.[4] The most
magnificent of all was found in the South-East House. It is
of purple gypsum and in the shape of a column. The capital
resembles that of the Egyptian papyrus columns, while the
shaft is decorated with spiral fluting divided by the ivy leaf
motive already mentioned as being found on a bronze cup from
Mokhlos.[5]

Libation tables of steatite were found in the Temple Repositories at Knossos and at Arvi, and inscribed examples at Palaikastro and the Diktaian Cave. The latter is the most elaborate,
consisting of a three-cupped table supported on four thin legs
resting on a base. From the base rises a kind of omphalos
which is attached to the underside of the table.[6] With these
must be taken the similarly inscribed limestone ladle from the
hill of Troullos near Arkhanais and one from the summit of
Juktas.[7] Breccia hammers were found near the Temple Repositories, at Agia Triadha and elsewhere. They are globular
with a projection back and front.[8]

Work in faience is now common. A group of inlays was *M.M.III*
found in a cist below the floor of the Long Gallery of Magazines *Faience*
at Knossos. They are mostly deep purple and of trefoil shape.
The border strips, however, were striped purple and green.
Some leaf-shaped examples have been covered with gold foil.[9]
The richest deposit, however, was found in the Eastern cist of
the Temple Repositories.[10] Here were small bowls with upright

[1] Ibid., I, 412. [2] *B.S.A.*, XXVIII, 251. [3] *P. of M.*, I, 390.
[4] Ibid., II, 297. [5] Ibid., I, 344. [6] Ibid., 625. [7] Ibid., 623.
[8] Ibid., 469. [9] Ibid., 451. [10] Ibid., 495 ff.

handles and cockleshells or figure-of-eight shields moulded round the rim.   A small jug is decorated with a band of running spirals in relief.   The colours vary from white through pale green to emerald and through pale blue to turquoise.   The designs were in dark brown, as in the case of the chalices, with sprays of leaves up the sides and a dark foot and lip (Pl. XXVIII, 1).   One of these chalices has a spray of rose-leaves in relief straying across the rim.   Flowers and fruit are reproduced in relief, as also flying fish, argonauts, and cockleshells, and other marine motives.   Exquisite panels in relief show a goat with her kids and a cow with her calf, which for their observation and sympathy have never been equalled (Pl. XXVIII, 3).   Votive robes and girdles are found, the former often elaborately decorated with a clump of saffron flowers. The central figures of this group were those of the Snake Goddess and her two votaries, the former nearly 35 cm. in height, the latter slightly smaller.   The Goddess wears a high tiara of purplish brown round which coils a snake.   Her black hair is cut in a fringe in front and falls back over her shoulders. Her face, arms and bare breasts are white, the features being added in black.   In her right hand she holds the head of a snake which coils over her shoulder.   The tail is held in her left hand. The tail of the snake which winds round the tiara descends and is entwined with another snake whose head is at her girdle and whose tail is beside her ear.   Her tight, short-sleeved bodice is laced in front below the breasts and is decorated with a spiral design in dark brown on yellow.   Her white bell skirt has been restored from that of one of her votaries, the upper half of whom had disappeared.   It has a pattern of brown lozenges at the bottom and lines round it.   Over it is a short apron which hangs down before and behind.   It is decorated with spots and a border of scrolls (Pl. XXVIII, 2).   The second votary is complete except for the head and left forearm.   Her arms are extended and she grasps a snake in each hand.   Her bodice is dark orange with brown bands.   Her skirt is flounced and decorated with pleats, which appear as a kind of panel pattern in brown on a pale ground.   Her apron has wide cross-hatchings.   Round her waist is a tight belt, perhaps of metal. Her flat cap surrounded by raised medallions was found separately, and a hole on the top corresponded exactly to a hole in the base of a miniature spotted cat or leopardess which thus appears to have been sitting on her head.

With this group, besides the steatite offering tables already

mentioned, was found a marble cross with arms of equal length
and quantities of seashells painted with brilliant colours.
Other fragments of faience mainly from the western cist included a large number of beads, globular, amygdaloid, and
segmented, and the remains of inlays for a gaming table.[1] Too
few of these latter were left to reconstruct the board, but
fortunately a magnificent example was found in a contemporary
deposit in the Corridor of the Draughtboard, the state of which
was sufficiently well preserved to admit of certainty in its
repair.

This magnificent object is nearly a metre in length by over   *M.M.*III
half a metre wide. The framework is of ivory probably laid   *Gaming Table*
on wood. The border consists of daisies in relief with a
central boss of rock crystal. In the two ' top ' corners are
a pair of argonauts in relief on a background of blue paste.
Next comes a group of four medallions set in crystal bars backed
with silver. The *cloisonné* work is again in ivory covered with
gold leaf and the interstices are again filled with crystal backed
by blue paste or silver. Below these a band of blue surrounds
the rest of the board and within this a band of ivory. The
central part of the board consists of six ribbed bars of crystal
backed with silver alternating with five of gold-plated ivory.
Below these is a group of ten simpler medallions surrounding
similar bars of crystal and ivory. Conical draughtsmen of ivory
were found in a somewhat earlier (M.M.III*a*) deposit near by,
and Evans suggests that the prism seals which show different
numbers of circles and dots on each side may have served for
dice.

In the House of the Sacrificed Oxen was found part of a   *M.M.*III
terra-cotta relief which must have stood originally nearly 30 cm.   *Figurines*
high. It represents the body and upper part of the legs of a
man bending slightly back from the waist as he strides forward.
Evidently he was bearing some heavy object. His buttocks
are covered with a short flap made in one with the typical codpiece. For the first time long locks of hair are shown on a
figurine.[2] Four reliefs in faience came to light by the South
Propylaeum. They represent women in flounced skirts holding
their breasts.[3] A small terra-cotta head, probably of this date,
was found in Tomb IV at Mokhlos. From the traces of white
paint it seems to be a woman. The face is very carefully
modelled and the hair is tucked away into a kind of turban.
The numerous bronze figurines it seems better to take as

[1] *P. of M.*, I, 470.   [2] Ibid., II, 753.   [3] Ibid., 702.

belonging to the transitional M.M.IIIb–L.M.1 Period next to be described, when Minoan sculpture reached its highest peak.

M.M.III Script

At the very beginning of M.M.IIIa the old hieroglyphic script was abandoned in favour of an advanced form of linear script in which only about a third of the signs can be traced to their hieroglyphic originals.[1] This script is always read from left to right and it further differs from contemporary writing in Egypt and elsewhere in that the animal and human forms never face the beginning of the inscription. The numerals have also changed. The vertical stroke is now universally employed for the unit. The dot is still used for ten in the earliest examples but is soon replaced by a short horizontal line. The hundreds are represented by circles, the thousands by circles with four short lines projecting, and the fractions by an L.

Graffiti in ink occur on the interior of cups and are incised on vases (Pl. XXVIII, 1). The most usual form of document was a nearly square tablet on which the signs were impressed. Clay roundels also are found which besides the inscription usually bear one or more seal impressions. Stone vases, ladles, and offering tables are also inscribed, and in some cases the same formulae occur on a number of similar objects such as libation tables. A clay figurine from Tylissos is inscribed on the back, and, in general, writing seems to have been a very widespread accomplishment, as can be seen from the graffiti on household pottery and on the walls at Agia Triadha. The use of ink rather implies that more perishable materials than clay were employed, leather or some form of papyrus, or according to Diodorus, palm leaves.

Fig. 28 shows a few of the characters with their hieroglyphic originals and their descendants in the Linear Class B of L.M.II. The script may be said to bear the same relation to its predecessor that hieratic does to hieroglyphic in Egypt, with the difference that it never became really cursive even in the most hastily written examples. A point of likeness to the Egyptian may be noticed in the number of compound signs, that is to say, combinations of two signs in one. The natural result of the introduction of a linear script is that it ceases to be used for decorative purposes on seal stones, only two examples being known. The gold ring from Mavrospelio, however, may well have been a signet of a religious nature for which the script seems to have been particularly adapted. It is unusual in that

[1] *P. of M.*, I, 612 ff.

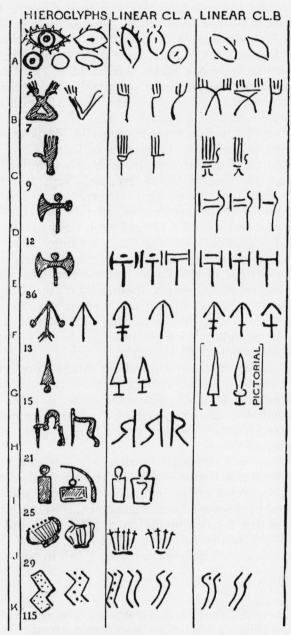

FIG. 28.—Middle Minoan III Linear Script

it reads spirally inwards from the rim to the centre like the Phaistos Disk to be described below. A number of the inscriptions from Mallia belong to this class ; the only point of difference from Knossos is the preference for the long label to the square tablet.[1] Only one tablet was found at Palaikastro ; it is of the Knossian shape. But a stone tablet of a similar shape and a bronze stylus now in the Fitzwilliam Museum are said to have been found in a tomb.[2]

In a cist at Phaistos, in company with M.M.III*b* vases and a square tablet incised with characters of linear Class A, was found a clay disk 16 cm. in diameter with an inscription running spirally from the rim to the centre, each separate character being impressed with a stamp.[3] Except for a few chance resemblances the characters have no relation with the Minoan script, the inscription seems to read from right to left and the human and animal figures face the beginning. The human figures are definitely un-Minoan ; the plumed head-dress is reminiscent of that of the Peoples of the Sea, who 400 years later are shown on Egyptian monuments ; the bow is an Asiatic bow ; the pagoda-like structure resembles later Lykian architecture, and we may safely assume an Anatolian origin for the disk even though nothing resembling it has as yet appeared in Asia Minor [4] (Pl. XXVIII, 4).

M.M.III
Seals

The seal stones attain an astonishing variety in material and design. The prism seal survives only in a very rounded form ; the flat-sided disk is rare. The most common types are the flattened cylinder, the amygdaloid, and the lentoid. The materials are carnelian, steatite, chalcedony, haematite, greenstone, agate, and onyx.

As has been said, the new linear script was unsuitable for the decoration of seal stones and on the whole the tendency is towards representations of natural objects and scenes. Architectural features are sometimes shown, conventional representations of the façades of buildings (Fig. 29*d*), but human and animal life is the favourite. Dolphins, skaros fish, and flying fish appear. A fisherman carries a fish in one hand and

[1] Chapoutier, *Ecritures Minoennes.*

[2] *B.S.A., Sup.,* 146.

[3] *Ausonia,* 1909, 255.

[4] Evans, *P. of M.,* I, 661, suggests that it is a hymn owing to the recurrence of certain groups of signs as if in a refrain. Macalister, *Proc. R.I. Acad.,* XXX, sect. C 342, compares the arrangements with that of a contract tablet with lists of witnesses. Of attempts made to translate it the less said the better.

an octopus in the other. Horned sheep, by themselves and in groups, are found, and a hunter lassos a wild ewe as she suckles her lamb. Recumbent oxen are shown sometimes with the head turned away. Scenes from the bull-ring are found for the first time, the performer turning a somersault over the back of the bull. In one case a huge bull has been grappled while drinking at a cistern. Hunter's gems are common, talismans perhaps for good fortune in the chase. The most beautiful and

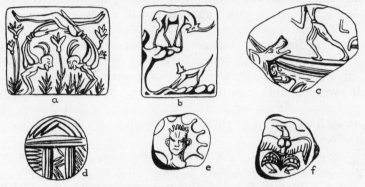

FIG. 29.—Middle Minoan III Seals

effective of these shows a pathetic picture of a wounded calf attempting to extract the arrow with his hoof. But so many and varied are the types that there is only space to give two more examples which are in their way masterpieces. A flat cylinder of bluish-white agate shows a rock ledge on which stands an ibex ready to defend himself against a hunting dog which barks below (Fig. 29b). A similar shape in blue chalcedony is engraved with two plumed tumblers throwing a long-arm balance. They are symmetrically arranged and the space between is filled with conventional flowers (Fig. 29a).

Besides the seals themselves, the clay impressions of them and apparently of signet rings of metal are frequently found. An example from Agia Triadha shows a battle scene recalling that on the gold ring from the Fourth Shaft Grave at Mycenae. Religious scenes appear. The goddess is offered a chalice in front of her shrine. Two female votaries in tall tiaras make an offering. Three great hoards of such sealings were found, in the Temple Repositories at Knossos, in House A at Zakros, and in the Room of the Seals at Agia Triadha, while a smaller group resembling the Zakros types but consisting of clay typical

of Vasilike came to light in the Harbour Town of Knossos.[1]
Many depict religious subjects and the figures are of great value
as showing varieties of costume. For women, besides the
flounced skirt, there is a shorter crinoline and a longer double
skirt. For men, besides the codpiece and the flap behind, there
is a short kilt and a pair of baggy breeches exactly like those of
the modern Cretan peasant.

The most interesting sealing from Knossos shows a man
on the deck of a boat desperately beating off the attack of a
dog-headed monster which appears out of the waves (Fig. 29c).

The Zakros hoard is remarkable for the fanciful nature of
many of the designs. Winged imps, goat-headed demons with
wings, bulls' heads with boars' tusks and animal heads growing
out of the horns. Bats and winged griffins appear, bird-
headed women and other nightmares (Fig. 29 e, f). Others are
less fantastic. Two lions are seen at a flying gallop over the
desert with a palm tree behind. A fortified city with tall towers
is shown.

The sealings from Agia Triadha, however, are of a much
simpler nature, the majority representing single animals. A
few show scenes of combat and one shows part of a chariot
drawn by two horses, the first representation of that animal
in Crete.[2]

A gold signet ring was found at Sphoungaras. The oval
bezel, in this case of crystal, is set at right angles to the hoop,
which consists of two rings. The gold ring from Mavrospelio
has already been mentioned. The bezel, nearly round in this
case, is made in one with the hoop, which is a simple plano-
convex band.

The beads have already been mentioned under the faience.

M.M.III
Foreign
Relations
The only Egyptian imports into Crete at this period are
the alabaster lid bearing the name of King Khyan, the Hyksos
Pharaoh, which was found in a M.M.IIIa deposit by the North
Lustral Area at Knossos, and the remains of three alabaster
vases, of a type which is common in Egypt during the Second
Intermediate Period, which were found in the isolated deposit
at Isopata.[3] With regard to the influence of late Middle
Kingdom designs it is rather hard to speak with certainty.

[1] *P. of M.*, I, 689 ff. *passim*. *J.H.S.*, XXII, 76, and *Annuario*,
VIII–IX, 1, 57. *Mon. Ant.*, XIII, 29, and *Annuario*, VIII–IX, 71.
P. of M., II, 254.
[2] *Annuario*, VIII–IX, Fig. 133.
[3] *P. of M.*, I, 419. *T.D.A.*, 3.

Several of the Zakros sealings and one from the Harbour Town
of Knossos have patterns which are eventually of Egyptian
origin. Whether, however, these designs were copied from
actual imports or whether they are descendants of similar
M.M.II designs, which were certainly derived direct from Egypt,
it is impossible to say. It is worth noting, however, that in
one case at least the M.M.III design is closer to the Egyptian
than that of M.M.II.[1]

The strong Egyptian influence shown in the design of the
lamp from the South-East House has already been noticed.
The beads from the Temple Repositories, particularly the
segmented variety, show distinct Egyptian affinities, but the
segmented ones bear a far greater resemblance to those of the
XVIIIth Dynasty than to earlier examples. The ' Notched
Plume ' found on the wings of a griffin in a fragment of the
Miniature Frescoes and on two votive arrows from the Temple
Repositories is found on the griffin on the axe blade from the
tomb of Queen Aah-hotep, mother of Aahmes, the first king of
the XVIIIth Dynasty, and the griffin, winged or wingless, is of
Egyptian origin, beginning apparently in the XIIth Dynasty.[2]
In which country the ' flying gallop ' originated one cannot
say. It was probably Crete. Examples of it have already been
described and it appears on the dagger hilt of Apepi I, the
Hyksos, and on the blade of Queen Aah-hotep's dagger.[3] The
vases combined with a ring-stand above mentioned are also
clearly connected with the pointed alabastra of Middle Kingdom Egypt.[4]

Direct connexions with Syria and Mesopotamia seem to have
ceased at this period.[5] No doubt this was the result of the
general disturbance of the Near East consequent on the irrup-
tion of the horsemen of Central Asia which resulted in the
' Aryan ' domination of the Kassites in Babylonia and the Hurri
in Mitanni, the wave of ' horse-breeding Minyans ' into Mainland Greece and the subsequent descent of the scum of Asia
on to Egypt in the shape of the Hyksos. Khyan may have been
an ' Embracer of Territories ' and his monuments may have
been found as far apart as Knossos and Baghdad, but though

[1] Ibid., I, Fig. 187, *f, o, p.*
[2] *P. of M.*, I, 548 ff., 709. In IV, 178, the term ' notched plume '
is altered to ' adder mark ' and derived from the markings on a snake's
sides.
[3] Ibid., I, 715 ff.   [4] Ibid., 417.
[5] Cf., however, the stone head, p. 121, above, which may have been
associated with the M.M.III rather than the M.M.I stratum.

we may grant him some temporary power outside Egypt, it is quite certain that during the rest of the period the Near East was in anarchy.

The sherds recently found by Woolley at Tell Atchana have been claimed as—if not Minoan—at least so nearly connected as to imply a branch of the Minoan stock resident in that part of Syria. The closest resemblances are said to be with M.M.iii, but it is noteworthy not only that a number of other sites, such as Nuzi and Tell Billah, have produced the same type of light-on-dark pottery, though the patterns are not Minoan, but also that on the present sherds the most Minoan part of the design is the rosette, which with its rounded petals has more connexion with M.M.iia, a date impossible for the present finds. At the same time the double axes and fleurs-de-lis are more reminiscent of L.M.i and the animal designs of L.M.iii, while the shapes of the vases bear no relationship to anything Minoan.[1]

The Anatolian connexions of the Phaistos Disk have already been mentioned.

Relations with the Aegean are intensified. At Korakou a certain amount of the light-on-dark pottery betrayed definitely Minoan associations.[2] At Tiryns two polychrome examples are very close to the Minoan.[3] At Mycenae some fragments of a gypsum relief representing a bull in the style of the painted relief at the North Entrance to Knossos were found. These were shipped to England by Lord Elgin with other antiquities from the site. It has been assumed that they were found in the entrance to the ' Treasury of Atreus ' and formed part of the decoration of the dromos. After going carefully over the evidence, I cannot see that this is proved, and while they are admirable evidence of close contact between the two regions they should not be used as proof of the early date of the tholos.[4]

Certain sherds from the Grave Circle are undoubtedly of M.M.iii fabric, two of them with sprays leaving a central disk at a tangent being apparently East Cretan.[5] In the opposite

[1] *J.H.S.*, 1936, 125 ff.   [2] *Korakou*, 32.
[3] *Tiryns*, Pl. XXVI, *d*, XXVII, *d*. ; Blegen, *Korakou*, 114, calls them Minoan, but the patterns, shapes and tone of the red paint disprove it. Light-on-dark and dark-on-light had already existed side by side in Early Helladic times. There is no reason why they should not appear together in the Middle Helladic Period without any Minoan influence.
[4] *P. of M.*, III, 192 ff.
[5] Ibid., I, 599. They are said to be from the Fourth Shaft Grave, but they are not claimed as such by Schlieman.

direction a fragment of Grey Minyan ware was found in a stratified deposit in the House of the Sacrificed Oxen.[1]

Phylakope in Melos was in close contact with Knossos. The Middle Cycladic culture seems to have been concentrated on this site and over twelve examples of the typical 'bird vase' of Middle Cycladic III were found in the Temple Repositories [2] (Pl. XXVII, 4). Other Middle Cycladic shapes, bowls with recurved rims and suspension handles, were found in the House of the Sacrificed Oxen.[3] But at Phylakope itself the 'Flying Fish Fresco' and the fragments of another fresco of the style of the 'Ladies in Blue' must be attributed, if not to an artist imported from Crete, indeed from Knossos itself, at least to one who had studied in the contemporary Minoan ateliers.

The positive chronology of M.M.III, then, is again fixed by Egypt. The beginning of the period must fall between 1800 and 1750, the end of M.M.IIIa must fall after Khyan's reign, say 1650, and the catastrophic earthquake probably comes about the beginning of the XVIIIth Dynasty, in 1580 B.C. *M.M.III Chronology*

SITES WHERE MIDDLE MINOAN III REMAINS HAVE BEEN FOUND

WEST CRETE
(a) Excavated Sites

APODHOULOU . . . House . . Contents (including inscribed vase found by the writer, 1933). Marinatos, *Arch. Anz.*, 1933, 297 ; 1935, 245.

(b) Surface Finds

GAVDHOS . . . . Sherds at Karavi. Levi, *Art and Archaeology*, 1927, 176 ff.

PATSOS. . . . . Sherds from cave at Khalara W. of village, found by writer, 1935.

PISTAGI . . . . Sherds at Palaiokapsou S. of village where a gold ring was found, seen by writer, 1935.

CENTRAL CRETE
(a) Excavated Sites

AMNISOS . . . . Settlement . Architectural and other remains. Marinatos, Πρακτικά, 1932, 76 ; 1933, 93.
Cave . . Sherds from Eileithyia cave. Ibid., 1929, 95.

---

[1] Ibid., II, 309.   [2] Ibid., I, 557 ff.   [3] Ibid., II, 309.

ANOPOLIS	. . . .	Burial . .	Pithos burial. Hazzidakis, 'Aρχ. Δελτ., III, 58.
ARKALOKHORI	. .	Settlement .	Vases from houses. Unpublished. Swords, &c., from the new cave. P. of M., IV, Supplementary Plate, LXVIII.
GAZE	. . . . .	Burial . .	Pithos burial. Hazzidakis, 'Aρχ. Δελτ., III, 60.
JUKTAS.	. . . .	Sanctuary .	Latest deposit of earlier sanctuary. Evans, P. of M., I, 157.
KASTELLOS TZERMI-ADHON		Settlement and Burials	Excavated, 1937, by the writer.
KNOSSOS	. . . .	Palace . .	New Era. P. of M., I, 315 ; II, 286, 547 ; III, 1, 397, 481.
		Town . .	Harbour town. Ibid., II, 229. Main town. Ibid., II, 296, 366, 391, 513. J.H.S., 1901, 80.
		Tombs . .	Temple tomb. Ibid., IV, 964. Isopata, T.D.A., 2. Mavrospelio, B.S.A., XXVIII, 234 ff. Pithos burials. P. of M., II, 554. J.H.S., LV, 168.
MALLIA	. . . .	Palace . .	Architectural and other details. Chapoutier, Mallia, I, II, 28. B.C.H., 1928, 377, 498 ; 1935, 303.
		Cemetery .	Burial in house. B.C.H., 1928, 502. By shore. Ibid., 1930, 521.
		Town . .	B.C.H., 1929, 527 ; 1931, 513 ; 1933, 296.
PSYKHRO	. . . .	Cave . .	Several sherds in the earliest deposit. B.S.A., VI, 101.
SPILIARIDHIA	. . .	Cave .	Earliest deposit. Xanthoudides, 'Eφ. 'Aρχ., 1907, 184, and B.C.H., 1922, 522.
TRAPEZA	. . . .	Cave . .	Latest Minoan sherds from excavations of 1936.
TYLISSOS	. . . .	Town and Palace .	Earliest elements in the main period. T.V.M., 79.

(b) Surface Finds

ANAGYROI	. . . .	Sherds from guard station on Minoan road. Evans, P. of M., II, 77.
ARKHANAIS	. . .	Inscribed ladle and vases from Troullos. Xanthoudides, 'Eφ. 'Aρχ., 1908, 108.

AVDHOU	Sherds from Strovili Hill to W. of village, found by writer, 1935.
DIA	Sherds from slope up to N. side of Island N. of Agia Pelagia bay, found by writer, 1935.
ELOUNTA	Vase from Kato Elounta seen by the writer, 1937.
GIOPHYRAKIA . . .	Sherds in cutting at the side of road, found by Miss Money-Coutts and Miss Eccles, 1934. *B.S.A.*, XXXIII, 91.
HERAKLEION . . .	Site at SW. corner of Candia. Evans, *P. of M.*, II, 231. Also E. of Trypete. Ibid., 229.
KALERGI MONASTERY .	Sherds and walls close to monastery, found by writer, 1934. *B.S.A.*, XXXIII, 81. Evans reports sherds of this period found by square vaulted tomb.
KANLI KASTELLI . .	Many sherds at Visala E. of the village. Evans, *P. of M.*, II, 71.
KARYDHAKI . . .	Sherds from fort S. of Knossos. Evans, *P. of M.*, II, 66.
KASTELLI PEDHIADHOS	Sherds at Petradhais to E. of village, found by writer, 1934. *B.S.A.*, XXXIII, 80.
MOUKHTARI . . .	Gem. Candia Museum, *Catalogue*, 609.
PETROKEPHALO . .	Burials and sherds seen by Miss Money-Coutts and Miss Eccles, 1934. *B.S.A.*, XXXIII, 91.
SKHINEAS	Sherds on Koprana, seen by the writer, 1937.
SKOTEINO	Sherds from the cave, seen by writer, 1933.
STAVROMENOS . .	Larnax and pithos fragments. Hazzidakis, *Ath. Mitt.*, 1913, 43.
TZERMIADHA . . .	Cup from the village, seen by the writer, 1937.
VATHEIA	Gem. Candia Museum, *Catalogue*, 972.
VATHYPETRO . . .	Walls and sherds at τῆς ᾿Αγίας ῎Αννας τὸ Φανάρι, seen by writer, 1934. *B.S.A.*, XXXIII, 82.

SOUTH CRETE

(a) Excavated Sites

AGIA TRIADHA. . .	Palace . .	Earliest remains. Halbherr, *Mon. Ant.*, XIII, 1. Levi, *Annuario*, VIII, 71. *Mem. Ist Lomb.*, XXI, 235. *Rend. Linc.*, 1903, 317; 1905, 315; 1907, 257.
GORTYNA	Deposit .	Stone vases, &c. Pace, *Annuario*, I, 372. Pernier, Ibid., VIII, 2.
KAMARAIS	Cave . .	A few vases. Dawkins, *B.S.A.*, XIX, 33.

STOU KOUSE . . . House . . Remains at τοῦ Βραχνοῦ ὁ Λάκκος. Marinatos, 'Αρχ. Δελτ., 1922–5, 53.

PHAISTOS . . . . Palace . . Later palace and contents. Halbherr, *Mon. Ant.*, XII, 7 ff. Pernier, Ibid., XIV, 313. *Rend. Linc.*, 1909, 297.

(b) Surface Finds

ALIKE . . . . . Sherds and traces of walls a little W. of Arvi, seen by writer, 1935.

AMIRA . . . . . Vase and stone objects from Χῶροι. Candia Museum, *Catalogue*, 1587–9.

ARVI . . . . . Sherds on hill called Komitas, seen by writer, 1935. Steatite libation table from Tartari. *P. of M.*, I, 630.

KASTELL BELVEDERE . Sherd from SW. slope just below summit, found by writer, 1936.

KERATOS . . . . Sherds in cave near summit, found by R. W. Hutchinson and Miss Money-Coutts, 1935.

KOMO . . . . . Sherds picked up by R. W. Hutchinson, 1937.

MEGALE VRYSIS . . Site described by Hazzidakis, 'Αρχ. Δελτ., II, 164.

SPHAKORIAKO . . . Sherds from guard station, seen by writer, 1935. *B.S.A.*, XXXIII, 89.

EAST CRETE.

(a) Excavated Sites

GOURNIA . . . . Deposits . Earliest elements in main period. *Gournia*, 44. *P. of M.*, I, 596, 611.

MOKHLOS . . . . Burials . . Inverted pithos burials. Seager, *Mochlos*, 37.

Settlement . Houses. Seager, *A.J.A.*, XIII, 274.

PAKHYAMMOS . . . Burials . . Pithos burials. Seager, *Pachyammos, passim.* At Khrysokamino to the E., traces of metal-working. Mosso, *Dawn of Mediterranean Civilization*, 289.

PALAIKASTRO . . . Town, &c. . Probable foundation of second settlement. *B.S.A.*, X, 202 ; XI, 273 ; *Sup.*, 18. Libation table from Plaka. *B.S.A.*, XII, 2.

PSEIRA . . . . Settlement . Rebuilding of town. Seager, *Pseira*, 10, 20.

SPHOUNGARAS . . Burials . . Pithos burials. Hall, *Sphoungaras*, 69.

ZAKROS . . . . Town . . Earliest Stratum in houses and pits. Hogarth, *B.S.A.*, VII, 121 ff. *J.H.S.*, 1902, 76 ; 1903, 248. Levi, *Annuario*, VIII, 157.

(b) Surface Finds

AMPELOS . . . . Carnelian gem seen by R. W. Hutchinson and others, 1936.

KALAMAFKA . . . Sherds on the NE. slope of the Kastellos, found by writer, 1935.

KALOKHORIO . . . Sherds near Kato Arniko to N. of village. Hawes, *Trans. Penn. Univ.*, III, 79.

MAKRYGIALOS . . Sherds on the beach, found by writer, 1934. *B.S.A.*, XXXIII, 100.

PHAZIPETRA . . . Guard station found by Evans. *Diary*, 1899. Sherds found by writer. *B.S.A.*, XXXIII, 94.

VRAKHASI . . . . Sherds from cutting of the road, seen by writer, 1935.

SPHAKA . . . . Sherds from the hill on the opposite side of the stream S. of the village, seen by R. W. Hutchinson, 1937.

Chapter IV

THE LATE MINOAN PERIOD

1. LATE MINOAN I (L.M.I)

(*See Map 10*)

LATE MINOAN II (L.M.II)

(*See Map 11*)

THE REAL break between the Middle and the Late Bronze Age exemplified by the earthquake at Knossos actually comes within the borders of what has always been called M.M.IIIb. No doubt if the original excavators had been gifted with prophetic knowledge of what they were going to find, they would have labelled the post-seismic M.M.IIIb pottery L.M.1a, and put the division between Middle and Late Minoan at that point. It would, however, be absurd to alter the terminology which has served for so many years, and in the following pages M.M.IIIb will still be used to describe the objects which fall within this short period with the concession to logic of expanding it to transitional M.M.IIIb–L.M.1a.

The earthquake at the end of M.M.IIIb seems to have acted as a spur, and a glance at the map shows the great increase in the number of settlements. L.M.I and II was the most flourishing period that Crete had known or was to know before Roman times. A number of sites, deserted after the final catastrophe at the end of L.M.I–II, were not reinhabited until the first century B.C. This catastrophe occurs at practically every site at the end of L.M.1b, but at Knossos at the end of L.M.II. L.M.II, in fact, was, like M.M.II, a true Palace style, though even more restricted in being confined to Knossos alone. That this is the case is proved by the occurrence of L.M.II vases of Knossian fabric in L.M.I deposits at Pseira, Palaikastro, Gournia, and elsewhere. This being the case, it seems best to take L.M.I and L.M.II together.

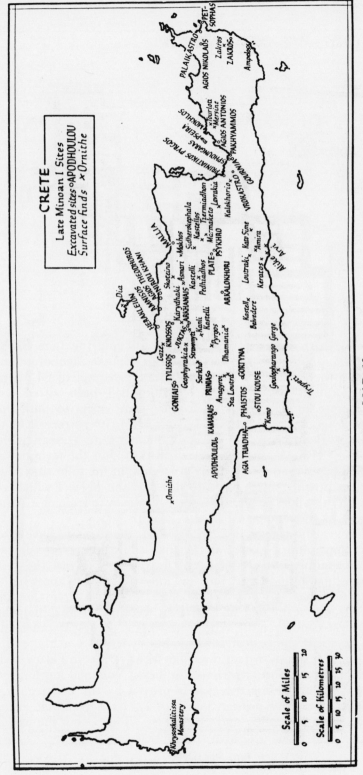

CRETE

Late Minoan I Sites
Excavated sites ○ APODHOULOU
Surface finds × Ornithe

Khrysoskalitissa
Monastery

× Ornithe

Dia

MALLIA
HERAKLEION
AGIOS THEODHORS
AGIOS NIKOLAOS INHANI
Sklavno
KNOSSOS
Amari × Mokhos
Gaza × Karydhaki
JUKTAS × Sidherokephala
TYLISSOS Kastelli × Kastellos
Geophyrakia × ARKHANAS ×Tzermiadhon
GONIAIS × Kanli Kastelli Lorakia ×
Sarkho × Pyrgos PLATE ○ Mac-maketa
KAMARAIS PIJINAS × PSYKHRO × Kalokhorio ×
Anagyroi Dhamania × ARKALOKHORI VROKASTRO ×
APODHOULOU Sea Loura PHAISTOS × Kastel × Loutraki × Kavo Sime GOURNIA
AGIA TRIADHA ○ STOU KOUSE Belvedere × × Amira PAKHYAMMOS
GORTYNA × Keratos
Komo ○ Goulopharango Gorge × Aloe × Alyi
× Tzyperi

PRINIATIKOS PYRGOS
PSEIRA × MOKHLOS
Tourloti
Mersine
AGIOS ANTONIOS
SPHOUNGARAS

PALAIKASTRO × × PET-
Zakros SOPHAS
ZAKROS
Ampelos ×

Scale of Miles
0   5   10   15   20

Scale of Kilometres
0 5 10 15 20 30

MAP 10

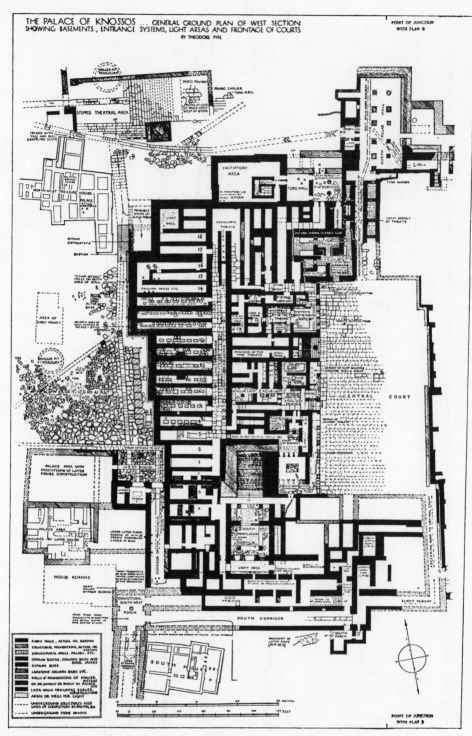

FIG. 30 (a)

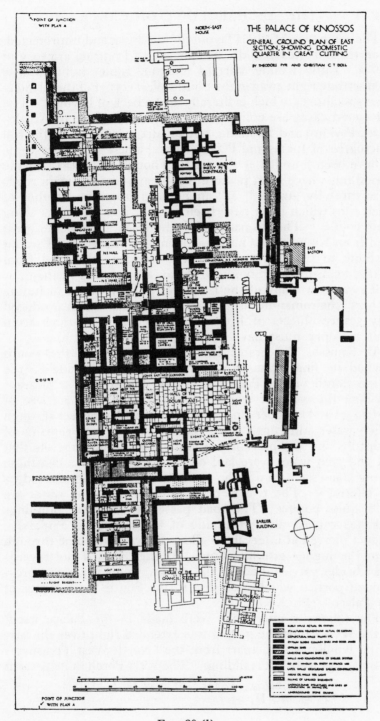

FIG. 30 (b)

The same type of site is favoured, low-lying and unprotected.
Even the hill sites of Sidherokephala and Loutraki are easy of
access.   Little fishing villages abound, some daring spirits
even settling right away in the South-West corner of the island at
Khrysoskalitissa, which is literally at the back of beyond.   The
old sacred caves are going out of use, except those of Arkalokhori, Psykhro and Skoteino, but repairs were done to the hill
sanctuaries of Juktas and Petsophas and a new sanctuary seems
to have been founded at Prinias.[1]   Though it is clear that the
period must have been peaceful in the extreme the main roads
were carefully guarded, as can be seen from the number of
small sites which must have been forts or police stations along
their course.   This is particularly noticeable along the great
road from Komo to the harbour town of Knossos, and I would
attribute to the same period the forts along the road from
Zakros to Ampelos, though no sherds were found in them, as
well as a great many of the buildings in East Crete, including
such as Kheiromandhrais and 'stas Tavernais, which produced
only scanty objects of Protogeometric date but which from
their masonry must have been built in Minoan times.

L.M.1
Architecture
At Knossos the grand entrance system from the South
reached its final form in L.M.1a.   On the far side of the
ravine South of the Palace is a little hostel with a pleasant
pavilion, the walls of which were decorated with a frieze of
partridges and hoopoes, and a bath for washing the feet through
which water still runs.   In a room close by were remains of
bath-tubs and the presence of carbonized wood suggests that
hot and cold water were laid on.   Just outside is a charming
spring chamber with a niche at the back for a lamp and ledges
for offerings.   The two steps leading down to the water are
worn quite hollow.   The road passed above these buildings
and was carried along the side of the ravine on a massive
viaduct pierced at intervals to allow the water to come through
from the higher ground above.   It then turned northwards
and a bridge carried it across the stream, where it joined a great
stepped portico which ascended to the South-West corner of
the Palace [2] (Pl. XXIX, 1).

The following alterations were made in the Palace itself.
In the West Court the paving was extended right over the surviving Kouloura and, apart from the ' North-West Treasury ',
no buildings were left standing.   The West Porch in its present

[1] But cf. below, p. 255.   It may be L.M.III.
[2] *P. of M.*, II, 93 f.

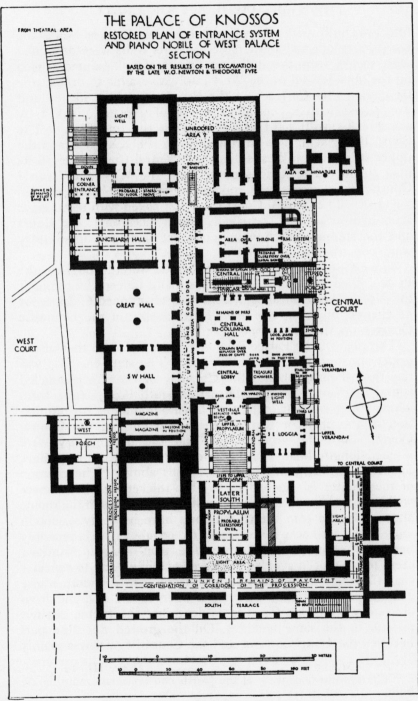

THE PALACE OF KNOSSOS
RESTORED PLAN OF ENTRANCE SYSTEM
AND PIANO NOBILE OF WEST PALACE
SECTION

BASED ON THE RESULTS OF THE EXCAVATION
BY THE LATE W.O. NEWTON & THEODORE FYFE

FIG. 31

form was built, with its low gypsum column base, as well as the reception-room and warders' lodge. Its walls were decorated with scenes from the bull-ring, and traces of painted stucco on the outside wall to the West imply a veranda to protect the frescoes. The Corridor of the Procession was widened and was paved with a central causeway of gypsum, flanked by schist slabs with hard red cement in the interstices. The South Propylaeum was narrowed down (Pl. XXIX, 2) and the upper story on the West side of the Central Court received its final shape. The façades on to both the West and Central Courts were extensively repaired, the latter being pushed forward. The Central Court itself was paved with rectangular slabs of limestone. The shrine which faces on to the Court and the stepped porch which gives access to the upper story were constructed.

The cists of the pre-earthquake period were, throughout the Palace, filled in.[1] The Lustral Basin and indeed the whole of the North-West entrance system was abandoned.[2] Little or no change, however, was made in the layout of the Domestic Quarter on the East slope.

The plan of the Palace is shown in Fig. 30 and that of the upper story on the West in Fig. 31. The state entrance was the West Porch, whence the Corridor of the Procession led round the South-West angle to the South Propylaeum, from which access was obtained to the ' piano nobile '. A continuation of the corridor turned North and entered the Central Court. Both the ground floor and the upper story were divided longitudinally by a corridor off which the magazines opened below and the main state halls above. The position of these latter is vouched for by the thickening of the lower walls to provide a firm base for walls and columns in the rooms above. In the plan shown windows have been given, but in view of the set-backs in the façade (p. 99, above), it is probably better to eliminate them from the plan—outside windows seem to have been avoided wherever possible—and to consider that sufficient light was obtained from the Corridor, whose cement paving implies that it was open to the sky, and from clerestory windows, for it is evident that the rooms did not all run to the same height.[3] On the ground floor the part between the Long Corridor and the Central Court was mainly

---

[1] *P. of M.*, 672 ff.   [2] Ibid., III, 12.
[3] The ground-floor walls at the North end are much more lightly built,

occupied by the pillared shrine, its façade being evidently of the type shown in the Miniature Frescoes, save that it seems to have had a single central column and two columns on either side at a lower level. It is clear that this group of rooms had always been of a sacred nature, for it embraces not only the two early pillar rooms but also the site of the Temple Repositories, above which two superficial cists were now sunk. The other important block is now occupied by the Throne Room System, built in L.M.II, and we have no means of knowing what preceded that.

The other main approach led up to and past the ' Theatral Area ' and went up into the Central Court via the North Entrance, which retained its previous form. The East Wing was entirely devoted to the Domestic Quarters and to the Craftsmen's area. The layout of the former is clear from the general plan. The first floor seems to have followed the lower almost line for line. A second floor lay on a level with the Central Court and marks on a landing block at this level show that the building rose at least one story above this. Reached by a flight of about twelve steps up from the Central Court was the great East Hall, which, there is evidence to believe, overlay the Corridor of the Bays, the Magazine of the Medallion Pithoi and the older basements East of this. It was fronted by three columns, supported on the piers of the Corridor of the Bays, and it is possible that there was a central ' impluvium ' in the South Cretan style.[1] The walls were decorated with high reliefs of wrestlers, and there was a frieze of winged griffins in similar painted stucco relief. Bronze locks of hair suggest the presence of a cult statue, probably a female figure of very large size.

From this wing of the Palace the only exit was by the East Bastion, remodelled and provided with an open conduit on the ' parabolic curve ' system whereby the rush of rainwater from the Palace roofs was automatically checked and led down through a series of settling tanks. An attractive suggestion has been made that the Palace laundry was here.[2] On the meadows below was no doubt the bull-ring, for they are the only place in the district suitable for an arena of any size.[3]

---

[1] *P. of M.*, III, 491. [2] Ibid., 233.

[3] Of course, a large ring on the Spanish pattern may not have been used. A narrow passage would mean that the bull charged direct. In this case perhaps even the Central Court could have been used with specially erected palisades.

The walls of the Palace are often of rubble faced with cut stone or stucco in place of the solid ashlar of the previous Palace. A most important feature of the architecture both of the restored Palace and of the contemporary houses is the use of tall slabs of gypsum for door jambs in place of wood on a gypsum base. This is practically universal and seems to imply a shortage of suitable wood. So also does the fact that the vertical posts, which tied in the masonry, are often omitted, while the horizontal beams are smaller. This has been taken to suggest further deforestation of the more accessible parts of the island at this period, whether due to the increase of population which cleared the old forests or to the widespread building and maritime activity.[1] The mason's marks on the stones are even more lightly scratched than in the previous period.

At the end of L.M.1a there seems to have been a slight earthquake which necessitated considerable repairs, though no structural alterations were made. A feature of these repairs was the plastering of whole walls to provide a larger surface for painted decoration.[2] Neither Agia Triadha nor Phaistos suffered much from the earthquake and their plans remain unchanged. Mallia also was unaffected.

L.M.11 Architecture

In L.M.11 at Knossos the most noteworthy structure is the Throne Room System, which was built in one of the oldest parts of the Palace, the rounded corner of the M.M.1a ' block-house ' still surviving.[3]

A short flight of steps leads down from the level of the Central Court to an antechamber, along the North and South walls of which ran gypsum benches broken in one place for the insertion of a wooden throne. A double door leads westwards to the Throne Room itself. The walls of this were decorated with the Griffin fresco to be described below, and the central part of the pavement was covered with red stucco. The southern section is taken up by a Lustral Basin to which steps descend. This has three columns in front of the balustrade. Facing it was the Throne. This was of gypsum, though it is a translation into stone of a wooden type. It is extremely well modelled and remarkably comfortable to sit in despite its

---

[1] *P. of M.*, II, 518, 565. This would merely mean that the Minoans would be sparing of wood owing to the expense of transport. It would not mean that supplies were completely cut off.

[2] Ibid., IV, 872 ff.

[3] Ibid., IV, 901 ff.

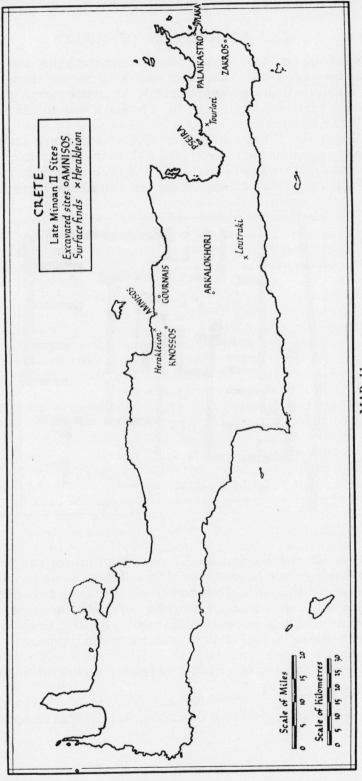

CRETE

Late Minoan II Sites
Excavated sites oAMNISOS
Surface finds ×Herakleion

PALAIKASTRO
PALAKA
ZAKROS o
PSEIRA
×Tourloti

Loutraki
×

ARKALOKHORI
o

GOURNAIS
o

AMNISOS

Herakleion×
KNOSSOS
o

Scale of Miles
0   5   10   15   20

Scale of Kilometres
0   5   10   15   20   30

MAP 11

formal appearance. Traces of plaster showed that the back had been decorated. On either side of the throne, though set a little apart, are gypsum benches. A small shrine with a raised altar slab opens off the Throne Room to the West (Pl. XXX, 1).

From the North-East corner of the anteroom a staircase leads up within the older curved wall to the upper story. It is possible that from here, as well as from a corridor to the North, access was obtained to the series of rooms which lie to

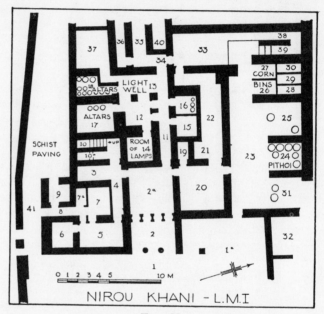

FIG. 32

the North and West of the Throne Room proper and which obviously belong to the system. One of these rooms was fitted out as a kitchen with a low plaster sideboard, a plaster mixing table and a stone seat. The whole group of rooms gives one the impression of a special suite to which the king might retire for a period of time during some particular ceremony.

As has already been said, the L.M.II Period is peculiar to Knossos, and the other sites, except for occasional imports, are unaffected by it.

The building at Nirou Khani seems to have been constructed immediately after the earthquake. It is an exceptional structure and the suggestion has been made that it was a storehouse for ritual objects, since four great double axes, obviously not for use, and over forty tripod altars of painted clay, were found.   Furthermore, on the South side of the East Court lay the remains of a large pair of sacred horns and the main corridor had a fresco of sacred knots.   As can be seen from the plan, the main room (2a) is entered direct from the court, which implies a public building of some kind.   Some of the partition walls of the lower story were of crude brick and much of the paving consisted of greenish-blue slate which was extensively used in the M.M.IIIb–L.M.Ia, transitional period.   Close by are traces of a mole running out into the sea.

We are fortunate in having two sites in East Crete where the whole town plan can be made out.   Gournia, one of the most fascinating sites in the world, covers a small hill close to the sea, (Pl. V, 4).   On the summit is the mansion of the Lord of the Manor facing on to a big public court and aping its betters in having a miniature ' Theatral Area '.   The rest of the houses are divided by paved streets.   One of these runs nearly all round the site rather more than half-way up and is connected with the lower ' Ringstrasse ' by stepped ascents.   The plans of the houses are difficult to determine for the walls as they stand are usually those of the basements which were entered from above.   Access to the main floor was obtained by short flights of steps which lead up from the street.   A small shrine containing an altar and cult images was approached by a well-worn alley.[1]   The arrangement of it is uncertain, but probably it had a ledge at the back.

Gournia must have been a town of farmers.   Pseira, on the other hand, was the home of sailors.   The town here covers the steep slopes on either side of a little harbour.   Whereas at Gournia the ordinary town houses were built of small stones, only the squire being able to boast cut masonry, at Pseira the masonry is all heavy, if sometimes roughly cut, and the floors are paved with large slabs of slate.   At neither site does brick seem to have been used.   The most usual plan seems to consist of a passage leading through a light-well to a reception-room, which in one case is provided with a lustration slab.   From here a flight of steps led up to what were no doubt the living-rooms.   The larger houses were terraced, apparently climbing

[1] Marinatos, in a forthcoming article, gives reasons for believing the contents to be L.M.III, but the shrine itself is almost certainly L.M.I.

the hill in tiers never more than two stories high [1] (Pl. XXX, 2).

At Palaikastro, a much bigger and more important site, a good deal of the town was cleared. The size of the houses was greater but the flat ground on which it was built deprives it of the charm given by the terracing of Pseira and Gournia. The finest example of a house is House B.[2] A flight of steps from the street led through a porter's lodge with a stone bench to a vestibule which in its turn led to an area containing four column bases. This has been regarded as a Megaron, but it is clear from the sunk rectangle enclosed by the columns that it is an impluvium in the South Cretan style. Adjoining this was a sunk lustral area or bathroom. Stairs led up to the second story, while to the South of the house is an open court with a veranda. A curious feature of the house on the opposite side of the street is the appearance of set-backs in the façade which in this case correspond to the rooms behind.

Although no large section of the town at Knossos has yet been cleared, enough important houses of this period have been excavated to give a good idea of their type. The most imposing of these is the ' Little Palace ' directly connected with the Theatral Area. A stately suite of reception-rooms including a peristyle, which was evidently universally adopted at this period, leads to the Great Hall, the two sections of which are lighted by the usual small colonnade and light-well. A lavatory, communicating with a drain without, opens off the North-West corner. From the South end of the Peristyle access was obtained to the great double flight of stairs which led to the upper story, and, from the North end, by means of a winding passage to a lustral area, the fluted columns on the balustrade of which have left their impression sharply cut on the clay and plaster of a later screen wall. The fluting is convex and the diameter seems to have been uniform. Across the whole southern section of the building a series of pillar crypts underlie the structures on the main floor, and Evans has brought parallels of chthonic worship to suggest that the Little Palace was an expiatory foundation after the terrible disaster which immediately preceded this period (Pl. XXXI, 1).

An equally magnificent building, though on a smaller scale, is the Royal Villa, the foundation of which probably dates from slightly later in L.M.1. This again was directly connected with the Palace by a road. The most interesting features

[1] *Pseira*, 14, House B.   [2] *B.S.A.*, VIII, 310 ; IX, 278.

of the house are the throne, set in a kind of apse behind a
balustrade at the back of the main hall and communicating by
means of a light-well with the room above, the staircase which
branches into two wings after the first landing, the gypsum
blocks, covered in some cases with red stucco, of which many
of the walls are built, and the pillar-crypt with gigantic roof
beams of cypress.

Of the better class of private houses the South House
(Fig. 33) offers the most complete example.   It is set in a cut-

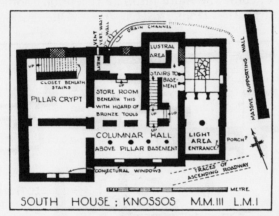

FIG. 33

ting just below the Palace and is entered either from the South-
East, through the usual light-well and reception-room, or
from the stepped Portico on a level with the first floor.   On
the ground floor is a pillar-crypt, in which the gypsum stand
for a double axe was found, and a sunk Lustral Area.   In
the basement is a series of cellars and store-rooms which could
be locked from either side by means of bronze pins passing
through holes in the reveals of the gypsum door jambs.

These important houses have a number of features in
common.[1]   They are entered, on the ground floor, through
a light-well.   Next comes a reception-room.   On the same
level is a pillar-crypt, except in the Little Palace where it is
in the basement, and a Lustral Area, except in the Royal Villa.
The more private quarters of the house are on the first floor,
and no doubt the bedrooms were on a still higher level.   We

[1] Many other good houses of the period were found close to the
Palace and *mutatis mutandis* have the same arrangements. *P. of M.*,
Index, 83.

must always remember that in ancient times, particularly in the East, the bedroom was comparatively unimportant. In the great Coptic and Arab houses of Cairo the master would sleep in whichever room he happened to be when he felt tired. The bedrooms therefore are small. The Knossian house on the whole resembles the Egyptian house of the Amarna Period in a vertical instead of a horizontal sense.

In the latter, after the chapel had been passed the first reception-rooms were entered. Behind these (instead of above as in Crete) come the more intimate reception-rooms, while at the back was the Domestic Quarter. One curious feature

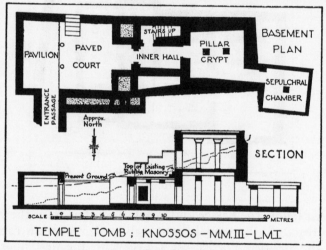

TEMPLE TOMB ; KNOSSOS —M.M.III—L.M.I

Fig. 34

remains to be mentioned. That is the absence of any regular kitchens, or servants' and slaves' quarters. One can imagine the meals being cooked over a brazier in some convenient room, but where were the bread ovens ?

The smaller houses of Knossos, such as the House of the Frescoes, show no regular planning. They consist, like the M.M.I houses of Vasilike, of a series of rectangular rooms, the use of which cannot be ascertained.

L.M.I Tombs

To the transitional M.M.IIIb–L.M.Ia Period must be put the great ' Temple-Tomb ' South of the Palace. This structure was approached from the side. The entrance led into a single-storied pavilion with two columns fronting on to an open, paved court. From the court a gateway, of which the lintel was found *in situ*, flanked by two heavy bastions, led into a passage, which in its turn opened into a pillar-crypt, the walls and piers freely incised with the double-axe sign. From the North-West corner of this the tomb chamber itself was entered, a square room lined with slabs of gypsum, three on each side, the central slabs holding the side ones in position and being themselves held up by great beams of wood which crossed a central gypsum pillar. The rough rock vault was painted a bright blue as if to imitate the sky. The body was presumably enclosed in a larnax of which all trace has disappeared (Pl. XXXI, 2).

From the passage leading to the pillar-crypt a door opens on to a flight of steps leading up parallel to it and emerging on to an open terrace above. A few stairs led up to the two-columned sanctuary chamber above the pillar-crypt. The whole is a remarkable illustration of the tomb of Minos in Sicily described by Diodoros as a concealed tomb beneath the earth and a temple to the goddess, Aphrodite, outside.[1]

Towards the end of L.M.1*a* an earthquake seems to have damaged the structure severely. The bastions on either side of the gate were partly shaken down and the pavilion was nearly razed to the ground. Stones from both these parts of the building were used to wall up the space in the pillar-crypt between the two pillars and the West and South walls. In the partitions thus formed were buried a large number of bodies, perhaps those of the victims of the earthquake. The passage through to the tomb chamber was, however, always kept open. Finally in L.M.II a hurried pit was dug for a final interment in the inner chamber.

The Royal tomb at Isopata must probably be put a little later in the period.[2] A long sloping dromos runs down from the surface of the ground. At the bottom is a built doorway the upper part of which is corbelled and was probably finished off with a flat lintel above on the same principle as the false doors or niches in the forehall which go back to the rock on either side. A similar door from the forehall leads into the main rectangular chamber. This had a lined burial cist in one corner and a niche at the back like those in the forehall. The whole may have had a keel vault, and if we take the height to be the same as its width, as is the case with the tholoi at

---

[1] *P. of M.*, IV, 960, 965.
[2] The finds were all L.M.II and later, but the mason's marks seem plainly L.M.I. Evans, *Man.*, 1937, No. 221, now puts it to M.M.IIIa.

Mycenae, we get the roof nearly 8 metres high.[1]   This implies
a great mound rising above the level of the ground.[2]   The
construction is rougher than that of the Temple Tomb, the
face of the stone being less well-dressed.   It may, however,
have been plastered.   This tomb continued in use in L.M.II,
to which period the main deposit belonged.

On a smaller scale is Tomb 1 in the same cemetery.   The
construction seems, from the scanty remains, very much the
same, the only points of difference are the absence of niches
except in the back wall and the lined burial cist which is
L-shaped.

Tomb 5 in this cemetery also was originally hollowed out in

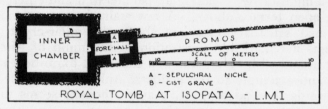

FIG. 35

L.M.I.   A chamber tomb was found West of the Palace [3] and
the Mavrospelio cemetery continued in use.

In South Crete at Agia Triadha square, lined tombs were
sunk in the earlier houses, while in the East the inverted pithos
burial was the most common.

*L.M.II
Tombs*

The majority of the tombs at Isopata and at least a third of
those at Zapher Papoura belong to L.M.II.   Three types of
grave are found, the ordinary chamber tomb, in which larnakes
may be used, shaft graves which descend some 2 or 3 metres
with a pit at the bottom covered with stone slabs, and ' pit
caves ' which are slightly deeper shafts with ledges at intervals
to facilitate descent, and a low, walled-up arch at the bottom
giving access to the tomb proper at one side.[4]

[1] Reference is made, *P. of M.*, IV, 776, to similar tombs in West
Crete.   The only one is at Malemo between Khania and the Diktynnaian promontory.   This has a square chamber with a round tholos
beginning about 1·50 metres up.   It is probably L.M.III like those at
Praisos, Plate, Mouliana, and Dhamania.   Of these the latter only
seems to have a vault similar to that at Isopata (see below, p. 242).

[2] If, however, it was finished off with a flat lintel like the niches or
had a lower barrel vault like some of the tombs at Ras Shamra, it
would hardly have projected at all.

[3] Ibid., 849.   [4] *P.T.K.*, 3.

The most interesting of the chamber tombs was the Tomb of the Double Axes, where the cist was dug in the shape of a double axe and the burial chamber was divided into two sections by a pier of rock projecting from the back wall and having a half-column cut on its face in relief.[1]

The frescoes and painted reliefs reach a very high standard of art. The House of the Frescoes produced some of the finest examples of the transitional M.M.iiib–L.M.ia style. These pictures represent scenes from nature and wild life. Monkeys, painted blue to represent the green monkey of West Africa, are seen mischievously plucking flowers amid clumps of vegetation and with the rocky landscape carefully shown. A blue bird, perhaps a roller, is shown rising from rocks which are covered with wild roses, lilies, irises, vetch, and other plants. Friezes of crocuses and myrtle are found, as well as a remarkable fragment depicting an artificial fountain. The preservation of these fragments is astonishing, the colours being in many cases, to use a hackneyed phrase which for once is true, nearly as bright as the day they were laid on.[2]

L.M.i Frescoes

The frieze of partridges and hoopoes which adorned the pavilion of the Caravanserai may also be attributed to this date, as may be the formal gardens with lilies, the outlines lightly incised, found at Amnisos.[3]

It is noteworthy that none of these show any signs of ' human interest ', and the same is true of the well-known frescoes of Agia Triadha which exclusively depict wild life. The cat sinuously stalking a pheasant and the roebuck leaping over rocks and flowers are instantaneously recorded impressions of nature which are unforgettable (Pl. XXXII, 2).[4]

Phaistos is devoid of frescoes, the walls of the later palace being covered with a plain wash, but the new buildings in the palace at Knossos are rich with decoration and human figures occur with great regularity.

To L.M.ia may be attributed the Palanquin Fresco which probably came from a small room opening off the continuation of the Corridor of the Procession.[5] This represents a figure in white robes seated on a kind of campstool in a carrying-chair borne by other white-robed figures. From the Queen's Megaron comes the upper part of a girl in a short jacket whose hair flies out as she dances.[6] The rather vulgar Shield Fresco

[1] *T.D.A.*, 33.   [2] *P. of M.*, II, 443.   [3] *Arch. Anz.*, 1933, 290.
[4] Shortly to be published in full by the Italian School.
[5] *P. of M.*, II, 770.   [6] Ibid., III, 369.

also belongs to L.M.1a.[1] This shows a row of figure-of-eight
shields, the dappled bull's hide represented by the same convention as that used in depicting the live bulls. The stitches
for the double thickness in the middle are shown and a hatched
stripe down the centre may either be intended for a metal
reinforcement or for the stiffer bristles along the spine of the
animal which are shown in the same way on the Taureador
Fresco.[2] The background is a bright orange and the shields
are shown hanging across a broad frieze of spirals with a central
rosette. Such spiral friezes are typical of the period.

The Taureador Frescoes, fallen from some apartment
above the ' School Room ' at Knossos, are in the nature of
panels, probably set above a dado at the height of about 2
metres.[3] Here we see both male and female acrobats performing somersaults over the backs of charging bulls. The female
figures are dressed exactly the same as the male, with the codpiece and short flap behind and the tight metal belt.

By the end of L.M.1a the painted reliefs seem to come to an
end. A ceiling pattern in this technique was found in the
area of the Miniature Frescoes, consisting of rosettes on a blue
field covered with linked spirals in white.[4] The ' Priest-King '
Relief is the only other example.[5] This relief is one of the
most successful figures made by the Minoans. The splendid
swing of the chest and the powerful muscles of the lean thighs
show the Minoan ideal of the human figure. He wears a
coronet of lilies with long peacock's plumes falling back.
His head, except for the ear, seems to have been painted flat
as were the flowing locks which come down over his chest.
Round his neck is a collar of lilies which one would like to
imagine were the insignia of some Minoan order of chivalry.
His costume is of the simplest. It is the same as that worn
by the athletes in the Taureador Fresco. Evidently, as in
Egypt, the king was depicted as wearing the simple primeval
garb long after in actual fact he had taken to wearing a much
more elaborate dress. He is walking in a paradise of fantastic
lilies and butterflies (Pl. XXXII, 1. The fragments of butterflies and flowers have not been inserted in this, the original).

[1] *P. of M.*, 304 ff.
[2] For the origin of this type of shield, see Murray, *Rise of the Greek
Epic*, 168, and Leaf, *Iliad*, I, 567.
[3] *P. of M.*, III, 209 ff.   [4] Ibid., 30.
[5] Ibid., II, 774 ff. In the index he is attributed both to L.M.1a
and *b*. The fact that he is in relief, however, is conclusive, though
he may still have been standing in the latter period.

To L.M.1*b* a good deal of fresco work can be attributed. Some of it is on a very large scale and it is typical of the period that the value of a whole wall as a basis for decoration was realized. The most impressive work of this period is the fresco which adorned the walls of the Corridor of the Procession, with which must be taken the famous Cupbearer from the South Propylaeum.[1] The Procession Fresco was probably in two rows, the lower of which alone survives, and of that only the bottom. It represented a procession of youths and maidens, the former apparently bearing vessels of precious metals, the latter perhaps musical instruments. At one point the procession is broken by a female figure in front of whom a group of four has turned round. She appears to be covered with a diaphanous veil which falls to her feet. Possibly she is a priestess or even the goddess herself. The Cupbearers of the South Propylaeum were certainly in two tiers and advance to meet the approaching procession, carrying great rhytons of silver, conventionally represented as blue (Pl. XXIX, 2). These figures provide excellent examples for reconstructing the actual formal costume of the time as opposed to the archaic ritual dress of the Priest King. The heads are bare and the long wavy hair falls back behind the ear, in contrast to the Priest King who has one lock falling in front of the ear on to the chest. Silver ear-rings, necklaces, bracelets, and anklets are shown. On the left wrist of the most complete figure is a lentoid gem of some banded stone set in silver. The broad metal belt which pinches the waist is of silver picked out in gold. A kilt is worn which descends at the back rather less than half-way to the knee, and falls in front to a point on a level with the knee from which depends a long network apparently of beads. The patterns on the kilts are very rich both in design and colour and betray the influence of tapestry weaving in their fondness for the quatrefoil motive which is also found in inlays. Of the female figures all that can be made out is that some of the skirts are flounced while some fall straight with an embroidered hem. The figure of the priestess or goddess has a distinctly architectural form of decoration with triglyphs and rosettes.

The background consists of conventional rock work which by now has degenerated into a series of contiguous wavy lines of various colours.

On a smaller scale and far more crudely executed is the

[1] Ibid., 719, 704.

'Campstool Fresco' from the North-West corner of the Palace.[1] This represents a number of figures, mostly youths, seated on campstools in pairs facing one another, each pair passing a two-handled goblet between them. The minx known as the 'Parisienne' is among them, the only female figure to have survived. The dress of the youths is most peculiar, consisting of long robes, reaching to the feet with flounces of alternate blue and yellow. Over the shoulders of some fall wing-like appendages. One figure has a red glove tucked into his belt, its fellow hanging on the cross-bar of the stool. The girl has a high bow, like a sacred knot at the back of her neck. It is noteworthy that no sign of the otherwise universal tight metal belt appears. There is an air of decadence about the whole work and a curious, unpleasant feeling of the inversion of the sexes which can only be paralleled in the art of Amarna, though there it is tempered by a delicacy and gentle melancholy which is quite absent from the present fresco.[2]

L.M.II
Frescoes

In L.M.II a considerable amount of redecoration was put in hand at Knossos, and a good many traces of the frescoes survive. A favourite device was a dado of imitation marbling, sometimes divided into panels.[3] Bull-sports were evidently still a favourite subject, though the small fragments that survive do not tell us whether they are treated in any new way.

The most complete example of fresco work was found in the Throne Room, where the recumbent griffins were still in some cases *in situ* on the walls [4] (Pl. XXX, 1). The background is red with a wavy white band at the bottom and another half-way up to indicate the rocks of a landscape. Stylized reeds ending in a papyrus flower grow from the base. The griffins themselves are remarkable in being wingless. The forepart is elaborately decorated with plumes and rosettes in green, red, and blue on the yellowish body-colour. The most interesting feature, however, is the cross-hatching to represent shading which is visible along the lower lines. This is the first appearance of any such attempt since the days of Altamira.

It is probable that the charming fragment, the 'Captain of the Blacks', which was found near the House of the Frescoes, belongs to L.M.II.[5] The background is blue and on it is

[1] *P. of M.*, IV, 384 ff.   [2] Pendlebury, *Tell el-Amarna*, 124 ff.
[3] *P. of M.*, IV, 893, 908.   [4] Ibid., 908.
[5] Ibid., II, 755. The evidence for the Sudanis is the knee of one figure on a blue background and the back of the head of another on a white background.

painted a smart Minoan officer in a yellow kilt and a horned
cap of skin, carrying two spears and leading a file of black
troops at the double.

Central and South Crete seem to have stepped comparatively
straight from the M.M.IIIb to the L.M.1a style of pottery.
East Crete, on the other hand, has a number of pieces which
can only be described as transitional. A good criterion seems
to be the use of white paint.   In this transitional period it is
used as a definite element in the decoration, as, for instance,
on a beautiful pedestalled bowl from Zakros, where the main
design consists of a band of star anemones in white on a dark
background, the rest of the vase being in dark on light.[1]   Later,
in true L.M.1a, white is used as a pure subsidiary to pick out
spirals or bands.   Several of the burial jars from the Pakhyammos Cemetery also belong to this transitional stage.
Pl. XXVII, 2a, shows a kind of ' double-axe plant ' with the
typical East Cretan tangential loops below.   Other examples
include a very fine jar with a school of dolphins.[2]   These and
other vases from Zakros, and Palaikastro, must have been
contemporary with the earliest phase of L.M.1a at Knossos
and elsewhere in the centre and South.

L.M.1a pottery is easily distinguishable from earlier fabrics
by its finer baking which produces a typical ' clink ' when a
sherd is dropped.   A fine yellow surface is produced either by
means of a slip or by polishing the body-clay of the vase.
White paint, as has been said, usually unfixed, tends to occupy
a less and less important position, and the invariable colour
scheme is in lustrous red-black paint on the yellow ground.
But at this early stage it is occasionally reinforced by bands of
a bright orange-red which is typical of early L.M.1a.

Of the unpainted pottery the most useful for dating purposes
is the small handleless cup which differs from that of M.M.III
by having the edge of the base sharp instead of rounded.   Of
cups with handles the ' Vapheio ' shape is the most common,
with a roll moulding round the middle and usually a spiral
decoration.   Others are lower and more rounded and are
generally adorned with sprays of leaves (cf. Fig. 36, 4 and 7).
These sprays are often in matt red, as are the similar sprays
which adorn the typical flower-pots.   These latter are of
varying shapes, some being like tall conical cups, some like
piriform amphoras with a wide mouth and no handle, some

[1] J.H.S., XXII, Pl. XII.
[2] Pachyammos, Pl. VI, IX, X, XVIII.

with a wide flaring lip and a comparatively narrow body and base. One from Palaikastro resembles a one-handled goblet with a thick stem. Like the flower-pots, however, it has a hole at the bottom.[1] Fruit-stands occur with a high pedestal and a bossed centre. A few examples of alabastra occur,

FIG. 36.—Patterns on Late Minoan Ia Pottery

imitating the baggy Egyptian shape and decorated with wavy lines to represent the veining of the original stone[2] (Pl. XXXIII, 1). Amphoras make their appearance and pedestalled bowls resembling the Zakros example already quoted are found. Cylindrical jars are decorated either with sprays of flowers or spirals. The false-spouted or stirrup

[1] P. of M., III, 277 ; IV, 364.
[2] e.g. also Gournia, Pl. VII, 15

vase makes its first appearance.[1] Jugs occur with high spouts
and usually rather a rough spiral decoration as well as with
the horizontal spout and a variety of patterns, one of which is
shown in Fig. 36, 11. Rhytons of all classes but particularly
the ovoid are becoming more popular. The ' peg-top ' class
tends to be decorated with linked spirals often enriched with
white dots. In the East of the island a greater variety of forms
appears. An example from Palaikastro is pear-shaped with
one handle at the back and another, like that of a basket, on
top formed by the horns of an ibex whose head projects from
in front.[2] Another from Pseira is in the form of a bull covered
with a net coat.[3] The peg-top type is often decorated with
red circles and dots imitating conglomerate. The long conical
rhyton in clay seems to have been introduced first in the East.
This usually has bands of running spirals or of connected
rosettes as in Fig. 36, 2.[4] The L.M.1 spiral is unmistakable,
for the outer ring is thick and the centre is a solid circle. Other
decorative patterns which make their first appearance are the
ivy leaf (Fig. 36, 6), which at this time usually, though not
always, has a single stem, and the lily (Fig. 36, 10), of which
so much use was to be made in L.M.II. The old tortoiseshell
ripple still survives. It is usually confined to the lowest
register, but examples occur where it forms the main element.[5]
The lines are much thinner and more neatly executed than
before, and sherds with this decoration are easy to distinguish.
An exceptional revival of polychromy was found at Knossos
in the cemetery at Isopata and in the Palace of Agia Triadha.
It appears on a series of large straight-sided goblets with two
double handles, like those of a pair of scissors. The vase is
actually covered with plaster and painted like a fresco. The
pattern is mainly a spiral design in blue on a Venetian red and
terra-cotta ground. In two cases from Isopata crested helmets
with ear-pieces and figure-of-eight shields are superimposed
(Pl. XXXIII, 2). Small hand-braziers also are found with
this decoration.[6]

Many of the larger vessels are highly decorated. A magnificent jar from Pseira has facing bulls' heads with double axes
between the horns and between each head (Pl. XXXIII, 3).

---

[1] *Gournia*, Pl. VII, 24.   [2] *P. of M.*, II, 537.   [3] *Pseira*, 22.
[4] e.g. *Gournia*, Pl. VII, 26, 31, 40. No doubt following the stone
and metal examples of the richer centres.
[5] e.g. *B.S.A., Sup.*, Figs. 13, 14.
[6] *P. of M.*, III, 311 f., and references.

In the background are sprays of olive leaves. Below are bands
of patterns among them that are shown in Fig. 36, 5.[1] Others
of similar shape are covered with linked spirals or have bands
of spirals, dark paint and leaves (Pl. XXXIII, 4).

Of pithoi the palaces of Knossos and Phaistos and the private
houses provide innumerable examples. And here we come
to a somewhat crucial question, that of the Medallion Pithoi.
A number of these were found *in situ* in the East Wing of the
Palace at Knossos. They stand on a gypsum floor below
which were found two earlier floors of plaster before the
' mosaiko ' floor, typical of M.M.iib, was reached. The pottery
in the three layers between the gypsum floor and the mosaiko
was uniformly M.M.iii except for a few M.M.ii sherds in
the lowest level. The original entrance to the Corridor of the
Bays, from which access was obtained to the present Magazine,
was blocked at the end of M.M.iiib. At all events vases typical
of that period were found *in situ* just within the blocking.[2]
Other examples of medallion pithoi were found in use in the
Sixth and Tenth Magazines along with L.M. examples as also in
the North-East House.[3] Thus it might be conceded that they
were originally M.M.iiib, though that would mean an extraordinary number of structural alterations in the floors of the
magazines for one period, and that a few had survived the
devastating earthquake towards the end of that period and
were re-used elsewhere. On the other hand, the shape is quite
unlike the elongated M.M.iiib shapes and corresponds exactly
to that of the painted jars just described. Furthermore, traces
of a possible doorway, communicating eventually with the
Corridor of the Draughtboard, are indicated by a great block
of gypsum resting on the foundations opposite which has been
cut as if to form an entrance and has holes in the side as if for
the attachment of jambs. Thus it is possible that only the
Corridor of the Bays fell into disuse while the Magazine of the
Medallion Pithoi remained open to serve the needs of the Great
East Hall above. At all events the pithoi, stylistically, seem
to approximate to the L.M.i type [4] and to have been in use
until the end of L.M.ii. They are between 5 feet and 5 feet

---

[1] *Pseira*, Pl. VII.   [2] *P. of M.*, I, 320 ff.
[3] Ibid., II, 415 ff. and 421, most of the pottery was L.M.ia, some
was of the transitional M.M.iiib–L.M.ia type.
[4] *P. of M.*, I, 562. Fragments of jars which may or may not have
survived the earthquake have the pattern of a broken M.M.iii gem
impressed on small rings.

9 inches high, with three rows of handles. Between each row are three bands decorated with small incised circles and between each handle a circular medallion with a raised border and a rosette in fugitive white painted on the bossed centre. With regard to the other pithoi it is hard to say which belong to L.M.1a and which are later, since no change in floor levels occurred in the Magazines at Knossos. We are probably justified in assigning to this period those which have plants moulded on them. The rope pattern has already degenerated into wavy bands, incised with slightly curved incisions, and ordinary bands surrounding the vessel. Occasionally small concentric circles are impressed round the rim, on the handles or on a band round the body.

The later phase of L.M.1 pottery, L.M.1b, though it is seldom distinguishable stratigraphically,[1] is easily distinguishable stylistically and from the fact that examples occur in Egypt in deposits of a later date than do those of L.H.1, a period corresponding in date to L.M.1a. Broadly speaking, the decoration of the pottery of L.M.1b, particularly in East Crete, is concerned with marine subjects as opposed to the vegetation of L.M.1a. The shapes vary little except for the introduction of that most beautiful shape of all—the ewer or oinochoe (Pl. XXXIV, 3). The pedestalled goblets have perhaps a trifle thinner pedestal, and the rhytons are more finely turned, but apart from very small points it is the decorative motives alone which need description.

The marine designs which are the hallmark of L.M.1b, embrace nearly every form of sea life. A globular stirrup vase from Gournia is painted with a really frightening octopus with glaring eyes (Pl. XXXIV, 1). The tentacles with their suckers wave all over the surface of the vase and one of them is gripping the neck. The spaces left are filled with bits of seaweed and coral. A less successful treatment of the same creature is found on a flask from Palaikastro and a vase on the borders of L.M.II from Knossos.[2] Argonauts with waving tentacles (cf. Fig. 37, 4) are found on the Marseilles oenochoe, a vase of the finest Knossian fabric probably found in Egypt,[3] and on many other examples (Pl. XL, 1). The conch shell (Fig. 37, 6) is a regular feature of decoration at Palaikastro and the rayed star with circles between the points (Fig. 37, 5) is also

[1] P. of M., IV, 291.
[2] Gournia, Pl. H., B S.A., Sup., 47. P. of M., IV, 280.
[3] Ibid., II, 508.

common at that site [1] (Pl. XXXIV, 2). Dolphins occur on a collared rhyton from Pseira, where they seem to be enclosed in the meshes of a net. [2] Always seaweed and coral provide a background, and the former is sometimes shown springing from

FIG. 37.—Patterns on Late Minoan 1b Pottery.

rocks which are shown as hollow trefoils and quatrefoils forming a decorative unit which was regularly used to fill in blank

[1] *B.S.A.*, *Sup.*, 50. Probably the example from Zakros, *J.H.S.*, 1902, Pl. XII, is an import from Palaikastro.

[2] *Pseira*, 29.

spaces. This type of decoration led to the custom which appears first in L.M.1*b* of leaving the design reserved while painting in the background. This technique appears rarely and always in a subordinate position [1] (cf. Fig. 37, 14, from the neck of a collared rhyton).

Plant designs are still common though somewhat more stylized than in L.M.1*a*. The ivy leaf tends to have a double or even treble stalk, and is conventionalized into the bands of the pattern of Fig. 37, 8, running round a rhyton from Palaikastro. The palm tree of Fig. 37, 3, on a rhyton from Pseira, is probably very late in the series and contemporary with L.M.II at Knossos.[2] Equally late must be the oenochoe from Palaikastro with the papyrus plant of Fig. 37, 1, since it also bears a rosette with distinct L.M.II affinities.[3] The lily motive is becoming formalized and will soon degenerate to a mere pattern. Pendent crocuses (Fig. 37, 9) are found at most sites and may be regarded as a typical pattern.[4]

Of pure patterns the ' adder mark ' or ' notched plume ' (Fig. 37, 10) is the commonest. It usually occurs on and below the rim of most shapes but on occasions it is found decorating the whole vase as on a goblet from Knossos.[5] The drop pendants of Fig. 37, 13, are usually used round the shoulders of jugs, but are also found as part of the design of the body (Pl. XXXIV, 3). The wavy frieze of Fig. 37, 11, occurs in various forms, the drops inside the loops being frequently replaced by dots. Fig. 37, 15, is also a neck design. Fig. 37, 12, occurs both as a frieze and as the main design of the whole vase.[6] Simple double axes occur on several fragments at Knossos, but the elaborate form shown in Fig. 37, 2, seems to be peculiar to the East, being found in four friezes round a curious basket-shaped vase from Pseira and hanging upside down on a rhyton from Palaikastro.[7]

The ' ogival canopy ' (Fig. 37, 7) is found on a spouted jug from Palaikastro, possibly an import, and a sherd from Knossos, but since these are the only case of its occurrence in Crete, and since it appears so regularly on the Mainland of Greece, it seems best to take it as a Mainland motive.[8]

[1] Ibid., 25. [2] Ibid., 25. [3] *B.S.A.*, *Sup.*, Pl. XVIII.
[4] e.g. Palaikastro, *B.S.A.*, *Sup.*, 53. Knossos and Tylissos, *P. of M.*, IV, 286–7.
[5] Ibid., IV, Fig. 145*a*.
[6] e.g. *B.S.A.*, *Sup.*, 51. [7] Ibid., Pl. XX. *Pseira*, 31.
[8] *P. of M.*, II, 489 f., Fig. 291*d*.; cf. *Archaeologia*, LXXXII, 153, where an origin for the pattern is suggested.

As has been said, the pithoi of L.M.1 as a whole are hard to separate. It is safe to say that the shapes of L.M.1*b* pithoi are identical with those of L.M.1*a*. A few examples from Agia Triadha and Phaistos which are comparatively well dated show the rope pattern in flat firmly incised bands instead of moulded.[1]

It will be noted that hitherto no mention has been made of the South. This is owing to the fact that its L.M.1*b* pottery is practically identical with the less-successful vases of Knossos and the centre. It would almost seem as if Knossos was so powerful that Phaistos and Agia Triadha were mere dependants, aping their masters, while in the East of Crete alone the seafarers of Palaikastro, Zakros, and Pseira kept a sturdy individuality of taste.

*L.M.*II
Pottery

L.M.II pottery is peculiar to Knossos. Imported examples have been found at Pseira, Palaikastro, and Gournia,[2] but it was clearly a Palace style, and as such no doubt overlaps L.M.1*b* even at Knossos. In essentials it is a formal, stylized type of decoration, a reversion from the increasing naturalism of L.M.1. Many of the vases show an almost architectonic scheme. It is the pottery of empire.

One frequently sees such terms as L.M.II*a* used, even since the general agreement to refer the bulk of the marine style to L.M.1*b*, but, for the present writer at least, it is impossible to distinguish any development in the decoration. Differences there naturally are, but there is no case where one can say that a particular L.M.II vase is later or earlier than another, with the possible exception of a few vases which, found in an otherwise pure L.M.II medium, show a degeneration towards L.M.III.[3]

A favourite shape is the amphora, usually with three vertical ribbed handles and a distinct narrowing to a moulded foot (Pl. XXXV, 1). On these the utmost resources of the painters' craft were lavished. The neck is dark sometimes with one or two wavy lines reserved. A very frequent decoration for the shoulder is a single or double row of drop pendants (Fig. 37, 13). These sometimes degenerate into the pattern shown in Fig. 38, 12, or are bordered by wavy lines as in 11. The adder mark or notched plume has been elaborated (Fig. 38, 10).

---

[1] *P. of M.*, IV, 639.
[2] *Pseira*, Fig. 11 ; *B.S.A.*, VIII, 313, &c., sherds in the Candia Museum.
[3] e.g. a few vases from the latest interment in the Temple Tomb.

The main design on these amphoras often consists of clumps
of formalized stately lilies of which the first three drawings in
Fig. 38 are examples.   Other forms of body decoration are
descended from L.M.1*b*.   Among these the octopus is most

Fig. 38.—Patterns on Late Minoan II Pottery from Knossos and Isopata

frequent.   It has become highly stylized and, in contrast to the
naturalism of the previous period, when the tentacles are always
shown crossing and re-crossing, they are now treated separately.   Dolphins also occur but very formally treated, for they
replace in one instance the drop pendant motive on the
shoulder.[1]   Architectonic motives are common.   Fig. 38, 7,

[1] *P. of M.*, IV, 304.

shows the triglyph and rosette and 9 obviously imitates the
spiral friezes on the palace walls.

The stirrup vase has developed more of a pedestal than it
had in L.M.i (Pl. XXXV, 3). The decoration, apart from
rosettes and drop pendants on the neck and shoulder, is uniform
all over the body of the vase, and usually consists of close wavy
lines or a scale pattern or network such as Fig. 38, 6. The
octopus is, however, still found, but again highly formalized,
though it still retains the rows of suckers on the tentacles.

A curious return to the tastes of the first Palace Style of
M.M.ii is shown in the preference for rosettes. Not only do
they occur as separate entities in the decoration of jugs, bottles,
goblets, and even pithoi, but they are introduced into every
possible motive as a secondary enrichment.

The jugs are lower and more rounded than those of L.M.i ;
they frequently have two handles or three. Their decoration
usually consists of one or more complete patterns repeated,
such as a rosette and a lily.

The two-handled goblets have a distinct pedestal like the
jugs and tend to have a single self-contained unit for decoration
(Pl. XXXV, 2).

The rest of the pottery contemporary with these few typical
shapes and patterns is indistinguishable from that of L.M.i,
except possibly for a somewhat cold, hard treatment of the
patterns which tend to be less carefully designed as if the whole
artistic talent of Knossos was exclusively employed on the
decoration of the splendid but, it must be admitted, sometimes
rather vulgar amphoras.

The pithoi, however, develop a number of new features which
are useful for dating purposes. All attempt at representing
rope is abandoned. Raised bands run round the body at
intervals with wavy bands between them. Almost every
variety of incision was employed, the herring-bone being the
most common. Impressed circles were also used. Even the
" adder mark " is found.[1] Two examples are worthy of a
more detailed description, since they show the most florid
Palace style enlarged to far too big a scale. The first was
found in the Royal Villa [2] (Pl. XXXV, 4). The decoration
consists of clumps of papyrus in relief with painted wavy lines
between them, perhaps representing water after the Egyptian
convention. Between the flowers above are raised medallions,
on one side impressed with stars, on the other having a white

[1] *P. of M.*, IV, 643 ff.   [2] Ibid., II, 400 ; IV, 329.

rosette in the centre much resembling the Medallion Pithoi described above. The other example was found in the North-West Quarter of the Palace.[1] It was painted with fringed reeds, like those in the Griffin Fresco, from which rise elaborate double axes with reduplicated blades.[2] In the background are rosettes.

Baths and larnakes are both of oval shape with a flat projecting rim. The best example of the former came from the bathroom of the Queen's Megaron.[3] Its interior was painted with sprays of grass reminiscent of the M.M.iii bath described above. Outside, the central band consisted of a stylized papyrus pattern running horizontally. The most complete larnax was found at Zapher Papoura.[4] It had a horizontal handle at each side and at each end, the ' adder-mark ' decorates the rim and two very conventional papyrus heads joined at the base diverge to the top corners of each side.

An exceptional group of pottery from near the North-West Treasury, which from its nature can hardly be called typical of the period, was found in an earlier pithos which had been paved round and was certainly in use in L.M.ii. This consisted of a complete set of vases for use in the worship of the domestic snake. Tubular vessels with cups projecting from the side seem to have provided a home for the creatures. They resemble earlier water pipes, and a very good case has been made out that this was their origin. Many bowls and small, handleless jugs were found, as well as a brazier with three double legs. But the most interesting objects were a low tripod table, with a ring for a vase in the centre and four grooves leading up to it from the edge, which has been wittily described and figured by Evans as a table for a *parti carré* of snakes, a pierced vessel in the shape of a honeycomb with a snake crawling round it and two miniature jugs, similarly pierced, with snakes crawling up them.[5]

The M.M.iii type of sword with a round shoulder and a short tang seems to have survived into L.M.i*a*, but, on the evidence of a bead seal, the horned sword, which is universal later, is coming in, and by L.M.i*b* it is well established.[6] This form is caused by the flanges of the tang and shoulder being projected upwards. In L.M.ii the horns so formed were drawn out more horizontally, resulting in a cruciform

L.M.i and ii Metalwork

---

[1] Ibid., IV, 342.   [2] Cf. a simpler example in Fig. 37, 2.
[3] *P. of M.*, III, 385.   [4] Ibid., IV, 329.
[5] Ibid., IV, 138 ff.   [6] Ibid., 849.

shape. In all cases the medial rib is well marked and in some cases engraved with a spiraliform design. Pommels of ivory and onyx are found, the actual grip being either of gold richly chased or of some material such as wood or ivory which has since perished. Daggers follow the same pattern, though an L.M.1a example from Gournia is of a type which is nearly cruciform and an isolated blade from Zapher Papoura which is probably of L.M.II date is leaf-shaped.[1] In East Crete a flat knife with a rounded end lasts from M.M.IIIb to L.M.II.[2] The spear-heads have a ringed socket and a sharply marked medial rib[3] (Pl. XXXVI, 1).

Many domestic tools were found in a deposit in the South House and in a house near by. These included axes and adzes of the normal shape and fine-toothed saws, one huge specimen of the latter being over 1·60 m. long. Cauldrons with three thin legs and two horizontal handles are common. A hoard of gigantic legless specimens came from Tylissos. Many basins with a small vertical ring handle are known. The finest examples were found in the North-West Treasure House, where the rims and handles were elaborately embossed with tufted lilies, ivy leaves or drop pendants. Ewers are also a common shape and often supply the prototypes of clay vases. They have the peculiar feature of a horizontal handle low down at the back. Lamps and ladles, cups and goblets are all found.[4] Curiously enough, very little development is visible during L.M.I and L.M.II (Pl. XXXVI, 2).

In the Arkalokhori cave were found a number of votive bronze axes engraved with various designs, one of them inscribed, and a few of gold and silver. The usual decoration consists of more or less elaborate bands running transversely across the blade between similarly engraved borders. One gold specimen, however, was covered with a pattern of drop pendants, while two of the bronze ones show scroll patterns[5] (Pl. XXXVI, 3).

Of copper were the ingots which occur at Agia Triadha, Tylissos, Mokhlos, and Knossos. These have incurving edges ; one side is flat, on the other the edges curve in, very much like an ox-hide.[6] They were clearly currency, for the weight is practically uniform, averaging just over 29 kilograms, and it is possible that they are the equivalent of the Homeric

---

[1] P of M., IV, 845 ff.   [2] B.S.A., Sup., 116. Mochlos, 107.
[3] P. of M., IV, 356.   [4] Ibid., II, 629 ff.
[5] Ibid., IV, 346.   [6] Seltman, Athens : Its History and its Coinage, 4.

talent—the price of an ox. A weight in purple gypsum carved in relief with an octopus of L.M.II style on each side weighs exactly 29 kilograms. Other contemporary weights are in the form of disks of stone engraved with numerals.[1]

The stone vases of L.M.I–II display a vitality which had not been seen since E.M. times. Most important is the conical rhyton shape which certainly precedes the examples in pottery. It is a natural shape for stone or metal but exceedingly difficult to turn in clay.

L.M.I and II Stone Vases, &c.

Earliest of all perhaps should be put the steatite vases from Agia Triadha.[2] The Boxer Vase at all events shows a marked likeness to the Miniature Frescoes and cannot be much later in date (Pl. XXXVII, 1). This is a conical rhyton divided into four zones, three of which show boxers in low relief, while the fourth has a spirited scene from the bull-ring. The boxers are splendidly rendered, the muscular development being just sufficiently over-emphasized to give an impression of brute strength as they knock their opponents flying. Interesting features of their costume are the leggings like puttees, traces apparently of a *cestus* worn on the hand and wrist, and the heavy helmet with cheek-pieces worn by the combatants on the lowest zone but one. A fragment of a similar vase from the North-East of the Palace at Knossos is shown in Pl. XXXVII, 4.[3] The Harvester vase is a peg-top rhyton (Pl. XXXVII, 3) and shows a rout of peasants in headcloths like those worn to-day. They have their winnowing fans over their shoulders and are bawling a song at the tops of their voices.[4] One party is led by a thick-set man in a skull-cap, rattling a sistrum, who looks remarkably like an Egyptian priest, the other by a rather cynical-looking old man who carries a rod over his shoulder and wears a quilted coat. The atmosphere of riotous inebriety is enhanced by the figure of a man who, blind drunk, has tripped and fallen on to the heels of the man in front, who turns round and roars a jest at him. For sheer spirit no other

---

[1] Ibid., 650 ff., for standards cf. *Corolla Numismatica*, 1906, 342 ff.
[2] *Mon. Ant.*, XIII, 80. *Mem. Ist Lomb.*, XX, Pl. II.
[3] *P. of M.*, I, 689.
[4] May it have been the Minoan equivalent of the Modern *matinadha* :

Οὖλα ἀπὸ τσὴ παραβολὴν μὲ βάνεις καὶ θερίζω,
Δέρνει μέ ὁ ἥλιος καὶ ὁ ἄνεμος καὶ πῶς δὲν θὰ μαυρίσω ;

You set me to reap all the stony parts,
The sun and the wind flay me. How can I avoid going black ?

vase approaches this rhyton and the mere technical skill in portraying in low relief groups four abreast is magnificent.

Part of a rhyton of this shape was found at Knossos and shows an octopus lurking among the rocks with one watchful eye visible [1] (Pl. XXXVII, 4).

From Agia Triadha comes a handleless cup showing a young prince giving orders to a subordinate officer and a file of men (Pl. XXXVII, 2). The contrast between the proud bearing of the Prince and the deferential attitude of the officer is admirably brought out.[2] From the same site comes a dolium-shell cut out of liparite.[3]

To the same transitional M.M.iiib–L.M.ia stage must be attributed the other two fragments found at Knossos shown in Pl. XXXVII, 4. One represents a procession of young men carrying bowls at arms' length. Behind them seems to rise a staircase. The other shows an archer disembarking from a boat reminiscent of the silver ' Siege Rhyton ' from Mycenae.[4]

Most of these vases have a counterpart in metal and, since an example from Palaikastro was found with gold leaf adhering to it, we have reason to believe that they were substitutes for vases in more precious materials.[5]

The bull's head rhyton from the Little Palace is probably of L.M.i date.[6] It is of steatite with, originally, gilded wooden horns. An inlay of white shell curves round the nostrils. The eyes are of rock crystal, the lower surface of which is painted to represent the pupil and iris. They are set in a rim of red jasper and the fierce bloodshot effect is quite startling. An alabaster rhyton, probably of L.M.ib date, in the shape of a lion's head, was found in the Central Treasury.[7]

Of other vases (Pl. XXXVIII, 1) the Vapheio cup shape was found in veined stone, in an L.M.ia deposit, and a variety of rhytons, some collared and fluted, some of an elongated pear shape, come from the Central Treasury, where was also a triton shell in hard white limestone. These latter vases can be attributed to L.M.ib, and the globular vessel with two high-swung handles in variegated stone which is carried by one of the figures in the Procession Fresco must also have been in use at this date. The ' blossom ' bowls are higher in the shoulder than in the previous period. The ' bird's nest ' vases which

[1] *P. of M.*, II, 227, 502.   [2] *Rend. Linc.*, XII, 324.
[3] *Orig. Civ. Med.*, 287.   [4] *P. of M.*, II, 752 ; III, 100.
[5] Ibid., I, 676. *B.S.A., Sup.*, 137.
[6] *P. of M.*, II, 527.   [7] Ibid., 822 ff.

persist in the East have the same characteristic. A considerable number of vases of varying shapes was found in a house
at Palaikastro with pottery of a date contemporary with
Knossian L.M.II.[1] This hoard provides an excellent example
of the dangers of dating by stone vases, for many of them are
obviously family heirlooms or chance finds from older graves
in the fields. Among the types, however, which are almost
certainly of L.M.I date, are bowls with a beaded edge and two
tilted horizontal handles also beaded, and the pear-shaped
rhyton, a magnificent example of which in breccia was found
at Pseira.[2]

The latest vases of all are from Knossos. A large alabaster
amphora decorated with running spirals on the rim and coils
in relief on the shoulder was lying unfinished where the sculptor
had left it when he fled from the final catastrophe.[3] Squat
alabastra were actually in use in the Throne Room at that
moment.[4] The lids, carved with a rosette and a figure-of-
eight shield for a central handle, are obviously contemporary
with the alabaster vase and lid from the last interment in the
Temple Tomb.[5]

Lamps are found with and without pedestals. A favourite
decoration for the rim is the drop pendant so common on
pottery. Pedestals are found either plain with a moulding
half-way up or with four stems opening out into a formal
flower.[6] At Pseira a particularly beautiful example resembles
a blossom bowl opened out almost flat [7] (Pl. XXXVIII, 2 and 3).

Faience is, of course, a very perishable material, but it is
surprising how little has been found belonging to L.M.I and II.
There are a few inlays from the Throne Room at Knossos and
from Phaistos which are interesting in that they are inscribed
with signs on the back.[8] The Knossian examples are purple
roundels with a central cross in pale green, those from Phaistos
fit together into a scale pattern and are blue with a light green
border. But apart from the mouth of a collared rhyton the
only vessel of faience is a spouted teapot with three handles and
a pedestal in bluish green picked out with lilac.[9]

L.M.I and II Faience

The great age of Minoan sculpture was undoubtedly the
transitional M.M.IIIb–L.M.Ia Period. To this period may be
put with all probability the masterpieces of Knossos, Tylissos,

L.M.I and II Figurines

---

[1] *B.S.A., Sup.,* 133 ff.   [2] *Pseira,* 37.   [3] *P. of M.,* IV, 896.
[4] Ibid., 938.   [5] Ibid., 1006.   [6] Ibid., II, 404, 523.   [7] *Pseira,* 38.
[8] *P. of M.,* IV, 941.   *Mon. Ant.,* XII, 92.   A similar practice is
common at Tell el-Amarna.   [9] *P. of M.,* II, 824.

and elsewhere. Unfortunately the stratigraphic evidence is slight. In most cases all one can say is that these figures are post-earthquake and from their vitality ought to be put in the same class as the Agia Triadha Vases. It may be noticed that such figures as the Fitzwilliam Goddess—the Toronto figure— or even the Boston Goddess are not included. This is not owing to any peculiar incredulity : indeed, I believe in the first and the last, which are second only to the ivory leaper described below ; but since a suspicion has been cast on them, it seems better to omit them and concentrate on those actually found in excavations or at least in circumstances which guarantee their genuineness. They fall into three classes ; female figures who may be goddesses, male votaries, and athletic figures. Clay, bronze, stone, and ivory are the materials used. The clay and the bronze may really be taken together since the latter were obviously originally moulded in clay or wax ; nor are they engraved after casting. The stone and ivory figures are made in several pieces, an obvious derivation from clay.

Very primitive examples in clay of the first class were found in the shrines of Prinias and Gournia, and from a house at Agia Triadha. They are shown with raised arms, almost featureless faces, breasts roughly indicated and a cylindrical skirt.[1] In one case from Gournia a snake is twined round the neck, and it is significant that in the same shrine were found pipes of the type described above but with snakes shown coiling round them.

The votaries are usually in bronze. They have the right hand raised to the brow. The men are dressed in the ordinary codpiece and short back flap, though on an example from the Diktaian Cave at Psykhro and another in the British Museum there is a long apron in front. In the latter case as in one from Tylissos an elderly man is shown who has given up the tight belt in favour of a free-spreading paunch. An interesting figure supposed to be from near Phaistos and now in Leiden shows both forearms raised in front of the chest and a *petasos* on the head.[2] Another figure, from the Harbour Town of Knossos, has his hands clasped in front of him away from his chest and a tall conical hat.[3] They range in size from 25 cm. to 10 (Plate XXXIX, 2).

---

[1] *P. of M.*, IV, 160. *Gournia*, 47. These, however, are attributed to L.M.III by Marinatos, see below.

[2] *Jahrbuch*, XXX, 65 ff. *P. of M.*, III, 461.   [3] *Ibid.*, II, 235.

Two examples will suffice to show the extraordinary skill and dash displayed by the artists in their representations of athletes. The first is the group in the Churchill collection of a man turning a somersault over a bull.[1] It is an extraordinary achievement, since the human figure has to be supported in some way and yet at the same time to give the impression of flying in mid-air. The effect has been realized by allowing the flowing locks of the acrobat to fall between the bull's horns and by curving the body so that the feet rest on the bull's back. For some reason the arms are cut short just above the elbow, and the stumps are in a position actually impossible during the course of the feat portrayed. Strictly speaking, they should be nearly vertically upwards. Clearly the athlete has not grasped the horns or his head could not conceivably be so far back, and for a clean somersault his hands must come over in time with his head. Evidently some technical difficulty arose and the artist tried to camouflage the arms, in which he has been most successful.

The second example is the most complete figure from the Ivory Deposit at Knossos [2] (Pl. XXXIX, 1). This ivory carving, 30 cm. in height, together with the other fragments from the same deposit, reaches the highest and most exquisite level of miniature sculpture attained in the ancient world, even including Egypt. The play of the muscles and the very veins are shown in such a way as not to give the effect of laborious detail but merely to heighten the impression of nervous energy. In contrast to the Boxer Vase from Agia Triadha it is the length of limb which is here emphasized in place of muscular development. They say that Lysippos was the first to realize that the head of a man in the pink of condition looks smaller in comparison with his body, but it is quite clear that the Minoan artist had got the same impression, for the head goes no less than nine times into the body. The figure, too, gives one the ideal of athletic development—the muscles are long and stringy, and obviously work quickly, the litheness of movement is quite different from the laboured attitudes of the professional Greek athlete. The figure is that

---

[1] *J.H.S.*, 1921, 247. The photograph in Fig. 2 is vastly preferable to the drawing, *P. of M.*, II, Fig. 416. Mr. C. H. Hawes tells me that he was shown this figure in 1905 at Kournas near Rhethymnos. The owner said it was found in one of the gorges leading down to Preveli.

[2] *P. of M.*, III, 428 ff.

of an intensely well-trained, highly-strung boy who will grow into a fine lean man and keep his condition until old age.

A head, also in ivory, found with this figure is of considerable interest.   Unlike most Minoan examples, the neck is remarkably thick, making the chin short in the extreme.   Such muscular necks are the natural result of prolonged practice in exercises which require niceties of balance.   Balance in most acrobatic sports, such as jumping or throwing, is attained mainly by the action of the head, which being the heaviest part of the body naturally gives the lead to the rest, and continual effort has the result of enlarging the neck muscles.

The figures were clearly ornamented with metal.   Holes in the heads show where locks of bronze, perhaps plated with gold, were attached to give even more spirited motion to the statuette.

*L.M.*I *and* II
Script

The linear class A of writing continues all over the island in L.M.I, with a tendency to employ rather larger tablets.   At Knossos, however, in L.M.II a more advanced type, B, was introduced which, though like L.M.II pottery, it was confined to the one site, yet naturally influenced the contemporary L.M.I*b* documents of class A elsewhere.[1]

The differences in the script are very small.   They are matters of detail not of fundamental importance.   Some twenty signs from class A fell into disuse.   Some ten new signs make their first appearance.   One cannot say that the writing is more stylized than before, since in some cases the signs are more elaborately written.   Evans suggests that it had an independent origin, some of the signs being closer to the hieroglyphic script of M.M. times.   I feel, however, that it is preferable to regard it as, in the modern sense, a ' script '—a scholarly writing taught to the Palace scribes and as such harking back to the more formal originals of the hieroglyphic type.

A few new features appear in the numerals.   A sign for 10,000 has been evolved consisting of the old 1,000 sign with a dash in the middle.   The horizontal line is now regularly used for ten and X appears for O.   That percentages were worked out is clear from a class of tablet which is inscribed in two registers with a sign which may mean flocks, followed by a number.   The two numbers invariably add up to 50, 100 or 200.

Most of the tablets are inventories and bear witness to the meticulous business methods of the Minoans.   Lists of men

[1] *P. of M.*, IV, 668 ff.

and women are found, flocks and herds are numbered, vases and their contents, olive trees and saffron. The 'Armoury', a building to the North of the road leading to the Theatral Area, contained a rich deposit of tablets which show the muster-roll of chariots and lists of weapons.[1]

The seal stones of L.M.i and ii do not display the vitality of those of M.M.iii. The flattened cylinder disappears in L.M.ia but the true cylinder makes its first appearance.[2] The amygdaloid shape begins with a smooth back, a fine example in cornelian showing a lion bringing down a bull.[3] In L.M.ia, however, grooves appear on the back and the

L.M.i Seals

Fig. 39.—Late Minoan i and ii Seals

shape lengthens and continues in its elongated form into L.M.ib and L.M.ii. The lentoid is the commonest shape.

The designs are best illustrated by a deposit of clay impressions well stratified in the South-West Basement at Knossos.[4] Among these was a curious representation of what appears to be a young Minotaur seated on a campstool while an attendant leans towards him and points to a kneeling ram. A very fine design, of which a number of impressions was found, is a bitch with a collar. Dogs are comparatively common, and Fig. 39a shows a young male figure holding two mastiffs. An interesting find was a clay matrix apparently for the reproduction, whether legitimate or not, of a gold ring. The design shows

[1] Ibid., IV, 785 ff.   [2] Ibid., 496.   [3] Ibid., 533.
[4] Ibid., II, 763 ff.

a female figure seated in front of a shrine while another offers her a two-handled goblet which resembles the polychrome type described above. The impression of the actual ring from which this matrix was taken was found at Zakros.[1] A magnificent gold ring was found in a tomb at Mokhlos. The design represents the goddess sitting naked in a boat taking leave of a small building on a rocky shore.[2]

In L.M.1b the elongated amygdaloid and the lentoid are the only shapes. The designs tend to be more heraldic. Genii or demons make their appearance. They seem to have their origin in the Egyptian Taurt, who is often represented as carrying a crocodile in the same way that the Minoan genii, who bear a remarkable resemblance to her, carry bulls, stags, or lions.[3] Lions gripping their prey, carrying it off or fighting over it are a favourite subject, and in these designs the symmetrical, heraldic tendency is most in evidence (Fig. 39b).[4] A curious outcome of this is seen in the case where the lion is gripping a horned sheep. The lion's head is invisible behind that of the sheep and the impression is given of a double-bodied animal with a single head. In the succeeding period two-bodied lions and sphinxes were deliberately made.

Cows and bulls recumbent or licking a hind foot are common (Fig. 39c). These do not display the naturalism of M.M.III, and the main object of the engraver seems to have been to fill up as much of the field as he could.

The human element is remarkably rare. One or two examples of huntsmen knifing ibex are found,[5] and there is a curious type with the figure set vertically on the amygdaloid which shows men in long robes not unlike those worn on the Campstool Fresco.[6]

L.M.II
Seals

In L.M.II the flattened cylinder seems to make a brief reappearance, though it is possible that the two examples known are survivals from L.M.1a.[7]

Amygdaloid and lentoid shapes again predominate, and impressions of signet rings are common on clay sealings.

[1] The minor differences noted by Evans, loc. cit., are probably due to inaccuracy on the part of the forger. It is hard to believe that two so nearly identical rings existed.

[2] *Mochlos*, 89. The hand is in the regular Near Eastern position of waving good-bye with the palm inwards.

[3] *P. of M.*, IV, 430 ff.   [4] Ibid., 582 ff.

[5] Ibid., 577.   [6] Ibid., 413.

[7] One from Tomb 1 at Isopata, one from the Archives. Ibid., 500, 602.

The designs are on the whole even more heraldic than those of L.M.1*b*, and in the case of the lentoids the engravers have gone further in their desire to fill the field and contorted the bodies of animals in quite an extraordinary way to fit the circular ground (Fig. 39*f*).

Heraldic supporters, lions as on the Lion Gate at Mycenae or protecting the Goddess on a hill summit, are common. Figures hold lions at arms' length in a style reminiscent of Gilgamesh.[1] Religious scenes and symbols are frequently found (Fig. 39*e*). Particularly interesting is the class on which grains of corn, or the sign in the linear script connected with corn, appear as secondary motives.[2] Bulls and cows are still favourite subjects. In one delightful example a farmer is leaning over a fence as though speculating on the chances of his prize bull in the local cattle show.[3] Scenes of the bull-ring are found, often showing the contortion of the body necessitated by the shape of the seal (Fig. 39*d*).

One of the most interesting seal impressions shows the transport of a horse, superimposed on a ship. Quite evidently the horse made a very late appearance in Crete. The ship also is noteworthy as showing, for the first time, a deck shelter to protect the rowers, a feature also present on another sealing.[4]

A number of beads were found in a well-dated L.M.1*a* deposit near the Temple Tomb [5] (Pl. XXXVI, 4). Gold, carnelian, amethyst, and paste were the materials. The shapes of the gold beads were segmented, spirally grooved tubular, amygdaloid, pear-shaped, and globular with and without fluting. One example of a lotos and a pendant in the shape of a recumbent calf appeared. The amethyst, carnelian and paste beads were globular and amygdaloid. A very similar deposit came to light in a larnax burial at Pyrgos with beads of precisely the same shape and materials.[6] These shapes persist into L.M.II, to which date may probably be attributed the lapis-lazuli drop pendants and the amulets in the shape of monkeys and a frog which came from the Royal Tomb at Isopata.[7] At the same time, or more probably in L.M.1*b*, appear gold beads in the shape of pairs of argonauts.[8] At Mokhlos, in a grave, probably of L.M.1 date, were found beads of the kind already described with the addition of globular examples in rock crystal and flat disks of gold pierced laterally and ornamented with a circle of

L.M.1 and II Jewellery

[1] Ibid., Fig. 597.   [2] Ibid., 625.   [3] Ibid., Fig. 564.
[4] Ibid., 827.   [5] Ibid., 963.
[6] Ibid., II, 75.   [7] *P.T.K.*, 152.   [8] Ibid., 58.

small bosses. The pendants included an ivy leaf and a whorl-shell in gold and a bull's head in amethyst.[1]

Relations with Egypt were intensified from the beginning of L.M.1*a*. In Crete itself the prince who was buried in the Royal Tomb at Isopata needed a whole service of Egyptian alabaster vases for his comfort.[2] More important is the circular seal of Queen Ty, wife of Amenhotep III, found in a chamber tomb at Agia Triadha with L.M.1*b* pottery,[3] which, as we have seen, is contemporary with the L.M.11 of Knossos. This is the latest datable object found in a stratum which precedes the final catastrophe, and since a scarab bearing the name of Queen Ty is the earliest object to be found with L.H.111 pottery, and the name of her husband Amenhotep III appears on objects found in similar deposits of which the pottery is unfortunately unpublished [4] on the Mainland, it provides us with a moral certainty that the destruction of the Minoan cities took place in the reign of Amenhotep III, i.e. between 1414 and 1378 B.C.

Though the number of actual imports is perhaps small, the evidence of considerable influence is overwhelming. Whether the idea of processional frescoes was copied from Egypt or not it is hard to say, but certainly the monkeys in the House of the Frescoes and the Hunting Cat of Agia Triadha owe a great deal to the Nile. The papyrus motive on frescoes and painted reliefs, and the stately clumps of lilies on L.M.11 jars, must also have their origin there, while the Captain of the Blacks Fresco implies the use of African mercenaries.

In Egypt the evidence is even more conclusive. In the tomb of Senmut, architect of Queen Hatshepsut, a procession of Minoan envoys is shown bearing gifts. Among these are typical L.M.1*a* vessels of metal and an enormous Vapheio cup decorated with bulls' heads. On the walls of the tomb of User-Amen, vizier in the earlier part of the reign of Thothmes

[1] *Mochlos*, Pl. X.

[2] *P.T.K.*, 146. As was said above (p. 202), the shape and the veins in the stone of these were copied in clay (Pl. XXXIII, 1).

[3] *Mon. Ant.*, XIV, 735.

[4] Of these, the scarab with Queen Ty's name found in a house South-West of the Acropolis, alone has L.H.111 pottery. 'Εφ. 'Αρχ., 1887, 169. Fragments of a plaque bearing Amenhotep III's name were found in a similar house North-East of the Lion Gate with two bronze pins. Pottery not given. Ibid., 1891, 18. A vase bearing his name was found in Tomb 49. Ivory cylinder. Pottery not given. Ibid., 1888, 156.

III, are more Cretans.   Among their offerings are metal vases, a bull's-head rhyton and the galloping figure of a bull.   User-Amen's nephew, Rekhmara, succeeded him in office and again shows us pictures of Minoans, Keftians as he calls them, one of whom bears a typical L.M.1b collared rhyton.   An interesting feature of one of these figures is the way in which the artist had begun to draw a codpiece and flap of the old L.M.1a type but had changed it to the new style of decorated kilt of L.M.1b.[1] Rekhmara's son Menkheperrasenb, High Priest of Amen at the end of Thothmes III's long reign, kept up the family tradition.   His Keftians, however, were evidently drawn from traditional copies, for the objects they bring are still of the same type, though L.M.1b was by now well advanced.[2]

The only two vases of obviously Minoan as opposed to Mainland fabric which have been found in Egypt both belong to L.M.1b.   One is the most beautiful vase ever made in Crete, the Marseilles Oenochoe (Pl. XL, 1).   Unfortunately no details of its discovery are known.[3]   The other is a tall alabastron from Sedment decorated with a very stylized imitation of alabaster veining (Pl. XL, 2).   The group in which it was found seems to date from about the reign of Thothmes III.[4]   No L.M.II pottery has appeared in Egypt with the exception of a single sherd in a later deposit at Tell el-Amarna.[5]   Other vases have been claimed as Minoan which on closer investigation appear to be of Mainland origin.   A squat alabastron was found in an early XVIIIth-Dynasty grave at Gurob.[6]   The squat alabastron seems, however, to be a purely Mainland shape.   Only five examples from Crete are known to me.   The first is from a chamber tomb at Knossos.[7]   This is decorated with the ' ogival ' canopy which, as we have seen, is a Mainland pattern.   A second is from Tomb 5 in the Mavrospelio cemetery.[8]   A third is from Tomb 5 at Isopata.[9]   A fourth is from the Little Palace.[10]

[1] P. of M., II, Fig. 473a.   In spite of Wainwright's extremely valuable article in J.H.S., 1931, 1.   I am still unable to dissociate Keftiu from Crete.   The finds at Ras Shamra and at Tell Atchana (see below) confirm me in my opinion that Keftiu could be applied to Crete, to its empire or to its sphere of influence.   J.E.A., XVI.

[2] The artist had, in fact, a number of Keftian types in his repertoire which he would reproduce to order without ever looking at the original.

[3] P. of M., II, 509.   [4] Sedment, II, grave 137.   P. of M., IV, 271.
[5] C. of A., II, 110.   [6] Gurob, Pl. XIII, 4.
[7] P. of M., IV, 850.
[8] B.S.A., XXVIII, 258.   [9] T.D.A., 25.   [10] Ibid., 37.

The fifth is of L.M.II date and was found in the Temple Tomb.[1] With this latter may be taken the examples in alabaster from the Throne Room, also dating from L.M.II, a period when mainland influence was very strong at Knossos.   This absence from Crete of a shape which is one of the commonest in Greece is a very powerful argument for assigning other vases of the same shape to a mainland source.[2]   A variant of this shape, or rather a squat jug with one vertical handle, was found in the tomb of Maket at Lahun.[3]   Only one example from Crete is known to me.[4]   It is extremely common, however, on the Mainland.[5]   The cup from Abousir is again of a mainland type with a distinct foot.[6]   The handled saucer from Saqqara like its companion alabastron is also not Minoan.[7]

One of the reasons no doubt for the presence of Mainland rather than Minoan vases is due to the fact that these squat alabastra were ideal shapes for travelling.   The lordly vases of L.M.II were too big and clumsy to be transported and were not of a shape which would hold anything safely at sea.   Something, too, might be claimed for the nice taste of the Egyptians.

But since L.H.I seems to be absolutely parallel to L.M.Ia and L.H.II to L.M.Ib and L.M.II, these vases are equally good evidence for dating purposes.   We can safely, then, take L.M.Ia as ending about the date of the accession of Thothmes III, i.e. c. 1510 B.C., and L.M.Ib as lasting at Knossos till about 1450, and in the rest of the island continuing parallel with L.M.II until the final disaster, which occurred probably in the earlier years of the reign of Amenhotep III, say between 1410 and 1405 B.C.

With Syria relations were close.   The earlier elements in the Minet el-Beida and Ras Shamra built tombs, which resemble the Royal Tomb at Isopata, and show all the three possible methods of vaulting the latter, must be contemporary with the end of L.M.I–II.   A silver bowl inscribed with Linear

[1] *P. of M.*, IV., Fig. 960*f*.

[2] e.g. Edgar, *Greek Vases in the Cairo Museum*, 26125, 26126. Firth and Gunn, *Saqqara*, Pl. XLII, and the famous Armant Vase. *B.M. Cat.*, A. 651.   The Aniba example, *P. of M.*, IV, 267, is a local imitation.

[3] *Illahun*, &c., Pl. XXVI.

[4] From Agia Triadha.   *P. of M.*, II, Fig. 315*a*.

[5] *Archaeologia*, LXXXII, 150, 157.

[6] *Arch. Anz.*, XIV, 57 ; cf. *Archaeologia*, LXXXII, Pl. I, 1, and contrast *P. of M.*, II, 475.

[7] Cf. *Saqqara*, loc. cit., with *Archaeologia*, LXXXII, Pls. I and II

Script B comes from the Library.[1] Syrian influence may perhaps be seen in the long robes of the campstool fresco and the amygdaloid gems on which the figures carry axes of a Syrian type.[2] An alabaster rhyton in the shape of a pregnant woman kneeling, from the Harbour Town of Knossos, though unstratified, probably belongs to this period.[3]

Farther afield at Ashur the neck of a faience rhyton of L.M.1*b* date [4] was found, and parallels to the script as well as to decorative patterns have been detected in finds from Amisos in Pontus,[5] though the date of these is not generally agreed.

In its relations with Mainland Greece and the islands, the influence of Crete is overwhelming. So Minoanized does the rest of the Aegean become that it is impossible for the present writer at least to avoid the conclusion that it was dominated politically by Crete.[6] Athenian tradition, always the most vocal, remembered the tyranny of Minos over the Saronic gulf. We cannot separate the legend of the youths and maidens, sent to be devoured by the Minotaur, from the bull-sports of Late Minoan Crete. Indeed, it would be an extremely good way of keeping down the old noble families of the Mainland if their best was taken and had the honour of being trained for the bull-ring. Many a king and country has been known by its badge, and as Lord Hastings was ' gored by the White Boar ', so the Mainland hostages might well be said to be devoured by the Bull of Minos.

A few remarks may be made on the differences between the remains on the mainland and islands and those in Crete. Architecturally the greatest contribution of the mainland was the Tholos tomb. Nothing like this was constructed in Crete until L.M.iii. It has been pointed out above that the E.M. circular tombs were certainly not vaulted and from the L.M.i Period when the construction of tholoi at Mycenae began the built tomb of Crete was something quite different, as one can see from the Temple Tomb at Knossos and the Royal Tomb at Isopata. The Palace at Mycenae, however, was naturally adapted to Minoan standards, at any rate, of decoration.

It has been almost impossible to determine the exact date of the various alterations but in the main it is quite clear that the old M.H. palace or manor house was in the L.H.i Period

[1] *Syria*, XIII, 5, 22.   Cf. *P. of M.*, IV, 775 ff.
[2] *P. of M.*, IV, 403.   [3] Ibid., II, 255.
[4] *J.H.S.*, 1928, 71.   [5] *P. of M.*, IV, 764 ff.
[6] But see below, p. 229, for a very different interpretation.

remodelled on Minoan lines with the major part of its decoration in the Minoan tradition if not actually done by Minoan artists.[1]

A great difference between Minoan and Mainland frescoes is the interest in action taken by the latter as opposed to the interest in the setting taken by the former. The fact that painted reliefs in plaster do not occur on the Mainland is good evidence for the L.M.1a date of what we believe to have been the conquest. But equally, as in India, the native princes must have been allowed to continue ruling as vassals. Otherwise the intensely mainland character of the known frescoes could hardly have existed. Just as in the palace of an Indian Prince European artists will be employed on the condition that their subject-matter is of interest to the Indian, so with the Mainland dominions of Crete the style is Minoan, but the subjects are Mainland.

We must naturally except purely decorative motives, such as the ' adder mark ' on the hearth at Mycenae, which the Minoan artist would include without thinking. But on the whole the impression we get is of a Cretan craftsman, not of the first class, working to the order of a master who had totally different ideas on the question of what the subject of a picture should be. That this is so is proved by the frescoes of the L.H.III Period, when the Mainland was quite independent of Crete.

In pottery as well Minoan influence was overwhelming, though as one would expect the traditional Minyan and matt-painted wares were still employed. A few points are note-worthy, the more so in that they seem to indicate definite Mainland characteristics which it may be useful to know if such pottery is ever found abroad. The typical L.M.–L.H.1 spiral, often enriched with white dots, has on the whole in the Main-land, far more convolutions than in Crete. On the whole this seems a safe distinction, particularly when thick dots are placed on either side of the connexion between the spirals. The ' Ogival Canopy ', already mentioned, occurs regularly on the Mainland, though only twice in Crete and is better regarded as a Mainland pattern. The squat alabastron is a Mainland shape, jugs with cut-away spouts have a broader lip on the Mainland and are apt to be squatter. The pedestalled goblet is commoner on the Mainland, and it is possible that we can

[1] *B.S.A.*, XXV, 147 ff., 268 ff. In its present form it is of L.H.III date and is a true Megaron, but many indications of earlier work survive and the Grand Stairway was very much in the Cretan style.

see a reaction on Crete in L.M.1*b*–L.M.II examples already given, since the Cretan pedigree is less direct than the Helladic. The tendency to use repeated single motives is certainly Minoan. When the Mainland does so the result is far more scrappy. Mainland decoration also tends to border broad bands with dots or short diagonal lines, and on the ' Palace Style ' vases the artists fill up every available vacant space. It is noteworthy that the L.M.II style appealed to the Mainland, whereas it was practically confined to Knossos in Crete and Egypt would have none of it.[1]

These distinctions are given only to distinguish in detail between the two sides of the Cretan Sea, since it is obviously an important matter if, in a particular foreign country, only Mainland or only Minoan vases are imported at a particular period. In any case, a detailed study of all patterns is needed, since the old distinction between the ' feel ' of the sherds, hard for Crete, soapy for the Mainland, can, as I can testify, no longer hold good.

As one might imagine, the Mainlander was a greater connoisseur of weapons. The sword with the sloping shoulder, common in Crete in M.M.III, is found in the Shaft Graves which date at the latest from the early part of L.H.I, but in those same graves are found both the horned sword and the cruciform type, the latter of which at least does not occur in Crete till later. The elaborate inlay of dagger blades shows the pride they took in their weapons, however Minoan may be the type of decoration.

Stone vases and lamps seem to be entirely Minoan in character.[2] The Medallion Pithos in steatite from the Tomb of Clytaemnestra has been the subject of considerable controversy. We have seen that the Medallion Pithoi of Knossos survived until the last days of the Palace, i.e. till the end of L.M.II, and that the manufacture of them can hardly be earlier than the transitional M.M.III*b*–L.M.I phase. Since copies of objects in other materials are not made when the originals have ceased to exist, this example in stone must have been made between those dates. But we have also seen that stone vases are apt

---

[1] Snijder, *Kretische Kunst*, 123, 124, indeed goes so far as to consider L.M.II an offshoot of the Mainland style, and having regard to the fact that this short-lived, locally restricted style can only have overlapped the latter part of L.H.II, it is hard to argue against him.

[2] There are practically no stone vases in the Shaft Graves, they begin in L.H.II (= L.M.1*b*).

to survive in use for a very long time and it would be very dangerous to date any deposit by the occurrence of such a vase in it.

The rings and seal stones are indistinguishable from those of Crete but, as in the case of the frescoes, the subjects are more frequently connected with hunting and warfare, though religious types are by no means rare, particularly those concerned with genii.

At Phylakope in the Third City L.M.1 vases are copied in the local clay, which did not admit of the highly glazed finish of the originals, and some very fine L.M.1a and b vases were imported from Crete.[1] Stone vases and lamps show strong Minoan affinities, but the architecture was unaffected. In Thera also appear Cycladic copies of M.M.111b–L.M.1a vases.[2]

The Downfall of the Minoan Power

The catastrophe which overtook the Cretan cities at the end of L.M.1b (or L.M.11 at Knossos) was practically universal. Knossos, Phaistos, Agia Triadha, Gournia, Mokhlos, Mallia, and Zakros all show traces of violent destruction accompanied by burning.[3] At Palaikastro, Pseira, Nirou Khani, Tylissos, and Plate there is a distinct break in the habitation, though no trace of burning was found.[4]

This overwhelming disaster must have taken place at one and the same time and it has been attributed to a severe earthquake.[5] Earthquakes, however, in ancient times are not liable to cause fires ; these are the result of gas and electricity. It has been seen, too, that woodwork was more sparingly used at this time than before, and that previous earthquakes, which were strong enough to fling great blocks of the Palace at Knossos into the houses below, had neither caused fires, though the woodwork was more extensive, nor had they caused such a complete break and set-back in the culture. Rather they had acted as a spur to fresh endeavours. Furthermore, at Knossos the first damage an earthquake of such magnitude would have done would be to shake down the Domestic Quarters and

[1] *B.S.A.*, XVII, Pl. XI. No. 163 with its ogival canopy and dotted lines is probably of Mainland origin ; so is No. 137, being a squat alabastron, and the vases on page 15, Fig. 2. Some of the pottery *Phylakopi*, Pls. XV–XXXI, seems Minoan.

[2] Åberg, IV, 136.

[3] *P. of M.*, IV, 942 ff., 786, 885. *Gournia*, 21. *A.J.A.*, XIII, 301. *Mallia*, I, 45. *B.S.A.*, VII, 142.

[4] *B.S.A.*, X, 259. *Pseira*, 10. ’Εφ. ’Αρχ., 1922, 24. *P. of M.*, IV, 786. *B.S.A.*, XX, 6.

[5] *P. of M.*, IV, 942 ff.

particularly the Grand Staircase, where four floors at least were supported on wooden columns. A very mild earthquake in 1931 snapped and shifted the upper part of a reinforced concrete column no less than 6 cm. But the Grand Staircase remained complete and practically undamaged long enough for it to be silted up with debris and earth which preserved the landing on a level with the Central Court to within 1½ metres of its original position. The marks of fire are most obvious on the Western or official wing.

Everything, indeed, points to a deliberate sacking on the part of enemies of the most powerful cities in Crete. We have seen the prosperity of the period and it is obvious that no mere Viking raid could have accomplished such destruction. It must have been a highly organized expedition with an avowed purpose. That this purpose was not to invade and colonize the island is clear from the way in which the Minoan culture continues, though in a very minor key, without any Mainland influence [1] until the very end of L.M.III. The object of this thorough, relentless destruction must have been purely political.

There are two theories which will account for this. Both have much to be said for them and, curiously enough, they are diametrically opposed. According to the first theory the Minoan domination over the Mainland has been grossly over-estimated.[2] It has been pointed out that if we lacked all historical documents we should, if we used similar arguments, maintain that there was an Athenian domination of Etruria in later days. On this theory the Mainland and Crete were separate independent powers, the former merely adopting the outward trappings of a higher civilization.[3] In L.M.II, however, the Mainland was strong enough to establish control over Crete. This would account for the extremely Mainland character of the Palace style.[4] In that case the destruction of the Cretan cities was due to a nationalist revolt against the foreign ' harmosts '. Evidence for this is the fact that in the succeeding, L.M.III Period, the civilization of Crete has little connexion with that of the Mainland; it is indeed, as will be seen, rather markedly Minoan.

[1] An unimportant exception to this will be stated below, p. 259.
[2] I am indebted to Professor Wace for bringing this theory to my notice. It has not, I think, previously appeared in print.
[3] Thus accounting for the Mainland pottery in Egypt and Syria. Crete and Greece, in fact, were commercial rivals.
[4] See above, p. 227, note.

The other theory,[1] to which the present writer adheres, would regard the Minoanization of the Mainland as too pronounced to be the result of mere influence.[2] It is certainly far more complete than was the influence of Egypt in that country's highly organized empire. We would regard the archaeological results as supporting legend, the latter admittedly only referring to the Saronic Gulf, that Crete had by the end of L.M.I–II established a considerable domination over the rest of the Aegean. Her main dealings abroad were with Egypt and the Egyptian Empire in Syria. Egyptian objects and influence are so rare on the Mainland that it would seem as if that part of the Minoan Empire was barred from direct traffic with Egypt. The presence of Mainland vessels in Egypt is easily explained by the fact that they were more suitable for travelling and that therefore the tribute of the Mainland to the Cretan overlord was sent direct to Egypt in payment of goods instead of being unloaded in Crete and reshipped thence.

We have seen that though superficially Minoanized, the Mainland still kept a good deal of its native culture and taste. The richest market in the world was barred and we may perhaps catch an echo of the attempt to find fresh markets in the story of Jason's voyage to the Black Sea. At all events it is not hard to imagine the rebellious feelings of the dominions, and we can well imagine things getting to the pitch of a concerted effort on their part to smash the capital state of the empire.

Now there is a name which is always associated, if not with the sack of Knossos, at least with the liberation of its subjects —Theseus. Names have a habit of being remembered when the deeds with which they are associated are forgotten or garbled. Who would recognize Alexander in Iskander of the two Horns, or Vergil in the necromancer of the Middle Ages? It has already been suggested that the seven youths and seven maidens may have been the Mainland quota for the bull-ring at Knossos. That is just the type of detail that would be remembered, the more so in that it may well have been the

---

[1] The theory propounded below is in essentials the same as that put forward by me in *J.E.A.*, XVI, 89 ff. I had then considered the Aegean vases in Egypt with one or two exceptions as Minoan, but even now that most of them seem to be of Mainland origin, it hardly affects the argument, as can be seen below.

[2] I would regard the sudden Mainland influence on the Knossian Palace style of L.M.II as resembling rather the Germanization of palace circles in England after Queen Victoria's marriage.

sentimental reason without which no purely commercial war can ever take place.   No doubt the rape of Helen was a very good rallying cry when the Mycenaean Empire wished to break through to the Black Sea trade which Troy was keeping for itself.

And in the last decade of the fifteenth century on a spring day, when a strong South wind was blowing which carried the flames of the burning beams almost horizontally northwards, Knossos fell.[1]

The final scene takes place in the most dramatic room ever excavated—the Throne Room.   It was found in a state of complete confusion.   A great oil jar lay overturned in one corner, ritual vessels were in the act of being used when the disaster came.   It looks as if the king had been hurried here to undergo too late some last ceremony in the hopes of saving the people.   Theseus and the Minotaur !   Dare we believe that he wore the mask of a bull ? [2]

Such imaginings may not be suitable to archaeology but, with this possibility in mind, I defy anyone to enter the Throne Room without a strange thrill.

Crete had fallen and henceforward she was to be a mere satellite of the world centring round Greece, gradually drawing nearer until she was absorbed in the general Hellenic culture which she herself had done so much to found.

SITES WHERE LATE MINOAN I REMAINS HAVE BEEN FOUND

WEST CRETE

(a) Excavated Site

APODHOULOU . . .   Settlement .   Architectural and other finds. Marinatos, *Arch. Anz.*, 1935, 245.

---

[1] *P. of M.*, IV, 943.   March mentioned as the month must be a slip.   Winds strong enough to blow smoke horizontally are rare at any other time than late April or early May.   One hardly likes to use the argument that Theseus traditionally sailed for Crete in the month of Munichion (April–May).

[2] For the wearing of the masks of divine animals by their human spokesman or communicant, cf. the forthcoming *Zeus*, III, by A. B. Cook.   Cf. also *Zeus*, I, 490 f.   L.H.III seal, *A.J.A.*, XXXVII, 540.

(b) *Surface Finds*

KHRYSOSKALITISSA   Sherds found close to the monastery by the
MONASTERY   writer, 1935.

ORNITHE . . . .   Stone vase from Tabia in the Rhethymnos
                        Museum.

CENTRAL CRETE

(a) *Excavated Sites*

AGIOS THEODHOROS . | Settlement . | Architectural and other remains. Xanthoudides, Πραϰτιϰά, 1925–6, 141. Marinatos, ibid., 1929, 94.
| | Tomb . . | Marinatos, ibid.
AMNISOS . . . . | House . . | Architectural and other finds. Marinatos, Πραϰτιϰά, 1932, 76.
ARKALOKHORI . . | Cave . . | Swords, axes, &c. Marinatos, *Arch. Anz.*, 1934, 245 ; 1935, 246.
ARKHANAIS . . . | Well-house . | Circular building. Evans, *P. of M.*, I, 623 ; II., Pl. XIV, also many remains of large settlement.
GONIAIS . . . . | House . . | Architectural and other finds. Marinatos, *J.H.S.*, 1930, 251. *B.C.H.*, 1930, 516.
JUKTAS . . . . | Sanctuary . | Present remains of building on summit. *P. of M.*, I, 158.
HERAKLEION . . . | Town . . | Architectural and other finds from E. of Trypete. Evans, *P. of M.*, II, 229.
KNOSSOS . . . . | Palace . . | See previous period and *P. of M.*, III, 280 ; IV, 858. Caravanserai. Ibid., II, 103.
| | Town . . | Little Palace. *Arch.*, 65, 159. *P. of M.*, II, 513. Houses. Ibid., 373, 396, 513 ; IV, 205. *B.S.A.*, VI, 70.
| | Tombs . . | Temple Tomb. IV, 962, 988. Chamber tombs. Ibid., II, 547 ; IV, 849. Isopata, *T.D.A.*, 1. *P.T.K.*, 136. Zapher Papoura. *P.T.K.*, 1. Mavrospelio. *B.S.A.*, XXVIII, 243 ff.
MALLIA . . . . | Palace . . | Latest deposit. Chapoutier, *Mallia*, I, II, 29. *B.C.H.*, 1935, 303.
| | Cemetery . | Graves by the coast. *B.C.H.*, 1930, 521.
| | Town . . | Ibid., 1931, 513 ; 1923, 296.

NIROU KHANI . . Building . Large house with religious furniture. Xanthoudides, *'Εφ. 'Αρχ.*, 1922, 1. Evans, *P. of M.*, II, 279.

PLATE . . . . . Settlement . A few of the earlier houses. Dawkins, *B.S.A.*, XX, 1.

PRINIAS . . . . Shrine . . Pernier, *Boll. d'Art.*, II, 455, calls it Archaic, but cf. Evans, *P. of M.*, IV, 160, and Marinatos' forthcoming article in *'Εφ. 'Αρχ.*

PSYKHRO . . . . Cave . . Deposit from Temenos. Hogarth, *B.S.A.*, VI, 94.

TYLISSOS . . . . Houses and Palace Architectural and other finds of the 2nd Period. Hazzidakis, *'Εφ. 'Αρχ.*, 1912, and *T.V.M.*, 6 and 79. House across the stream at Daverona.

(b) *Surface Finds*

ANAGYROI . . . . Walls and sherds from guard station. Evans, *P. of M.*, II, 77.

ASMARI . . . . Sherds and walls at Mandrais, seen by writer, 1934. *B.S.A.*, XXXIII, 82.

DIA . . . . . . Sherds and walls on promontory above Agia Pelagia bay. Sherds in walled field on saddle to N., and to S. of summit, seen by writer, 1935.

GAZE . . . . . Sherds from cutting of road, seen by Miss Money-Coutts and Miss Eccles, 1934. *B.S.A.*, XXXIII, 92. Evans, *P. of M.*, II, 231, speaks of settlement at the mouth of the river. Hazzidakis describes vases found in illicit dig here. *T.V.M.* 73.

GEOPHYRAKIA . . . Sherds by the side of the road E. of the village, seen by writer, 1933.

KANLI KASTELLI . . Main surface deposit at Visala. Evans, *P. of M.*, II, 71.

KARYDHAKI . . . Walls and sherds of guard-house. Evans, ibid., 66.

KASTELLI PEDHIADHOS Sherds in cave of Khristos, walls and sherds at Koutsounaria, seen by writer, 1934. *B.S.A.*, XXXIII, 81. Is the former the cave mentioned by Hazzidakis, *T.V.M.*, 76 ?

KASTELLOS TZERMIADHON Sherds on summit, seen by writer, 1935. Cf. Evans, *Academy*, 20/6/96. Taramelli, *Mon. Ant.*, IX, 415. No trace of this period in areas already excavated.

MARMAKETO . . . Sherds from Phakidia, seen by writer, 1935. Cf. Dawkins, *B.S.A.*, XX, 4.

MOKHOS . . . . Stone vase from Mouri, seen by writer, 1933.

PYRGOS . . . . Objects from a larnax burial. Evans, *P. of M.*, II, 75.

SARKHO . . . . Stone vase in the Candia Museum. *Catalogue*, 114. Miss Money-Coutts and Miss Eccles could find no site, 1934. *B.S.A.*, XXXIII, 92.

SIDHEROKEPHALA . . Traces of walls to N. of hill. Walls on top (Taramelli, *Mon. Ant.*, IX, 402) have disappeared. One pithos sherd found by writer, 1935.

SKOTEINO . . . . Many sherds in the cave. Evans, *P. of M.*, I, 163.

STRAVOMYTI . . . Sherds by the spring near Agios Ioannes, below the cave. Evans, *P. of M.*, II, 71.

SOUTH CRETE

(a) Excavated Sites

AGIA TRIADHA . . Houses . . Surrounding palace. *Mem. Ist Lomb.*, XXI, 245. *Rend. Linc.*, 1903, 340 ; 1905, 387.

Palace . . Main occupation. Halbherr, *Mon. Ant.*, XIII, 1. Levi, *Annuario*, VIII, 71. *Mem. Ist Lomb.*, XXI, 235. *Rend. Linc.*, 1903, 317 ; 1905, 315 ; 1907, 257.

Tombs. . In earlier buildings. Paribeni, *Mon. Ant.*, XIV, 719.

GORTYNA . . . . Deposit . Stone vases from Volakais. Pace, *Annuario*, I, 372 ; VIII, 2.

KAMARAIS . . . . Cave . . Small deposit of sherds. Dawkins, *B.S.A.*, XIX, 1.

STOU KOUSE . . . House . . Latest deposit at τοῦ βραχνοῦ ὁ Λάκκος. Marinatos, ᾿Αρχ. Δελτ., 1922–5, 53.

PHAISTOS . . . . Palace . . Later palace. Halbherr, *Mon. Ant.*, XII, 7. Pernier, *Mon. Ant.*, XIV, 313.

(b) Surface Finds

ALIKE . . . . . Sherds and traces of walls, seen by writer, 1935.

AMIRA . . . . . Sword, spindle whorls, beads, perhaps from a tomb. *P. of M.*, II, 174, n. 2.

ARVI . . . . . Swords, beads, &c. Evans, *T.D.A.*, 43. Sherds on knoll of Komitas, seen by writer, 1935.

DHAMANIA. . . . Sherds and obsidian flakes, seen by writer, ½-hr. N. of village, 1934. *B.S.A.*, XXXIII, 84. ? the same as Τροχάλοι. Xanthoudides, *Ἀρχ. Δέλτ.*, II, Παρ., 24.

GOULOPHARANGO GORGE Sherds and walls at Agios Savas, seen by writer, 1934. *B.S.A.*, XXXIII, 87.

KASTELL BELVEDERE . Sherd from SW. slope below summit, seen by writer, 1936.

KATO SIME . . . Stone vessel and pottery. Evans, *Diary*, 1896.

KERATOS . . . . Sherds from cave and from settlement on summit, seen by R. W. Hutchinson, 1935.

KOMO . . . . . Large building on the shore. Evans, *P. of M.*, II, 88.

STA LOUTRA . . . Votive cups from near stone tank. Ibid., 76.

LOUTRAKI . . . . Sherds on summit of Kandiliero, seen by writer, 1935.

TRYPETI . . . . Sherds from settlement. Evans, *P. of M.*, II, 82.

EAST CRETE

(a) Excavated Sites

AGIOS ANTONIOS . . House . . Walls and vases. Boyd, *Trans. Penn. Univ.*, 1, 21.

AGIOS NIKOLAOS . . Burial . . Pithos burial. Tod, *B.S.A.*, IX, 336.

GOURNIA . . . . Town . . Main occupation. *Trans. Penn. Univ.*, 1, 29. *Gournia*, passim.

Burials . . Pithos burials. Seager, *Mochlos*, 89.

MOKHLOS . . . . Settlement . Latest houses. Seager, *A.J.A.*, XIII, 274.

Burials . . Pithos burials. Hall, *Sphoungaras*, 73. Seager, *Mochlos*, 89.

PAKHYAMMOS . . . Burials . . Pithos burials. Seager, *Pachyammos*, 9 ff., and *passim*.

PALAIKASTRO . . . Town . . Main period of town. *B.S.A.*, VIII, 380; IX, 281; X, 202; XI, 272.

PETSOPHAS. . . . House . . Remains at Plate to N. Dawkins, ibid., XII, 2.

Sanctuary . Remodelling. Ibid., IX, 358.

PRINIATIKOS PYRGOS . Settlement . Later remains. Hall, *Vrokastro*, 79.

PSEIRA . . . . Town . . Architectural and other finds. Seager, *Pseira*, 8, 21.

SPHOUNGARAS . . Burials . . Pithos burials. Hall, *Sphoungaras*, 65.

VROKASTRO . . . House . . Vases, &c., from house on Kopranais. Hall, *Vrokastro*, 84.

ZAKROS . . . . Town . . Main period. *B.S.A.*, VII, 121. *J.H.S.*, 1902, 333; 1903, 248. *B.S.A.*, XVII, 265. Levi, *Annuario*, VIII, 157.

(b) Surface Finds

AMPELOS . . . . Sherds from Agios Nikolaos, seen by writer, 1934. *B.S.A.*, XXXIII, 100. Vase from Pharmakokephalo. Evans, *Academy*, 20/6/96.

KALOKHORIO . . . Sherds at Kato Arniko. Hall, *Vrokastro*, 79.

LAVRAKIA . . . . Sherds from several guard stations, seen by the writer, 1937. Cf. Evans, *Diary*, 1898.

MERSINE . . . . Sherds from Khalinomouri, seen by R. W. Hutchinson, 1936.

TOURLOTI . . . . Remains at Kastellos, seen by Bosanquet, unpublished. Sherds seen by R. W. Hutchinson, 1936.

ZAKROS . . . . Sherds from Skinarais E. of Apano Zakros, found by writer, 1934. *B.S.A.*, XXXIII, 99.

SITES WHERE LATE MINOAN II REMAINS HAVE BEEN FOUND

CENTRAL CRETE

(a) Excavated Sites

AMNISOS . . . . Stratum. . In cistern. Marinatos, Πρακτικά, 1933, 93.

ARKALOKHORI . . Cave . . Some of the gold and bronze axes, &c. Marinatos, *Arch. Anz.*, 1934, 245 ; 1935, 246.

KNOSSOS . . . . Palace . . Redecoration. *P. of M.*, IV, 291, 901.

Town . . Houses. *B.S.A.*, VI, 70. *P. of M.*, II, 400 ; IV, 138. Harbour town. Ibid., II, 234.

Tombs . . Last burial in Temple Tomb. Ibid., IV, 1002. Harbour town. Ibid., II, 235. Isopata. *P.T.K.*, 136. *T.D.A.*, 1. Zapher Papoura. *P.T.K.*, 1 ff. Mavrospelio. *B.S.A.*, XXVIII, 243.

GOURNAIS . . . . Tombs . . A few sherds from chamber tombs with larnax burials. Hazzidakis, 'Aρχ. Δελτ., III, 62 ff.

(b) Surface Finds

HERAKLEION . . . Tombs . . By small stream just E. of Candia. Evans, P. of M., II, 229.

SOUTH CRETE
(b) Surface Finds

LOUTRAKI . . . . Sherds found on the summit of Kandiliero to the E., by writer, 1935.

EAST CRETE
(a) Excavated Sites

PALAIKASTRO . . . Town . . A few deposits. B.S.A., Sup., 21 ff., and passim.

Tomb . . ? remains of built tomb below larnax burial. B.S.A., XI, 273.

PLAKA . . . . . Cave burial   Larnax burial. Dawkins, B.S.A., XII, 2.

PSEIRA . . . . Town . . A few imported vases found in L.M.1 strata. Seager, Pseira, 26.

ZAKROS . . . . Town . . A few imported sherds. B.M. Cat., I, 116.

(b) Surface Finds

TOURLOTI . . . . Pithos fragments from Kastellos, seen by R. W. Hutchinson, 1936.

2. LATE MINOAN III (L.M.III)
(See Map 12)

The disaster at the end of the previous period had broken the spirit of the Minoans. Some sites such as Pseira, Mokhlos, and Nirou Khani remained deserted. Other sites are re-occupied but on a much smaller scale. With the destruction of the great centres and palaces the concentration of power ceased. Perhaps the ruling caste was wiped out. At all events the map clearly shows the tendency for the population to scatter. Particularly noteworthy is the extension of habitation in the West. Thrown back on to their own resources,

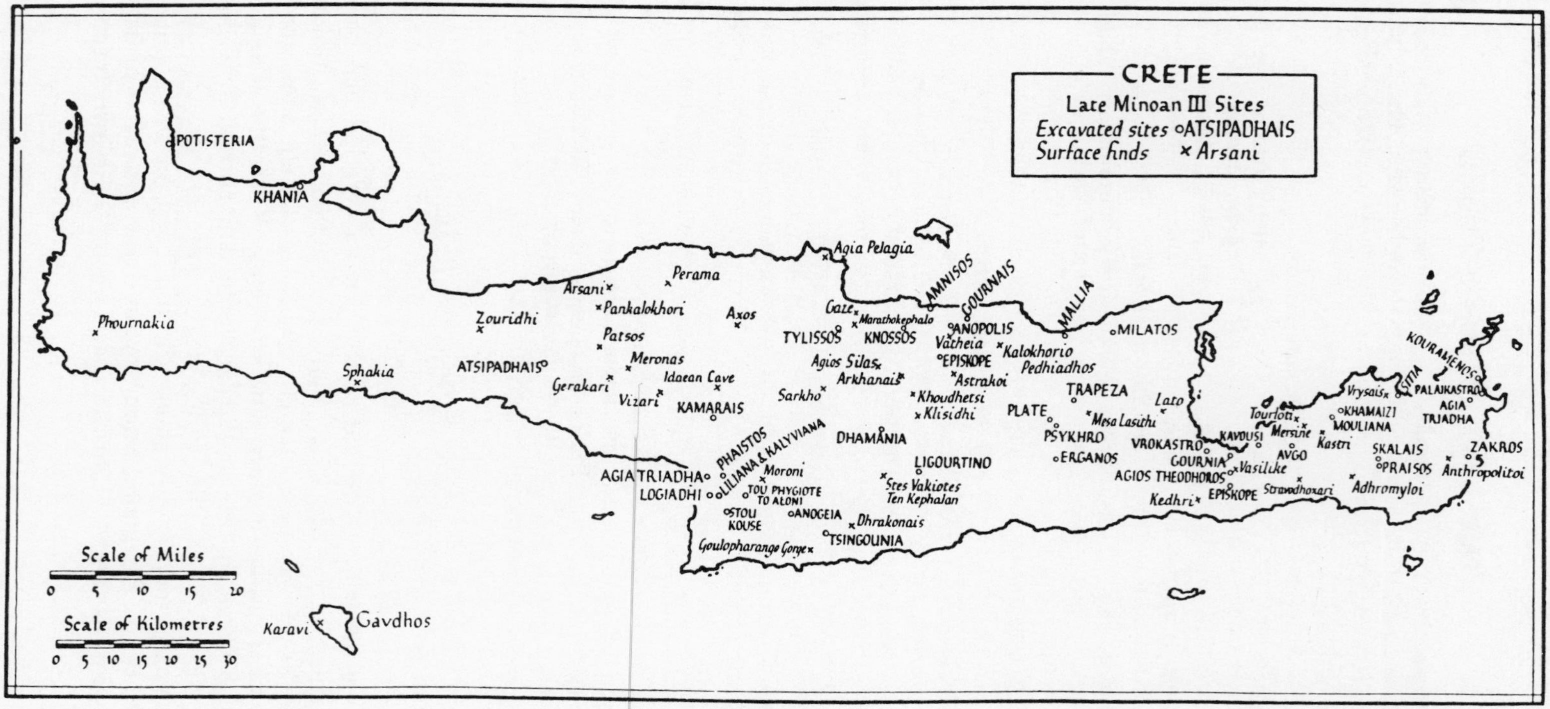

CRETE

Late Minoan III Sites

o Excavated sites o ATSIPADHAIS

x Surface finds x Arsani

POTISTERIA

KHANIA

Phournakia

Sphakia

Zouridhi

ATSIPADHAIS

Arsani

Pankalokhori

Patsos

Perama

Axos

Meronas

Idaean Cave

Vizari

Gerakari

KAMARAIS

AGIA TRIADHA

LOGIADHI

PHAISTOS

MELIDHOKHORIA

Meroni

STOU
KOUSE

TOU PIYIOTE
TO ALONI

CANOKEIA

Dhrakonais

Gouloparanga Gorge

TSINGOUNIA

Agia Pelagia

KNOSSOS

Monastiraphalo

Gazi

TYLISSOS

Agios Silas

Sarkho

Arkhanais

KALIVIANA

DHAMANIA

Kliisidhi

Khoudhetsi

Ini

Astrakoi

EPISKOPE

Vathcia

KNOSOS

KALLONI

AMNISOS

SISNINY

GOURNAIS

MALLIA

MILATOS

Kalokhorio

Pedhiadhos

TRAPEZA

PLATE

Mesa Lasithi

PSYKHRO

Lato

ERGANOS

AGIOS THEODHOROS

VROKASTRO

GOURNIA

Vasiliki

Ten Kephalan

Sres Vokiates

LIGOURTINO

Keahri

EPISKOPE

Sravokhoari

KAVUSI

Vasilike

AVGO

Mersini

Kastri

OUAMANZI

VOULIANA

MOULIANA

Vrysais

Tourloti

SKALAIS

PRAISOS

Adhromyloi

Anthropolitoi

ZAKROS

AGIA
TRIADHA

PALIKASTRO

KOURALES

SITEIAS

Gavdhos

Karavi

Scale of Miles
0 5 10 15 20

Scale of Kilometres
0 5 10 15 20 30

MAP 12

their great fount of wealth, Egypt, apparently cut off from them and their trade in the hands of others,[1] the Minoans were forced to exploit and tame the wild country West of Ida, where before there had been only isolated outposts. We can see the routes they took. The folk of the Messara would colonize the rich Amari Valley and get by Patsos to Rhethymnos. Some would turn off before, and the cemetery at Atsipadhais shows them on their way to Sphakia and even farther West to Phournakia near Voutas. The northerners expanded along the Mylopotamos Valley by Axos, Perama, Pankalokhori, Mesi, and Arsani. West of Rhethymnos, Zouridhi marks the route to Khania and the West.

As one would expect, many of the sites of the pioneers in West Crete are in commanding positions, though in the centre, South, and East the old low-lying sites are still favoured, a proof that life was still comparatively peaceful. Once her wealth had gone and her power was broken, Minoan Crete offered no attractions to the Mainlander.

Architecturally there is no difference between the earlier and later phases of the period. The Palace at Knossos seems to have lain deserted for a while.[2] But the East bastions of the North Entrance were pulled down early in L.M.iii and the entrance attained two-thirds of its original width. The West bastions, however, with their painted plaster relief of the charging bull, remained *in situ*.[3] Somewhat later a number of floors were repaired.[4] But large parts of the Palace were cleared of debris and inhabited with little or no alteration.[5] The two most important relics, however, are in the nature of shrines.

L.M.iii Architecture

In a small chamber South of the Lily Vase Magazine a shrine was found, the objects in which date from the middle stage of L.M.iii.[6] Half the floor was paved with water-worn pebbles and the ledge at the back, 40 cm. high, was similarly paved.

---

[1] No L.M.iii sherds have been found at Komo, for instance, nor at the Harbour Town of Knossos.

[2] *P. of M.*, II, 335. [3] Ibid., III, 160. [4] e.g. *B.S.A.*, IX, 26.

[5] e.g. *Guide to Stratigraphical Museum*, Magazine 8 (D., XII), South Propylaeum (G., II, 8) West of Corridor of the Chess Board (K., II, 3). East Bastion Area (L., IV, 1 and 2). The Queen's Megaron Area (N., II, 18) and the whole Domestic Quarter (N. and O., *passim*).

[6] *P. of M.*, II, 335 ff., called L.M.iii*b*, and certainly with a post Tell el-Amarna style of pottery.

In front of the ledge was a low tripod altar of white stucco round which were laid vases. On the ledge were two pairs of sacred horns with a hole for the insertion of the shaft of a double axe between them, a figure of the goddess with upraised hands, two handmaids and a male votary offering a dove.

In the Little Palace the Lustral Area was paved over and the columns walled in. The coping was used as a ledge similar to that in the above-mentioned Shrine of the Double Axes. On this ledge were plaster horns and the roughly modelled

BLOCK J

KATO ZAKROS – L.M. III

Fig. 40

figure of an ibex. Near by were three stones, shaped by nature into a rude resemblance to the human figure. No doubt these were fetish stones for the worship of the inhabitants of the Reoccupation Period when the old country beliefs had ousted the more urbane religion of the Palace.[1]

These country shrines, as we may call them, are common at this period. One existed at Gaze, though it was destroyed by the peasants, and at Pankalokhori. The small shrine at Agia Triadha must also be put to this date, though probably it is later than the rest, and Dr. Marinatos would, on hitherto unpublished evidence he tells me, make the Prinias and the Gournia shrines of the same period.

At Agia Triadha appears a simple rectangular building divided into four sections, which overlies the Palace. This seems to have been built at the very end of the period and must

[1] *B.S.A.*, XI, 6 ff., and compare the ritual figures in the bathroom of house Γ at Palaikastro. Ibid., *Sup.*, 84 ff.

be the first occurrence of the Mainland type of megaron in Crete.[1]

The extreme East end of Crete seems to have attained considerable prosperity after the disaster. Dawkins remarks that ashlar masonry is rare at Palaikastro before L.M.IIIa.[2] The plans correspond in the main to those of the previous period. In one house in block △ were found objects from a shrine.[3] Three dancers surround a central female figure playing a lyre. Since figurines of doves were also found, it is clear that we have to do with some sanctuary not unlike the shrine of the Double Axes at Knossos.

At Zakros an exceptionally fine house was cleared. This house bears an astonishing but obviously fortuitous resemblance to the contemporary houses of Tell el-Amarna.[4] A

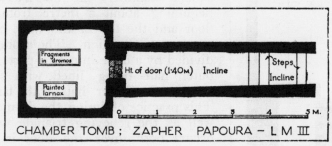

FIG. 41

doorway on to the street leads to a large reception-hall—or possibly court—(9) from which access was obtained to the main living-room (5), which was no doubt run up higher than the surrounding rooms and lit by clerestory lighting. Behind this were the domestic quarters. There seems to have been a bathroom (16) and a service-room (4). The reoccupation houses at Gournia (blocks *Eh* and *He*) show the same good work and resemble in plan the Zakros house.

So good and prosperous are these L.M.IIIa houses in the East that, taking into consideration their practical abandonment before L.M.IIIb,[5] one wonders whether perhaps the invasion of the Mainlanders had had only a temporary effect and whether owing to renewed energy on the part of the

[1] Ibid., XI, 220 ; XII, 250, where it is suggested that it is the result of the introduction of the fixed hearth.
[2] Ibid., 283, 286. [3] Ibid., X, 216 ff., and *Sup.*, 88.
[4] *J.E.A.*, XIX, 1 ff. [5] *B.S.A.*, XI, 250.

eastern sites, perhaps of a piratical nature, the treatment had had to be repeated.   But this is pure conjecture.

The larnax burial is now the regular method of interment, and except for a single group at Alissa Langadhi near Gournia the pithos burial has died out.   The old rock shelter has now developed into a well-cut chamber tomb (Fig. 41).   At Zapher Papoura both the shaft grave and the pit cave continue in use (Fig. 42) as well.

The built tomb is still found and we can see the gradual infiltration of Mainland types in the development from the

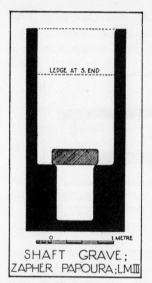

SHAFT GRAVE:
ZAPHER PAPOURA:LMⅢ

Fɪɢ. 42

rectangular tomb, barrel-vaulted, keel-vaulted or with a flat top, to the true tholos.   Earliest must be put the tomb at Dhamania.   This has a square chamber, the c o r b e l l i n g beginning about a metre from the floor and the top of the vault being nearly 3 metres high.   The dromos is divided by a door into two parts, the outer half being lined with small stones, the inner half with larger. This practice of lining the dromos as well as the relieving triangle which occurs both over the door in the middle of the dromos and over that into the tomb are new features for whose origin we must look to the Mainland.

Next comes the tomb at Praisos, which is $2\frac{1}{2}$ metres square with an unlined dromos.   About 1.20 metres up begins a circular vault formed of overlapping stones, which probably ran up to something over 2 metres.   Of exactly the same type is the tomb at Malemo, West of Khania.[1]   It is larger than that at Praisos, being 5 metres square.   The vault begins at 1.75 metres and the total height is nearly 5 metres.   The doorway is fortunately preserved and shows a relieving triangle above the heavy lintel.   Somewhat later are the tombs at Mouliana.

This type of tomb, square with a circular vault above, con-

[1] Since I could find no sherds here I have included it in the catalogue (p. 293, below) of L.M. sites in general.

tinues in Lasithi and the neighbourhood into Proto-geometric times.

Finally comes the true tholos of Agios Theodhoros. It is 2 metres in diameter and the vault, still formed roughly of overlapping stones, reaches the height of 1.80 metres. The dromos is unlined, but a blocking of stones was found in the doorway. This is the only true tholos of the Bronze Age yet found in Crete,[1] and from the contents it seems to belong to the very end of L.M.III. At the beginning of the Iron Age the type is fairly common.

To the latter part of L.M.III belongs the cremation burial at Tylissos. This is the first case of deliberate cremation found in Crete, if we except, as we must, the traces of burning in the E.M. tombs of the Messara. Possibly the tomb is that of a foreigner ; at all events it has no parallel in Crete until the succeeding period.

The evidence of the pottery confirms that of the architecture. The Minoan culture continued unbroken but on a lower level. The Mainland elements which appear both in the shapes and in the decoration are not numerous enough to imply any sort of conquest or settlement from without.

L.M.III Pottery

The most characteristic features of L.M.III pottery are the use of a smooth chalky slip, the greater proportion of painted to unpainted vases, and the sudden raising of what seems to have been an old taboo against the representation of birds and animals on pottery.

Various examples of what may be called a transitional type are known. The best perhaps is the squat alabastron from the Macebearer's Tomb at Isopata.[2] Round the neck are stiff drop-pendants and between the handles are disks, below which runs a band of loosely linked scrolls (Fig. 43, 16). The lower part is filled with a confusing jumble of designs. Among these are very degraded forms of lilies, a rough imitation of a clump of papyrus, crosses, a one-handled ewer, and a waterfowl. The effect is, at first glance, rich, but the decoration is scrappy in the extreme, being thrown together with no leading motive.

From Palaikastro comes a pedestalled strainer.[3] Between the drop pendants below the rim and a frieze of double axes,

---

[1] The comparison given in the publication with the Palaikastro tomb (*B.S.A.*, VIII, 303) is inaccurate. The latter is not a built tomb at all but a rock-cut chamber tomb with a stone blocking.

[2] *T.D.A.*, 16.   [3] *B.S.A., Sup.*, 77.

both of them L.M.I–II designs, is a scrappy band of closely painted chevrons. From the same site comes a squat-beaked jug with a double row of S's round the shoulder and a large lozenge pattern, formed of two rows of chevrons on the body.

Very nearly contemporary with these must be the contents of a pithos burial near Gournia.[1] An early feature here is the quatrefoils between the ' adder mark ' band round a jug. The ' adder mark ' itself has, however, already almost become stylized into chevrons. The care with which the drop pendants are painted and the fact that the outer band of the spirals is still the thickest combine to put this group at the very beginning of L.M.III. Another criterion of the transitional style which seems to hold good, is the junction of the handles of jugs with the rim. In mature L.M.IIIa the handle is set slightly lower on the neck.[2]

Good deposits of early L.M.IIIa pottery were found in the bathroom of block Γ at Palaikastro,[3] in some of the larnax burials from the same site,[4] in a larnax burial near Gournia,[5] in the Temple Tomb at Knossos,[6] in chamber tombs at Kalyvia.[7]

A few new shapes appear. The tall alabastron, still imitating the Egyptian examples,[8] has a rather longer neck.[9] The smaller varieties of jugs have often a round mouth instead of a beak and, as said above, the handle is set lower.[10] The open-mouthed crater has come into fashion [11] (Pl. XL, 3). Practically every variety of stirrup vase is made. A transitional example from Grave 1 at Zapher Papoura narrows down to the foot.[12] From the reoccupied parts of Gournia come an almost globular type, with a foot ranging from a mere ring to what is practically a pedestal, a type where the shoulder is almost flat, making a sharp angle with the lower part of the body and a well-rounded squat type with a ring base.[13] It is noteworthy that the decoration tends to be confined to the shoulder and rarely, as in L.M.II, covers much of the body of the vase. The pilgrim bottles, of which few examples have been found, are probably imported, as may be the stemmed kylix with one handle

---

[1] *Gournia*, Pl. X, 13–26.   [2] *B.S.A., Sup.*, 79.   [3] Ibid., 84.
[4] Ibid., 79.   [5] *Gournia*, Pl. X, 27–43.
[6] *P. of M.*, IV, 1016.   [7] *Mon. Ant.*, XIV, 560.
[8] See above, pp. 202 and 222.
[9] *Mon. Ant.*, XIV, 568. *B.S.A., Sup.*, 79.
[10] Ibid.   [11] e.g. *P. of M.*, IV, 1017.   [12] *P.T.K.*, 22.
[13] *Gournia*, Pl. X.

of Mainland type from Palaikastro,[1] though the two-handled
example from the Diktaian Cave is certainly Minoan from the
thickness of the outer whorl of the spirals.[2]   The normal type,
however, is still really a goblet with a hollow pedestal and two
handles, indistinguishable except for the pattern from L.M.II [3]
(Pl. XL, 3).   The normal cup, which is now almost always
decorated with a narrow band of dark brown paint below the
rim and amorphous splashes, is more carefully made than
before ; it has a swelling body and narrows down to a low
foot.[4] The ' Vapheio ' shape has died out.   At Palaikastro
a small straight-sided vase with a handle perched on the flaring
rim makes its appearance.   It is always painted and examples
occur with a small cup on the rim beside the handle and with
two handles one within the other.[5] Bridge-spouted saucers
are also a characteristic shape of L.M.IIIa in the East.   They
occur both handleless and with a single handle either opposite
the spout or at the side.[6] The circular pyxis has come into
favour again, and round, domed covers for lamps are found.[7]
The rhytons are invariably of the conical shape.

The pithoi are squat, almost barrel-shaped, and are frequently painted on the upper half of the body.   They have a
low neck on to which fitted large flanged lids.   The handles
are set just below the rim and are four in number, two vertical
and two horizontal.[8]

In Central Crete the chest larnax is the most common form.
These larnakes have a single panel on each side which is framed
either by a thickening of the edges or by an imitation in paint.
The lid is gabled and the ridge pole projects at either end to
enable it to be raised.   In East Crete the sides are usually
divided into two panels and the division is continued on to the
lid, which is provided with handles corresponding to those on
the body so that it could be tied on.   These, however, are in
a minority in this part of the island, the most usual shape
being the bath-type already described in L.M.II.   These were
covered either with fragments of their predecessors, for
secondary burials were still common, or by a plain pottery
slab.   While the chest larnax was copied no doubt from the
wooden chests in the houses, there is little doubt that the bath

---

[1] *B.S.A.*, *Sup.*, 84. *P.T.K.*, No. 76e.   [2] *P. of M.*, IV, 369.
[3] Examples ibid., Fig. 306, from the Temple Tomb.
[4] *B.S.A.*, *Sup.*, Fig. 68, 2.   [5] Ibid., 86.
[6] Ibid., and *Gournia*, Pl. X, 29, 30, 38.
[7] Ibid., X, 5. *B.S.A.*, *Sup.*, 89.   [8] Ibid., 98.

FIG. 43.—Patterns on Late Minoan III Pottery

246

larnakes were actually in domestic use before they were employed as coffins.[1]

The patterns used in L.M.IIIa are on the whole a stylized form of those of L.M.I–II. The ' adder mark ' and the waved line tend to become chevrons, which themselves, as we have seen, are combined into lozenges. A typical flower is shown in Fig. 43, 8, but a further stylization soon occurs, when the perianth is merely filled with a series of arcs and finally they are laid on their side so that one side of a flower becomes the top of the next.[2] The papyrus has become a simple necklace (Fig. 43, 18),[3] or has been elaborated into a palmette (Fig. 43, 5). The double axe has already been mentioned. It seldom occurs, but when it does it keeps its character and is not stylized. The same is true of the ' sacred horns ' (Fig. 43, 10), which one would expect to degenerate into a meaningless frieze very quickly.[4]

The octopus is still a favourite form of decoration (Pl. XL, 3).[5] The tentacles are reduced in number to six, though suckers are still on the two lower pairs, and are symmetrically prolonged beyond nature. A still further degeneration is seen on a contemporary crater from Palaikastro, where the top pair of tentacles have been reduced to mere antennae, the two middle pairs have become long straggling lines and the lowest pair form a single loop round the bottom of the body.[6]

But the most distinctive departure from previous Minoan tradition lies in the figures of birds and animals as motives on vases. Waterfowl had been comparatively common on the Mainland from M.H. times, a particularly fine specimen of L.H.II date coming from Argos, but they make their first appearance in Crete in L.M.IIIa.[7] That they are an introduction from without with no local tradition behind them is clear from the purely conventional patterns with which they are decorated and from the already stiff, stylized form in

---

[1] B.S.A., Sup., 151, for a study of the evidence.

[2] Ibid., Fig. 60b, eventually they cover the whole vase as a scale pattern. Ibid., Fig. 76.

[3] This is from Amnisos. Cf. Gournia, Pl. X, 6.

[4] e.g. B.S.A., VIII, Pl. XVIII, Sup., Fig. 88a.

[5] P. of M., IV, 311.

[6] B.S.A., Sup., Fig. 66b. It has the same vandyking round the neck as the example from the Temple Tomb.

[7] P. of M., IV, 335, gives an example found in a confused L.M.I–II deposit in the West Court (B., III, 14, in the Palace Museum). It is the only one so found and may well be an import.

which they are shown, very different from the chance resemblances which induced the E.M. potter to add animal heads to a pattern he had already completed.

They are rare in the North, but are found on a series of tall alabastra from the cemetery of Phaistos and on the well-known larnax from Anogeia (Fig. 43, 5 and 6). Fishes and water plants appear with them and on an example from Ligourtino the birds are shown chasing butterflies. Frequently the tail of the bird spreads out almost into a fan and the wings, when spread, are treated in the same way.[1] In other cases the bird is tailless, and, except when rudimentary wings show that it is flying, wingless.[2]

Animals appear very seldom. Greater naturalism is attempted in their rendering but less success is obtained (Pl. XL, 4).[3] That this should be so is clear proof that the effectively stylized waterfowl are an introduction from without. It may seem strange that the fine tradition of the representation of animals on the frescoes of only a few years previously and on the contemporary sarcophagus of Agia Triadha left no trace in pottery, but we must remember that the two arts were quite distinct in ancient times. The same artist seldom attempted to work on both a flat and a curved ground.[4]

The human figure is only depicted once.[5] This is on a larnax from Tomb 9 at Zapher Papoura. There are traces of a chariot on one side, while on the other two men are roping a wild goat. The drawing is extremely rough and the larnax has the further distinction of being the only Central Cretan example to be divided into separate panels, by a vertical band at the sides and by two horizontal bands at each end.

That the power of representing human figures had not died out, however, is proved by the famous painted limestone sarcophagus from Agia Triadha.[6] The panels are bordered above and below with bands of rosettes. The frame is decorated at the sides with rosette-centred spirals, at the ends with an imitation of variegated stone like that below the Griffin Fresco in the Throne Room at Knossos. So typical indeed of L.M. I–II

---

[1] e.g. *B.S.A.*, VIII, Pl. XIX.   [2] Ibid., *Sup.*, Fig. 72.
[3] *Gournia*, Pl. X, 44. Cf. the griffin from Palaikastro. *B.S.A.*, VIII, Pl. XVIII.
[4] If the Minoans were on the whole ' eidetics ' (see below, page 275), they would naturally tend towards the abstract when painting designs on surfaces on which they could not project the image.
[5] *P.T.K.*, 29.   [6] *Rend. Linc.*, XIII, 343.

work is this framework, that, in spite of its discovery in an unmixed L.M.IIIa deposit, it is hard to believe that it does not date from the earlier period, the more so in that the paintings in the panels are unique if the later date is adhered to.[1] But the attitude of many of the figures in which the near shoulder is on a level with the far one and the introduction of the chariot into the end panels is opposed to Minoan usage and most easily paralleled by examples from L.H.III frescoes. At each end is a chariot ; one drawn by winged griffins contains two female figures, one of whom, perhaps the goddess, has a headdress resembling in some ways that of the Priest King ; the other, drawn by horses, also contains two female figures, probably worshippers. That the horse is still a somewhat rare beast is shown by the mistakes and hesitation in drawing which contrast with the practised representation of the griffins. On one side a procession of women headed by a flute-player is passing behind an altar on which lies a trussed ox. Its throat has been cut and the blood streams into a bucket-shaped vase. Below the altar crouch two calves. In front stands a woman in a short decorated jacket and a baggy kilt, evidently representing the skin of some mottled animal, for a tail hangs down behind. She is making some liquid offering on an altar. Beyond the altar is a double axe with a long shaft on which perches a raven. This stands in front of a highly decorated shrine surmounted by the ' sacred horns ' and apparently surrounding an olive tree. The other side is divided into two sections. To the left a woman, similarly attired to the one already described, pours some liquid, perhaps the blood of the ox, into a cauldron which is set between two double axes, the long untrimmed shafts of which are set on the stepped stands so often found at Knossos. Again, on each axe perches a bird. Behind the first woman stands a second, in more normal Minoan costume, who bears, slung over her shoulder, two more buckets. Behind her again is a man playing a seven-stringed lyre and dressed in the style of the Campstool Fresco. The right-hand half of the panel faces the other way. Here are three men, clad in the same baggy, tailed kilt as the priestess, but with bare chests. The foremost carries a model boat with a high swung prow, each of the others either a calf or more probably a model calf—for the attitude is that of the ' flying gallop '. They approach an elaborately painted flat-topped doorway in front of which stands the figure of a man

[1] *P. of M.*, IV, 295, 426.

clad in a long dappled robe which does not show his arms. By him is a tree and in front of him a stepped platform on which no doubt the offerings are to be laid. Unfortunately the lower right-hand corner is broken away and the legs of the man with it. Since, however, his head is on a lower level than that of those who bring the offerings, it is reasonable to suppose that he is rising out of the ground. In any case we are safe in concluding that the scene represents the offerings made at the tomb of the dead man and to compare it with the common Egyptian scene where relatives bring offerings to the mummy of the ' justified ' which stands between persea trees before the tomb door. It may be remarked in passing that the frame doorway shown in this painting approximates far more to that of the Egyptian door with torus and cavetto than to the simple frame known elsewhere in Crete.

The second phase of L.M.III pottery is well represented at Knossos by two deposits, both of which were separated by some 30 cm. of deposit from the previous stratum. On the floor level above the Room of the Stirrup Vase Tablets were found several stirrup vases. Here the degeneration of the octopus has gone a stage or more further. On one the head and eyes of the creature have become two thick-centred spirals from which the tentacles meander in two symmetrical series of loops round the body of the vase. On another the body of the octopus has been omitted and a single wavy line goes right round. The first vase is very tall and thin, coming down to a splayed foot. The other is more globular and has on its shoulder three long S's in double line which may well be descended from the two-stalked ivy. With these was a disk-shaped strainer, the centre being decorated with a seven-rayed star, the rays consisting of a form of the old ' adder mark '. The Shrine of the Double Axes provided an even better series. The most typical shape is a low one-handled cup in plain clay with a neat flaring foot. A stirrup vase, like the first of those described above, was found, but with a better glaze and the decoration confined to the upper part of the body. The small plain jugs with a plain circular mouth are not unlike M.M.1a examples, while the open-mouthed store jars resemble those of M.M.III. The big two-handled water-pots are precisely like the water-jars of to-day. Two low straight-sided vases were found like those of L.M.IIIa at Palaikastro, but with two handles standing straight up from the rim.[1] Many of the vases show

[1] Cf. from Palaikastro, *B.S.A.*, *Sup.*, Fig. 81.

both within and without the ridges made by the potter's fingers when turning them. The pithoi are well illustrated by several specimens from the North-East angle of the South Propylaeum. They are small and undecorated, with wide mouths and a flat, spreading rim. They narrow down to a ring base and have only two horizontal handles, just below the rim.

The vases from the chamber tomb at Milatos are contemporary, or at any rate they overlap the groups above described. In the first group [1] the central vase is a crater of much the same shape as that shown in Pl. XL, 3, but with a narrower pedestal. The octopus has become a truncheon-shaped object with concentric circles attached at the top for eyes. The lower pair of tentacles alone is joined to the body ; the upper pair has become a disconnected series of loops. This vase contained a one-handled cup of the type found in the Shrine of the Double Axes and stood on an openwork base. Other vases included a long-stemmed kylix type with high swung handles and a curious triglyph decoration at intervals below the rim, a low bridge-spouted saucer on a pedestal with a series of concentric semicircles, a small beaked jug with a pattern resembling that shown in Fig. 43, 9, at intervals round the shoulder and two stirrup vases. One of these latter link on to the very latest true Minoan examples from East Crete with a very rich and elaborate design on the shoulder. The central vase of the second group [2] is a crater of the normal type with a series of highly conventionalized triton shells set vertically round the body and divided by rows of dots. Below each handle is a panel containing a design of four leaves arranged as a star. A stirrup vase of the type found in the Room of the Stirrup Vases at Knossos, a kylix with a band of circles surrounded by dots below the rim and a deep dipper with a high swung handle are the most important shapes. A larnax was found with each group. Both were of the usual Central Cretan type but with a handle at each end of the lid. That found with the second group of vases was plain, but at one end of the other is a rude drawing of a male figure with long floating locks. The right hand is raised, with the palm spread, the left grasps what appears to be a floppy figure-of-eight shield. Below is a fish.

At Palaikastro a good deposit, parallel in date, was found in a store-room, Γ 9.[3] A crater of the normal shape is divided into four panels by vertical bands of spiral, or wavy lines.

[1] *P.T.K.*, Fig. 105.   [2] Ibid., Fig. 106.   [3] *B.S.A.*, *Sup.*, 106.

These are decorated with sprawling chevron patterns, the angles filled with concentric semicircles with dashes outside, the last degradation of the flower, or with a rough-scale pattern, the same semicircles filling the points of juncture. A large, finely formed amphora has an octopus as stylized as that from Milatos but with the body playing a more important if no more accurate part. Another amphora has a well-moulded splaying foot. Wavy lines descending from the handles divide it into three panels. Two of these have treble lines running diagonally across them, every angle being filled with the usual concentric semicircles, but one has a great quatrefoil dividing it diagonally, the leaves of which are filled in solid in the style associated with the end of the period in East Crete. In the field are rosettes, which again make their appearance on a tankard with waterfowl from near by.[1] Another tankard has a design of pot hooks and this shape, whether with one or two handles (cf. Pl. XL, 3, for an example from Knossos), is typical of the period.

It has already been noted that a vase decorated in the close, elaborate style always associated with the very end of L.M.III was found in the tomb at Milatos. Another was found in an intrusive burial in one of the entrance niches of the Royal Tomb at Isopata.[2] The most distinctive feature of this style is the use of thick solid elements in the decoration usually fringed and combined with a forest of fine lines and closely hatched subordinate figures. The octopus motive is a favourite one, and, though still clearly distinguishable, it has become divorced from all reality and is treated as a pure pattern. On the shoulder of a stirrup vase from Tomb B at Mouliana one pair of tentacles only are of any size. These have become thick S scrolls the top coils of which have been turned by cross-hatching into argonaut shells.[3] On one side of a bridge-spouted tankard from the Diktaian Cave the ' octopus ' has no less than twelve thick coiling tentacles as well as two ' antennae '. On the other side is a chequer panel above which is a stylized triton shell pattern. The vase from Isopata, like that from Mouliana, shows the ends of the coils turned into argonauts, while hatched squares and other figures fill the field. That from Milatos has an elaborate design of hatched arcs. The

[1] *B.S.A.*, Fig. 77.
[2] *P.T.K.*, 141 ; cf. a simplified form from Tomb V at Mavrospelio. *B.S.A.*, XXVIII, 258.
[3] 'Εφ. 'Αρχ., 1904, Pl. 1.

stirrup vase from the tholos at Agios Theodhoros [1] shows two
thick coils ending in solid-centred spirals. No body is shown,
only the eyes, but two elaborate rosettes appear in front, the
rest of the background being filled with a diaper of small
arcs. The basket-shaped vase from the same tomb has a
pattern of the same triton shells as appeared on the tankard
from Psykhro, arranged in panels. Part of a stirrup vase with
the same type of pattern was found at Palaikastro [2] but the
centre of this elaborate style must have been what one may
call the 'Middle East' of the island.[3] The rarity of vases of
this style in Crete and their restriction to a single area, in
contrast to their widespread popularity on the Mainland and
in the Islands, preclude one from making a fresh chronological
—L.M.IIIc—division for them. The pottery of L.M.III in fact
falls very easily into two divisions. First the transitional style
exemplified at Palaikastro and leading immediately on to that
of L.M.IIIa typified by the popularity of the bird and octopus
motives. Next L.M.IIIb, typified by a degeneration of the
octopus motive and by a general coarseness of fabric in the
larger vessels. Connected with a good stratum of this phase
at Palaikastro was the tankard with a design of birds which
must be very close in date to L.M.IIIa, while in an equally pure
contemporary group at Milatos was found a vase of the rich,
closely decorated style which, we know from the evidence at
Mouliana, links on to the succeeding sub-Minoan and Protogeometric. At all events one of the greatest necessities for
Minoan archaeology is the excavation of some such site as
that which probably exists on the mainland opposite Mokhlos,
to give a series of strata which might settle these questions
once and for all.

The long rapiers remain the same as those of L.M.II, the *L.M.III Metalwork*
horned and cruciform type still surviving until the end of
L.M.IIIa.[4] In Tomb 95 at Zapher Papoura was found a short
sword of triangular shape with square shoulders and the flange
extending right round the hilt, which widens out into a frame
for the pommel. From a chamber tomb at Palaikastro, on the
borders of L.M.IIIb, came a dagger of the cruciform type, but
with a hilt like the preceding.[5] Latest of all the two swords

[1] *Trans. Penn. Univ.*, II, Pl. XXX. [2] *B.S.A., Sup.*, Fig. 98.
[3] Cf. *Gournia*, 45, Fig. 25. *Vrokastro*, 149.
[4] *P.T.K.*, 105 ff. *B.S.A.*, XXVIII, 282.
[5] Ibid., *Sup.*, 117. This shape seems to go back to L.M.II, as it
appears on the Sword Tablets from Knossos. *P. of M.*, IV, 854 ff.

from Tomb B at Mouliana, of the type of that from Zapher Papoura but increasing in width towards the point, bring us to the threshold of the Iron Age. The only spearhead found, that from the Macebearer's Tomb at Isopata, is of the socketed L.M.II type.[1] The knives often bear a remarkable likeness to a modern carving knife.[2] Razors, both of a single-edged curved variety and double-edged and leaf-shaped are found ; the first type is favoured in the East,[3] while the latter is confined to Knossos, where it had appeared in the last interment in the Temple Tomb. Bronze vases are rare. Two were found in Tomb 99 at Zapher Papoura.[4] One was a shallow straight-sided bowl with horizontal handles placed low down, from the middle of which project knobbed vertical off-shoots. The other is a globular vase with a short wide neck, flat rim, and single ribbon handle. Remains of scales and lead weights were found at Mavrospelio.[5]

L.M.III Stone Vases

There is little falling off from L.M.I to II in the manufacture of stone vases—that is to say if the few that are known are not merely heirlooms.[6] No example from L.M.III*b* is known. The bird's-nest vases and blossom bowls are still in use.[7] A tall cylindrical pyxis with moulded bands at top and bottom has come into fashion for the first time since M.M.I and a smaller pyxis has been found as well as a double example.[8] Two very fine pieces, however, have no parallel elsewhere. One is a low basin with moulded vertical handles from Tomb 99 at Zapher Papoura. The other is a beautiful goblet in steatite from a larnax burial at Gournia. This has a low pedestal, a carinated body, and two grooved handles. It is strongly reminiscent of some of the finest Minyan goblets.[9]

At Palaikastro, the only L.M.III site where stone lamps were found, it was noted that the pedestal at this period was longer than before, or rather that it approximated to the pedestals of L.M.I–II lamps elsewhere. The floral bowl is the same as has already been described. The pedestal has a moulded band half-way up.[10]

L.M.III Figurines

The figurines of L.M.III are made of terra-cotta only. Those

[1] *T.D.A.*, 15.   [2] e.g. *P.T.K.*, 25.
[3] Ibid., Figs. 71, 98. *B.S.A.*, *Sup.*, 118.   [4] *P.T.K.*, 89.
[5] *B.S.A.*, XXVIII, 253. The weight standard was not given.
[6] e.g. in Tomb III at Mavrospelio there was a very fine L.M.I pegtop rhyton in marble.
[7] e.g. Mavrospelio, XII, 1 ; XX, 6.
[8] Ibid., III, 23. *T.D.A.*, 33. *Gournia*, Pl. X, 27.
[9] Ibid., 28.   [10] *B.S.A.*, *Sup.*, 139.

from Gournia and Prinias have already been described under L.M.i, though there is a distinct possibility that they should be attributed to L.M.iii.[1] The great majority, if not all, were found in L.M.iiib deposits, though from the technique of those from the Shrine of the Double Axes and Tombs 3 and 4 at Mavrospelio one would be inclined to believe that they were made in the first half of the period and continued in use.

In the East of Crete, at Palaikastro, was found a group of three women dancing with linked hands round a central figure holding a lyre. The style is lively in the extreme. The vandyke pattern on the skirt and the vases found with them go to show that they belong to the early part of the period.[2]

L.M.iiia is a blank except for this and the unique series of figurines from the cemetery of Atsipadhais. These were almost certainly imported from the Mainland where they are at home,[3] and the pottery that accompanies them, like most West Cretan L.M.iiia pottery, is simpler and nearer to the L.H.iiia style than elsewhere.

The central figure in the Shrine of the Double Axes is the goddess. She wears a tubular crinoline and what appears to be a decorated jacket. Necklaces and bracelets are indicated by dots. Her breasts are placed at the base of the throat. Her enormous hands are raised, the palm of the right hand facing the spectator, that of the left, inwards.[4]

Her features are rude but clearly modelled. Her hair descends in a single plait down her back and on her head is a dove. On either side of her stood slightly smaller figures of her attendants, the head of one being inclined, of the other turned towards her. Their arms, which are mere cylindrical pieces of clay, are curled over their breasts. At the far end of the ledge is a male figure standing on a square base and offering a dove. He wears a closely fitting jacket laced up

---

[1] Further arguments in favour of a late date are the treatment of the hair and the presence of figures of birds which the excavators themselves thought might originally have been on the heads of the figures. Both of these features are exactly paralleled in the figures from the Proto-geometric Shrine on Karphi in Lasithi recently excavated by the writer.

[2] *B.S.A.*, X, 216, *Sup.*, 88.

[3] The three types mentioned in *Archaeologia*, 82, 215, are present.

[4] A similar hand with a dove instead of a plain line on the palm was found at Knossos in 1937. The peculiar position of the hands is paralleled by a seated figurine probably of early Iron Age date from N. Greece, in the possession of Professor A. B. Cook.

at the back and a sketchy version of the codpiece. Besides, there was a very primitive seated figurine in the Neolithic tradition.[1]

Of the same date are two figurines from the Mavrospelio cemetery.[2] Both are rather rougher in feature than those already described. One is a simple figure with outstretched arms. The other, who has a peaked cap or lock of hair at the back of the head, holds out in front of her an infant with raised elbows and a general attitude resembling the bronzes of the M.M.III–L.M.I transitional period. This figure is squatter than the rest, and her dress is decorated with short vertical lines of paint not unlike the dappled robes on the Agia Triadha Sarcophagus. Rather later must be put the large figure from Pankalokhori with a chequered skirt, a small conical hat, and very pronounced features. Last of all come

a   b   c

FIG. 44.—Late Minoan III Seals

the figures from Gaze, one of which with its refined features and elaborate headdress links on to the recently discovered Proto-geometric figures on Karphi in Lasithi (see below).

L.M.III
Inscriptions

The only inscribed object from Knossos is a sherd painted with three signs of Class B Linear Script. It may well be an import from the Mainland, where the script had been taken over in its entirety at this period, for the good glaze is not characteristic of Crete.[3]

L.M.III
Seals

Only one seal stone has been found in a clear association with L.M.IIIa pottery. From Agia Pelagia, presumably from a chamber tomb, comes a haematite cylinder on which a goddess rides a bushy-tailed beaked creature through a thicket of papyrus while an attendant behind her carries a dead griffin over his shoulder (Fig. 44, *b*). The latter figure is extremely well drawn and the sagging body of the griffin is the best representation of death accomplished by a Minoan artist.

[1] *P. of M.*, I, 52.   [2] *B.S.A.*, XXVIII, 291.
[3] *P. of M.*, IV, 738.

Other cylinders, also of haematite, have been attributed to this period.[1] They all betray a queer mixture of Oriental and Minoan subjects, lions and winged figures being especially common. Most of the male figures show the Minoan belt and loin-cloth but their attitudes and the rigidly vertical grouping is un-Cretan. The same is true of a steatite cylinder from Palaikastro, though the daemon is in the Minoan tradition.[2] One or two lentoid bead-seals may also be mentioned here. One from Arkhanais, in agate, represents a bull, bound for sacrifice, laid on an altar. The scene recalls that on the sarcophagus from Agia Triadha. Another, in green jasper, shows three wild duck swimming among the papyrus [3] (Fig. 44a). A third, from the Idaean Cave, shows a goddess blowing on a conch shell before an altar crowned with a pair of horns.[4] Two from Tomb 100 at Zapher Papoura show lions attacking bulls, and one from the Macebearer's Tomb at Isopata shows an ibex and kid.[5]

The lentoid shape continues in L.M.IIIb, usually in steatite. A group in process of manufacture was found in the Lapidary's Workshop at Knossos.[6] The cow and calf still appears as a type and on the trial impressions of clay were found scenes of a dog seizing his quarry, goats, sheep, and oxen. To this period Evans has referred an impression from the Little Palace of a lion springing on a bull (Fig. 44c) and a seal from Arkhanais showing a hunting cat attacking wild duck. To the very end of L.M.IIIb must be put a bead-seal found in the Knossos district showing a convoluted argonaut design.[7]

In seals as in ceramics it is L.M.IIIa which breaks away from the Minoan tradition and L.M.IIIb which returns to it.

A good deal of jewellery was found in the cemeteries of Knossos. Tomb 7 at Zapher Papoura contained a gold-plated bronze ring with the design of a winged sphinx and a gold necklace of beads showing a double argonaut design which is also found at Phaistos.[8] In Tomb 66 was a gold necklace of

L.M.III Jewellery

---

[1] Ibid., 426, 458, 498, and cf. a faience example *P.T.K.*, 71.

[2] *B.S.A.*, VIII, 302.   [3] Ibid. *P. of M.*, IV, 492.

[4] Ibid., 210 ; note the vase with a long spout in front of the altar is identical with that found in conjunction with a similar altar at Knossos (ibid., Fig. 163).

[5] The latter is, I think, a family heirloom from M.M.III, and the same may be said of many of the seals from the tombs at Phaistos. *Mon. Ant.*, XIV, 627 ff.

[6] Ibid., 595.   [7] Ibid., 535, 588. *Index*, 183.

[8] Also found on the Mainland.

rosettes and a chain of ribbed faience beads. Cornelian, crystal, ivory and gold beads of varying shapes were found in Tomb 99, in Tombs 3 and 6 at Isopata, and at Mavrospelio. None of the shapes is new. In the last cemetery, however, there appears in the same deposit as the goddess and child granulated conical earrings of gold with horns which are not unlike facing bulls'-heads.

L.M.III Foreign Relations

Foreign relations at this period are rather difficult to describe. Although direct intercourse with Egypt, or rather, perhaps one should say, state intercourse with official trading between the two countries had ceased, yet the indirect influence exercised by both Crete and Egypt on the other is as strong or stronger than ever.

Only two Egyptian imports have been found in L.M.III deposits, a scarab from Tomb 100 at Zapher Papoura and an alabaster vase from a tomb at Isopata—the latter perhaps an heirloom.[1] No single L.M.III object has yet been found in Egypt. All the pottery which has appeared at Tell el-Amarna is of the Mainland-Rhodes-Cyprus type.[2] On the other hand, the new-found fondness for waterfowl and the conventionally represented papyrus and water background of L.M.IIIa pottery taken in conjunction with an overwhelming predominance in the artistic standards of Tell el-Amarna of the Minoan point of view shows a closeness in the mutual interchange of ideas which had never before been seen.[3]

That, however, is natural. With no more grandiose work for the great palaces, the fine artists and craftsmen would assuredly seek employment overseas. Some, no doubt, were retained by the Mainland lords who had succeeded to the Minoan Empire and who were to make of L.H.III so brilliant a period at Mycenae. Others, however, like the scholars and artists of Constantinople after the sack in 1453, would prefer to try their fortune in the country with which Crete had been so long in contact. In Amenhotep III and in his son Akhenaten they found ideal patrons, and the fresh outlook which they gave to the Egyptians, though short-lived, for political reasons, was enough to revolutionize an art which had become stereotyped and stiff in the course of ages. Conversely we find Egyptian influences coming into Crete. That again is to be expected. Though the official trade between the two countries had no doubt completely ceased with the downfall of Crete, it is evident

[1] *Aegyptiaca*, Nos. 46, 47.   [2] Ibid., 54.   C. of A., II, 110.
[3] P. of M., IV, 336.   *Tell el-Amarna* (Pendlebury), 124 ff.

that there was no Mainland domination of the island, and just as you find to-day an inhabitant of Melidhoni hailing you in Egyptian Arabic and leading you to a room decked with imitations of the products of the Cairo bazaars, so in L.M.III you would have found the returned native of Phaistos busily painting pseudo-Egyptian scenes on his vases.

Relations with Syria must have been on very much the same footing. Quantities of Aegean pottery have been found in this area, but all of it seems to be of Mainland fabric.[1] The ivories, too, have more in common with Mycenae and Cyprus than with Crete.[2] But we have already seen the very strong Asiatic influence on the seals of this period found in Crete, not only in shape but in design.

In the West, Italy and Sicily, again the Aegean imports of this period are from the Mainland.[3]

Most important of all is to distinguish between Crete and the Mainland and Islands in L.M.III. It is quite clear to begin with that no such domination as the Minoan rule in L.M.I–II was enjoyed by the Mainlanders over Crete. A certain number of what one may call Mycenaean features appear, but not enough to imply any control of, or indeed interest in, the island. Among these the introduction of the tholos has already been mentioned, and in pottery the comparatively common appearance of the squat alabastron, the pilgrim bottle, the kylix and the small three-handled amphora. In Crete the decoration of the pottery begins with an elaboration of the Palace style of L.M.II. On the Mainland it harks back to the simpler forms of L.M.–L.H.I. It is noteworthy that in Crete white paint is not used as a subsidiary in L.M.III. L.M.IIIa is on the whole a close style. L.M.IIIb, until the appearance of the ' Middle Eastern ' style, is more open. The opposite is the case on the Mainland. As one would expect, seal stones and rings are commoner on the Mainland than in Crete at this period, and it is clear that many of the best engravers were pressed into the service of the conquerors. The fresco painters, too, who seem to have had no work in Crete, must also have been partly responsible for the production

---

[1] Cf. the various preliminary reports on Miniet el-Beida and Ras Shamra in *Syria*. One vase only is of the Minoan type. *Syria*, XIII, Pl. IV. *P. of M.*, IV, Fig. 756a. In Palestine the pottery from Tell abu Hawam covers the whole period. Not one piece is Minoan. *Q.D.A.P.*, IV, 1 and 2, *passim*.

[2] e.g. *Syria*, 1929, Pl. LVI.   [3] *Mon. Ant.*, II, 9 ; VI, 121.

of the numerous frescoes of Mycenae, Tiryns, and Thebes, adapting their subjects to Mainland tastes.

Since no product of L.M.III has been found in Egypt, the positive dating of the period is difficult. It is hard, however, to dissociate the close style of the Mainland from the Middle Eastern Cretan style of L.M.IIIb, and since none of the former has been found in Egypt and since it appears most likely that the breaking off of the relations between Egypt and the Aegean was due to the first sea raid in Merenptah's reign, i.e. 1232 B.C., it is best to put the change in Mainland styles to somewhere about the middle of the thirteenth century. It is probable, however, that the change from L.M.IIIa to L.M.IIIb came rather earlier in Crete, and we shall not be far wrong if we allow L.M.IIIa to cover the first two-thirds of the fourteenth century, L.M.IIIb the last third of the fourteenth, the thirteenth, and part of the twelfth with the introduction of the Middle Eastern style about 1250.

If this is so, where does the Achaean domination of Crete come ? In Homer, Idomeneus is King of Crete and vassal of Agamemnon.[1] In his realm are Achaeans, Eteocretans, Kydonians, Dorians, and Pelasgians.[2] The Achaeans may well be little more than Idomeneus' house-karls, though the mention of different languages in the island implies that they were a recognized element in the population. The Eteocretans had their home in East Crete in later times and even in Homer's day may well have been considered of particularly pure stock. The Kydonians evidently mean the inhabitants of the recently settled Western parts. Khania is near enough to the Mainland to make a mixed settlement of Minoans and Mainlanders very possible.[3] The Dorians are a difficulty. They ought not to appear for a hundred years or more. Most probably it is a Grecized form of some Minoan tribal division.[4] The Pelasgians are ' aborigines '.

The Trojan War is now generally accepted as being in the second decade of the twelfth century, and the rise of the House of Atreus and the Achaean Empire about 1250. That is the date to which we have provisionally put the appearance of the ' Middle Eastern ' style. Now this style seems not to be native

[1] *Iliad*, II, 645. [2] *Odyssey*, XIX, 175.
[3] The Western L.M.III pottery is nearer the Mainland type and we have already mentioned the Mainland ' dolls ' at Atsipadhais.
[4] The Zakkaray (? Teucrians or ? connected with the modern Zakros which is no Greek word) held Dor in Palestine and Syria.

to Crete. It is far more common in the islands of the Dodecanese and at Mycenae.[1] It is therefore possible to put forward as a tentative theory that after letting Crete alone for some hundred and fifty years the Mainlanders, with the rise of the new Dynasty at Mycenae, decided to bring it into the empire, which probably implied little more than the granting of the fief to some *condottiere* who made his home at Knossos and concocted himself a pedigree reaching from the old royal family of Minos. It was in no sense an act of colonization. If we are right, the pottery of Mouliana is that of an Achaean lieutenant of the eastern marches and in no sense a native product.[2]

SITES WHERE LATE MINOAN III REMAINS HAVE BEEN FOUND

WEST CRETE

(a) Excavated Sites

ATSIPADHAIS	Cemetery	Pithos burials with vases and figurines. Petroulakis, ' 'Εφ. 'Αρχ., 1915, 48.
KHANIA	Cemeteries	B.S.A., VIII, 305. Mariani, Mon. Ant., VI, 203. Ath. Mitt., 1900, 466.
POTISTERIA	Cave	Sherds in first large ' room '. Marinatos Mitt. über Höhlen und Karstforschung, 1928.

(b) Surface Finds

ARSANI	Alabastron in the Rhethymnos Museum.
AXOS	Vase and figurine. Taramelli, Mon. Ant., IX, 310.
GAVDHOS	Vases and sherds from Karavi. Levi, Art and Archaeology, 1927, 176 ff.
GERAKARI	The writer heard in 1935 of figurines said to have been found in a cave on Kokkino Dheti in 1912.
IDAEAN CAVE	Crystal Seal. Evans, J.H.S., 1901, 142.

---

[1] B.S.A., XXV, 48.

[2] Dare we adduce as further proof the gold mask from the tomb ? That would be in the Mainland tradition.

MERONAS . . . .   Emm. Akoumianos remembers vases decorated with octopuses being found above the village in 1912.

PANKALOKHORI . .   Statuette of goddess. Marinatos, *Arch. Anz.*, 1933, 198.

PATSOS . . . . .   Sherds from cave by church of Agios Antonios in the gorge, seen by the writer, 1935. Figurines from cave of Hermes Kranaios. Halbherr, *Mus. It. Class. Ant.*, II, 913.

PERAMA . . . .   Sherds at τὰ Γρέβελα, seen by the writer, 1935.

PHOURNAKIA . . .   Sherds and burials, seen by the writer, 1935.

SPHAKIA . . . .   Vases in the Ashmolean Museum from Τὰ Φαράγγια. *B.S.A.*, *Sup.*, 90, Fig. 73.

VIZARI . . . . .   A larnax burial said to have been found at Ellenika; no sherds could be found by the writer, 1935.

ZOURIDHI . . . .   Burial, sherds, and figurines at Xenageorgi, seen by the writer, 1935. Cf. Evans, *Diary*, 6/3/99.

CENTRAL CRETE

(a) Excavated Sites

AMNISOS . . . .   Tomb . .   Chamber tomb with larnax burials, at Mapheze. Marinatos, 'Αρχ. Δελτ., XI, 63.

ANOPOLIS . . . .   Burial . .   Larnax burial at Artsa. Xanthoudides, 'Εφ. 'Αρχ., 1904, 1.

EPISKOPE . . . .   Tombs . .   Larnax burials at Markabousa. Xanthoudides, 'Αρχ. Δελτ., II, Παρ., 25. Cf. Taramelli, *Mon. Ant.*, IX, 368. *B.C.H.*, 1931, 517.

ERGANOS . . . .   Tombs . .   A few vases from the tholoi. Halbherr, *A.J.A.*, 1901, 270.

GOURNAIS . . . .   Tombs . .   Chamber tombs with larnax burials. Hazzidakis, 'Αρχ. Δελτ., III, 62.

KNOSSOS . . . .   Palace . .   Reoccupation period. Shrine of Double Axes. *P. of M.*, II, 335. Other deposits. Ibid., IV, 734.

Town . .   *B.S.A.*, VI, 70.

KNOSSOS	Tombs . .	Deposit in Temple Tomb. *P. of M.*, IV, 1015. Isopata, *T.D.A.*, 1. Zapher Papoura, *P.T.K.*, 1. Mavrospelio, *B.S.A.*, XXVIII, 243, and VI, 81.
MALLIA	Cemetery .	Larnax burials at Agia Pelagia. *B.C.H.*, 1921, 536. *Ἀρχ. Δελτ.*, II, 186; IV, *Παρ.*, ii, 17. At Agios Demetrios. *B.C.H.*, 1923, 532.
	Deposit . .	South of the Palace. Ibid., 1933, 296.
PLATE	Town . .	Houses and tombs. Dawkins, *B.S.A.*, XX, 1.
PSYKHRO . . .	Cave . .	Deposit in the temenos. Hogarth, ibid., VI, 94.
TYLISSOS . . .	Town . .	Reoccupation period. Hazzidakis, *Ἐφ. Ἀρχ.*, 1912, and *T.V.M.*, 6.
	Tombs . .	Cremation burial at Alotzou. Marinatos, *Ath. Mitt.*, 1931, 112. Larnax burials W. of the site. Hazzidakis, *T.V.M.*, 81.

(b) *Surface Finds*

AGIA PELAGIA . .	Cemetery described by Evans, *P. of M.*, I, 299. Cylinder seal. Ibid., IV, 497. Vases in Ashmolean Museum.
AGIOS SILAS . . .	Vase in Candia Museum from Sokhoro. *Catalogue*, 9182.
ARKHANAIS . . .	Lentoid seals. *P. of M.*, IV, 588, and 41.
ASTRAKOI	Cypro-Minoan Cylinder. Ibid., 425.
GAZE	Clay figurines of goddess, from a stone hut. *A.J.A.*, XL, 371 ff.
KALOKHORIO PEDHIADHOS . .	Clay head. Levi, *Annuario*, X–XII, 619.
KHOUDHETSI . . .	Vase in the Candia Museum. *Catalogue*, 254.
KLISIDHI	Sherds from the hill to the right of the road beyond Partheni Metokhi, seen by writer, 1937.
MARATHOKEPHALA .	Settlement and cave. Mariani, *Rend. Linc.*, 1894, 180.
MESA LASITHI . .	Sherds in road-cutting, seen by the writer, 1936.

SARKHO		Vase in the Candia Museum. *P.T.K.*, 96.
VATHEIA		Vases from Kamina, in the Candia Museum, *Catalogue* 9173/4.

SOUTH CRETE

(a) Excavated Sites

AGIA TRIADHA. . .	Settlement .	Latest Settlement. Halbherr, *Mon. Ant.*, XIII, 71. Levi, *Annuario*, X–XII, 613. *J.H.S.*, XXXII, 388.
	Tombs . .	Square tombs. Larnax burials. Paribeni, *Mon. Ant.*, XIV, 715 ; XIX, 5.
ANOGEIA	Tombs . .	Chamber tombs with larnax burials. Orsi, *Mon. Ant.*, I, 203 ; XIV, 679.
DHAMANIA . . .	Tomb . .	Corbelled vaulted tomb. Xanthoudides, *Ἀρχ. Δελτ.*, II, 171.
KALYVIANA . . .	Tombs . .	Chamber tombs, excavated by Marinatos. *B.C.H.*, 1925, 473.
KAMARAIS	Cave . .	A few sherds. Dawkins, *B.S.A.*, XIX, 1.
STOU KOUSE . . .	Burials . .	Two larnax burials at *Τοῦ Βραχνοῦ ὁ Λάχχος*. Marinatos, *Ἀρχ. Δελτ.*, 1922–5, 53.
LIGOURTINO . . .	Tombs . .	Tholos and others. Evans, *Diary*, 8/5/94. Taramelli, *Mon. Ant.*, IX, 423. *B.C.H.*, 1907, 116. Savignoni, *Mon. Ant.*, XIV, 655.
LILIANA	Tombs . .	Larnax burials. *Rend Linc.*, 1902, 318. *Mon. Ant.*, XIV, 627.
LOGIADHI	Tombs . .	A few poor burials. *Mon. Ant.*, XIV, 653.
PHAISTOS	Settlement .	Reoccupation. Halbherr, *Mon. Ant.*, XII, 7. Pernier, *Mon. Ant.*, XIV, 313.
TOU PHYGIOTE . . TO ALONI (KALYVIA)	Tombs . .	Chamber tombs and contents. *Rend. Linc.*, 1902, 318. *Mon. Ant.*, XIV, 503.
TSINGOUNIA . . .	Settlement .	One house excavated. Xanthoudides, *Panathenaia*, 1907, 92.

(b) Surface Finds

DHRAKONAIS . . . Sherds found near the circular tomb. *V.T.M.*, 77.

GOULOPHARANGO . . Sherds at Agios Savas, seen by writer, 1934.
GORGE   *B.S.A.*, XXXIII, 87.

MORONI . . . . Traces of larnax burials seen by the writer, 1933. *B.S.A.*, XXXIII, 90.

STES VAKIOTES . . Sherd, seen by writer, 1934. *B.S.A.*,
TEN KEPHALAN   XXXIII, 85.

EAST CRETE

(a) Excavated Sites

AGIA TRIADHA . . . Cemetery . Larnax burials. Bosanquet, *B.S.A.*, VIII, 297. House near by. Dawkins, *B.S.A.*, XIII, 1. Moulds. Xanthoudides, 'Εφ. 'Αρχ., 1900, 25 ; 1903, 187.

AGIOS THEODHOROS . Tholos . . Larnax burial. Hawes, *Trans.*
   tomb   *Penn. Univ.*, II, 113, 129.

AVGO . . . . . Guard-house Walls and pottery. Hawes, *Trans. Penn. Univ.*, I, 18. Evans, *Diary*, 14/4/94. Hastings, *A.J.A.*, 1905, 277.

EPISKOPE . . . . Tombs . . Chamber tomb and larnax burials. Hall, *Trans. Penn. Univ.*, II, 111. Xanthoudides, 'Αρχ. Δελτ., VI, Παρ., 157.

GOURNIA . . . . Town . . Reoccupation period. *Gournia*, 20, 45.

   Tombs . . Larnax burials at Alazzomouri and pithos burials at Alissa Langadhi. Ibid., 46.

KAVOUSI . . . . Tombs . . Unpublished, at Petrino Tigani in the village. Vases in the Candia Museum.

KHAMAIZI . . . . Fort . . Few finds. Xanthoudides, 'Εφ. 'Αρχ., 1906, 117.

KOURAMENOS . . . Houses . . Few finds. Dawkins, *B.S.A.*, IX, 329.

MILATOS . . . . Tombs . . Chamber tombs. Orsi, *Mon. Ant.*, I, 208. Evans, *P.T.K.*, 93. Xanthoudides, 'Αρχ. Δελτ., VI, 154.

MOULIANA . . . . Tombs . . Earliest deposit in built tombs. Unexcavated settlement. Xanthoudides, 'Εφ. 'Αρχ., 1904, 21 ff.

PALAIKASTRO . . .	Houses and cemetery	At Kastri. Bosanquet, *B.S.A.*, VIII, 287 ; XIV, 429. In main town latest deposit. Ibid., IX, 314, 8208, *Sup.*, 74 ff. Larnax burials. Ibid., VIII, 297 ; X, 227 ; XI, 290 (at Aspa), 293, and *Sup.*, 148. Chamber tomb. Ibid., VIII, 303.
	Tomb . .	Shrine. Ibid., X, 216 ; XIV, 429.
PRAISOS	Tomb . .	Larnax burial. In built tomb. Bosanquet, ibid., VIII, 245. Gem from later deposit. Ibid., 251.
SITIA	Burial . .	Larnakes from Papourais, E. of the town. Xanthoudides, *Ἐφ. Ἀρχ.*, 1904, 52.
SKALAIS	Cave . .	A few sherds. Bosanquet, *B.S.A.*, VIII, 235.
VROKASTRO . . .	Deposit .	In houses on summit. Hall, *Vrokastro*, 91.
	Tomb . .	At Kopranais. Ibid., 149.
ZAKROS	Houses . .	Latest deposit in town. *B.S.A.*, VII, 121 ff.

(b) Surface Finds

ADHROMYLOI . . .	Larnax burial. Evans, *Diary*, 7/4/94.
ANTHROPOLITOI . .	Sherds from settlement, found by writer, 1934. *B.S.A.*, XXXIII. Cf. Hogarth, *B.S.A.*, VI, 147. Bosanquet, ibid., IX, 176. Evans, *Academy*, 20/6/96.
KASTRI.	Gem. Unpublished. Bosanquet Note-book.
KEDHRI	Larnax burials. Evans, *Diary*, 1896. Vase in the Candia Museum. *Catalogue*, 541.
LATO	A few sherds. Demargne, *B.C.H.*, XXV.
MERSINE	Sherds from Khalinomouri, seen by R. W. Hutchinson, 1936.
STRAVODHOXARI *or* STAVROKHORI	Two stirrup vases in the Candia Museum. *Catalogue*, 9125. Cf. Evans, *Diary*, 1896.
TOURLOTI	Cemetery. Seager, *A.J.A.*, 1909, 286. Bosanquet saw remains at Kastellos ; sherds, seen by R. W. Hutchinson, 1936.
VASILIKE	A few sherds on the N. slopes of the Kephala, seen by the writer, 1936.
VRYSAIS	Site uncertain. Evans, *Diary*, 1898, saw an askos from here.

Chapter V

A SURVEY OF THE MINOAN CIVILIZATION

THE RISE and fall of the Minoan civilization has been sketched in the previous pages, but of necessity many general topics have been omitted.

Racially, as far as the limited data go, the inhabitants of *Physical* Crete remained unchanged from the earliest times down to the *Characteristics* end of the Bronze Age at least. The skeletons of Agios Niko- *of the Cretans* laos differ in no way from those of Milatos. Thus it is clear that any invasion must have been by people of an identical stock, a conclusion in which the steady progress in arts and crafts would incline us to believe.

The Minoans were long-headed and such few skulls of a brachycephalic type as have been found may either be mere freaks of nature or those of actual foreigners resident in the island. In stature they were short, shorter on an average than the Cretan of the present day. Increase in height, however, with the passage of centuries is a phenomenon which appears almost universally. It cannot be said to be due to any influx of invaders, who, while responsible for shortening the skull, were certainly no taller than the aboriginal inhabitants. The present-day Cretan has, indeed, much of the Minoan in him, for the Minoan stock, like the Egyptian, was evidently one which readily absorbed new elements. All over the island to-day you see the wasp waists, no longer artificially restricted but still emphasized by the long silk girdle, the slim hips, the high square shoulders and the long legs. Many a village boy might be the direct descendant of the Cup-Bearer or the Priest King, and who can deny the possibility that he may be ? Minoan, too, is the sense of style which your modern Cretan has above all other Greeks. His very dress, the baggy breeches (βράχα), the headcloth (μαυρομαντίλι or σαρίκι), the belt (ταράβολουσι), can all be paralleled in Minoan times. The Zouave jacket (μειτάνι) seems to have been confined to the women, but the well-cut riding-boots of white, red, or black leather remind us of the leggings shown on the Agia Triadha vases, on one of which the frieze cape (ϱασίδι) is also shown.[1]

It has often been said that the scanty Minoan costume is an indication of the eventual origin of the race in a warmer climate. Admittedly the codpiece has Libyan affinities, but it would be unsafe to argue from that that the Minoan stock as a whole was of Libyan origin. How far it was the artistic convention to omit everything but the simplest garb one cannot say. But their fondness for the human figure may well have caused the artists to show as much of it as they could, and it must be remembered that in Egypt men were portrayed wearing the old kilt for centuries after long robes of gauffered linen were in fashion.

One item of costume remains to be mentioned, the seal. This was probably worn in the case of a cylinder or signet, suspended round the neck, in the case of a bead-seal, lentoid or amygdaloid, round the wrist as in the Cupbearer Fresco. Finger-rings are rare and those which have survived are all of precious metals. No case is known of a stone seal set as a bezel. Such signets are particularly necessary where writing is the accomplishment of few.[2]

Minoan Language

How much of the language survived one cannot say. A number of Cretan words—some of them current in ordinary Hellenic speech—have been preserved by such writers as Hesychius.[3] As one would expect, many of them are words for plants, flowers, or animals for which the intrusive Greek language had no equivalent. Some have to do with navigation, the terminology of which is always liable to be a hotch-potch of languages. The -nth- and the -ss- terminations are particularly common, τερέβινθος (terebinth), σμίνθος (mouse), κυπάρισσος (cypress), and θάλασσα (sea). These terminations frequently appear in place-names of a pre-Hellenic character, Knossos, Tylissos, Tiryns, Corinth, and, in Asia, Labranda.[4]

[1] See, however, Gerola, *Monumenti Veneti*, II, 327, where a different type of breeches is shown in the 14th.–16th. cent. Note also that most of the names are foreign. Ταϱάβολουσι, for instance, is ' the stuff of Tripolis '.

[2] Any one who has been in charge of a piece of Government work in a country like Egypt, where the labourers, mostly illiterate, are expected to sign a receipt for their wages, knows the dialogue on pay-day :—' Can you sign ? '—' No ! '—' Have you your signet ? '—' I forgot it ! '—' Give me your thumb print.'

[3] *Lexikon*. See useful list of words, Glotz, *The Aegean Civilization*, 386 ; also a list of Cretan Months, Reinach, *Epigraphie Grecque*, 487.

[4] Cf. Haley and Blegen, *A.J.A.*, XXXII, 141 ff.

One or two words may even survive to the present day, such as ἐπά or ἐπάϋγε (*here*), ἐδά (*now*) and ἐτά (*there*), or the old-fashioned word ἄχλα (*tomb*), sometimes heard in Lasithi. Certainly place-names of a Minoan character lasted well down into Classical times, as one can see from the names of streams and hills in such documents as the Olous-Lato boundary treaty. Unfortunately the only name that is still applied to-day is purely Greek. The Kalos Lakkos, near Ellenika village, still marks the boundary between the districts of Elounta (Olous) and Agios Nikolaos (Lato pros Kamara).

What the language of the Minoans was it is as yet impossible to say, except that it was not Greek. The L.H.iiib inscription from Asine,[1] where the Minoan characters approximate to the Cypriote syllabary, has indeed been translated into Greek. But that is precisely what one would expect at this period when the courtly Minoan tongue, which was no doubt used for all official purposes like our Norman French in England, had died out and the common tongue of the native population was written in its stead. For if one thing is clearer than another it is that neither the Minoan script nor the Cypriote syllabary was composed for a language of the Greek type, and racially there is a world of difference between the two peoples.

It would be a profitless task to guess at it. The material is there and is arranged. We can only hope for a bilingual clue ; perhaps a bill of lading in Egyptian and Minoan will one day be found at Komo. Even then it may turn out to be a dead language which has left no descendant behind to help in its decipherment. All that we can safely say is that the probabilities lie in the direction of its being an Anatolian language, perhaps allied with Lykian, Cilician, or Carian, since, as we have seen, it is from those parts that the race seems to have come. Two documents which should help us have unfortunately little to offer. One is a schoolboy's writing-board from Egypt of early XVIIIth-Dynasty date.[2] On one side is a list of names headed ' to make names of Keftiu '. Some of the names, however, are Egyptian, such as Sennefer and Sennefert ; one, Benjeber, is Semitic. One, however, is of considerable interest, Akesh, which it has been reasonably suggested is the same name as Achish (Ikausu), the Philistine friend of David. With it must go another name, Akesht, perhaps the feminine.

[1] Persson, *Schrift und Sprache in Alt-Kreta*.
[2] Peet, in *Essays in Aegean Archaeology*, 90 ff.

The other document is a Keftian spell for the eyes. How much this is pure mumbo-jumbo and how much it is an unsuccessful attempt on the part of the Egyptian scribe to write Minoan in Egyptian characters, it is hard to say. At all events a careful study by Wainwright [1] has made it clear that many of the words have affinities with names common in Asia Minor.

Of the famous post-Minoan ' Eteocretan ' inscriptions from Praisos it is again unsafe to say anything with certainty. A strong case has been made out for their being in an Indo-European language,[2] but that is all. It seems impossible, then, that they should represent a late stage of the Minoan language.

It is conceivable that there was a Libyan element in the language, since, as we have seen, North Africa played its part in the development of civilization in its early days in Crete. Owing to the absorbent powers of the Minoan physical type and to the fact that the Libyans themselves may well have been a branch of the same Mediterranean race, one cannot call the Messara skulls in evidence. But it is a possibility that should be borne in mind.

That the language was connected with Egyptian is unlikely. Such hieroglyphs as are common to both are definitely foreign to Crete and are clearly borrowed. It would be most unsafe to attempt to give them their Egyptian values. Many of them give the impression of determinatives, a very necessary addition to a script where the vowel sounds are not written.

Minoan Life

Much might be gained from a really close study of every available scrap of evidence as to the life of the Minoans. There is space here for only the briefest survey. Corn, vines, and olives, ' the Mediterranean Triad ', were certainly cultivated, but we know nothing of the methods. The plough, for instance, is very like the Egyptian plough, but was it drawn by oxen ? The lack of interest on the part of the Minoan artist in everyday life at home and in the fields has deprived us of a great source of knowledge. Sheep and goats were kept, as well as oxen. We know that from the bones. But what were the draught animals ? We know from a clay model found at Palaikastro that the four-wheeled cart was known as early as M.M.I, but we never see one in use on a fresco or a seal stone. The chariot probably came in with the horse in L.M.I–II, but Crete was too rough for its regular use. The normal method of progression for the rich man was a palanquin. Riding seems to have been unknown.

[1] *J.E.A.*, XVII, 26 ff.   [2] *B.S.A.*, VIII, 125 ff.

Naturally the sea played a large part in Minoan life. Fishing
must have been the occupation of most of the coast towns. But
from the earliest times Crete had been in contact with overseas
powers, and her domination of the East Mediterranean has
come down to us in the tradition of Minos the Thalassocrat.
Now it seems clear that it was the Minoans who did the trading,
and it must certainly have been in their interests to keep the
high seas free of pirates. Indeed, we no doubt have an echo
of the downfall of Crete in one of the Amarna Letters.[1] Here
we find that Amenhotep III has to increase the coastal police
owing to the sudden increase of piracy on the part of the
Lukki (Lycians ?) and others. Curiously enough, we have no
scenes of a sea-battle, though possibly the wild-looking archer
on the fragment of an L.M.i rhyton (Pl. XXXVII, 4) may
have been part of a scene in which a pirates' nest was smoked
out.

A few models of boats have been found, but our chief source
of information comes from the seal stones.[2] The prow is
always high and frequently ends in a forked prong, but in
many cases there is a raised after-castle in the stern. Both
sails and oars were used. The steering seems to have begun
with a fixed rudder like a spur projecting from the stern, but
by M.M.ii, no doubt under Egyptian influence, two steering
oars are substituted. In two L.M.ii seal impressions a deck-
house, or at least a shelter for the rowers, is shown.[3] Heavily
built-up cogs as well as lighter galleys were used. Of their
methods of navigation we know nothing, but it is probable that
a good deal of their lore was handed down to be incorporated
in later itineraries, for Skylax and the *Stadiasmus* are both
particularly well informed about Crete.

On the whole the Minoans seem to have been a peaceful folk.
In contrast to the Mainland, scenes of combat are rare. Body
armour until L.M.ii [4] was unknown, but the great figure-of-
eight shield ($\dot{\eta}\dot{v}\tau\varepsilon\ \pi\dot{v}\varrho\gamma o\varsigma$) protected the warrior from the
neck to the feet, while a helmet, perhaps covered with boars'
tusks, covered his head.[5] For this defensive armour the

[1] Winkler, 128.
[2] Marinatos, *B.C.H.*, 1933, 170 ff. A careful study of all the
evidence.
[3] *P. of M.*, II, 244.
[4] Ibid., IV, 803. Corselets appear on tablets from the Armoury
(L.M.ii), but are never shown in scenes of combat. Is this another
Mainland feature of L.M.ii ?
[5] Ibid., 868. *Archaeologia*, LXXXIII, 212.

weapon was the spear. The sword was, except for the great broadsword of Mallia, a rapier adapted for thrusting only and incapable of guarding except by skill. The speed necessary for such play rendered the use of the huge shield impossible, and since we have no representation of any smaller shield, it is most probable that some skill in fencing had already been attained, while the size of some of the daggers may imply that sword and dagger were used together, though we have no other warrant for supposing so. The bow is rarely used. Evidently the Minoans were not the celebrated archers that the later Cretans became.[1] Sling stones are found but, in Crete, no representation of a slinger is known.

Minoan Religion

The religion of the Minoans has been the subject of many studies.[2] Its possibilities and its ramifications are endless, and a very brief account must suffice here.

Of the places of worship in E.M. times we know nothing. But in M.M.1 we find mountain sanctuaries such as those on the windy peaks of Juktas and Petsophas.[3] At that time also it is possible that the caves, which had provided a home for the Neolithic population and a cemetery for the Early Minoans, became sacred. Whether this implies some sort of worship of the dead it is hard to say. Many of the M.M.1 deposits by the circular tombs in the Messara are votive deposits rather than offerings made at the funeral. More probably it was the fantastic nature of the places and the natural pillars of rock and stalactite which gave the caves of Kamarais, Skoteino, and Trapeza their sacred character. For the worship of pillars and of sacred stones in the shape of *omphaloi* was evidently deeply ingrained.

With the rise of the Palaces in M.M.1, however, a more dignified form of chapel appears in the Palaces themselves, and we find a steady rise in splendour from the simple pillar-rooms of Knossos and the small sanctuary at Phaistos to the elaborate shrine shown on the Miniature Frescoes, which still, however,

[1] We do not know where they learnt the art. Certainly not from Egypt, the only country in the ancient world to draw properly to the ear.

[2] The best are Evans, *Mycenaean Tree and Pillar Cult, The Earlier Religion of Greece, P. of M., passim*, and Index, s.v. *Religion*; Nilsson, *The Minoan-Mycenaean Religion*.

[3] It is a point worthy of attention that whereas in the rest of Greece the peaks of mountains once dedicated to Zeus have now a chapel of Prophetes Elias, in Crete the place of whatever deity had power over them has been taken by Aphendes Khristos, or more simply Aphendes.

keeps the pillars as a central feature. The private houses also begin to have their own shrines, though these seem to keep to the old simple form of pillar-room. Finally, after the fall of the Palaces in L.M.I–II, we see the simpler rustic sanctuaries returning, probably as centres of worship for the whole community, not merely for the nobility. That this is a return to an old fashion which had never died out is evident from the scenes on earlier rings and gems where a goddess is often shown seated with her attendants in a sacred grove.

Throughout their history, indeed, the Minoans were worshippers of nature, who was represented from M.M. times by a great Mother Goddess, Mistress of Trees and Mountains and Lady of the Wild Animals. As representing the fertility of nature she is often credited with a son—a boy-god. In Greek times her attributes were divided among a number of goddesses, Athene takes her snakes, Aphrodite her doves and her son, Artemis, her stags, and various nymphs her mountains, streams, and forests. But there was always the tendency in Crete to combine these goddesses into one, and Britomartis or Diktynna was more truly the goddess of Crete than the politely Hellenized Athene or Artemis.

When pictured on the rings and seal stones, the goddess is always bareheaded, with her long tresses floating in the wind. In the more urbane statuettes destined for Palace use she wears a tiara or crown, and no doubt it is this tradition which is followed in the capped figures of L.M.III. In either case she follows the women's fashion of the period. Her son is shown either naked or wearing the normal loin-cloth. Occasionally he wears a peaked cap. He is one of those soulless, faun-like, heartless boys whom you meet in the wilder parts of Crete to-day.

Being divinities of the earth, the water, the air, and all that in them is, they were evidently considered to be resident in pillars, trees, or queer stones, and Evans has made out a very good case for the ritual means of evoking them by invocation, by summoning on a conch-shell, or by dancing, and for the outward manifestation of their presence by the appearance of birds perching upon the cult object.[1]

Two objects must be mentioned in connexion with religion.[2] The first is that known as the ' horns of consecration '.[3] A

---

[1] *P. of M.*, Index, 147. [2] Nilsson, *M.M.R.*, 152.
[3] Cook, *Zeus*, I., 508, gives reasons for supposing their origin to lie in the setting of actual horns on an altar.

detailed discussion by Nilsson shows that they mark a place
of consecration where the cult objects are laid, the libation
jug, the double axe, or the sacred bough.   On the other hand,
they may be used as an architectural decoration on buildings
of a sacred character, whether actual shrines or a building like
the Palace at Knossos whicn was a kind of sanctuary itself.
The double axe itself [1] is found as a votive offering and as a
cult object between the horns of consecration.   On rings and
seals it is seen ' handled by ministers of the cult or carried by
women.   It is never in the hands of a male god '.   This makes
it practically certain that it is in no sense a thunder weapon
or a symbol of the male counterpart of the Mother goddess.[2]
The most likely explanation is that it was originally a sacrificial
axe which had in course of time become both a cult symbol and
a cult object.

The most common living creatures to appear in a religious
context are the bull, the dove, and the snake.   The splendid
Cretan bull was a natural symbol of power and strength.   We
have no archaeological reason to believe that it was worshipped.
It was certainly sacrificed, and if the bull-leaping sports were
of a religious character at all, no doubt some of that sanctity
would attach itself to the central figure, but there is no direct
authority for speaking of a bull-god.   On the other hand, the
sky-god common to nearly all the Near East is frequently given
the form of a bull.   Was Crete one of the few exceptions ?
It is hard to think so.   The doves frequently accompany the
goddess and are seen perching on double axes, pillars, and
trees.   Again we can say that such birds are the natural
attributes of a divinity of the woods.   The snake, however, is in
a rather different category.   It seems to have been a kind of
beneficent spirit looking after the welfare of the house, as it is
considered in many parts of the world to this day.[3]   Mention
has already been made of the paraphernalia of its cult found
in an L.M.II house in the West Court at Knossos (see p. 211),
and in several shrines ' snake tubes ' have been found.   It
may have been actually worshipped or merely propitiated in
a friendly way, but at all events it is the only living creature to
which tribute was paid.

Another class of figure which is associated with religious
scenes is the animal-headed daemon, which is particularly

[1] *M.M.R.*, 192.
[2] But cf. a slightly later gem from Melos. Cook, *Zeus*, II, 544.
[3] *P. of M.*, IV, 138 ff.

popular in the Late Minoan Period.[1] These daemons appear as attendants both on the goddess and the boy-god, to whom they bring libations and for whom they often act as heraldic supporters. The type certainly owes much to the Egyptian goddess Taurt, but it is also conceivable that they may represent human attendants masked with the heads of the usual animal companions of the divinity.

The Minoan view of death, and the cult of the dead, is hard to determine. The presence in the tomb of such objects as were used in daily life implies a belief in some existence after death. It is dangerous to rely on the Ring of Nestor,[2] since it was found on the Mainland, and though it is no doubt the work of a Cretan artist, we have seen that the subjects depicted by such artists for Mainland consumption were often very different from those popular in Crete. It is safe, however, to say that offerings were made to the dead at their tombs from M.M.1 onwards,[3] and that it appears from the Agia Triadha sarcophagus that the dead man was summoned by some ritual to rise from his grave and partake of them.[4]

It was no doubt the influence of the Palace worship which *Minoan Art* led to the curious mixture in the Minoan character of religious formalism and a real *joie de vivre* of a somewhat heartless and childlike nature. Minoan art shows clearly that, while much of the artist's work consisted of depicting scenes of a religious or semi-religious nature, yet he certainly had a quick observant eye for wild life and a sense of the country which is unparalleled in antiquity. His natural vitality was expressed in his representation of such sports as boxing and the bull-leaping which, however much they may have become bound up with religion, must in origin have been purely secular, and the outcome of a love of physical exertion which is only now returning to the Aegean. His observation of nature is brought out in the almost photographic representations of animal life. His art is intensely subjective and Snijder has produced some remarkable parallels between Minoan art and that of a class of people known as ' eidetics '.[5] Just as one can look away from a window and

[1] Ibid., 431 ff.
[2] Ibid., III, 146 ff., and *The Ring of Nestor, &c.*
[3] e.g. in the annexes to the Messara tombs and in the Temple Tomb at Knossos.
[4] Nilsson, *op. cit.*, 378, believes that the dead man was actually deified and is receiving divine rites.
[5] Snijder, *Kretische Kunst.*

still see its shape clearly on a blank wall, so some people have the power of conjuring up an actual object which they have seen, printing it as it were from the negative of their memory on to the bare wall or canvas to be decorated. It appears that this was how the cave artist of Altamira worked—by drawing in the picture he could flash at will on the rock wall. To-day it is mostly confined to the comparatively simple-minded, for once knowledge, one might almost say scholarship, with its accompanying conventions comes in, this gift ceases to work. It is noteworthy that in Crete it is most in evidence in the frescoes, which were drawn quickly before the image faded, less so in the plaster reliefs and hardly at all in the seal stones which required a longer time to work. It is also the case that the human figure is almost always formalized, perhaps owing to the same kind of tabu which precluded its inclusion in the repertoire of the vase painter.[1] But in their representations of wild life, of animals and birds, and in their sense of the surroundings in which the action takes place, the Minoan artists are not approached in ancient art until the days of Tell el-Amarna, the peculiar style of which they may well have done much to influence.[2]

As a rule the Minoan artist worked best on a small scale. His miniature vases, painting, and sculpture are excellent. But when he comes to work on a larger scale, although many individual figures such as the Priest King are magnificent, he does not seem capable of taking it all in and, from what one can judge from the fragments of the Procession Fresco and others, his grouping leaves much to be desired.

A curious gap in the Minoan mentality is the lack of historical sense. No picture exists of any scene which can be described as a record of an historical event. No inscriptions were put up on the Palace walls or on the cliffs recording wars or expeditions or the reception of tribute.[3] Indeed, they never realized the possibilities of writing as decoration on a large scale, which is the more strange in that not only were they in close contact with Egypt, where the inscribing of walls had

---

[1] As has been said above, however (p. 248), the rounded surface of a vase practically forced an abstract form of decoration on the artist.

[2] See above, p. 258 ; also Frankfort's chapter in *The Mural Painting of El-Amarneh*.

[3] This leads one to believe that when the script is deciphered it will make extremely dull reading.

reached a fine art, but also their developed hieroglyphic script had been used quite effectively on M.M.II seal stones. Admittedly the linear script is not well adapted for decorative purposes, and even on documents calligraphy in the Egyptian sense seems never to have been attempted, but one would have expected them to keep on the hieroglyphic script for this very purpose parallel with the linear.

We have therefore been forced to decipher the history of Crete from the material remains and a brief résumé of the results may not be out of place. *Résumé of Minoan History*

In the Neolithic Period (before 4000–c. 3000 B.C.) a folk whose nearest cultural connexions were with South-West Anatolia and Syria, entered Crete. Comparatively few in number, they occupied sites in the rocky uplands of East Crete, the isthmus of Hierapetra, and the fertile valley of Messara, as well as scattered settlements along the North coast, whence they obtained access to the mountain plain of Lasithi (Map 3). Originally they were a seafaring race. This is clear from the occurrence of Egyptian artefacts in Neolithic strata and from the fact that the settlements divide themselves up into groups, each one reached from some point on the coast. There is no string of sites leading from one original landing-place whence the rest were colonized. Indeed, it would appear that their main idea was to avoid the coast at all costs. The eastern group of sites has Zakros alone for a port. The Messara has Komo. Mokhos, the Lasithiote sites, and those on the western slopes of Lasithi have Mallia. Knossos has Amnisos. It may well be that other coastal sites await discovery, but we cannot get away from the fact that on those which have already been excavated the Neolithic deposit is meagre in the extreme. *The Neolithic Period*

For the most part caves served them for habitation and naturally a smaller version of their dwelling acted for a burial-place. Only on one site in each of the main groups are there built houses, Magasa, Knossos, and Phaistos. Perhaps we may regard these as capitals of each small state. What was the fear which drove them to seek shelter in caves we shall probably never know. It is explicable at a wild site like Potisteria but for pastoral communities, as the rest seem shortly to have become, we cannot say. We certainly cannot maintain that it was only in the course of time that they learned to build, for although no traces were found it is quite certain that even in the Lower Neolithic Stratum at Knossos there was some form

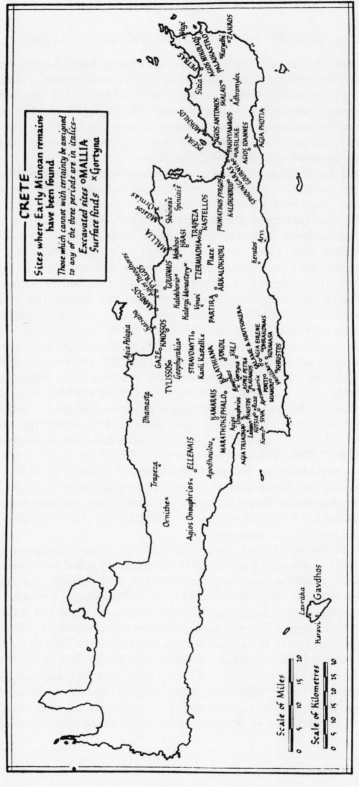

CRETE

Sites where Early Minoan remains
have been found

*Those which cannot with certainty be assigned
to any of the three periods are in italics—*

Excavated sites ○MALLIA
Surface finds ×Gortyna

MAP 13

of artificial structure, while on most other sites they were still inhabiting caves until the very end of the period.

In the Early Minoan Period (*c.* 3000–*c.* 2200 B.C.) the population of the island increased rapidly (see Map 13).[1] The most noteworthy feature is the foundation of important towns on the coast such as Palaikastro, Pseira, Mokhlos, and Gournia. The most prosperous settlements are in the East and there is little doubt, taking into account the evidence of the finds also, that this new wave of colonization came as did the original stock from Asia. In the South, however, where the Messara is thickly settled, there is some reason to see a wave, perhaps a small one, of immigrants from Libya. At all events, life becomes far easier, and ordered communities are springing up. But the island is still divided into three main groups, Central, Southern, and Eastern, and it may well be that these groups correspond to tribal divisions on the Asiatic side, each of which reinforced during the third millennium its original emigrants. Further excavation in Anatolia and Syria alone can tell us. *The Early Minoan Period*

In every department of life great strides have been made. House architecture, for which the eastern end of the island affords us the best evidence, had reached a very high pitch. The old ' but and ben ' hut of Neolithic days was enlarged by throwing off additional rooms though little regular planning is yet to be seen. As always, in primitive times, funerary architecture reflects the fashions of a previous generation and we find in the East the old ' but-and-ben ' surviving for tombs. Even this concession to fashion must have seemed new-fangled to some for the rock-shelter, which is still practically universal in the centre, is frequently found. In the South by E.M.II the circular tomb, no doubt reminiscent of Libya, had ousted other forms of burial.

It is impossible to say what kind of social order existed. Glotz has drawn a delightful picture of a patriarchal community which he bases on the multiple burials in the tombs both of South and East Crete.[2] He sees each clan or *genos* with its own house and its own tomb and he traces the breaking up of the clan in the introduction of separate interments in later times. Attractive as this theory is, there is not sufficient weight of evidence to support it. Individual burials are common

[1] In this and the following maps are included, in italics, sites which cannot be more accurately dated than to E.M., &c. A list of these is at the end of the chapter.

[2] *The Aegean Civilization*, 134 ff.

everywhere except in the South.   Few of the rock-shelters
could have held more than one body at a time and a secondary
interment would only be possible when the first had become
skeletized.   We can allow, also, the existence of one or more
charnel-houses to each settlement, as indeed exist to-day in
Crete, without postulating a patriarchal régime based on the
genos.   All the evidence, indeed, points to the appearance of a
settled urban community which took the place of the scattered
farmsteads of Neolithic times.

It was this concentration of the population into towns and
villages which made the advance in artistic achievement
possible.   In a purely pastoral stage, such as that in which
most of the Cretan settlements had previously been, the professional artist does not exist.   The pots are made by the
women of the house, and so is such jewellery as can be made
from teeth and pebbles.   The man confines himself to the
building and the manufacture of weapons.   It is with the
appearance of towns and villages that the arts of the potter
and engraver became professions.

In ceramics the Early Minoan Period saw the introduction
of painted decoration and the imitation in pottery of metallic
and leather shapes.   With better firing a lighter colour was
given to the wares and as a result dark-on-light decoration
was at first the rule.   The tricks played with the background
of the vases by the potters of Vasilike, however, rendered a
pattern of dark lines useless, and once the artists had tired of
the novelty of a decoration which they could not successfully
control they introduced white paint, which alone would show
up on the now darker background.   As a result the mottled
ground was abandoned and a black wash substituted.   Light-
on-dark decoration had come to stay, on the finer pottery, for
800 years.   By the end of E.M.III almost every shape of vase
which was to appear in Minoan times was already in use.

In metalwork the Minoans were backward.   Much use was
still made of obsidian.   But no doubt it was the possession of
metal tools which made possible the perfection of the stone
vases, though great use was still made of the reed drill.   In
sculpture, however, they as yet gave no sign of the heights they
were later to reach, and except in the Messara, where a strong
foreign influence had made itself felt in E.M.III, the seal stones
are comparatively poor.   The rendering of natural objects was
as yet in its infancy.   The finest artists concentrated on pure
design.

The foreign relations at this time were with Asia, Egypt, and Libya. From the first came the bulk of the increased population, with the second a certain amount of direct trade must have been carried on, from the third there possibly came a small band of immigrants thrust overseas by the overthrow of the West Delta Kingdom by Khasekhemui, and from the same quarter comes the influence felt in E.M.III which we must connect with the Syrian domination of parts of Northern Egypt in the First Intermediate Period. Relations with the Cyclades were constant, though it is often hard to say what is the result of direct intercourse and what the natural parallels between populations of the same stock.

The Middle Minoan Period (*c.* 2200–*c.* 1600 B.C.) sees two *The Middle* most important changes : the rise of the Palaces and, allowing *Minoan* for local differences due to natural difficulties of communica- *Period* tion, a unity of culture. The map (Map 14)[1] shows a great increase in the number of settlements in the centre and South of the island and a corresponding decline in importance if not in number in the East. The three main divisions are still there but a string of sites is now beginning to connect them up and the trunk road from Komo to Knossos has been laid. The population has begun to spread in a systematic way West of Ida, in which region excavation would no doubt bring to light a good deal more evidence. Overseas trade and relations are evidently regularized and sites are found all round the coast. But it is significant that with the rise of the palaces it is the Palace style pottery, M.M.II, alone which is found in Egypt and Asia. The occurrence of the statue of a private individual of the XIIth Dynasty at Knossos implies the residence there of some Egyptian representative. Is it too early to talk of state-controlled commerce ?

Into how many states Crete was divided we cannot tell, but it certainly looks as if Knossos had established herself as the chief political power, though there is no reason to deny the independence of Phaistos. The East end of the island was almost certainly subservient to one or the other, as is shown by the sudden rise of the hitherto small town of Palaikastro and the appearance at that site and at the murex fisheries on Kouphonisi of imported M.M.II pottery.

The unity of culture is shown not only by the close similarity of building methods and ceramic styles all over the island but also by the gradual adoption of a common type of burial. The

[1] See note on Map 13.

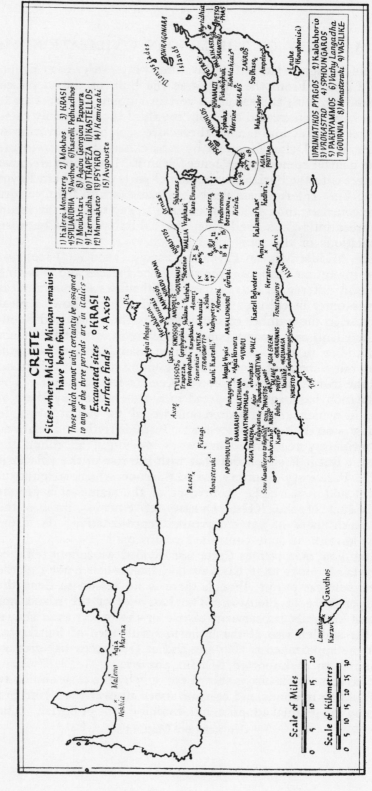

CRETE

Sites where Middle Minoan remains
have been found

Those which cannot with certainty be assigned
to any of the three periods are in italics —

Excavated sites   o KRASI
Surface finds   x Axos

1) Kalergi Monastery 2) Mokhos 3) KRASI
4) SPILIARIDHIA 5) Avdhou 6) Kastelli Pedhiadhos
7) Moukhtari 8) Agiou Georgiou Papoura
9) Tzermiadha 10) TRAPEZA 11) KASTELLOS
12) Marmaketo 13) PSYKRO 14) Kaminaki
15) Avgouste

1) PRINIATIKOS PYRGOS 2) Kalokhorio
3) VROKASTRO 4) SPHOUNGARAS
5) PAKHYAMMOS 6) Vathy Langadha
7) GOURNIA 8) Monasteraki 9) VASILIKE

MAP 14

Scale of Miles
0 5 10 15 20

Scale of Kilometres
0 5 10 15 20 30

circular tombs of the Messara and the rectangular ossuaries of East Crete fall out of use in favour of the pithos burial.   This becomes universal by M.M.iii whether under rock-shelters as in Central Crete or isolated in the sand as in the East.

The introduction of bronze instead of copper had a great effect on the architecture.   From the very beginning of M.M.i, good ashlar masonry was being produced and attention was being paid to the outward appearance of buildings.   Gypsum was being used as a facing stone and the possibilities of plaster as a decoration and not merely as an element in the structure were realized.   Before the end of M.M.iii some of the finest frescoes of the ancient world had been produced.   The plans of the buildings now begin to take a more definite shape.   At first it was merely the grouping of a number of rambling ' insulae ' round a central court as at Knossos.   But by the beginning of the second millennium the palaces, at least, had become comparatively ordered entities, while the private houses, if we may take Khamaizi as an example, had followed suit.   The plan adopted had obvious advantages for the climate.   The absence of outside windows guarded against the heat of the sun and the icy winds.   The elaborate drainage system obviated the unhealthy dampness which would result from the rain collecting in the light-wells.

The arrival of the potter's wheel, probably from Asia, had given tremendous impetus to vase-making.   M.M. pottery needs a complete study to itself, for it is a complete and satisfying whole from its comparatively crude beginnings to the decadence of M.M.iii.   We see the beginnings of polychromy in M.M.i, the realization of its possibilities in the Palace style of M.M.ii and its gradual disappearance in M.M.iii.   This abandonment of polychromy is coupled with generally inferior pottery and is probably due to the employment, by the upper classes, of richer materials.   In M.M.iii, indeed, pottery held much the same position as ' earthenware ' to-day.   The vase painter still wisely kept to patterns.   If he introduced natural forms such as palm-trees, he stylized them to suit the shape of the vase.   He never, fortunately, when engaged on the decoration of the finest eggshell vases, fell into the error of trying to make them imitate something.   The result was a charming and necessary touch of formality.

As a natural sequel to the use of metal vases the art of making stone vases practically died out, and the hard variegated stones gave place to the dull, easily cut steatite.   Easily worked

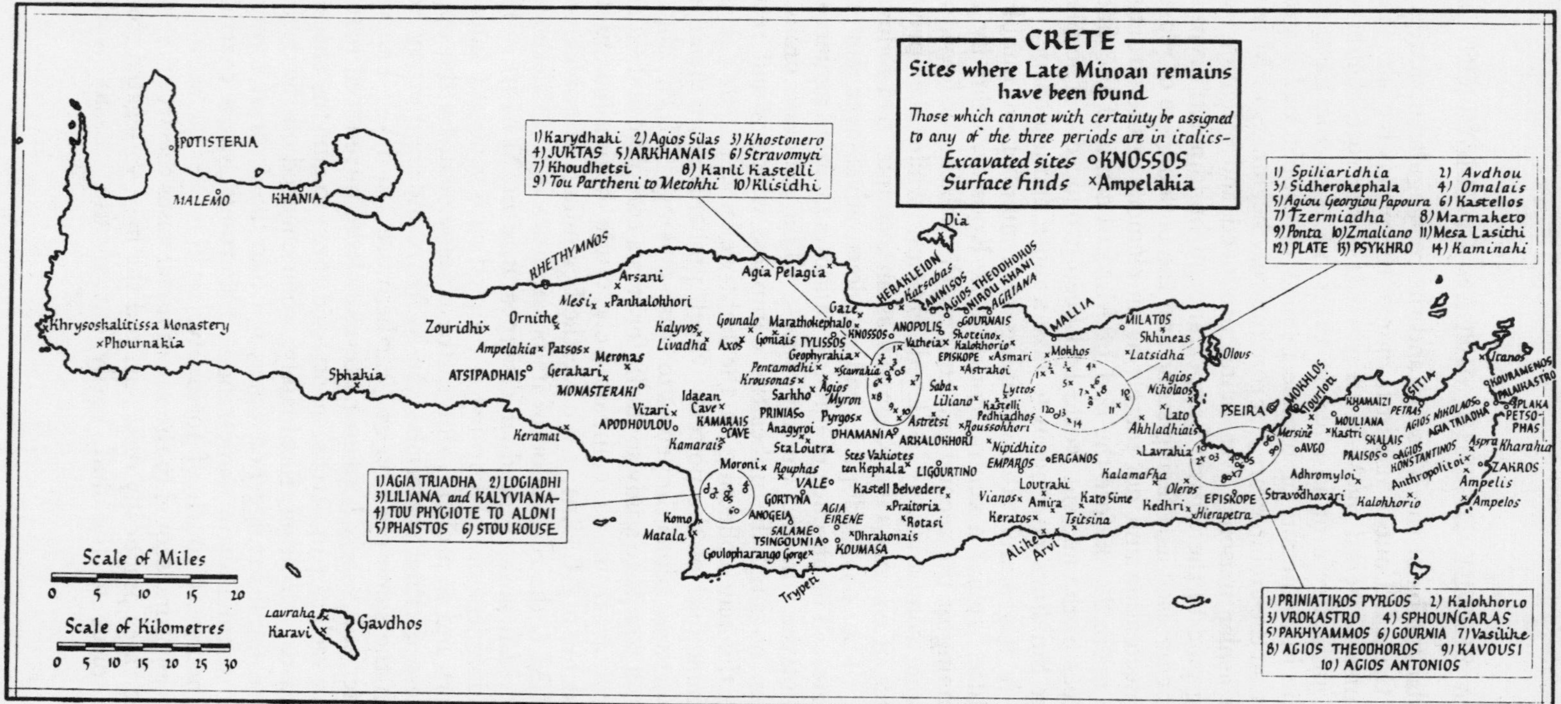

CRETE

Sites where Late Minoan remains
have been found

Those which cannot with certainty be assigned
to any of the three periods are in italics—

Excavated sites oKNOSSOS
Surface finds ×Ampelakia

Box (top left, Rethymnon region):
1) Karydhaki 2) Agios Silas 3) Khostomero
4) JUKTAS 5) ARKHANAIS 6) Stravomyti
7) Khoudhetsi 8) Kanli Kastelli
9) Tou Partheni to Metokhi 10) Klisidhi

Box (bottom left, Phaistos region):
1) AGIA TRIADHA 2) LOGIADHI
3) LILIANA and KALYVIANA
4) Tou Pyngiote to Aloni
5) PHAISTOS 6) STOU HOUSE

Box (top right, Siteia region):
1) Spiliaridhia 2) Avdhou
3) Sidherokephala 4) Omalais
5) Agiou Georgiou Papoura 6) Kastellos
7) Tzermiadha 8) Marmaketo
9) Ponta 10) Zmaliano 11) Mesa Lasichi
12) PLATE 13) PSYKHRO 14) Haminaki

Box (far right):
1) PRINIATIKOS PYRGOS 2) Kalokhorio
3) VROKASTRO 4) SPHOUNGARAS
5) PAKHYAMMOS 6) GOURNIA 7) Vasilike
8) AGIOS THEODHOROS 9) KAVOUSI
10) AGIOS ANTONIOS

Scale of Miles

Scale of Kilometres

MAP 15

materials were the order of the day. Clay replaces stone for figurines, which still lag behind the other branches of art until the end of M.M.III. In the latter period, however, the improvement in the technique of working faience evidently captured the attention of some of the best artists of the time. Though the Snake Goddess and her attendants are still rather primitive, the animal reliefs found with them could hardly be bettered. The gem engravers, too, have settled down to a native style, no longer dependent on foreign influence. Patterns of Egyptian origin are naturally found, but they are adapted to Minoan tastes and in M.M.III the seal stones reach the highest point of beauty.

The art of writing also no doubt owed much to Egypt in its early stages, but the development from the hieroglyphic to the linear script is purely native. We can see the stages by which the use of writing passed from mere identification purposes, personal signets, labels for packets of merchandise, to the advanced system of careful inventories. Perhaps it is justifiable to trace in this the rise of a centralized, bureaucratic power. No illiterate state can carry on systematic commerce.

The Late Minoan Period (c. 1600–before 1100 B.C.) is *The Late* divided into two by the disaster at the end of L.M.I–II. This *Minoan Period* disaster, however, seems to have had little effect on the density of population, its result being rather to break up the large communities into smaller ones. The Map (Map 15) [1] shows how thickly the towns and villages cluster. The unifying process, which had begun in M.M. times, is now complete. Except for the L.M.II style of pottery, which was exclusively Knossian and which was seldom exported to other sites, it is in very rare cases only that we can tell from what part of the island a particular object comes. There are no gaps now in the map and we can no longer talk about groups of sites except in so far as there will naturally be in every district one site which is the ' county town '.

In L.M.I a regular network of roads is in evidence with guard-stations at intervals.[2] The impression we get is of an ordered state with a highly centralized bureaucracy, the whole being ruled from the royal city of Knossos, where, as all Greek legends agree, was the seat of Minos, lord of Crete and many overseas dominions. How deep an impression this empire made has

[1] See note on Map 13.
[2] See also Map 16 and the accompanying list of sites which are probably Minoan but where no datable objects have been found.

been fascinatingly brought forward by J. K. Frost, who pointed out the extraordinary resemblances between Plato's Atlantis as described in the *Critias* and Minoan Crete.[1] Even more interesting is Leaf's suggestion that the Phaiacia of the *Odyssey* is no less than a picture of the Minoan realm transferred to fairyland,[2] while Miss Lorimer has shown that many of the early elements in the Homeric poems are a reflection of the golden days of L.M.i–ii.[3]

One of the reasons for the depth of this impression was no doubt the fact that for the only time in the history of the Greek world until Alexander's days the civilized parts of the Aegean were under a single ruler. Agamemnon is overlord of the Mycenaean Empire, but he is only *primus inter pares* and at the mercy of his barons. Just as in Egypt the fall of the Old Kingdom, with its strong, bureaucratic government centred on the Pharaoh, was followed by the feudal age of the First Intermediate Period with the local barons technically owing allegiance to the king of the moment, so the destruction of Knossos was followed by the splitting up of its empire into small baronies which might or might not pay lip service to an overlord.

Crete in the sixteenth century became a world power. That she is not mentioned as such in contemporary Egyptian documents must be due solely to the fact that she was in peaceful relationship with that country. Her warlike exploits were confined to the extension of her empire to the North, over the Mainland and islands, and according to legend westwards to Sicily. The acquisition of that empire probably began in very much the same way as the British Empire in India. First of all, come the trading stations. All over the Aegean the name Minoa survived into historical times.[4] There is one in Siphnos, one in Amorgos, an island off Megara, one in Delos, one in Laconia, and others on the coasts of Syria, the West and even Arabia. These may have been the names given by the original inhabitants to the station occupied by the traders of Minos or by the traders themselves. The next stage is when a local prince calls on the traders for help against a neighbour, which is given at a price. And so, gradually and probably peacefully, most of the country comes under the power of the new-comers. Finally comes the stage when further acquisitions become necessary owing to the need of putting down piracy or rather

[1] *J.H.S.*, XXXIII, 191 ff.   [2] *Homer and History*, 183.
[3] *J.H.S.*, XLIX, 145 ff.
[4] Fick, *Vorgriechische Ortsnamen*, 27.

of ensuring against other seafarers poaching on their preserves. The peace of the seas is essential to an empire whose wealth is based on trade, and the thalassocracy of Minos is no myth. But that the empire was not obtained by a deliberate policy of fire and sword seems clear from the lack of a general catastrophe on the Mainland at the beginning of the Late Bronze Age.

The great material prosperity of Crete in L.M.I–II is reflected in all branches of art. Architecturally the Palaces remain much the same but the private houses become much more luxurious. Indeed, the fact that one or two of the houses at Knossos encroach on what had previously been palace property implies a rise in power of the nobles at the expense of the king. The old rock-shelter is now well and deeply enough cut to be termed a chamber tomb. Built tombs appear as a natural sequel to these chamber tombs, since the latter are always inclined to collapse when cut in such soft rock.

No doubt it was the very close relations with Egypt which suggested to the Minoans at this time the idea of treating whole walls as a suitable background for frescoes instead of contenting themselves with small panels. The striated limestone and crystalline gypsum of the island not being suitable materials for reliefs in the Egyptian manner, the painted plaster relief was substituted.

Vase painting begins to represent nature, flowers, and grasses in L.M.Ia, marine life in L.M.Ib. As a result the light-on-dark decoration gives place to the dark-on-light which allowed far more delicate gradations of colour and which was to last throughout the Aegean for a thousand years. The stiff formal vases of L.M.II from the Knossian workshops have the appearance of intrusions, and this style must be brought into close relationship with the 'Palace Style' vases of the Mainland, whose beginnings seem rather earlier.

In weapons, also, Crete owed a debt to her overseas dominions. Both the horned and the cruciform sword seem to have been introduced from these more warlike regions. In the small arts we find the highest point of carving reached in such figures as the ivory leaper from Knossos and the steatite rhytons with relief decoration from Agia Triadha. But the seal stones cannot live up to the standard of M.M.III, and though fine examples are known they display a stiffness and formality which had before been absent.

At the very height of prosperity came the crash. We have dared to suggest an economic reason for this and to bring the

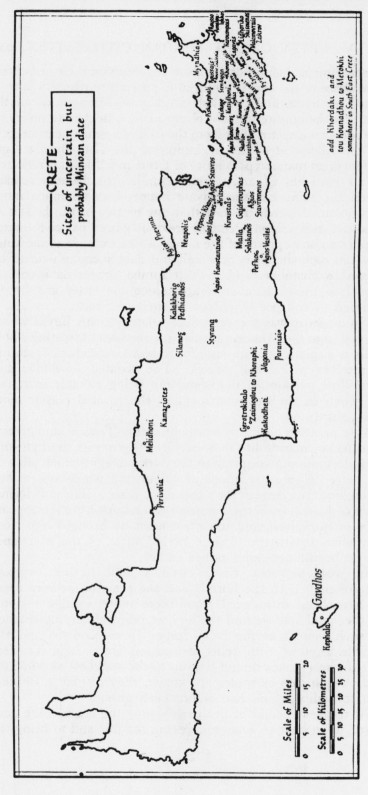

CRETE

Sites of uncertain but
probably Minoan date

Myrtidhia
Kokolampali
Episkopi
Sirinagos
Aghia Roadheros
Aghia Photia?
Katsidhonis
Selatia
Kalamaula
Prone
Marathokephalo
Kelaki
Krephi
Klados?
Naussus?
Etraia
Skiaves ta Kalampali
Aghia Antoni
Aspes Lasides
Selianou
Zakhro

add Kthordaki and
tou Kounadhou to Kteokhi
somewhere in South East Crete

Aghai Prevmna
Neapolis
Peponi Khani
Aghios Ioannis
Aghios Scavros
afrisos
Kroustais
Malia
Selakanos
Perkos
Aghios Vasiles
Aghios Stavromenos
Gojderouphas

Kalabhorig
Pedhuadhos

Silamos

Styrang

Aghas Konstantnos

Kamariotes

Melidhoni

Gerotrokhalo
Zaimoglou to Kharaphi
Nagonia
Parasise

Perivolia

Kakodheri

Gavdhos

Scale of Miles
0   5   10   15   20

Scale of Kilometres
0 5 10 15 20 25 30

Kephala

MAP 16

evidence into line with the Greek legend of Theseus. But certainty is obviously impossible. At all events it seems to have been the ruling classes and the cities which suffered, and small communities replace large ones. No real break in the indigenous culture, however, is visible and the annexation of the island by the Achaean Empire seems to have been peaceful enough, though it is possible that the desertion of Palaikastro before the end of L.M.III may imply an expulsion of ' Eteo-cretans ' who had made a last stand in that part of the island. For it must not be forgotten that the prosperity of that site did not end with its destruction at the end of L.M.I–II.

By the end of the twelfth century Crete had been absorbed into the common culture circle of the Aegean and in the following chapter we shall briefly sketch the course she took.

SITES WHERE REMAINS HAVE BEEN FOUND WHICH ARE OF EARLY MINOAN DATE BUT CANNOT BE ASSIGNED TO ANY PARTICULAR PERIOD

(See Map 13 where they are in italics)

WEST CRETE

APODHOULOU . . . . Small settlement at Gournais below the village. Sherds found by writer, 1933.

DHAMASTA . . . . . Small E.M. figurine with suspension hole instead of a face. Candia Museum. *Sculpture Catalogue*, 96.

ELLENAIS AMARIOU . . . Cave. Sherds and vases. Marinatos, *Arch. Anz.*, 1932, 77.

GAVDHOS . . . . . Sherds, at Lavraka. Levi, *Art and Archaeology*, 1927, 176 ff.

TRAPEZA . . . . . . Between Arkadhi and Margaritais, jug seen by the writer, 1935.

CENTRAL CRETE

AGIA PELAGIA . . . . E.M. settlement, mentioned by Evans, *P. of M.*, I, 299.

AGIOS THEODHOROS . . E.M. tombs, mentioned by Xanthoudides, ᾿Αρχ. Δελτ., IV, Παρ. 2, 19. Close to Nirou Khani.

GEOPHYRAKIA . . . . E.M. figurine of stone. Candia Museum. *Sculpture Catalogue*, 261.

GOURNAIS . . . . . E.M. sherds and cups from a walled pit. Hazzidakis, ᾿Αρχ. Δελτ., I, 59.

KALERGI MONASTERY . . Traces of what seems to be a circular tomb, found by writer, 1934. *B.S.A.*, XXXIII, 81.

KALOKHORIO PEDHIADHOS . Gem. Candia Museum. *Catalogue of Gems*, 77.

KATSABA . . . . . Axe. Candia Museum. *Catalogue*, 2318.

PYRGOS . . . . . . Settlement, unexcavated, on the hill. Xanthoudides, *J.H.S.*, 1925, 276. A stone axe was found here by Miss M. Chubb in 1933.

VONOI . . . . . . Gem. Candia Museum. *Catalogue*, 644.

SOUTH CRETE

APESOKARI . . . . . Traces of circular tomb at Vigla with obviously E.M. sherds exposed by rain, seen by writer, 1934. *B.S.A.*, XXXIII, 88.

ARVI . . . . Evans mentions early cist graves, *J.H.S.*, XIV, 285.

ASPRE PETRA . . . . E.M. tombs and early scarab (wrongly said by writer in *Aegyptiaca*, 29, to come from Marathokephalo). Xanthoudides, 'Aϱχ. Δελτ., IV, Παϱ. 1, 15.

KERATOS . . . . . Cave, found by Miss Money-Coutts and R. W. Hutchinson, 1935. A few sherds.

KOMO . . . . . . Sherds from S. summit (Viglais). Evans, *P. of M.*, II, 88.

KOTSIA . . . . . . Square building, possibly ossuary. Xanthoudides, 'Aϱχ. Δελτ., II, Παϱ. 25.

LANGOS . . . . . . Indeterminate sherds, hand-made, found in gorge between Kamilari and Komo by the writer, 1934. *B.S.A.* XXXIII, 89.

RIZA . . . . Possibly rectangular bone enclosure. Xanthoudides, 'Aϱχ. Δελτ., II, Παϱ. 25.

ROUPHAS . . . . . Sherds, from settlement. Evans, *P. of M.*, II, 80.

VALI . . . . Circular tomb. Marinatos, *J.H.S.*, 1927, 258.

VASILIKE MESSARAS . . . At Plakoura and Merthiais near by seem to be circular tombs. A few sherds on the surface. At Girokephala, walls and sherds found by writer in 1934. *B.S.A.*, XXXIII, 86.

EAST CRETE

ADHROMYLOI . . . . Traces of two circular tombs at Pedhino, ½ hr. W. of the village, hand-made sherds, seen by the writer, 1934. *B.S.A.*, XXXIII, 96.

KALOKHORIO MIRABELLOU . Cave at Kato Arniko. Hall, *Vrokastro*, 79.

KARYDHI . . . . . Remains found in rock pocket. Dawkins, *B.S.A.*, XI, 268.

PRINIATIKOS PYRGOS . . Sherds from settlement. Hall, *Vrokastro*, 79.

SITIA . . . . . . Cycladic marble figurine (more probably from Petras). Evans, *P. of M.*, I, 115.

SKALAIS . . . . . . Some sherds from the cave. Bosanquet, *B.S.A.*, VIII, 235.

SPINIAIS . . . . . Small stone vase. Evans, *Diary*, 18/4/94.

VAGI . . . . . . Stone vases, in Candia Museum. *Catalogue*, 990.

SITES WHERE REMAINS HAVE BEEN FOUND WHICH ARE OF MIDDLE MINOAN DATE BUT CANNOT BE ASSIGNED TO A PARTICULAR PERIOD

(*See Map 14 where they are in italics*)

WEST CRETE

AXOS . . . . . . Gem. Xanthoudides, 'Εφ. 'Αρχ., 1907, 164, No. 39.

GAVDHOS . . . . . Sherds at Lavraka. Levi, *Art and Archaeology*, 1927, 176 ff.

MALEMO . . . . . Sherds reported from Tholos. Prinz, *Ath. Mitt.*, 1910, 150.

MONASTERAKI . . . . Site at Kharakas, E. of village, seen by writer, 1933.

NOKHIA . . . . . Sherds by church of Agios Konstantinos, N. of village, seen by writer, 1935.

CENTRAL CRETE

AGIA PELAGIA . . . . One sherd which seemed to be of this date, found by writer, 1933.

AGIOU GEORGIOU PAPOURA . Pottery seen by Taramelli. *Mon. Ant.*, IX, 407.

ARKHANAIS . . . . . A few sherds and walls. *J.H.S.*, LIII, 293.

ASMARI . . . . . . Stone vases from Prinos. Candia Museum. *Catalogue*, 241–3.

ASTRETSI . . . . . Seal stone. Xanthoudides, 'Εφ. 'Αρχ., 1907, 162.

GERAKI . . . . . . Seal stone in Candia Museum. *Catalogue*, 130.

KAMINAKI . . . . . Seal stone in Candia Museum. *Catalogue*, 1258.

KASTELLOS TZERMIADHON . Sherd from summit and amygdaloid gem, in the Candia Museum. *Catalogue*, 639.

MOKHOS. . . . . Sherds, at Phragmena, NE. of village, seen by writer, 1935.

NIROU KHANI . . . Dump of sherds outside main building. Xanthoudides, Πρακτικά, 1922-4, 126. Ἐφ. Ἀρχ., 1922, 25.

SABA . . . . . Seal stone in the Candia Museum. Catalogue, 1359.

STAVRAKIA . . . . Sherds from road cutting. Marinatos, Ἀρχ. Δελτ., IX, Παρ. 12.

STRAVOMYTI . . . Sherds from cave. Evans, P. of M., II, i, 68.

SOUTH CRETE

AGIA EIRENE . . . Lamp from tomb E. Xanthoudides, V.T.M., 53.

AGIA VARVARA . . . Stone statuette. Xanthoudides, Ἀρχ. Δελτ., II, Παρ. 22.

AGIOS ONOUPHRIOS . . Some of the pottery from the find. Evans, Pictographs, Sup., 105.

BOBIA . . . . . Sherds and walls to E. of village, seen by the writer, 1934. B.S.A., XXXIII, 90.

KALYVIANA . . . . Stone vase in Candia Museum. Catalogue, 2173.

STOU KAVALLIEROU TO . . Sherds from fort above Agia Triadha, KEPHALI   seen by the writer, 1933.

KOMO . . . . . Sherds and walls on the S. headland. Evans, P. of M., II, i, 88.

KOUMASA . . . . Settlement and shrine. Xanthoudides, V.T.M., 49. Nilsson, M.M.R., 90.

ROUPHAS . . . . Sherds from settlement. Evans, P. of M., II, i, 80.

SALAME . . . . . Sherds from settlement, W. of the tomb. Xanthoudides, V.T.M., 73.

TSOUTSOUROS . . . Stone vases in Candia Museum. Catalogue, 3, 4.

VALI. . . . . . Later deposit from circular tomb. Marinatos, J.H.S., 1927, 258.

VASILIKE . . . . A few sherds from Girokephala, seen by the writer, 1934. B.S.A., XXXIII, 87.

EAST CRETE

DIONYSIADES ISLANDS . . Pottery from Cave of Dhragonara. Bosanquet, B.S.A., XIV, 429.

KALAMAFKA . . . . Vase from Lagou, above the village to the NW., seen by the writer, 1935.

KOKHLAKIAIS . . . Vases mentioned by Bosanquet. B.S.A., IX, 276.

KRITZA . . . . . Seal stone in Candia Museum. Catalogue, 974.

MERSINE . . . . . Sherd seen by R. W. Hutchinson, from Khalinomouri, E. of village, 1936.

MONASTERAKI . . . . Seal stone from near the village fountain, seen by the writer, 1935.

MYRTIDHIA . . . . . Seal stone in the Candia Museum. *Catalogue*, 956.

PETRAS . . . . . Settlement on plateau. Bosanquet, *B.S.A.*, VIII, 282.

PRINIATIKOS PYRGOS . . Sherds from settlement. Hall, *Vrokastro*, 79.

SARANTARI . . . . . Ossuaries on ridge. Hawes, *B.S.A.*, XI, 293.

SKALAIS . . . . . A few sherds from the cave. Bosanquet, ibid., VIII, 235.

VATHY LANGADHA . . . Seal stone in Candia Museum. *Catalogue*, 1257.

VROKASTRO . . . . . Small deposit in lowest stratum on summit. Hall, *Vrokastro*, 79.

SITES WHERE REMAINS HAVE BEEN FOUND WHICH ARE OF LATE MINOAN DATE BUT CANNOT BE ASSIGNED TO ANY PARTICULAR PERIOD

(See Map 15 where they are in italics)

WEST CRETE

AMPELAKIA . . . . . Walls of guard-station and sherds at τὰ Μανδράκια ¾-hr. SW. of village, seen by the writer, 1935.

GAVDHOS . . . . . Sherds from Lavraka. Levi, *Art and Archaeology*, 1927, 176 ff.

GONIAIS . . . . . . Pithos fragments, loomweights, &c., at Stephane, W. of the village, seen by the writer, 1935.

GOUNALO . . . . . Traces of circular wall and pithos fragments, 1 hr. W. of Axos, seen by the writer, 1935.

KALYVOS . . . . . Seal stone, published by Xanthoudides, 'Εφ. 'Αρχ., 1907, 173.

KERAMAI . . . . . Some sherds at Visala, seen by the writer, 1929 and 1932.

LIVADHA . . . . . Seal stone, Xanthoudides, 'Εφ. 'Αρχ., 1907, 177.

MALEMO . . . . . Square stone-lined tomb with round tholos roof. Sherds mentioned, Prinz, *Ath. Mitt.*, 1910, 150.

MESI . . . . . . Larnax found at Phoukianos, said by peasants to have been from a built tomb. Cf. Evans, *Diary*, 23/3/94.

MONASTERAKI . . . . Site at Agia Kyriake, seen by the writer, 1933, partly excavated by the school-master.

RHETHYMNOS . . . .   Graves at Stavromena. Mariani, *Mon. Ant.*, VI, 211. Seal stone. Xanthoudides, *'Εφ. 'Αρχ.*, 1907, 173.

CENTRAL CRETE

AGIOS MYRON . . . .   Seal stones. Xanthoudides, *'Εφ. 'Αρχ.*, 1907, 181. Vase in the Candia Museum. *Catalogue*, 7765.

AGIOU GEORGIOU PAPOURA .   Sherds from E. and S. slopes, seen by the writer, 1935. Cf. Taramelli, *Mon. Ant.*, IX, 407.

AGRIANA . . . . .   Larnax. Marinatos, *'Αρχ. Δελτ.*, IX, 12.

ARKHANAIS . . . . .   Remains found by peasant. *B.C.H.*, 1925, 473.

ASTRETSI . . . . .   Seal stone. Xanthoudides, *'Εφ. 'Αρχ.*, 1907, 168.

AVDHOU. . . . . .   Seal stone. Xanthoudides, ibid., 175.

EMPAROS . . . . .   Pottery from Patela. Halbherr, *A.J.A.*, 1901, 281.

GOURNAIS . . . . .   Larnax burial E. of the village. Hazzidakis, *'Αρχ. Δελτ.*, I, 59.

KAMINAKI . . . . .   Seal stone from Trokhaloi, in the Candia Museum. *Catalogue*, 947. Cf. Dawkins, *B.S.A.*, XX, 4.

KATSABA . . . . .   Stone vase in the Candia Museum. *Catalogue*, 2083.

KHOSTONERO . . . .   Statuette from cave on Juktas. Candia Museum. *Catalogue*, 8558.

KROUSONAS . . . . .   Sherds from Κοῦπο, described by Taramelli, *Mon. Ant.*, IX, 332. The spot could not be found by Miss Money-Coutts and Miss Eccles, 1934. *B.S.A.*, XXXIII, 92.

LILIANO. . . . . .   Seal stone. Xanthoudides, *'Εφ. 'Αρχ.*, 1907, 184.

LYTTOS . . . . . .   ditto. Ibid., 169.

MALLIA . . . . . .   Settlement, probably at Agio Pnevma.

NIPIDHITO . . . . .   Stone vase, published by Halbherr. *A.J.A.*, 1901, 232.

NIROU KHANI . . . .   Larnax burials W. of the main building. Xanthoudides, *Πρακτικά*, 1922–4, 126. Settlement between the main building and the sea. *'Εφ. 'Αρχ.*, 1922, 25.

OMALAIS . . . . .   Evans, *Academy*, 20/6/96, describes the ' City of Castles '. Very extensive site. Sherds seen by the writer, 1935, round the forts in Rodhakinia Lakkos.

TOU PARTHENI TO METOKHI   Sherds on the W. slope below the car road, seen by the writer, 1934. *B.S.A.*, XXXIII, 84.

PENTAMODHI . . . .   Larnax burials described by Orsi, *Mon. Ant.*, I, 209.

PONTA . . . . . . A few sherds round Barboulio spelio, seen by the writer, 1936.

ROUSSOKHORI . . . Seal stone. Xanthoudides, *'Εφ. 'Αρχ.*, 1907, 180.

SABA. . . . . . Sherds from a guard-house E. of the village, seen by the writer, 1934. *B.S.A.*, XXXIII, 80.

SPILIARIDHIA . . . Earliest deposit in the cave. Xanthoudides, *B.C.H.*, 1922, 522.

STAVRAKIA . . . . Vases seen by Mariani, *Mon. Ant.*, VI, 230.

STRAVOMYTI . . . Latest sherds from the cave. Evans, *P. of M.*, II, 68.

TZERMIADHA . . . Seal stone. Xanthoudides, *'Εφ. 'Αρχ.*, 1907, 183. Probably from the Kastellos or some other site ; pithos burial at Kavallares Volakas. Evans, *Academy*, 20/6/96.

VATHEIA. . . . . Seal stone. Xanthoudides, ibid., 173.

ZMALIANO . . . . Pithos burial found during the making of the road at Palaiomandra, seen by the writer, 1936.

SOUTH CRETE

AGIA EIRENE . . . A number of larnakes and sherds in earth above circular tomb. Xanthoudides, *V.T.M.*, 51.

GORTYNA . . . . Surface finds at Agios Ioannes, W. of the Acropolis. Pace, *Annuario*, I, 372.

KALYVIANA . . . . Burials. *Rend Linc.*, 1902, 318.

KAMARAIS . . . . Settlement in valley W. of village. Taramelli, *A.J.A.*, 1901, 437.

KOUMASA . . . . . Pottery from the settlement at Korakiais. Xanthoudides, *V.T.M.*, 3.

MAKHAIRA . . . . Fimmen, 19, mentions finds on the report of Hazzidakis. The writer could hear of no site in 1933.

MATALA . . . . . Seal stone in the Candia Museum. *Catalogue*, 135.

PRAITORIA . . . . Fimmen, 21, mentions finds on the report of Hazzidakis. The writer could hear of no site in 1934.

ROTASI . . . . . Pithos fragments seen by the writer, 1934. *B.S.A.*, XXXIII, 86.

ROUPHAS . . . . Sherds and traces of buildings. Evans, *P. of M.*, II, 80.

SALAME . . . . . Sherds from the settlement. Xanthoudides, *V.T.M.*, 73.

TSITSINA . . . . Stone vase seen by Evans. *Diary*, 1896.

VALI. . . . . . Latest burial in circular tomb and larnax burials. Marinatos, *J.H.S.*, 1927, 258.

VIANOS . . . . . . Statuette from Kato Vianos, in the Candia Museum. *Catalogue*, 8737.

EAST CRETE

AGIOS ANTONIOS . . . Chamber tombs. Hall, *Vrokastro*, 183.

AGIOS KONSTANTINOS . . Tombs. Bosanquet, *B.S.A.*, VIII, 286.

AGIOS NIKOLAOS MIRA-BELLOU . Kernos. Xanthoudides, *B.S.A.*, XII, 18.

AGIOS NIKOLAOS SITIAS . House. Tod, *B.S.A.*, IX, 336.

AKHLADHIAIS . . . . Tripod legs and cooking-pots found by the writer, 1936, at fine defensive works. Below in the ravine are traces of another road at the ' Kitten's Cistern '. Cf. Evans, *Academy*, 1894. Taramelli, *Mon. Ant.*, IX, 410.

AMPELIS . . . . . Group of houses. Hogarth, *B.S.A.*, VI, 147.

AMPELOS . . . . . House at Ellenika. Evans, *Diary*, 1896. Good walls at Agios Nikolaos, seen by Bosanquet, unpublished.

ASPRA KHARAKIA . . . Houses. Evans, ibid., but is this the same as Galana Kharakia or Stas Tavernais ? See p. 316.

HIERAPETRA . . . . . Vase in the Candia Museum. Fimmen, 18.

ITANOS . . . . . . Stone vase in the Candia Museum. *Catalogue*, 236. Evans, *Diary*, 1896, saw Minoan settlement here.

KALAMAFKA . . . . Sherds on the Kastellos, seen by the writer, 1935. Cf. Evans, *Academy*, 13/6/96.

KALOKHORIO SITIAS . . Houses. Bosanquet, *B.S.A.*, VIII, 239.

LATSIDHA . . . . . Seal stone. Xanthoudides, 'Εφ. 'Αρχ., 1907, 175.

OLEROS . . . . . . One or two sherds at Myrtokoudhia, seen by the writer, 1936. Heard report of statuette at Kokkala.

OLOUS . . . . . . Seal stone. Evans, *J.H.S.*, XVII, 334.

PETRAS . . . . . . Houses on plateau. Bosanquet, *B.S.A.*, VIII, 282. Sherds from next hill to the E., seen by the writer, 1934. *B.S.A.*, XXXIII, 98.

PETSOPHAS . . . . . Larnax burials. Dawkins, *B.S.A.*, XI, 290 ; XII, 2.

SITES WITH REMAINS OF UNCERTAIN BUT PROBABLY MINOAN DATE

(*See Map 16*)

AGIO PNEVMA . . . . 2 miles W. of Mallia. Evans, *P. of M.*, II, 233, mentions borings in the rocks on the shore, presumably for quarrying.

AGIOS IOANNES . . . To the N. of the pass out of the Lakonian Plain to Agios Nikolaos. Evans, *Diary*, 1898, saw the walling of a fort.

AGIOS KONSTANTINOS . . About 10 min. above the church at the E. end of the Lasithi Plain are fortifications and terracing of an ancient road to Katharos. Evans, *Academy*, 1/6/95.

AGIOS STAVROMENOS . . N. of Anatole. Bosanquet bought a stone table and bronze axe. Unpublished.

AGIOS STAVROMENOS . . In the Katalione Plain. Evans, *Academy*, 20/6/96, reports a prehistoric acropolis. Bosanquet noted polygonal and isodomic walls.

AGIOS STAVROS . . . At the E. end of the pass from the Lakonian Plain to Agios Nikolaos. Evans, *Diary*, 1898, saw a fort.

AGIOS THEODHOROS . . S. of Dhaphne. Evans, *Diary*, 7/4/94, and 1896, saw large acropolis and city on the N. side of the river. Marked in *P. of M.*, I, Map 1.

AGIOS VASILES . . . . Near Vianos. Bosanquet mentions the find of a steatite cup and clay cups in a garden called Στὰ Δραϰιανά.

ARMENOI . . . . . E. of Khandhra. . Evans, *Diary*, 8/4/94, bought seal stones here.

ARNI . . . . . . S. of Zakros. Evans, *Diary*, 1896, saw forts. Marks a town site. *P. of M.*, I, Map 1.

STEN ASPAN . . . . Near Katsidhoni. Bosanquet mentions the find of a dozen unpainted cups.

EPISKOPE . . . . . S. of Sitia. Bosanquet mentions foundations of houses and vases in a cave at Dhrogara, ½-hr. NW.

GAIDEROUPHAS . . . . An hour W. of Kalamafka, a fort found by Evans, *Diary*, 1898 ; there is a bronze dagger in the Candia Museum, *Catalogue*, 624, said to be from here.

GAVDHOS . . . . . Walls, &c., on Kephala. Levi, *Art and Archaeology*, 1927, 176 ff.

GEROTROKHALO . . . . On the left bank of the Messara river. *Rend. Linc.*, 1902, 318, mentions burials. No excavations, however.

GRAS . . . . . . Now Agios Stephanos, W. of Khandra. Evans, *Diary*, 1898, saw Cyclopean wells close to the village.

KAKODHEI . . . . . A headland between Komo and Sphakoryako. Good walls but no sherds, seen by the writer, 1934. *B.S.A.*?

KALOKHORIO PEDHIADHOS . Taramelli, *Mon. Ant.*, IX, 377, 434, gives plan of acropolis S. of the village at τῆς Μασᾶς ἡ Κορφή.

KAMARIOTES . . . . NE. of Axos. Fragment of a bronze knife in the Candia Museum, *Catalogue*, 2220, from Armanogeia.

KAROUMPAIS . . . . Between Zakros and Palaikastro. Hogarth, *B.S.A.*, VII, 122, saw two groups of prehistoric houses. Mariani, *Mon. Ant.*, VI, 298, gives a plan. Cf. also Post-Minoan remains of uncertain date, p. 377.

KASTRI . . . . . . Between Pyrgalais and Ampelos. Evans, *Diary*, 1896, saw a fort here.

KATSIDHONI . . . . NW. of Sitanos. Bosanquet mentions graves at Melokepos called the Τάφοι τῶν Σαρανταπήχων. Cf. Mariani, *Mon. Ant.*, VI, 176.

KHONOS. . . . . . NW. of Karydhi. A fragment of a bronze axe in the Candia Museum, *Catalogue*, 985.

KHORDHAKI. . . . . Somewhere in SE. Crete. Bosanquet, *B.S.A.*, VIII, 239, mentions ancient house site.

KORPHE STO KOPRANI . . Near Gras. Evans, *Diary*, 1896, saw a prehistoric acropolis and fort.

TOU KOUNADHOU TO . . Somewhere in E. Crete. Bosanquet
METOKHI   mentions coarse painted pottery from here.

KOUNENI . . . . . Four clay statuettes of indeterminate date in the Candia Museum, *Catalogue*, 806–9.

KRITSA . . . . . . Evans, *P. of M.*, I, Map 1, marks Minoan remains W. of the town.

KROUSTAIS . . . . . S. of Kritsa. Evans, *Academy*, 1/6/96, mentions a series of Minoan forts ½-hr. above the village on the road to Mallais.

LAGAVAS . . . . . Near Zakros on the Sitia road. Evans, *Diary*, 10/4/94, saw many antiquities but could not find the site.

LAMNON PLAIN . . . Evans, *Diary*, 1896, saw rock-shelters and a hollow with prehistoric pottery.

LITHINAIS . . . . . S. of Sitia. Evans, *Diary*, 1898, saw Minoan guard-stations on a col above the Sitia road.

MALLA	Evans, *Diary*, 1896 and 1898, saw forts in the valley between here and Khristos. The writer in 1935 heard of further antiquities 1-hr. S. at Xerasterna.
MARATHIA	Near Stravodhoxari. Evans, *Diary*, 1898, saw a fort.
MELIDHONI	The Candia Museum has a bronze axe, *Catalogue* 2270, from Kamaroto.
MERONI	On the Zyros-Praisos road. Evans, *Diary*, 1898, saw early walling.
MYRTIDHIA	Near Palaikastro. Bosanquet speaks of burials and vases found by a hill to the SW.
NEAPOLIS	A lamp in the Candia Museum, *Catalogue*, 7764.
ORNO	S. of Roukaka. Evans, *P. of M.*, I, Map 1, marks Minoan remains here. *Diary*, 1898, at Elleniko are traces of a guard-house and at Skaphe are walls and tombs.
PARANISI	S. of Pyrgos in the Messara. Small chamber with part of corbelled roof, seen by the writer 1936, at Vropigaïdho.
PEPONI KHANI	In the pass between the Lakonian Plain and Agios Nikolaos. Evans, *Diary*, 1/6/95, saw a fort and traces of roadway.
PERIVOLAKIA	SW. of Khandra. Bosanquet, *B.S.A.*, VIII, 239, mentions a house site.
PERIVOLIA	E. of Rhethymnos. Evans, *P. of M.*, I, Map 1, shows Minoan remains.
PEFKOS	E. of Vianos. Evans, *Diary*, 1896, saw a cave with walling, E. of the village.
PISKOKEPHALI . . .	S. of Sitia. Evans, *Diary*, 12/4/94, saw walls.
PYRGALAIS	In the SE. corner of the Omalais Plain near Zyros. Evans, *Academy*, 4/7/96, saw a guard-station.
ROUSSAIS ? ROUSSE. EKKLESIA	SE. of Sitia. A bronze axe in the Candia Museum, *Catalogue*, 1023, a vase, 3824.
ROUSSO AMALOULAKKOS	Near Cape Plaka. Evans, *Diary*, 1898, heard of large ancient buildings.
SELAKONOS	Above the site of Malla. Bronze axes in the Candia Museum, *Catalogue*, 301–8, and in the Ashmolean. Evans, *Diary*, 1898, saw rock-shelters.
SKALLIA I	A mile NE. of Stravodhoxari. Evans, *Diary*, 1898, saw a settlement and a fort.
SKALLIA II	Between Zakros and Zyros. Evans, *Academy*, 4/7/96, saw a settlement.

STYRANA . . . . . S. of Alagni Pedhiadhos, a bronze axe in the Candia Museum, *Catalogue*, 2162.

SYLAMOS . . . . . Between Knossos and Juktas. Station by the Minoan road, architectural and other remains. Evans, *P. of M.*, II, i, 66. Miss Eccles saw pithos fragments between here and Sterianos, 1935.

SYKIA . . . . . . W. of Praisos. Evans, *Diary*, 1898, saw a Minoan fort.

VAGONIA . . . . . N. of Vasilike Messaras. Seal stones in the Candia Museum, from Perivola, *Catalogue*, 1363-4, 1436.

ZAKROS . . . . . . Two forts and traces of coast road running S. to Ampelos at Lidhoriko Skismenes and Malamourais Zakrou, seen by the writer, 1934. *B.S.A.*, XXXIII, 99.

ZYMOGLOU TO KHORAPHI . A few poor tombs. *Mon. Ant.*, XIV, 652, near Liliana.

ZYROS . . . . . . SE. of Khandra. Evans, *Academy*, 4/7/96. *Diary*, 1898, describes fort in the opening W. into the Plain of Khandra. *P. of M.*, I, Map 1, shows remains. The writer found no sherds, 1934. *B.S.A.*, XXXIII, 100.

No satisfactory substitute has yet been formulated for the existing terminology of the periods. There might be something to be said for abolishing M.M.II, which is only a local development of M.M.I, and there is more to be said for reverting to the old terminology and describing L.M.Ib as L.M.II since the present L.M.II is a style of vase-painting found only at Knossos. The resulting confusion, however, would more than counterbalance any doubtful advantage to be gained from such simplification.

One point, however, cannot fail to strike the reader, and that is the tremendous length of time allotted to E.M.II and III. With the dates at present accepted for Egyptian history this is unavoidable. But, while admitting that in primitive times progress is extremely slow, it is very hard to make the existing remains cover the six hundred years demanded by the usual chronology, and any lowering of dates by Egyptologists would be most welcome.

It is therefore the more gratifying to find that Scharff is already well on the way to doing so. He has suggested that the beginning of the Ist Dynasty can easily come down to 3000 B.C. and has since worked out a scheme for the First

CHRONOLOGICAL TABLE OF THE BRONZE AGE

The following table gives, very diagrammatically, the results arrived at in the text. Its provisional nature may best be realized from the admission that, until the end of the Middle Bronze Age, any of the dates may be nearly a century out either way.

Date	Egypt	Central Crete	South Crete	East Crete	Dates suggested by Scharff	Mainland	Islands
3300	Predynastic	Neolithic Period				Neolithic to varying dates	Uninhabited ?
3200							
3100	Ist to IIIrd Dynasties						
3000					3000		
2900		Sub-neolithic	Period				
2800	IVth Dynasty	Early Minoan I	Early Minoan I	Early Minoan I	2800		
2700	Vth and VIth Dynasties	Early Minoan	Minoan			Early Helladic	Early Cycladic
2600		Early	Minoan	II	2600		
2500							
2400	VIth to Xth Dynasties First Intermediate Period	Early	Minoan				
2300				III	2300		
2200		Middle Minoan Ia					
2100	XIth Dynasty	Middle Minoan Ib	Middle Minoan I		2100		
2000		Middle Minoan IIa	Middle Minoan I	Middle Minoan I	2000	Middle Helladic	
1900	XIIth Dynasty	Middle	Middle Minoan IIa	Middle Minoan I	1900		Middle Cycladic
1800		Middle	Middle Minoan IIb		1800		
1700	XIIIth to XVIIth Dynasties 2nd Intermediate Period including Hyksos	Middle	Minoan	IIIa	1700		
1600		Middle Minoan III	Minoan IIb. Pre-earthquake		1600		
1500	XVIIIth Dynasty. Thothmes III 1500–1447 Akhenaten c. 1386–69 (Tell el-Amarna)	Late	Post-earthquake and Late Minoan Ia		1500	Late Helladic I	Late Cycladic
1400		Late Minoan II (Knossos only)	Minoan	Ib	1400	Late Helladic II	
1300	XIXth Dynasty	Late	Minoan	IIIa	1300	Late Helladic IIIa	
1200		Late	Minoan	IIIb	1200	Late Helladic IIIb	
1100	XXth Dynasty	Sub-Minoan and Proto-geometric	Minoan and Proto-geometric		1100	Sub-Mycenaean, &c.	

Intermediate Period whereby the VIth Dynasty ends about 2300 and the XIth begins locally in 2150 and is supreme in Egypt from 2065. The date of the XIIth Dynasty remains of course unchanged.[1]

[1] *J.E.A.* XIV, 275, and *Der Historische Abschnitt der Lehre für König Merikarê*, 54.

Chapter VI

POST-MINOAN CRETE

I. THE SUB-MINOAN AND PROTOGEOMETRIC PERIODS

(See Map 17)

WE HAVE traced the course of Cretan civilization down to the end of the Bronze Age, at some time late in the twelfth century. The new period is characterized by the appearance of iron and the increasing absorption of the island both racially and culturally into the general civilization of the Aegean.[1]

The breaking up of the Mycenaean or Achaean empire, of which Crete for a short time formed a part, no doubt began some time before the actual destruction of Mycenae.[2] The dark ages of which history has nothing and legend little to tell us, had begun. Crete suffered a tremendous loss of population, as she was to do again after the Venetian and Turkish conquests and after the revolt of 1821.[3] The map shows an extraordinary change after L.M.III. Most of the coastal sites, particularly to the South, have been abandoned. Few of the inland towns have survived. Their inhabitants have fled to mountain eyries, such as those of Karphi, Vrokastro, and Kavousi (Pl. VI). We seem to be back in the Neolithic Period with its life of terror, the only difference being that some building skill had survived and robber castles take the place of caves. It will be noticed that the West of Crete seems to have been completely abandoned except for Eleutherna, which may have offered a refuge where the surviving inhabitants of the newly founded towns collected. It is possible that other such cities

---

[1] See for all this early period, Mackenzie, *B.S.A.*, XIII, 428 ff.

[2] *B.S.A.*, XXV, 125, 245.

[3] Pashley, II, 326, suggests 500,000 as the population when the Venetians first landed, reduced to half by the sixteenth century and to less than 80,000 a few years after the Turkish conquest. It rose to about 260,000 by 1821, but had fallen to half that number in 1834. In 1881 it was 280,000. To-day it is half a million.

CRETE

SubMinoan & Protogeometric Sites
Excavated Sites °KOURTAIS
Surface finds ×Prinias

STOU KOUKOU
TO KEPHALI
PALAIKASTRO ×Stou Tavernais
Galana Kharakia
MOULIANA ×Kheiromandrais

AGIOS KONSTANTINOS
KAVOUSI PRAISOS°

Skhineas
ANAVLOKHOS ×Vrakhasi
Vrakhasi
KARPHE ×Mesa
Sidherokephala× ×Astresi Lasithi
ANAPOLIS PSYKHRO
ARKHANAIS VROKASTRO°
Klisidhi AMYGDHALI
KNOSSOS° PANAGIA° ERGANOS
Phoinikia× PHRATI× EMPAROS BRAIMIANA°
Stravomyti× Ligourtino×
AGIA PARASKEVE°
×Prinias
VATHIANOS ×KOURTAIS
KAMPOS °TOU PHYSIOTE
AMNISOS TO ALONI

Kytaion×

LILIANA

ELEUTHERNA

Kamarais×

add KOLLYVA METOKHI
one hour west of Herakleion.

MAP 17

Scale of Miles
0   5   10   15   20

Scale of Kilometres
0 5 10 15 20 25 30

of refuge exist and will be brought to light when excavation
has gone below the later remains. But the possibility must be
borne in mind that, since the West was still no doubt largely
virgin forest land which was only just being opened up at the
end of the Bronze Age, with the failure of communications the
inhabitants continued in the L.M.III stage of culture. We shall
see the way in which the Lasithiote sites continued the Minoan
tradition, though they were certainly in communication with
the outside world, and it would not be surprising if the same
was true of the West in an even greater degree. Knossos and
the harbour town of Amnisos alone can be said to have survived

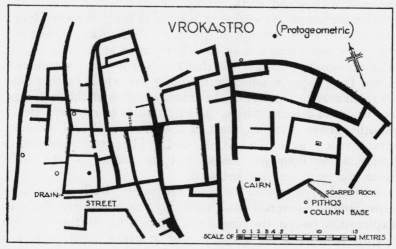

FIG. 45

all shocks from the first arrival of human beings in Crete,
through the Bronze Age and Iron Age, down to modern times.

At Knossos the final desertion of the Palace site took place.
Whether this was due to some further disaster or to super-
stition, at all events, it is clear that the area was regarded as
tabu in later times. Our knowledge of the house architecture
is confined to two sites in the East, Kavousi (Pl. VI, 1) and
Vrokastro (Fig. 45), and will be extended when the excavation
of the equally wild site of Karphi in Lasithi is continued.
Inaccessibility and strength are the main factors.

Architecture as an art has ceased to exist. At Kavousi, on *Proto-*
'Thunder Hill' (Vronta), there is a distinct forecourt and *geometric*
circular and square column bases appear in one or two rooms *Architecture*
at Vrokastro, but of any sort of amenities there is no sign.

As to plan, the Vrokastro group, with a stretch of imagination, could be divided up into three houses, two entered from the South, one running East and West with no sign of an entrance. If this is really so we have a kind of Megaron arrangement, the chief room of the house lying at the back and approached through one or more antechambers, but we cannot be certain. The construction at Vrokastro is of small undressed stones laid without bonding. At Kavousi, however, were slabs of local shale bonded with clay. Frequently the lower part of the wall consists of the native rock which has sometimes, though not always, been cut back. The inequalities of the floor were covered with a red earth filling.

The contemporary shrine at Karphi is built of rather larger stones with some attempt at dressing. The plan consists of a big outer room which may have been open at the North end. The probability, however, is that the North wall has collapsed down the precipice which runs along the whole of that side. Immediately to the left of the door, which is at the East end, are traces of a ledge where the cult statues (see below) stood. Another ledge occupies most of the West wall and a square altar existed near the North end. The same method of levelling the floor was noted, but the stones of the walls were laid with no clay between.

Proto-
geometric
Tombs

Of tomb architecture we know far more. Built tombs were now almost universal and naturally, in the early days of exploration (when the vexatious restrictions of the Turkish régime hampered the archaeologist at every turn), were the easiest form of excavation to undertake. Frequently, however, the excavator was even, in such cases, prevented from completing his work and further excavation at such sites as Erganos and Kourtais is desirable. In the publication of these they are said to be true tholoi, i.e. circular from the foundations. Of those which have been excavated since conditions were easier, almost all are rectangular and their domes do not begin until about a metre from the ground. The present writer knows from his own experience the length of time which it takes to decide, when there is no bonding clay, what is fallen stone jammed against the side and what is not. At Karphi the two tholoi had actually been planned as rough circles when it was noticed in cleaning them for photography that a sherd ran under one of the blocks which, when duly raised, proved not to be part of the construction at all. The Praisos example is certainly a true tholos, but is probably fairly late in the period, bordering on Geometric times. Furthermore, it is built of regular courses of cut stone and has a kind of chapel in front.

The normal type is shown in Fig. 46. It is a lined rectangular chamber tomb. The size varies from 2 to 3 metres across. The height is usually about 2 metres. The building

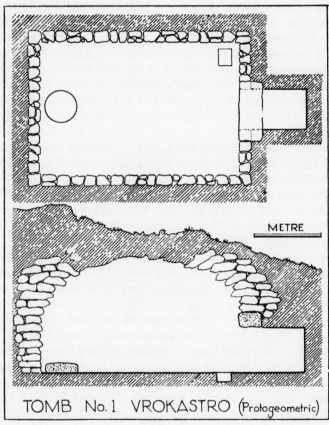

TOMB No. 1 VROKASTRO (Protogeometric)

FIG. 46

blocks are comparatively small slabs, with the result that the roof has usually collapsed in spite of the pressure of the earth outside. There is a fairly well-dressed lintel, though no slabs for the jambs. There is sometimes a very short unlined dromos which is more in the nature of a pit to facilitate entrance to the door, which is only a metre high. In Lasithi, however, a new style makes its appearance. The two tholoi so far excavated are somewhat smaller in size, being under 2 metres square, and the doors are even lower than usual. The tholos is surrounded by a mass of rough masonry roughly square in shape and in thickness equal on three sides to the diameter of the tomb. The West or entrance side, however, is only the thickness of the door. This buttressing extends to within less than a metre of the top of the tomb, which appeared above it as a cupola. A terrace wall extends along the back of both these tholoi and from it other walls extend enclosing them. It appears also that there are other tombs in the same line and enclosed by the same system of walls. This is the first appearance of free-standing built tombs, though probably the top of the vault at Isopata and of most of the Mainland tholoi projected out of the ground or were covered by a mound of earth. The idea, also, of a regularly spaced group of tombs is quite new.

Another type of tomb found at Vrokastro and probably slightly later than the tholoi is the ossuary resembling those of E.M. and M.M. times at Palaikastro.

A few unlined chamber tombs exist, most of which are probably of L.M.III date re-used, for there was evidently little or no break wherever the settlements were able to remain in the same place, since sometimes even the larnakes were re-used. A third form of burial, in caves, was found by Hogarth at Τοῦ Κούκου τὸ Κεφάλι near Apano Zakros. Cremation was practised at Mouliana and Vrokastro but not at Kavousi.[1]

Pottery

The pottery of the period can be divided into two subdivisions. First comes the transitional, Sub-Minoan style, best exemplified by the later interment at Mouliana, the deposit from the Spring Chamber at Knossos and sites such as Vrokastro and Erganos. With this will have to be put, no doubt, the vases from Karphi when they are mended and studied, though in such troubled times it is quite possible that so remote a site continued the Sub-Minoan style for generations after it had died out elsewhere. Next comes the developed Protogeometric style of the Knossos tombs and elsewhere.

1. Sub-Minoan

Minoan shapes, such as the globular stirrup-vase with a knob on the false spout, survive into Sub-Minoan times. But the most typical vase of the period is a new introduction, the open-mouthed krater with horizontal handles. The usual

[1] For a good discussion see Lorimer, *J.H.S.*, 1933, 163 ff.

decoration of such kraters is in panels, a style which now becomes common in Crete. A smaller version of the same shape was used as a cup and decorated by having the upper part dipped into black paint. Other kraters exist not unlike those of L.M.iiib, but with the widest part of the body lower. Slightly domed lids, usually painted with concentric circles, were found to fit these last.[1] Another common shape is the straight-sided pyxis with tilted horizontal handles projecting up from the shoulder but applied to the vase as far down as the base.[2] With this must be taken the basket or kalathos with a flaring body and low horizontal handles similarly clinging to the body which is also found in open-work, the openings being apparently cut out when the vase was partly hardened.[3] Duck vases also are widely spread.[4] The pilgrim bottle is a not uncommon shape in East Crete, where also are found deep two-handled goblets on a long thick stem.[5]

The patterns tend to the linear. Hatched triangles are nearly the only form of decoration found on the shoulders of stirrup vases. But the close style, with fringed lines and thick, bold designs, is still found at Mouliana, Karphi and in the spring chamber at Knossos. Most interesting, however, is the appearance of human figures on the bell-krater from Mouliana. On one side is a very rude drawing of a huntsman pursuing two *agrimis*, or wild goats, on the other is the first representation of a man riding. He wears a peaked or plumed helmet and holds a spear and small round shield. His legs are not shown, for the artist evidently conceived of him as part of his mount.

Mention must also be made of a series of vases, as yet unmended, from Karphi. The clay of these has turned with firing to a bright blue and in one case to a deep metallic purple. They form a strange contrast to the soft yellowish clay which is otherwise characteristic of the period.

The fully developed Protogeometric style is best illustrated from the tombs at Knossos.[6] The stirrup vases have a high foot. The bell-kraters are deeper and less swelling. Small pithoi are found, some with a low flaring neck, some with a

2. Proto-geometric

[1] *Vrokastro*, 131, and Pl. XXXII.
[2] Ibid., Pl. XXX. *A.J.A.*, 1901, Pl. VI, 4. *B.S.A.*, XXIX, Pl. VI, 11.
[3] Ibid., Pl. V, 11. *P. of M.*, II, Fig. 69g. Also found on Karphi open-work: *Vrokastro*, Pl. XXXI.
[4] *B.S.A.*, XXXI, 58, n. 5.
[5] Ibid., 126, 150. [6] *B.S.A.*, XXIX, 232 ff., 267.

FIG. 47.—Patterns on Protogeometric Pottery from Knossos

fairly high cylindrical one. A tall neck amphora with two handles appears, probably under Mainland influence.[1]

The decorative patterns are shown in Fig. 47. Many of them, such as the triangles with various forms of hatching and the chequers, are linear versions of Minoan ornament. The most typical designs, however, are the concentric circles and semicircles, sometimes with a cross inside, always with a mark showing where the point of the compass was placed. The patterns are usually widely spaced and the decoration of large- and medium-sized vases with broad bands at considerable intervals is common.

Iron gradually supersedes bronze throughout this period. An iron sword was found at Kavousi. It has a broad concave blade and seems a mere translation into iron of a bronze type.[2] Probably the fragments from the later interment at Mouliana are from a weapon of the same shape. Knives with a single concave or convex edge and the tang continuing the line of the back of the blade are found at Vrokastro. Iron spear-heads are found at the same site of a broader type than the Minoan.

Proto-geometric Metalwork

The iron axe and adze from Tomb 1 at Vrokastro are not illustrated and have perished. It is not certain from the description whether the former is a single or a double axe.

Fibulae are found for the first time. They occur on most sites in both iron and bronze. Both the bow fibula and the stilted type appear in the earliest tombs of the period, and every example has the coiled spring to the pin, which shows that they were not introduced into the island until they had been in use elsewhere long enough for this refinement to be adopted. The broad plate in which the pin catches is beginning to appear. If further argument were needed that a new type of garment had appeared necessitating the use of something to keep it up on the shoulder, it is provided by the greater number of pins, usually of bronze, with a knobbed end which are now found. Small plain rings and ear-rings of bronze are common on most sites. The gold finger-rings from Vrokastro and Mouliana have a plain bezel at right angles to the flat hoop. The finest object of metal, however, is a bronze tripod nearly 40 cm. high from Tomb 1 at the former site. No trace of the cauldron which it was to support was found. The legs have ridges down each side which end at the top in volutes. These are

[1] Cf. ibid., Pl. V, 6, with *B.S.A.*, XXXV, Pl. IX, *a*.

[2] *A.J.A.*, 1901, 137; for a contemporary short bronze type, cf. *Vrokastro*, Pl. XXI, *g*.

joined by the two branches into which the medial rib splits. Above the volutes is a low abacus on which rests the ring. Slanting supports run from the legs to the ring, and three horizontal braces meet in a smaller ring low down.[1] Plain tripods combining cauldron and legs in one have been found in tombs at Knossos, as yet unpublished.

Proto-
geometric
Figurines

The figurines of the period are, with a few exceptions, of clay. A bronze figurine from Vrokastro with upraised arms bears a strong resemblance to Minoan examples and may well be a survival.[2] At Knossos a hut-shaped vase was found in the Spring Chamber. Through an opening in the front of this appears the upper part of a female figure with upraised arms. But the most impressive examples were found in the sanctuary on Karphi. Pl. XLI, 1 and 2, shows the only two yet to have been mended. They are obviously in the Minoan tradition, with their bell-skirts and their raised arms. The features, however, are much more strongly marked even than those of the L.M.IIIb goddesses from Gaze. In both cases the crown was surmounted by disks and birds. The strangest point, however, is the presence of the feet and lower part of the legs, which are moulded separately and appear through openings in the front of the skirt. The goddess must have needed them to reach her lofty shrine.

The head of a similar figure from Kalokhorio is shown in Pl. XLI, 3. The modelling of the face is exactly the same but a twisted wreath, perhaps of hair, replaces the crown.

Small figurines of animals, perhaps bulls or sheep, were frequently found round about the tholoi on Karphi. They are very roughly made and are covered with small shallow holes. Painted examples occur in the Spring Chamber at Knossos, one of which is in the attitude of a sphinx.

Proto-
geometric
Seals, &c.

No trace of writing has yet been discovered in deposits of this date, and such few seal stones as have been found are probably heirlooms and date from L.M.IIIb.[3] The finer stones had gone out of use, as had the making of faience. The beads, which are usually of globular shape, fluted or of flat disk shape, are clay or steatite. Small flat slabs of the latter material

[1] *Vrokastro*, 132.
[2] Ibid., 121. Miss Lamb, *Greek and Roman Bronzes*, 35, assigns some of the figures from Psykhro to this period. The bulk are Geometric (see below, p. 322).
[3] e.g. *Vrokastro*, Figs. 72, 88, 95, and a very well-cut example with a rosette from Karphi.

pierced at the top and incised with rough patterns were used as pendants.[1]

Crete at this time was almost completely cut off from intercourse with the world outside the Aegean. A few seals of faience with rough hieroglyphs and a string of beads were found in Tomb 1 at Vrokastro, and a similar seal comes from Eleutherna. They belong to the XXth–XXIInd Dynasty.[2] A few more objects of faience come from the unpublished tombs at Knossos. No imports of this date have been found in Egypt.

Protogeometric Foreign Relations

Whence comes the vase shown in Pl. XLII, 1, which was found in a small burial by the Temple Tomb, I do not know. The paint is a dull purple, and the shape reminds one of the predynastic stone vases of Egypt.

It is likewise impossible to say from what part of the Aegean came the introduction of iron and the new style of dress which needed the fibula.

The dating for the end of the Sub-Minoan Period is probably about 1050, and for that of the Protogeometric Period about 900 B.C.[3]

Protogeometric Chronology

SITES WHERE SUB-MINOAN AND PROTO-GEOMETRIC REMAINS HAVE BEEN FOUND.

WEST CRETE

(a) *Excavated Site*

ELEUTHERNA . . . Deposit . . At Orthe Petra, W. of the acropolis, near where the famous (later) statue was found. Payne, *B.S.A.*, XXX, 266. Hartley, ibid., XXXI, 108. Egyptian seal. Ἐφ. Ἀρχ., 1907, 163.

CENTRAL CRETE

(a) *Excavated Sites*

AGIA PARASKEVE . Tomb . . *A.J.A.*, XL, 371, excavated by N. Platon, 1935.

AMNISOS . . . . Deposit . . Marinatos, *Arch. Anz.*, 1935, 245.

ANOPOLIS . . . Cemetery . Halbherr, *A.J.A.*, 1897, 254.

---

[1] e.g. ibid., 121 f.   [2] Ibid., 136.

[3] Schweitzer, *Untersuchungen zur Chronologie der geometrischen Stile in Griechenland.*

ARKHANAIS . . .	Pits . . .	Two pits at Vromonero. *A.J.A.*, XL, 371. Cf. *B.S.A.*, XXXI, 72.
EMPAROS	Deposit .	Vases with many mounds of large stones at ὁ Δραος. Halbherr, *A.J.A.*, 1901, 281.
ERGANOS	Cemetery .	Tholos tombs. Halbherr, *A.J.A.*, 1901, 270.
KARPHI	Settlement . Tombs Sanctuary	Excavation begun in 1937 by the writer. The settlement extends on to both Megale and Mikre Koprana (cf. Evans, *Academy*, 20/6/96). Vase in the Candia Museum. *Catalogue*, 525.
KNOSSOS	Deposits .	Spring Chamber. *P. of M.*, II, 136. W. of Theatral Area, *B.S.A.*, XXXI, 77, 94. Little Palace, 91.
	Tombs . .	N. of Makryteikhos. *B.S.A.*, XXIX, 232. Fortezza, *B.S.A.*, XXXI, 56. *J.H.S.*, LV, 166; LIII, 289.
PANAGIA	Tombs . .	Vaulted tombs. Halbherr, *A.J.A.*, 1901, 283. Levi, *Annuario*, X–XII, 389.
PHRATI	Tombs . .	Vaulted tombs, square and round, on the west slope. Levi, *Annuario*, X–XII, 174.
PSYKHRO . . .	Cave . .	Deposit in the Temenos. Hogarth, *B.S.A.*, VI, 105.
VATHEIANOS KAMPOS	Tomb . .	Larnax burial in chamber tomb. Marinatos, *Arch. Anz.*, 1934, 246.

(b) Surface Finds

ASTRETSI	Sherds found by T. W. Dunbabin, 1937.
KALOKHORIO PEDHIADHOS	Head of Statuette in Candia Museum, similar to those from Karphi. *Annuario*, X–XII, 618.
KLISIDHI	Sherds from the hill, seen by the writer, 1937.
KOLLYVA METOKHI .	Vases from a chamber tomb, found by the peasants. Marinatos, ᾿Αρχ. Δελτ., 14, 1. 1 hr. W. of Herakleion.
KYTTAION . . .	Sherds picked up by R. W. Hutchinson, 1937, at Palaikastro Rodhias.
MESA LASITHI . .	Group of larnax burials at Vlykistra, found while making the car road, seen by the writer, 1936.
PHONIKIA . . .	Vases from burials, in the Candia Museum, seen by the writer, 1930. Marinatos, ᾿Αρχ. Δελτ., 14, 2.

PRINIAS . . . . Crater, published by Orsi. *A.J.A.*, 1897, 252.
SIDEROKEPHALA . . Tholos tombs. Taramelli, *Mon. Ant.*, IX, 402.
SKHINEAS . . . . Sherds seen on Koprana by the writer, 1937.
STRAVOMYTI . . . Traces of larnax burials seen by Miss Eccles, 1935, at Kampariane.

SOUTH CRETE

(a) Excavated Sites

KOURTAIS . . . . Cemetery . Tholos tombs. Halbherr, Taramelli, Mariani, *A.J.A.*, 1901, 287.
LILIANA . . . . Cemetery . Re-used larnakes. *Rend. Linc.*, 1902, 318.
TOU PHYGIOTE . . Tombs . . Later deposit in chamber tombs.
TO ALONI   *Rend. Linc.*, 1902, 318.

(b) Surface Finds

KAMARAIS . . . Tholos tombs at Τῆς Καϋμένης τὸ Σώπατο. ½ hr. NW. of the village. Evans, *Diary*, 30/3/94. Taramelli, *A.J.A.*, 1901, 437.
LIGOURTINO . . . Settlement on the Kephala, found by Wace and Blegen, 1920 (cf. *B.S.A.*, XXXIII, 85).

EAST CRETE

(a) Excavated Sites

AGIOS KONSTANTINOS House . . Bosanquet, *B.S.A.*, VIII, 236.
AMYGDHALI . . . Tomb . . Chamber tomb. Hall, *Vrokastro*, 84.
ANAVLOKHOS . . . Tombs . . Tholoi at Lami. *Demargne*, *B.C.H.*, 1931. Cf. Evans, *Diary*, 1896.
BRAÏMIANA . . . Tombs . . Small tholoi. Marinatos, *J.H.S.*, 1932, 255.
KAVOUSI . . . . Settlements . Houses on Vronta, Kastri, and
                  Tombs   Azorgia Mouri. Boyd, *A.J.A.*, 1901, 125 ff. Tholoi, at Vronta. Ibid.
MOULIANA . . . Settlement . The latter only excavated.
                and Tombs   Xanthoudides, 'Εφ. 'Αρχ., 1904, 21 ff.
PALAIKASTRO . . . Settlements . At Kastri, *B.S.A.*, VIII, 239. At Kouramenos., ibid., IX, 330.
PRAISOS . . . . Tomb . . Tholos near A c r o p o l i s 3. Bosanquet, *B.S.A.*, VIII, 240.
STOU KOUKOU TO . Burials . . Cave burials excavated. Hogarth, ibid., VII, 148.
KEPHALI

| VROKASTRO . . . | Settlement . | Houses on the summit. Hall, *Vrokastro*. |
| | Tombs . . | Chamber tombs, tholoi, and pithos burials at Karakovilia, Khavga, Kopranais, Mazikhortia. Ibid. |

(b) Surface Finds

GALANA KHARAKIA . or STAS TAVERNAIS	Site and plan given by Halbherr, *Antiquary*, 1892, 155.
KHEIROMANDRAIS .	Proto-Geometric (misprinted in text Geometric) sherd, found by the writer, 1934. *B.S.A.*, XXXIII, 98, near the fort dug by Hogarth, *B.S.A.*, VII, 147.
VRAKHASI. . . .	Vases in the Candia Museum, from Τεφροδόχος Κάλπη. *Catalogue*, 5914, 9029–35.

II THE GEOMETRIC PERIOD

(See Map 18)

It is clear from the map (Map 18) that very much the same conditions prevailed in Crete during the course of the Geometric Age as in the previous period. Perhaps some slight improvement is to be inferred from the fact that a few of the old Minoan sites, such as Agia Triadha, Phaistos, and Mallia, were reoccupied, as was also the harbour town of Komo.[1] In the first two cases it is the old site itself which is settled; in the last two, as at Kanli Kastelli, the Geometric remains are a little way from the Minoan site, though the fact that the new spot is equally low and undefended probably implies more of a tabu, as at Knossos, than any necessity for change.

Coast towns, too, are slightly more common, though both Trypeti and Ampelos have wild enough country behind them to act as a refuge in case of trouble. The West is again being opened up and probably by the end of the period the island was comparatively peaceful and ready for the tremendous expansion of population which was to come in Archaic times.

The architecture is indistinguishable from that of the previous period. Indeed, at most of the settlements so far excavated, the same buildings were inhabited. At Kavousi, *Geome Archit*

[1] It is possible that there may have been a Protogeometric site at the first two. Practically none of the material has been published, and in the days of the excavation the distinction between the two periods had not been drawn.

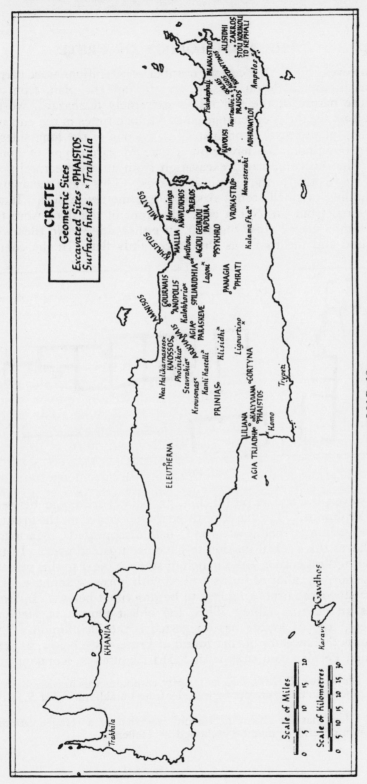

CRETE

Geometric Sites

Excavated Sites °PHAISTOS
Surface finds ×Trakhila

Trakhila

KHANIA

ELEUTHERNA

Nea Halikarnassos
KNOSSOS°
Phoinikia×
Stavrakia×
Krousonas×
Kami Kasteli×
PRINIAS°

AMNISOS

MILATOS

PHALSTOS

GOURNAIS
ANOPOLIS°
Kalekhoria×
ARDHANA°
AGIA° PARASKEVE
SPILIAROIDHIA°
Lagou×

Klisidhi×
Ligourtino×
LILIANA
AGIA TRIADHE° °KALYVIANA °GORTYNA
°PHAISTOS
Komo×
Trypeti

Merminga
MALLIA°
Avdhou×

AGIOU GEORNOU°
PAPOURA
°PSYKHRO

PANAGIA
°PHRATI

VROKASTRO°
KalamaFka× Monasteraki
ADHROMYLOI

DREROS°
ANAVLOKHOS°

KAVOUSI

Piskokephalo× PALAIKASTRO
ISTS° °KONSTANTINOS
Tourtoullas×°× °ROUSSOLAKKOS
PRAISOS× °
Ampelos S×

.KLISIDHI
ZAKLOS
STOU KOUKOU
TO KEPHALI

Karavi
Gavdhos

Scale of Miles
0   5   10   15   20

Scale of Kilometres
0 5 10 15 20 30

MAP 18

however (Fig. 48), a certain number of alterations were carried out in the castle on Kastro, and though the plan, from the mere nature of the ground, is extremely haphazard, we can at least see the great change since Minoan times in the entrance being placed at the end instead of on one of the long sides of the building. We have now a true Megaron type of house.

The most important excavation from an architectural point of view is that of the temple at Dreros. This was a rectangular building of small stones 10·90 × 7·20 metres in size. It was entered from the North end. In front of the door were two columns placed close together on either side.[1] No tiles were found and the roof was almost certainly flat. In the centre,

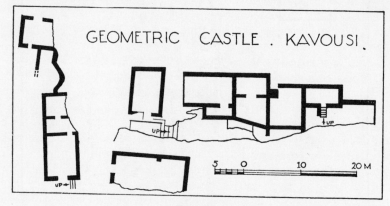

GEOMETRIC CASTLE . KAVOUSI

FIG. 48

however, is a square pit (cf. Fig. 51, below) or ἐσχάρα between two columns. The bases of these merely rested on the ground. The columns, being of wood, had disappeared. Marinatos believes this central portion to have been gabled over. In the South-West corner was a bench of stone. Next to this was the κερατών, or 'altar of horns', filled with horns of animals. On this stood the bronze figures to be described below. In front was an offering table. This, the oldest temple in Hellenic Crete,[2] the excavator has suggested is the Delphinion. The plan is the ancestor of that found at Prinias (see below, p. 331), which Pernier compares with L.H.III houses at Korakou and

[1] Marinatos, *B.C.H.*, LX, 214, aptly compares this arrangement to that shown in the contemporary model from Perakhora. *J.H.S.*, LIV, 191.

[2] I feel that the shrine at Karphi was that of a refugee Minoan population and cannot be reckoned as Hellenic.

considers a type of building imported from the Mainland
and foreign to Crete.

In most cases the old Protogeometric tombs were re-used *Geometric Tombs*
for secondary interments, as in the tholoi of Phrati, the ossuaries of Vrokastro and the larnax burials at Liliana. But in
Lasithi the local style of tholos had new developments. At
one end of the Papoura, about a quarter of an hour below the
tholoi of Karphi, is a group of Geometric tholoi, one of which
has been excavated. It resembles its predecessors in plan
except that the chamber is circular from the foundations.
Furthermore, the rectangular block of masonry surrounding
the tholos shows a later addition, probably lower in height,
which extended beyond the doorway and formed a narrow
dromos. The tomb then would have appeared with two terraces, the uppermost surmounted by the projecting dome of
the tholos. The lintel which spanned the low door was
relieved from undue pressure by the recessing of the courses
above it in a semicircle.

Pithos burials still occur at Anopolis and Phrati. Cremation
is practically universal in all types of burial.

The Geometric pottery of Crete [1] never attained the high *Geometric Pottery*
standard of the Attic School. At Knossos alone is there a
definite marked advance. In the rest of Crete only a few vases
show much progress. The clay is better sifted and the turning
is more careful than in Protogeometric times. Many of the
shapes are different. The kraters and pithoi tend to have their
greatest breadth rather higher. The amphoras with a tall
neck have a much better proportioned body. A new type of
oenochoe with a slimmer body and a taller neck makes its
appearance. The saucers and plates are flatter and have a
more pronounced rim. Before the end of the period double
horizontal handles joined in the middle are found on ovoid
pithoi as well as three loops at the base, forming a tripod. The
conical lids of such vessels are frequently topped themselves by
miniature vases. The stirrup vase seems to have died out
completely. One example was found in the tomb on the
Papoura in Lasithi, but it may well have been an heirloom or
merely another example of the conservatism of that district.

The designs show an almost complete break with those
found on Proto-geometric vases (Fig. 49). The cross-hatched
triangles and lozenges and the concentric circles are the only

[1] *B.S.A.*, XXIX, 271. Cf. also *Annuario*, X–XII, 551.

survivals,[1] while the meander, the quatrefoil, and the diagonalled square are all typical of the new style. Compared with the magnificent Dipylon vases of Athens the motives

FIG. 49.—Patterns on Geometric

are few and the decoration is scanty. Birds appear fairly frequently, but human figures are almost unknown, though an example from Kavousi shows a six-wheeled chariot on one side and three figures on the other.[2] The paint used is rather duller than on Attic vases and ranges from a rusty black to light brown. Before the end of the period a few vases are found with white paint on a dark ground, usually confined to rings round the lower part of the vessel, the upper part being

[1] The concentric circles can always be distinguished by the fact that the mark of the compass point does not appear.

[2] *A.J.A.*, 1901, 111. Cf. *Vrokastro*, 98.

in dark-on-light, but sometimes on small vases constituting the whole of the decoration. This has been regarded as a survival of Minoan technique, but there is a great gap between

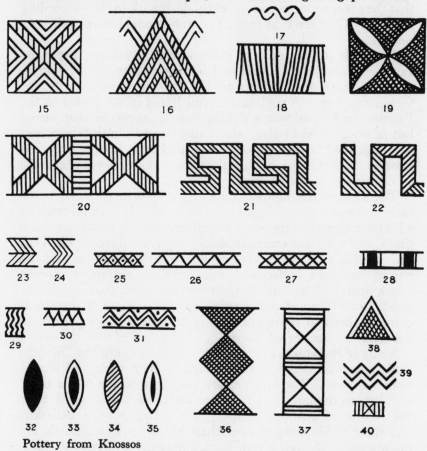

Pottery from Knossos

L.M.1a, which was the last period in the island when white paint, and that only as an accessory, was used, and Geometric times. White paint, again as an accessory, appears in L.H.III on the Mainland but is universally absent in Protogeometric pottery.[1] In Crete it is confined to the Knossos district, with the exception of one or two vases obviously imported from that region.[2] A few *bucchero* vases were found in the tombs at Knossos, the nearest parallel being the Rhodian ware.[3]

[1] The one exception is the goat krater from Mouliana of Sub-Minoan date.

[2] *B.S.A.*, XXIX, 276. [3] Ibid.

Before the close of the eighth century when the Geometric Period comes to an end a class of polychrome vases makes its appearance.   These betray such strong orientalizing influences that they will be more conveniently dealt with in the succeeding section.   They are best treated as transitional between the two periods.

Geometric Metalwork

The tools and weapons of iron show no advance.   From the examples found at Kavousi and Vrokastro it would be impossible to assign them either to the Protogeometric or to the Geometric Age.   A curious survival found in the tholos on the Papoura in Lasithi was a double axe of purely Minoan shape but of iron.   The fibulae, which still occur in both bronze and iron, are now frequently of the beaded type with a large flat plate to catch the pin.   This plate, however, is never decorated as elsewhere in the Aegean.

Geometric Figurines

The best of the figures come from Vrokastro.   The heads seem to have been mounted on tubular stands with no trace of a body.   The eyes are more prominent than in Protogeometric times, but only one example shows any real advance (Pl. XLI, 4).   In this case the modelling is careful throughout and the parted lips and half-closed eyes give an extremely lifelike appearance.[1]   The animal figurines are often hard to distinguish from those of the previous period.   Paint, however, is common both to represent bridles and for a mere pattern to decorate the manes of horses.

Many of the votive figurines of bronze found in the Diktaian Cave are to be dated to this period.[2]   Both male and female figures appear.   The former show the continuation of the L.M. tradition in the left hand raised to the brow, and in some cases the kilt is of Minoan shape.   The latter have a bell-skirt and their hands clasped over their breasts.   The animals are mainly oxen, though a ram occurs drawing a chariot in company with an ox.   The nearest parallels are from Olympia.[3]

Geometric Seals

The art of writing is still a dead one.   The seal stones are comparatively few, or rather perhaps one should say that comparatively few have been published.   Three good examples exist in the British Museum.   All are of green steatite, a soft, easily cut stone, and are engraved with spirited if rude pictures

[1] *Vrokastro*, 101, 112.
[2] Miss Lamb, *Greek and Roman Bronzes*, 35, suggests that some of the human figures with disproportionately long bodies may be attributed to the Protogeometric Period.
[3] *Olympia*, IV, 28 ff.

of a lion, a lion and an eagle, and two lions devouring a stag.[1] The old Minoan spirit had not quite died out. It only needed a fresh impetus, which in this case seems to have come from the islands and from Melos in particular.

No foreign import can be dated with certainty to this period. *Geometric Foreign Relations* The fine bronze statuette of Amen-Ra from the Diktaian Cave belongs most probably to the same deposit as the rest of the bronzes, but its date has been put as early as XVIIIth to XIXth Dynasty, and as late as the Saite Period.[2] Crete, indeed, seems to have been in a backwater at this time, though imported Attic vases appear at Knossos and Vrokastro.[3] The nearest parallels to the pottery have been found in Rhodes for Central Crete and Thessaly for East Crete.[4]

The most probable dating for the end of the true Geometric *Geometric Chronology* Period is about 700 in the East, and about 750 in Central Crete, where it was followed by a transitional semi-orientalizing period, to be described in the next chapter, for which we may allow about fifty years.

SITES WHERE GEOMETRIC REMAINS HAVE BEEN FOUND

WEST CRETE

(a) Excavated Sites

ELEUTHERNA . . . Deposit . . At Orthe Petra, W. of the acropolis. Payne, *B.S.A.*, XXX, 266 ; Hartley, ibid., XXXI, 109.

KHANIA . . . . Cemetery . Graves in the main road near Touzla. Stavropoulos, *J.H.S.*, 1929, 235.

(b) Surface Finds

GAVDHOS . . . Sherds at Karavi. Levi, *Art and Archaeology*, 1927, 176 ff.

TRAKHILA . . . Sherds seen by the writer, 1935.

---

[1] *B.M. Catalogue of Gems*, 180, 181, 183.

[2] *J.H.S.*, LII, 126. *Aegyptiaca*, No. 15, and *Journal des Savants*, 1931, 326.

[3] *Vrokastro*, Pl. XXVI. *B.S.A.*, XXXI, 89, 92.

[4] Ibid., XXIX, 272, 277 ; XXXI, 105. *Prehistoric Thessaly*, 208 ff.

CENTRAL CRETE

(a) Excavated Sites

AGIA PARASKEVE	Tomb	*A.J.A.*, XL, 371. Excavated by N. Platon.
AGIOU GEORGIOU PAPOURA	Tombs	Tholos excavated in 1937 by the writer. (Cf. Evans, *Academy*, 20/6/96.)
AMNISOS	Deposit	Marinatos, *Arch. Anz.*, 1935, 245.
ANOPOLIS	Cemetery	Pithos burials. Halbherr, *A.J.A.*, 1897, 254.
ARKHANAIS	Pits	Two pits at Vromonero. Ibid., XL, 371 ff. Cf. *B.S.A.*, XXXI, 72.
GOURNAIS	Settlement	Between the sea and the village. Hazzidakis, *'Aρχ. Δελτ.*, I, 59.
KHRISTOS ISLAND	Deposit	*B.C.H.*, 1925, 473.
KNOSSOS	Town	Deposits. *P. of M.*, I, 404; II, 432. *B.S.A.*, XXXI, 76, 77, 92, 94, 95; VI, 79. *J.H.S.*, LVI, 159.
	Tombs	*P. of M.*, II, 154; IV, 1018. *B.S.A.*, XXIX, 271; XXXI, 97; VI, 82. *J.H.S.*, LV, 166; LIII, 289.
MALLIA	Tomb	At *Τροχάλοι*. Xanthoudides, *'Aρχ. Δελτ.*, IV, *Παρ.* ii, 18. Burials in dromos of L.M.III tomb (at Agia Pelagia), *B.C.H.*, 1921, 536.
MILATOS	Tomb	Vases from a chamber tomb. *P. of M.*, IV, 164.
NEA HALIKARNASSOS	Cemetery	*A.J.A.*, XL, 371 ff.
PANAGIA	Tombs	Vaulted tombs. Halbherr, *A.J.A.*, 1901, 283. Levi, *Annuario*, X–XII, 389.
PHRATI	Tombs	Pithos burial. Levi, *Annuario*, X–XII, 79. Deposit in vaulted tombs, ibid., 174.
PRINIAS	Deposit	Below Temple A. Pernier, *Annuario*, I, 40. Levi, ibid., X–XII, 620.
PSYKHRO	Cave	Deposit in temenos and lower grotto. Hogarth, *B.S.A.*, VI, 94.
SPILIARIDHIA	House	Earliest deposit from house near cave. Xanthoudides, *B.C.H.*, 1922, 522.

(b) Surface Finds

AVDHOU . . . . Sherds by Aphendes Khristos church, seen by writer, 1935.

KANLI KASTELLI . Settlement to the NE. Evans, *P. of M.*, II, 71. Tomb at Riza to the N. Xanthoudides, *'Αρχ. Δελτ.*, IV, *Παρ.* 10.

KLISIDHI . . . . Sherds from the hill, seen by the writer, 1937.

KROUSONAS . . . Vases from Prinori. Xanthoudides, *Αρχ. Δελτ.*, IV, *Παρ.* 10. Sherds on *Κοῦπο*, seen by Miss Money-Coutts and Miss Eccles, 1934. *B.S.A.*, XXXIII, 92.

LAGOU . . . . Sherds at Bagali and Stou Stavrakou ton Lakkon, seen by Miss Money-Coutts, 1937.

PHOINIKIA . . . Vases from tombs, seen by the writer, 1930. Marinatos, *'Αρχ. Δελτ.*, 14, 4.

STAVRAKIA . . . Vases, published by Orsi, *A.J.A.*, 1897, 259. Mariani, *Mon. Ant.*, VI, 230.

SOUTH CRETE

(a) Excavated Sites

AGIA TRIADHA . . Deposit . . Unpublished except for one clay head. Levi, *Annuario*, X–XII, 620.

GORTYNA . . . . Deposits . . At Agios Ioannes. Pace, *Annuario*, I, 372. *Jahrbuch*, XIV, 40. Below the Odeum. Pernier, *Annuario*, VIII, 6.

KALYVIANA . . . Burials . . Sherds only. *Rend. Linc.*, 1902, 318. *Mon. Ant.*, XIV, 654.

LILIANA . . . . Burials . . Re-used larnakes. Ibid.

PHAISTOS . . . . Deposit . . Immediately above the Minoan. Halbherr, *Mon. Ant.*, XII, 21.

(b) Surface Finds

KOMO . . . . . Sherds on the S. headland. Evans, *P. of M.*, II, 88.

LIGOURTINO . . . Settlement on the Kephala. See previous period.

TRYPETE . . . . Large settlement on the shore, exposed by rain, seen by the writer, 1934. *B.S.A.*, XXXIII, 87.

EAST CRETE

(a) Excavated Sites

ADHROMYLOI . . . Tomb . . Over a hundred vases. Bosanquet, *B.S.A.*, VIII, 249. Droop, ibid., XII, 43.

AGIOS KONSTANTINOS   House . .   Bosanquet, *B.S.A.*, VIII, 236.
ANAVLOKHOS. . .   Fortifications   On main summit.
    Tombs . .   Pithos burials at *Κακὸ Πλάϊ.* Demargne, *B.C.H.*, 1931.
DREROS . . . .   Temple . .   Ibid., LX, 214. Cf., *Ἀϱχ. Δελτ.*, IV, *Παϱ.* ii, 25.
KAVOUSI . . . .   Settlement .   Later deposit at Kastro. Boyd, *A.J.A.*, 1901, 139.
KLISIDHI . . . .   Fort . . .   Galana Kharakia or Stas Tavernais. Hogarth, *B.S.A.*, VII, 148, found sherds here.
STOU KOUKOU TO KEPHALI   Burial . .   Cave burial. Hogarth, ibid., VII, 148.
    Settlement .   On both sides of the river. Ibid.
PALAIKASTRO. . .   Deposit . .   Vases near the surface on the town site. Ibid., IX, 320.
PRAISOS . . . .   Tombs . .   Built and shaft graves, Bosanquet. *B.S.A.*, VIII, 245. Droop, *B.S.A.*, XII, 37, 39.
    Settlement .   On Altar Hill. *B.S.A.*, VIII, 254 ; XII, 39.
SKALAIS . . . .   Cave . . .   Latest deposit. Bosanquet, *B.S.A.*, VIII, 235.
VROKASTRO . . .   Settlement .   Latest deposit in the houses on the summit. Hall, *Vrokastro*.
    Tombs . .   Bone enclosures at Karakovilia. Ibid.
ZAKROS . . . .   Settlement .   At Ellenika up the gorge. *B.S.A.*, VII, 145.

(b) Surface Finds

AMPELOS . . . .   Geometric seal stone, seen by R. W. Hutchinson, 1936.
KALAMAFKA . . .   Pithos fragments on the Kastellos, seen by Bosanquet. Unpublished.
MERMINGA . . .   Vases published by Droop, *B.S.A.*, XII, 37, 38. Candia Museum, *Catalogue*, 517.
MONASTERAKI . .   Settlement at the top of the Khaos gorge at Katalimata. Hall, *Trans. Penn. Univ.*, I, 18.
NEAPOLIS-MIRABELLO ROAD   Group of vases published by Droop, *B.S.A.*, XII, 37.
PISKOKEPHALO . .   Base published by Droop, *B.S.A.*, XII, 37.
TOURTOULLOI . .   Vases, published by Xanthoudides, *'Ἀϱχ. Δελτ.*, IV, *Παϱ.* i, 13.

III. THE ORIENTALIZING AND ARCHAIC PERIOD

(See Map 19)

With the eighth century the true Hellenic Period in Crete begins. The map is particularly instructive as showing the drift westwards of the population, or more probably the settling of that part of the island by immigrants from the Mainland. The great cities of Axos, Polyrrhenia, and Hyrtakina are founded, and very probably excavation would show that Phalasarna, Elyros, and Sybrita also, have remains of this period. Only slightly smaller are the new foundations of Rhokka, Bene, and Ornithe, the latter probably the ancient Osmida. Eleutherna and Kydonia have expanded rapidly. Most interesting of all, however, is the votive deposit in the cave of Ida, the earliest elements in which are about contemporary with the latest elements in the Diktaian cave. Since the birthplace of Zeus was placed by different legends at both these sites, the apparent transference of the centre of worship from one to the other at this period gives us a very good idea of the shift of power. The worship of Diktaian Zeus, however, was still carried on at Palaikastro in the East end of the island, where by now the population seems to have concentrated on the one big site of Praisos. Farther West the sites of Lato and Dreros, in Lasithi the city on the Papoura, and Phrati on the slopes of Dikte, all show the wealth of the island. In the South Rhytion, Gortyna, Pyloros, and Phaistos, in the centre Knossos, Prinias (the ancient Rhezenia ?), and Astretsi (the ancient Diatonion ?) make us feel that at last we are in touch with Greek literature and history.

The desperate conditions of the early Iron Age have disappeared. The type of site now favoured is strong and defensible enough—that was inevitable with the petty inter-city wars—but it is not inaccessible and is more in the nature of an acropolis with the city built on the slopes (Pl. VII). The coast still seems to be avoided, probably more because of the absence of dignified sites than because of any specific danger. No doubt excavation below the classical and Roman strata of later harbour towns would reveal at least a dockyard of the Archaic Period.

Of the constitution and laws of these cities we have some information.[1] The island was by now thoroughly ' Dorian ' and the constitution was much the same as that of Sparta.

[1] Particularly Aristotle, *Politics*, II.

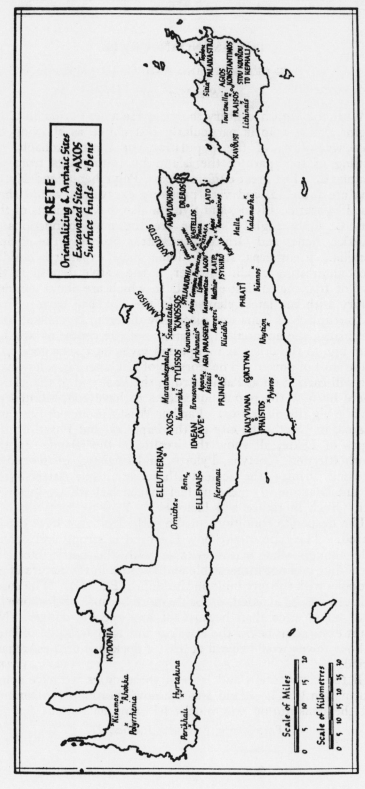

CRETE

Orientalizing & Archaic Sites
Excavated Sites   °AXOS
Surface Finds   ×Bene

KYDONIA

Kisamos
×
×Nokka
Polyrrhenia×

Hyrtakina
×

Perikhali
×

ELEUTHERNA

AXOS°
Marathokephala°
Kamaraki× TYLISSOS
Ornithe×
Bene×
Krousonas×
IDEAN
CAVE°

Sxamataki
KNOSSOS
SPILIAROUDHIA×
Apano× Aprou Gonums Prepvana×
Arkhanais°
Kounavoi×
Kastamonitza×
Apani×
Aristais°   NEA PARASKEVE°
PRINIAS°   Mathia×
Kliadhi
Aroreti×
LAGOU°
SKALAGA

KHERSITOS
SOSINWV

AMNISOS

AMNILOKHOS
DREROS°
Ganais×
Gulas×
KASTELLOS
Priniz
Kastellosxxx×Agios
Nixxxxxx× Kastambos
LATO°
Malle×
Kalamafka×

Kavõust
Lidinais

Toutzelia× AGIOS
PALAIKASTRO
KONSTANTINOS
Situ×
PLAISOS°
STOU KRINÕOU
TO KEPHALI

PHLAT°
Biannos×

ELLENAIS
Keramai
KALYVIANA
PHAISTOS°
GORTYNA
×Pyloros

Rhytzon
×

Kliadhi
Mathia×
PLATE×
PSYKHRO°
Kastambos×
Kaunfabmos×

Scale of Miles

0   5   10   15   20

Scale of Kilometres

0   5   10   15   20   25   30

MAP 19

Lykourgos, indeed, is said to have borrowed much from Crete, and on the whole the Cretans were considered to have kept the Dorian ideal purer than in other parts where it had to be adapted to local conditions.   At the head of each city-state were the ten *kosmoi*, elected for a year from aristocratic families.   They combined the functions of the Spartan kings and ephors.   The Council or *Βωλά* was composed of ex-kosmoi, who sat for life. The Assembly merely ratified decisions already taken.   The old population was divided into free subjects, *περίοικοι*, and serfs, *μνοῖα* or *μνοῖται*, in which name it is perhaps permissible to trace some connexion with Minos.[1]   The whole of the constitution and the education of the young was drawn up with a view to war.   If their own small bickerings were not enough they hired their swords abroad, and among them were the most famous mercenaries of ancient times.[2]

Up to the present the ruins of Lato provide us with the best idea of an archaic city.   Lato has a double acropolis (Pl. VII, 1), which rises steeply on all sides.   The fortification walls are well preserved in places about half-way down the western

Archaic Architecture

---

[1] Hybrias, 5, *τούτῳ δεσπότας μνοίας κέκλημαι.*
[2] In spirit they have hardly changed.   Compare the last verse of Hybrias :

> ' τοὶ δὲ μὴ τολμῶντ' ἔχειν δόρυ καὶ ξίφος
> καὶ τὸ καλὸν λασήϊον, πρόβλημα χρωτός,
> πάντες γόνυ πεπτηῶτες ἁμὸν
> πάντες χαμαί με προσκυνέονθ' ἅτε δεσπόταν
> καὶ μέγαν βασιλῆα φωνέοντες.'

> ' But your wights that take no pride to wield
> A massy spear and well-made shield,
>   Nor joy to draw the sword,
> O I send those heartless, hapless drones
> Down in a trice on their marrow bones
>   To call me king and lord.'

(T. CAMPBELL)

with the words of the modern Cretan equivalent—the Pentozales dance :

> ' ὅποιος δὲν εἶνε μερακλῆς καὶ στ' ἄρματα τεχνίτης
> πρέπει του νὰ μὴν τὰ πατεῖ τὰ χώματα τσῆ Κρήτης.
> ὅποιος δὲν εἶνε μερακλῆς του πρέπει νὰ ποθάνη,
> γιὰ τὶ στὸν κόσμον γιὰ νὰ ζῆ μόνο τὸ τόπο πιάνει ; '

> ' He who is not a man of taste and skilled in arms
> Has no right to tread the soil of Crete.
> He who is not a man of taste had much better die.
> Why should he clutter up the earth by merely living ? '

slope.[1] The road of approach runs along these walls and ascends to a fortified gate, whence a narrow paved street leads up and over the saddle between the two summits. At a point before the top of the saddle is reached lies the Agora. This is a comparatively large open space, at the North end of which is a flight of steps leading up between two towers to the Prytaneion, in the main hall of which is an altar. Along the West side of the Agora runs a portico. Facing the Prytaneion is a simple, probably hypaethral shrine consisting of a single chamber. On the South side of the road and forming the South end of the Agora is an exedra. A comparison with Gournia (p. 191) is inevitable. At Lato the group of public buildings has taken the place of the manor house as the centre

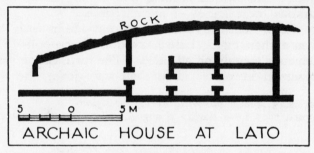

ARCHAIC HOUSE AT LATO

FIG. 50

of the city. There is no regular system of roads. The buildings seem to lie quite haphazard.

A typical house is shown in Fig. 50. It is built of large, rather rough stones, except for the door jambs which are square-dressed and are often monoliths. The rock is cut back to form one of the walls. This is a feature which is particularly common in West Crete,[2] where almost every ancient acropolis shows a quantity of rock-cuttings, but rare in East Crete, where, owing to the hardness of the native stone, the inhabitants preferred to terrace up the foundations rather than to cut back. At one end is a courtyard from which the entrance-hall is

---

[1] Fortification walls are always dangerous things to date. Most of the examples in mainland Greece are later than the fifth century. It is difficult, however, in this case to dissociate them from the houses, since the masonry is identical.

[2] The best example is at Rhokka, where the rock wall often ran up two stories, the holes for the beams of the ceiling being clearly visible.

reached. Behind this are more rooms. As usual these are divided into two groups either for men and women or for master and servants. At Kolonna in Lasithi a baetylic stone is set upright in the paving before the front door.

The simplest form of temple is the earliest Pythion at Gortyna, which is a plain chamber entered from the East, screen-walls running back on either side of the door for about a metre. Next comes those at Lato, which consist of a pronaos, often projecting at one side, and a cella. There are no traces of columns and the suggestion has been made that they are hypaethral. The most elaborate example is Temple A at Prinias (Fig. 51). This has a pronaos and cella. The entrance, over which was a sculptured frieze of horsemen, is divided into two by a square pillar. There seems to have been a column also in the middle of the doorway leading to the cella. The lintel of this was elaborately carved with figures of the goddess on its under surface and of animals on its sides, while it was surmounted at each end by seated statues of the goddess in the round (see below). The arrangement of the cella resembles that of the earlier temple at Dreros, with a *bothros* or ἐσχάρα, lined in this case with slabs of limestone, which show traces of fire, between two columns. Like the Dreros temple, this part was probably hypaethral. No remains of an altar were found,

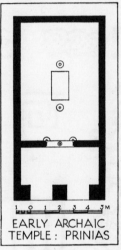

EARLY ARCHAIC
TEMPLE : PRINIAS

FIG. 51

but traces exist of a bench running along the South side. Of the Temple of Diktaian Zeus at Palaikastro nothing remained but the *sima* and a few objects, and the small shrine in the Palace at Knossos had been entirely destroyed.

There is a tendency in the Archaic Period to dress the stones better, even for ordinary houses. The walls on the whole are roughly polygonal but with a tendency to isodomy. They are usually laid dry and the ' cement ' mortar reported from Lato is probably the result of repairing in later times. The frieze and lintel of Prinias and the *sima* from Palaikastro give us some idea of the entablature, but what order of columns was in use we do not know. Probably they were still of wood and very likely of the old Minoan type. The earliest known Doric

FIG. 52.—Patterns on Orientalizing

Pottery from Knossos

capital from Crete was found at Knossos on the top of the
Acropolis (Monasteriako Kephali), whither it had been taken
in much later times to be used as a millstone. It cannot date
to much before the very end of the sixth century, in spite of
its rounded *echinus*, and the site of the temple from which it
came is unknown.

*Archaic
Tombs*

The burial customs remain much as before. Indeed, there
are few Geometric tombs which were not in use down to at
least the end of the Orientalizing Period. The building of
tholoi, however, has died out. Pithos burials were found at
Phrati, and at Agios Konstantinos a shallow grave was found
in one of the rooms of an earlier house. Possibly some of the
rock-cut tombs, such as are to be seen at Patela near Prinias,
on Koutsoulas, the hill East of Polyrrhenia, and at Rhokka, may
have originally been hollowed out at this date, though the very
rare sherds that have been found in them are Classical and
Hellenistic.

*Archaic
Pottery*

The pottery begins with a transitional phase which, as has
been said, overlapped with the end of the Geometric Period,
and displays the beginnings of a marked Oriental influence.[1]
At first the patterns show, as Payne says, a reluctance to depart
from the Geometric tradition, but gradually free curvilinear
designs appear. The most typical of these are the cable pattern
and floral designs (Fig. 52). The shapes show little development, being all variants of forms already in use. The polychrome vases are confined to tombs. No example has yet been
found in any settlement. There are only three shapes so
decorated, and of these, two, bowls and suspension bowls with
a plastic *protome*, are very rare. The rest are tripod pithoi.
Both shape and decoration are traceable to Cyprus.[2] The
designs are painted on a thick white slip. The colours employed are red and dark grey, which is often very nearly blue,
but yellow is also found. How popular this form of decoration
became is shown by vases from Knossos originally painted in
the Geometric style but later covered with a white slip and
painted in the new technique. Payne sees a clue to the
chronological order of these vases in the substitution of grey
for red as the chief colour. Figures of birds become much
more common, and on one vase is a regular forest of leaves

[1] See Payne, *B.S.A.*, XXIX, 277 ff., for the best discussion of this
pottery.
[2] Payne, loc cit. Their funerary character is there compared to
the Attic fifth-century polychrome ware.

with fledgelings picking their way through. Round the top
of this same vase is a frieze of fish. The old Minoan love of
nature has come to the fore again, for the composition of the
panel containing the birds owes nothing to outside influence.[1]
On one vase only appear human figures. A warrior in a
plumed helmet approaches a woman in a long skirt and a thick
fillet on her hair. Both figures stand on bases, which seem
to have been an artistic convention.[2] The drawing is very rude,
particularly when compared with the fishes and the floral designs.

In dating this pottery we shall probably be fairly correct if
we suggest the second half of the eighth century for the first
arrival of the orientalizing influences, and the last quarter of
the same century to about the middle of the seventh for the
polychrome vases.

The vases from Phrati are a peculiar group of their own.
Human figures are common, and so are plastic vases. An
interesting example is a bucket-shaped vase, which shows a
figure of the goddess holding very stylized trees with a bird on
each side of her. Her head is facing and her hair has been
added in relief.[3] These vases, which cover practically the
whole of the Orientalizing Period, have few parallels elsewhere,
even in Crete. To the present writer they seem to bear more
resemblance to contemporary Attic vases than to any other
style.

Many fine examples are known of pithoi decorated in relief
with animals, sphinxes, and human figures. Fragments of
these are among the most common objects to be found on the
surface of a site of this period. Courby,[4] in his study of such
vases, divides them into three groups: Neo-Mycenaean, to
include those from the Diktaian cave and examples from
Lyttos, which he seems to date to the Geometric Period ;
Orientalizing, which he dates from 750 to 650 ; and Architectural, 650–550, where the impression is given of a frieze on a
building. It is probable, however, that his Neo-Mycenaean
and his Orientalizing are contemporary at any rate during the
existence of the former.

This pottery is the last Cretan ware which is of a distinctive
local type. From now onwards Cretan vases are poor imitations of the contemporary styles prevalent elsewhere. One

[1] Ibid., 283.
[2] Cf. the Rhethymnos mitra. *Greek and Roman Bronzes*, 61.
[3] *Annuario*, X–XII, 330, Fig. 431.
[4] Courby, *Vases Grecques à Relief*, 40 ff.

example alone is worthy of mention. This is a pinax from a tomb at Praisos. The interior shows a horseman very much in the style of the Prinias frieze (see below). Outside is the fragment of a magnificent scene in which a hero wrestles with a sea-monster (Pl. XLII, 2). The clean sweep of the outlines and the splendid swing and vigour of the body are reminiscent of the best Minoan work, and it is hard to believe that it is not of local manufacture.[1] The white object below the monster's tail has been explained as a female foot, and it has been suggested that the scene represents Thetis attempting to escape from Peleus in the likeness of a fish.

Archaic
Metalwork

In the Orientalizing Period a number of important works of art in bronze was produced in Crete.[2] Earliest of all are the famous bronze shields found in the cave on Mt. Ida.[3] These are votive offerings of thin bronze, the smaller examples which show no central boss being more accurately described as gongs or cymbals. The designs are hammered out—more rarely incised. The shields have a central boss, projecting in one case enough to be made into the head of a bird in the round, in another to form a lion's head in high relief. Round this are circular friezes of animals. Sphinxes and snakes also appear. One of the gongs shows a god, bearded in the Assyrian style, swinging a lion above his head.[4] On either side are winged attendants. The nearest parallel to these bronzes are the Phoenician bowls, made from the ninth to the seventh centuries, which have been found at Nimrud, in Cyprus, Italy, and Greece. The character is purely Oriental, a hotchpotch of Assyrian and Egyptian motives. The 'shields', however, are probably of local manufacture, since not only do they seem a regular form of offering but certain details in the drawing are not of Oriental origin.[5] In date they probably cover the last half of the eighth century.[6]

---

[1] Hopkinson, *B.S.A.*, X, 149 ff., would make it an import from the Melos–Delos group. Buschor, *Greek Vase Painting*, 32, maintains its Cretan origin and finds a connexion between it and the Odysseus and Ram vase from Aegina, which has been assigned to almost every orientalizing fabric and is possibly Proto-attic.

[2] Cf. Kunze, *Kretische Bronzereliefs*.

[3] Other examples from Palaikastro and Phrati.

[4] He is the young hunter god of the Gilgamesh type, one of whose homes was the Zagros range. It is significant that Zagreus appears early in Crete. [5] *C.A.H.*, IV, 583.

[6] Kunze would push some back to the ninth century, but cf. Payne's review, *J.H.S.*, LIII, 122.

To the end of the eighth or very beginning of the seventh century belong the bronze reliefs from Kavousi and Knossos, both perhaps by the same hand. Their Oriental features are very marked, particularly in a human figure wrestling with two lions and in a scene of a chariot advancing against bowmen.[1]

To the seventh century belong a number of figures cut from sheets of bronze probably for attachment to a wooden chest or some such object. The finest of these represents two huntsmen, one a boy carrying a wild goat over his shoulder, the other a bearded man with a bow. The relief is very low and the details are incised. The narrow waists, the peculiar short loin-cloth, and the curls on the boy's forehead show the survival of Minoan tradition.[2] With these must be taken the *mitrai* from Axos.[3] They are in low relief, *repoussé* work with the details incised. Of the same class are the breast-plates from Olympia engraved with figures of animals, heraldic sphinxes, and in one case a frieze of divine figures.[4] The fine engraving and the clean sweep of line is characteristic of the Cretan school as well as a fondness for zigzags, dog tooth, and varieties of honeysuckle patterns and linked spirals. To the early sixth century can be attributed a magnificent helmet from Axos with reliefs of winged horses and rosettes. The brow is engraved with lions' heads and the patterns along the bottom are those typical of Crete.

The earliest statues in the round are those found in the temple at Dreros.[5] They are made of bronze plates, hammered into shape and riveted over a wooden core mould.[6] *Archaic Sculpture and Figurines* The two female figures have a straight tubular skirt with a double band of small knobs down the front. The torso is bare but a short cloak is indicated over the shoulders and upper arms. The hair is dressed in a heavy straight bob and is surmounted by a *polos*. The arms are held tightly to the sides. The male figure is nude except for a *mitra* and a round skull-

---

[1] Kunze, op. cit., Pl. 56. *J.H.S.*, 1933, 290.

[2] *C.A.H.*, IV, 586. Lamb, loc. cit., 59 f. Cf. another example from Dreros, *B.C.H.*, LX, Pl. XXX. This is a pure silhouette.

[3] *Annuario*, XIII–XIV. There is good reason to believe that the example in Candia, said to come from Rhethymnos, Lamb, loc. cit., is really from this site.

[4] *Olympia*, IV, Pls. LVIII and LIX.

[5] *B.C.H.*, LX, Pl. LXIII, and forthcoming *Monument Piot*.

[6] The σφυρήλατος method of *Pausanias*, III, 17, 16, and elsewhere. Pausanias describes a statue of Zeus at Sparta made in this technique by Klearkhos, a pupil of Dipoinos and Skyllis, the Cretan artists.

cap. The arms are bent at the elbow and held slightly away from the body. Collar-bones and ribs are lightly marked. The features of all three are well-marked but intended to be viewed from in front only. Holes in the bronze are left for the insertion of eyes of a different material. The modelling is remarkably good and, since it is impossible to put the figures later than the end of the eighth or the very beginning of the seventh century, considerably better than is to be found for many generations.

The seventh century is covered by the ' Daedalic ' series of sculptures and terracottas which have recently been the subject of a detailed discussion by Jenkins.[1] His Proto-daedalic phase, dated by him from about 680 to 670, is represented by a head in New York. It shows a triangular face with a heavy nose. The face is framed in a wig or possibly in hair elaborately dressed in horizontal bands which are typical of Crete. The eyes show a double groove to the lids. The Early Daedalic figures from 670 to 655 show a fuller face. The lids of the eyes and the brows are well-defined but the features are still coarse. To this period belong the seated figure in stone from Malla and a few terracotta heads from the Diktaian Cave. Middle Daedalic 1, from 655 to 645, shows better modelling, as on a head from the Little Palace at Knossos. The mouth curls upwards at the ends in a smile. The eyes are heavily ringed. To this period probably belongs the frieze of horsemen from Prinias and the original figures of the goddess on the lintel, of which the existing remains are an archaizing copy of about 600. Hitherto the figures have been intended to be seen from in front only. With Middle Daedalic 2, however, from 645 to 640 the craftsman begins to consider the profile. The stone statue from Auxerre, which is claimed as Cretan, shows a firm angular chin, and, with certain terracotta heads from Phaistos, has the eye treated so that it can be seen from the side, though the correct angle is not given till later. In this approach to three-dimensional modelling Crete is ahead of the contemporary Aegean world. This tendency is carried a step further in Middle Daedalic 3 (640–630), to which period belong a head vase from Arkhanais and a small bronze *kouros* from Delphi. The small eye and the double fold above are still typical of Cretan modelling, but the face is shorter and squarer. Last of all comes the Late Daedalic Period from 630 to 620,

[1] *Dedalica*, 1936, 25, 29, 34, 42, 45, 51, 58, 79, and references there given.

of which the best example is the well-known stone figure from Eleutherna.   In this statue the chin is quite square, the mouth is straight and well-modelled, the nose short and projecting sharply and the eyes still defined by the double groove above (Pl. XLIII, 2).

In the sixth century Cretan art declined sadly, and except for a bronze statuette of a boy carrying a ram [1] the figures are mere poor relations of the products of the Peloponnesian School. A few terracottas from Praisos are of interest.   The most important is one of a series of figurines from a small temple at Mesavrysis which is clearly the direct descendant of the Minoan goddess type though her arms are not raised.[2]   A number of large painted figures of lions of varying dates was found on the Altar hill, and from the same site comes the upper half of a male figure three-quarters life-size,[3] whose sharp, clear-cut features are in contrast to the softer contours of the seventh century.   It may probably be attributed to the last half of the sixth.   The middle of the sixth century is the most likely date for the terracotta *sima* from the Diktaian Temple at Palaikastro (Pl. XLIII, 1).   This consisted of a number of blocks all cast from the same mould and showing a warrior entering a chariot, which by a strange error is shown as being drawn at full speed by two horses below which runs a dog.[4]   Other terracotta plaques and moulds of various dates in the sixth century display no peculiarly Cretan characteristics.

The ivories from the Idaean Cave are discussed by Kunze.[5] He finds parallels to them from Ephesus, Nimrud, Arslan Tash, and Syria, though mostly of a date as early as the eighth century.   His conclusion is that they are all Asiatic imports.

The first Greek inscription in the island is the earlier code of laws from Gortyna, which has been dated to the early sixth century.   The alphabet employed is, with small differences, that of Thera and Melos and approaches most closely the ' Phoenician ' alphabet.   The inscription is deeply cut and reads from right to left throughout.   Coins were not minted in Crete until the beginning of the fifth century, and from this inscription it appears that fines were reckoned in cauldrons or tripods.

Archaic Inscriptions

---

[1] Lamb, op. cit., 84.
[2] *B.S.A.*, VIII, 278.
[3] Ibid., 272, Pl. XIII.
[4] Ibid., XI, 300.
[5] *Ath. Mitt.*, 60/61, 218 ff

SITES WHERE ORIENTALIZING AND ARCHAIC REMAINS HAVE BEEN FOUND

WEST CRETE

(a) *Excavated Sites*

AXOS	Temple .	Levi, *Annuario*, XIII–XIV.
ELEUTHERNA . . .	Deposits .	Payne, *B.S.A.*, XXX, 266. Hartley, ibid., XXXI, 110. Cf. *Rev. Arch.*, XXXI, 10.
ELLENAIS . . .	Cave . .	Sherds. Marinatos, *Arch. Anz.*, 1932, 77.
IDAEAN CAVE. . .	Cave . .	Bronze. *Ath. Mitt.*, X, 62. Kunze, *Kretische Bronzereliefs, passim.* Halbherr, *Mus. It. Ant. Clas.*, II, 689. Kunze, *Ath. Mitt.*, 60/61, 218 ff.
KYDONIA . . .	Graves . .	Unpublished, contents in the Museum of Khania. Also many vases from the district in both this Museum and that of Candia.

(b) *Surface Finds*

BENE	Walls seen by Spratt, II, 105, at N. end. Walls and sherds at S. end, seen by the writer, 1935.
HYRTAKINA . . .	Description by Pashley, II, 111. Inscription, Doublet, *B.C.H.*, XIII, 175. Cf. Savignoni, *Mon. Ant.*, 1901, 408. Sherds scattered over large area, seen by the writer, 1935.
KERAMAI	Sherds and walls at Visala, seen by the writer, 1929, 1932.
KISAMOS	Vases in the local museum.
ORNITHE	Perhaps the ancient Osmida. Fine fortification walls and relief pithos sherds seen by the writer, 1935.
PERIKHALI . . .	Lekythos, published by Savignoni, *Mon. Ant.*, 1901, 459.
POLYRRHENIA . .	For general description see Pashley, II, 46. Many of the bases of the walls are archaic. Many sherds all over the site. Vases in the Khania Museum.
RHOKKA	Site on low ground NW. of the village, vase seen by the writer, 1935. Acropolis above.

CENTRAL CRETE

(a) *Excavated Sites*

AGIA PARASKEVE . .	Tomb . .	Latest deposit in rock-cut tomb. *A.J.A.*, XL, 371.

AMNISOS	Deposit .	From house. Marinatos, Πρακτικὰ, 1933, 93. *Arch. Anz.*, 1934, 246 ; 1935, 245.
KASTELLOS TZERMIADHON	Deposit .	Vases in M.M.III house excavated, 1937, by the writer.
KERASA	Deposit .	Vases, &c., by a Hellenistic Tomb. Excavated in 1937 by the writer.
KHRISTOS ISLAND .	Deposit .	*B.C.H.*, 1928, 502.
KNOSSOS	Deposits .	In palace. *P. of M.*, II, 6. *B.S.A.*, XXXI, 76, 77. Outside palace. *J.H.S.*, LVI, 159.
	Tombs . .	*B.S.A.*, XXIX, 277. *J.H.S.*, LV, 166 ; LIII, 289.
KOLONNA. . . .	Houses . .	Outskirts of the City on the Papoura, excavated in 1937 by the writer.
LAGOU	Houses . .	Two houses at Donadhes, excavated in 1937 by the writer.
PHRATI	Settlement .	Houses and Fortifications on Prophetes Elias. Levi, *Annuario*, X–XII, 32 ff.
	Tombs .	Pithos burials on W. slope. Ibid., 79. Latest deposit in vaulted tombs, 174. At Selli, 381.
PLATE	Deposit .	From above the Minoan settlement, mainly pithos fragments. Dawkins, *B.S.A.*, XX, 1.
PRINIAS	City . .	Perhaps the ancient Rhezenia. Architectural and other finds. Pernier, *Annuario*, I, 18. *Mem. Ist Lomb.*, XXII, 53, and *Bolletino d'Arte*, I, 28, II, 455. Cf. Halbherr, *A.J.A.*, 1901, 399. Savignoni, ibid., 404. *A.J.A.*, 1934, 171.
PSYKHRO . . .	Cave . .	A few sherds from the temenos. Hogarth, *B.S.A.*, VI, 94.
SPILIARIDHIA. . .	House . .	Latest deposit in a house near the cave. Xanthoudides, *B.C.H.*, 1922, 522.
TYLISSOS	Deposit .	A few objects. Hazzidakis, *T.V.M.* 109.

(b) Surface Finds

AGIOU GEORGIOU PAPOURA	Sherds and very fine terracotta plaques from SE. slope, seen by the writer, 1936.
AGIOS KONSTANTINOS	Sherds and walls seen by the writer at Kharakia, 1937.

APANO ASITAIS .   .   Vase in the Candia Museum. *Catalogue*, 587.

ARKHANAIS .   .   .   Clay figurine. Candia Museum. *Catalogue*, 3262 ; also report of bronzes.

ASTRETSI .   .   .   .   Possibly the ancient Diatonion. Mariani, *Mon. Ant.*, VI, 235. Taramelli, ibid., IX, 349. Relief pithos. Marinatos, *Arch. Anz.*, 1933, 313.

GAITANOU .   .   .   Stamped pithos fragments found by Emm. Akoumianos, 1935.

GONIAIS .   .   .   .   Site at Phakistriais S. of the village, found by Emm. Akoumianos, 1935. Also at Lefteroi or Stolos above the latter. Xanthoudides had seen this.

KAMARAKI .   .   .   Statuette from Philerymo in the Candia Museum. *Catalogue*, 5238.

KASTAMONETZA .   .   Remains of votive deposit seen by Evans, *Diary*, 15/3/95 ; relief pithos, Marinatos, *Arch. Anz.*, 1934, 246.

KEPHALA .   .   .   .   Jug in hands of villager, from burial on NW. side, seen by the writer, 1936.

KLISIDHI .   .   .   .   Sherds on the hill, seen by T. J. Dunbabin, 1937.

KOUNAVOI .   .   .   Possibly the ancient Eltyna. Inscription. Xanthoudides, 'Ἀρχ. Δελτ., IV, Παρ. ii, 24.

KROUSONAS .   .   .   Terracotta figurines in the Candia Museum. *Catalogue*, 6342–4. Mariani, *Mon. Ant.*, VI, 38.

LAGOU .   .   .   .   Sherds at Bagali and Stou Stavrakou ton Lakkon, seen by Miss Money-Coutts, 1937.

LYTTOS .   .   .   .   Stamped pithoi in the Candia Museum.

MARATHOKEPHALA .   Pithos fragments and traces of walls found by Mariani. *Rend. Linc.*, 1894, 180.

MATHIA .   .   .   .   Pinax from Kharakia. Levi, *Annuario*, X–XII, 621.

PONTA .   .   .   .   Extensive site, many good relief pithos fragments seen by the writer, 1935–6. Cf. Evans, *Diary*, 1898.

STAMATAKI .   .   .   Archaic terracotta figurine. Mariani, *Mon. Ant.*, VI, 39.

SOUTH CRETE

(a) Excavated Sites

GORTYNA.   .   .   .   City   .   .   Temple of Apollo Pythios. *Mon. Ant.*, i, 8 ; III, 1 ; XVIII, 381. Odeum, *Annuario*, II, 303 ; VIII, 9.

KALYVIANA .   .   .   Tombs .   .   Poor burials. *Mon. Ant.*, XIV, 654.

PHAISTOS.   .   .   .   Deposit   .   Above Geometric on palace site. Halbherr, *Mon. Ant.*, XII, 21. Marinatos, *Arch. Anz.*, 1933, 312 ; 1935, 244.

(b) Surface Finds

BIENNOS . . . . Sherds on Korakia above the village, seen by the writer, 1935. Cf. Mariani, *Mon. Ant.*, VI, 174.

RHYTION . . . Cf. Spratt, I, 333. Evans, *Diary*, 2/4/94. Walls and sherds seen by the writer, 1934. *B.S.A.*, XXXIII, 86.

PYLOROS . . . . Inscription from Ἀγκέραμαι to the E. Halbherr, *Mus. It. Ant. Class.*, III, 719.

EAST CRETE

(a) Excavated Sites

AGIOS KONSTANTINOS   Grave . . Bosanquet, *B.S.A.*, VIII, 239.

ANAVLOKHOS. . . Deposit . . On Κακὸ Πλάϊ. Demargne, *B.C.H.*, 1931. Cf. Mariani, *Mon. Ac. Linc.*, VI, 244.

DREROS . . . . City . . Houses and public buildings. Xanthoudides, Ἀρχ. Δελτ., IV, Παρ. ii, 23. Later deposit in Temple. Marinatos, *B.C.H.*, LX, 219. Ibid., 1933, 299.

KAVOUSI . . . . Tomb . . Vaulted tomb on Skouriasmenos latest deposit. Boyd, *A.J.A.*, 1901, 143.

STOU KOUKOU TO   House . . Terracotta figurines and
KEPHALI   plaques. Hogarth, *B.S.A.*, VII, 148.

LATO . . . . . City . . Houses and public buildings. Demargne, *B.C.H.*, XXV, 282 ; XXVII, 206, and further remains at Melissakia near by. *B.C.H.*, 1929, 382.

PALAIKASTRO. . . Temple . Temple of Diktaian Zeus. Bosanquet, *B.S.A.*, XI, 298. Cf. Kunze, *Kret. Bron. Rel.*, 247 and *passim*, and *Ath. Mitt.*, 60/61, 218 ff.

PRAISOS . . . . City . . Mainly on the SW. Acropolis ' Altar Hill '. Bosanquet, *B.S.A.*, VIII, 254; XV, 281. Halbherr, *A.J.A.*, 1901, 371. Comparetti, *Mus. It.*, II, 673. Tombs. Hopkinson, *B.S.A.*, X, 148. Marshall, ibid., XII, 63. Forster, ibid., XI, 243.

(b) Surface Finds

KALAMAFKA . . . Sherds on the East slope of the Kastellos, seen by the writer, 1935.

LITHINAIS . . . Stamped pithos in the Candia Museum, *Catalogue*, 1578. Bosanquet saw vases and terracottas from a knoll to the S. of the road.

MALLA . . . . Daedalic statue from Patela, in the Candia Museum, *Catalogue* 245. Pernier, *Annuario*, II, 312.

SITIA . . . . . Terracotta figurine. Mariani, *Mon. Ant.*, VI, 175. XXVIth-Dynasty *shawabti*, seen by the writer.

TOPLOU . . . . Traces of archaic burials, seen by Emm. Akoumianos, 1936.

TOURTOULLOI . . Hydria in the Candia Museum, *Catalogue*, 7417.

IV. THE CLASSICAL PERIOD

(*See Map 20*)

In the fifth and fourth centuries a further drift westwards is noticeable and practically every city of importance has been founded. Most of the sites of the previous period are still inhabited and the type of site favoured remains the same, that is to say, a city centring round a strong acropolis. A few new features are noteworthy. At Kastri South of Phalasarna and Kastri East of Milatos are small, well-built structures which may be forts or watch-towers, like the towers of Siphnos, Amorgos and other islands, but which may equally well have been lighthouses marking the most dangerous headlands near the big harbour towns. The same may be true of the tower at Minoa, which, together with Aptera, marked the entrance to Soudha Bay, the finest harbour in Crete. Some regularization of roads, at any rate in the West of the island, is to be deduced from the bridges at Eleutherna and Philippos. The former might be considered merely as of local importance, since they directly served the city, but the latter is a far cry from a site, though it is on the regular route eastwards from Kydonia and Aptera. The number of coastal towns has increased and we should probably add Ampelos, Lebena, Metallon, Soulia, and Herakleion, and consider that the classical remains are buried beneath those of later date. At all events it is significant that Lissos, Tarrha, and Lyttos are all important enough to strike coins of this date, though no remains are visible on the surface. It is, however, improbable that much building was done. Apart from fortification-walls no structure of importance survives. Indeed, it would seem that in almost every case the

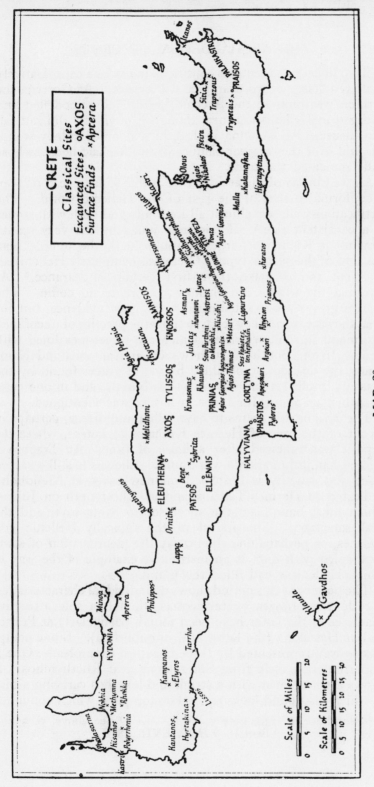

CRETE

Classical Sites
Excavated Sites ○AXOS
Surface Finds ×Aptera

Itanos
PALAIKASTRO
Trapezous ×PRAISOS
Sitia ×
Trapezous ×
Psira ×
Agios × Nikolaos
Olous ○
Kalamafka ×
Hierapytna
Malla ×
Agios Georgias ×
Ponza ×
Kastri ×
Milatos ×
Khersonesos ×
KOLONNE ×
Agios × Georgias ×
Apoinaphapous ×
Nirou × Georgias ×
Astritsi ×
Lytos ×
Kounavoi ×
Stou Partheni × to Metokhia ×
Metaxia ×
Juktas × Klisidhi ×
Rhauhos × Mesari ×
Krousonas × Ligourtino ×
Asmari ×
Aylhos × Ermterphala ×
Aylhos ×
Kolyani na ×
TRAPEZA ×
Xteros ×
Stes Rakietes ×
ten Kephalen ×
Argeon ×
Rhytim × Priansos
AMNISSOS ○
KNOSSOS ○
Milatos ×
Nkasti ×
Kyaeon ×
Hyealon ×
Agia Pelagia
TYLISSOS ○
AXOS ○
Melidhoni ×
ELEUTHERNA ×
PRINIAS ○
Agios Georgias ×
GORTYNA ○
Apeshari ×
PHAISTOS ○
Pyloros ×
KALYVIANA
ELLENAIS ○
PATSOS ○
Sybrita ×
Bene ×
Ornithe ○
Lappa ○
Drchymnos ×
Philippos ×
Aptera ×
Minoa ×
KYDONIA ○
Niokia ×
Nissamos ×
Methymna ×
Rhokka ×
kastro ×
Polyrrhenia ×
Chalasarna ×
Rantanos ×
Hyrtakina ×
Kampanos ×
Elyros ×
Tarrha ×
Lissos ×
Klimaru ×
Gavdhos ×

MAP 20

Scale of Miles
0   5   10   15   20

Scale of Kilometres
0 5 10 15 20   30

Archaic houses and temples continued in use in a comparatively unaltered state.   Two examples will suffice.   At Gortyna the Pythion was built in the Archaic Period and remodelled and enlarged in Hellenistic times, though it obviously did not fall into disuse.   At Kolonna in Lasithi a floor of kidney-stones was laid over the original plaques of the Archaic house, whose walls remained the same.

Classical Architecture and Tombs

All we can say of the architecture is that as far as can be seen it conforms to that of the rest of the Hellenic world.   The fortification-walls are almost all isodomic and built with stones of a consistent size.[1]   If one may judge by the very scanty remains at Kounavoi (largely unpublished), the temple plan was now of the normal type.   Crete was completely Hellenized. Rock-cut tombs make their first certain appearance.[2]   At Kydonia the graves are shallow ; there is no coffin.   The Praisos graves are too disturbed to be good evidence, but for what they are worth they seem to show the practice of uncoffined interments in shallow graves, which are sometimes lined with stone.   In the South-West, however, at Kantanos and Kampanos, the description obtained by me of graves found by the peasants implied a survival of pithos burials, and in one case, on Atheniais above Kantanos, a larnax was mentioned.

The cave on Ida seems to have fallen into disuse, perhaps in favour of the cave of Hermes Kranaios at Patsos, where the deposit was renewed after a lapse of time.   At Trapeza a meagre handful of sherds was found.   Ellenais is still a sacred place and sanctity is bestowed on new caves at Melidhoni, dedicated to Hermes Tallaios, and at Khostonero on Juktas, which must have been the successor to Stravomyti and the peak sanctuary.   The arrival of the typically Hellenic god Hermes, or perhaps one should say the identification of some local spirit with him, is an instructive example of the way in which Hellenism had filled the island.

Classical Pottery, Metalwork and Sculpture

The pottery at this period shows no individual characteristics, nor do the bronzes or terracottas, though a few attractive examples of the latter have been found, particularly at Praisos and at Hyrtakina (the latter still unpublished).   Stone sculpture is well represented by three beautiful examples.[3]   One is a marble grave stele from Stavromena near Rhethymnos.   It shows a young man with a strigil and lekythos carrying a bird at which his hound looks up.   The top part, which contained

---

[1] See above, p. 330, note 1.   [2] See above, p. 334.
[3] Benton, *J.H.S.*, LVII, 38 ff.

the head, is missing, and the upper half is worn but enough remains to display an excellent style. The legs are rather heavy for the rest of the body, but in the lack of emphasis on the muscles we must recognize a national characteristic inherent from Minoan times however much overlaid by Hellenic art. This relief dates from between 465 and 460. The second example is a much-worn marble metope found covering a Roman drain at Knossos. The relief shows a very spirited scene of Herakles throwing the boar at Eurystheus who has taken refuge in a pithos. The surface is badly worn, and what at first sight looks like modelling often turns out to be a wearing away of the stone. It is probably this that gives one the impression that the figure of Herakles is slimmer and longer in the leg than is usual in contemporary art, i.e. just before 450. The third piece is the top of a marble stele showing the head and shoulders of an archer. It was found in a well at Agia Pelagia, which perhaps occupies the site of the ancient Dion [1] (Pl. XLIII, 3).

Miss Benton regards the first and the last as possibly imports from Paros or from some island in the Parian circle.[2] But it seems just as probable that they are of local production and that the resemblance to the works of the so-called Parian school is due to the influence of that school on Crete, or indeed vice versa.

The most famous inscription is the later version of the laws of Gortyna, which now forms the back wall of the Roman Odeum. The alphabet is a modified form of that used in the earlier inscription. *Classical Inscriptions*

At the beginning of the fifth century the cities of Crete began to issue a coinage.[3] The standard is the Aeginetic and the chief denominations are the didrachm and drachma. For the classical period the coins fall roughly into two divisions, *c.* 500–*c.* 430 and *c.* 430–*c.* 300. The two earliest pieces are from Gortyna (obverse Europa riding on the bull : reverse a facing lion's scalp in an incuse square round which runs the retrograde inscription Γόρτυνος τὸ Φαῖμα) and Phaistos (identical *Classical Coins*

---

[1] Not Akhladha, which is a village nearly an hour above, though as being the more important place its name figures in the Museum register.

[2] She does not, however, mention whether the material is Parian or some other marble.

[3] Svoronos; *B.M. Cat., Crete and the Aegean Islands*, 1 ff.; Head, *Historia Nummorum*, 457 ff.

types with the inscription Φαιστίων τὸ Φαῖμα). Other cities to issue coinage during the first period were Knossos (running Minotaur : Labyrinth), Itanos (Triton and trident : star in incuse square), Eleutherna (Apollo with stone and bow between trees : Artemis shooting with a bow, hunting dog), Lyttos (Flying eagle : Head of boar in incuse square), and Praisos (Gorgoneion or cow suckling an infant : Herakles (?) shooting with a bow ; or Herakles shooting : Eagle in incuse square). After 430 or thereabouts other cities begin to strike coins. Kydonia [1] (Wreathed female head : Archer with or without dog, or bitch suckling an infant (Kydon ?)) employed an engraver Neuantos. Aptera (Head of Artemis : Warrior saluting a tree, Πτολίοικος) and Polyrrhenia (Head of Diktynna : Bull's head facing) employed Pythodoros. Axos (Rude head of Apollo : Tripod), Khersonesos (Head of Britomartis : Apollo on the omphalos, or Herakles), Elyros (Goat : Bee), Hierapytna (Triskeles and wreath : Fore part of boar and wreath, or Head of Zeus : Palm tree and eagle), Hyrtakina (Head of Ibex and arrow head : Bee), Lappa (Female head, or head of bull : Bull's head facing with one horn turned down), Lissos (Head of Artemis : Dolphin, Goat's head : Bee), Olous (Head of Britomartis : seated Zeus, Tripod or Star), Phalasarna (Head of Diktynna : Trident or monogram), Priansos (Goddess beneath palm tree or head of Artemis : Poseidon with trident and dolphin, Fore part of goat, Trident or Palm tree), Rhaukos (Poseidon Hippios and horse : Trident), Rhethymnos (Head of Apollo or Athene : Apollo, Trident or dolphins), Sybrita (Dionysos : Hermes), Tarrha (Head of goat : Bee), Tylissos (Head of Hera : Apollo) strike coins for the first time. Knossos (Female head in meander : Zeus or Minos, or star or bull's head in labyrinth), Gortyna (Europa in tree : Bull), and Phaistos (Europa on rock with bull advancing : Hermes ; or Herakles : Bull ; or Velkhanos : Bull ; or Talos : Bull) change their designs. In addition are fourth-century coins of Moda (Head of Zeus : Bull's head facing), Myrina (Bull's head on both sides), and Tanos (Head of Dionysos : Bull between crescents or Head of Hermes) which are hitherto unidentified sites.[2] In the fourth century appear the only gold coins struck in Crete. They marked an alliance between

[1] Kydonia may have used and stored Aeginetan turtles from the earliest days. Seltman, *Greek and Roman Coins*, 169.

[2] Svoronos, 244, suggests Modhe near Polyrrhenia as the site of the first. I could hear of no such place locally.

Hyrtakina and Lisos, bearing on the obverse a dove, a dolphin or a star and on the reverse the names of the two cities.

In artistic quality the coins vary considerably. There is a great interest in nature and in the setting of the main figures which has been attributed to religious causes, i.e. the local legends of Europa in the tree, &c., but which is more probably the emergence of the old Minoan love of scenery visible on gems and rings of which these coins are the true descendants. There is also a love of perspective and foreshortening, but while many of the types have admirable designs there exist alongside with them unskilful copies some of which verge on the barbarous. A particularly instructive example is a didrachm of Gortyna showing Europa in the tree. Here are a whole range of similar designs from the most beautiful coins produced in Crete to an example which bears the same relationship to it as do British coins to those of Philip of Macedon. It is noteworthy that the roughest example might well be the design on an inferior M.M.III gem.[1]

SITES WHERE CLASSICAL REMAINS HAVE BEEN FOUND

WEST CRETE

(a) Excavated Sites

AXOS . . . . . City . . Levi, *Annuario*, XIII–XIV (incomplete).

ELEUTHERNA . . . City . . Bridges. Spratt, II, 89. Walling, &c. Payne, *B.S.A.*, XXX, 266. Coins. Svoronos, 128 ; Head, 464.

ELLENAIS . . . Cave . . Sherds. Marinatos, *Arch. Anz.*, 1932, 77.

KYDONIA . . . Tombs . At E. end of the town. Marinatos, ibid., 1934, 246. Coins. Svoronos, 96. Head, 463.

PATSOS . . . . Cave . . Of Hermes Kranaios. Halbherr, *A.J.A.*, 1896, 593.

(b) Surface Finds

APTERA . . . . Some of the walls on the N. and E. sides. Also coins. Cf. Svoronos, *Num. Cret. Anc.*, 11. Head, 458.

BENE . . . . . Walls seen by Spratt, II, 105. Vases and lamps from here in Padhanasos village, seen by writer, 1935.

---

[1] *B.M. Cat.*, Pl. IX, 5–10.

ELYROS . . . . Coins. Svoronos, 140. Head, 465. Some walling on the E. side, seen by the writer, 1935.

HYRTAKINA . . . See previous period. Sherds and terracottas, found at SE. corner. Coins. Svoronos, 196. Head, 469.

KAMPANOS . . . Tombs at Πλάϊ, walls at Κάραβος, both SE. of the village. Fine bronze tripod handle from village itself, seen by writer, 1935.

KANTANOS . . . Pashley, II, 116. Walls on the acropolis. Tombs at Atheniais, Bizilia, and Patella. Savignoni, *Mon. Ant.*, 1901, 400.

KASTRI . . . . Perhaps Kale Akte of the ancients. Pashley, II, 57. Well-built fort or lighthouse, seen by writer, 1935.

KISAMOS . . . . Vases in the local museum. Savignoni, *Mon. Ant.*, 1901, 304, publishes small objects.

KLAUDA . . . . The modern Gavdhos. Spratt, II, 276, saw a small site on an eminence over the NW. end of the island. Presented British Museum with marble statue. Sherds seen by Levi, on hill of Agios Ioannes. *Art and Archaeology*, 176.

LAPPA . . . . Good wall on the E. side of the site. Also remains at Ellenika on the other bank of the river, seen by the writer, 1935. Coins. Svoronos, 209. Head, 470.

LISSOS . . . . Coins. Svoronos, 222. Head, 471. No remains on surface.

MELIDHONI . . . Many votive cups in the cave now buried, also inscription to Hermes Tallaios. Pashley, I, 126. *C.I.G.*, II, 426. Ancient cuttings by road to the village, seen by the writer, 1935.

METHYMNA . . . At Nopigia. Pashley, II, 38. Spratt, II, 210. A few sherds seen by the writer, 1935.

MINOA . . . . Sherds on the promontory of Limne, seen by the writer, 1935. Walls and tower. Spratt, II, 130.

NOKHIA . . . . Perhaps the ancient Pergamos. Walling at Agia Eirene. Spratt, II, 205.

ORNITHE . . . . Sherds and some walling seen by the writer, 1935 ; see previous period.

PHALASARNA . . . Best description by Spratt, II, 227. A good deal of walling. Coins. Head, 474.

PHILIPPOS . . . The lower courses of the bridge over the Almyros river. Spratt, II, 126.

POLYRRHENIA . . Cf. Pashley, II, 46. Many good stretches of walling, architectural fragments and sherds all over the site. Coins. Svoronos, 275. Head, 474.

RHETHYMNOS . . Grave stele from Stavromena, *J.H.S.*, LVII, 42. Walls at Palaikastro, coins at Agrion

	(perhaps the site of the ancient town of that name). Xanthoudides, 'Ἀρχ. Δελτ., IV, Παρ. i, 14 ; VI, Παρ. 163. Coins, Svoronos, 309. Head, 477.
RHOKKA	Rock-cut tombs at Ellenika, seen by the writer, 1935. Cf. Spratt, II, 207.
SYBRITA	Description by Spratt, II, 102. Walls and sherds seen by the writer, 1933. Coins. Svoronos, 313. Head, 477.
TARRHA	Description by Pashley, II, 264. Spratt, II, 247. Coins. Svoronos, 320. Head, 478.

CENTRAL CRETE

(a) Excavated Sites

AMNISOS	Deposit .	Both on town site and in cave of Eileithyia. Marinatos, Πρακτικά, 1929–34. Arch. Anz., 1934–5.
KNOSSOS	Deposit .	In palace. Temple. P. of M., II, 6. B.S.A., XXXI, 92. Outside palace. P. of M., II, 546. B.S.A., XXXI, 92.
	Tombs .	Near Fortezza, J.H.S., LV, 166.
KOLONNA	House .	Later deposit in archaic house, excavated by the writer, 1937.
PRINIAS	City . .	Possibly ancient Rhezenia. Pernier, Boll. d'Art, I, 28 ; II, 455.
TRAPEZA	Cave . .	One or two sherds from the excavations of 1936.
TYLISSOS	Altar . .	Hazzidakis, T.V.M., 66. Coins. Svoronos, 328. Head, 478.

(b) Surface Finds

AGIA PELAGIA . .	Very fine tomb stele in the Candia Museum. J.H.S., LVII, 42.
AGIOS GEORGIOS . .	Sherds from Kastellos to W., seen by writer, 1935. No traces of fortifications seen by Evans. Academy, 1/6/95.
AGIOU GEORGIOU PAPOURA	Settlement. Evans, Academy, 20/6/96. Sherds and plaques from SE. slope, seen by writer, 1936.
ASMARI	Sherds and stone troughs at Bagalou Khoraphi, seen by writer, 1934. B.S.A., XXXIII, 82.
ASTRETSI	See previous period. Good walling and sherds seen by writer, 1933. Cf. Spratt, I, 90. Evans, Diary, 15/4/95.
AVDHOU	A few sherds on Strovili hill to the W., seen by the writer, 1935.
GAITANOU . . .	Sherds found by Emm Akoumianos, 1935.
JUKTAS	Cook, Zeus, I, 160, mentions that Bosanquet saw a cave on the left of the path up from Arkhanais with sherds, probably Khostonero.

KARPHI . . . . Sherds at Τὰ Μνήματα and on the summit, seen by the writer, 1935.

KASTRI . . . . Fort and sherds on the cliff, seen by the writer, 1937.

KHERSONESOS . . Sherds and tombstone at Piskopiano, sherds at Τὸ Παλάτι, seen by R. W. Hutchinson, 1935. Silver ring from Atrivolos in the Candia Museum, *Catalogue*, 542. Coins. Svoronos, 48. Head, 460.

KLISIDHI . . . . One sherd on the hill, seen by the writer, 1937.

KOUNAVOI . . . Remains of Doric temple at Zagourianoi. Xanthoudides, ᾿Αρχ. Δελτ., IV, Παρ. ii, 24.

KROUSONAS . . . Sherds from Κοῦπο, seen by Miss Money-Coutts and Miss Eccles, 1934. *B.S.A.*, XXXIII, 92.

KYTTAION . . . Sherds at Palaikastro Rodhias, seen by writer, 1933.

LIGOURTINO . . . Sherds on the Kephala, seen by the writer, 1934. *B.S.A.*, XXXIII, 85.

LYTTOS . . . . Coins. Head, 471. No remains visible on surface.

MATHIA . . . . Pinax from Kharakia in the Candia Museum. *Catalogue*, 6340.

STOU PARTHENI TO METOKHI   Sherds below the car road and traces of walls, seen by the writer, 1934. *B.S.A.*, XXXIII, 84.

PONTA . . . . A few sherds seen by the writer, 1935.

RHAUKOS . . . Sherds NE. of the village over large area, seen by Miss Money-Coutts and Miss Eccles, 1934. *B.S.A.*, XXXIII, 91. Coins. Head, 477.

SIDHEROKEPHALA . A few sherds seen on the summit by the writer, 1935. Cf. Taramelli, *Mon. Ant.*, IX, 402.

SOUTH CRETE

(a) Excavated Site

GORTYNA . . . . City . . Excavated areas by the Odeum. *Annuario*, II, 304 ; VIII, 19.

KALYVIANA . . . Tombs . Poor burials. *Mon. Ant.*, XIV, 654.

PHAISTOS . . . . City . . Remains of Temple, &c., above the Palace. Halbherr, *Mon. Ant.*, XII, 21.

(b) Surface Finds

AGIOS GEORGIOS APANOSYPHIS   Sherds from Knoll ½ hr. NE. of monastery close to the car road, seen by writer, 1934. *B.S.A.*, XXXIII, 84.

AGIOS THOMAS . . Probably the ancient Pannona. Mariani, *Mon. Ant.*, VI, 184. Taramelli, *Mon. Ant.*, IX, 340. Tombs, &c.

APESOKARI . . . Sherds from large site at Ellenika, seen by writer, 1934. *B.S.A.*, XXXIII, 88.

ARGEION . . . . A few sherds seen by writer, 1934. *B.S.A.*, XXXIII, 86. See Xanthoudides,ʼ *Ἀρχ. Δελτ.*, II, *Παρ.* 24.

KERATOS . . . . Sherds on the summit, seen by R. W. Hutchinson, 1935.

MESARI . . . . Sherds by the Dhamania-Melidhokhori road, seen by the writer, 1934. *B.S.A.*, XXXIII, 84.

PRIANSOS . . . . A few traces of walling. Cf. Spratt, I, 340.

PYLOROS . . . . Extensive site covering Lagarotopos and Ragavas W. of Plora, seen by the writer, 1934. *B.S.A.*, XXXIII, 88.

RHYTION . . . Large site on the Kephala. Spratt, I, 333. Evans, *Diary*, 2/4/94. Sherds seen by the writer, 1934. *B.S.A.*, XXXIII, 86.

STES VAKIOTES TEN KEPHALAN — Small town site with rock-cut tombs. *Arch. Anz.*, 1916, 156. Xanthoudides,ʼ *Ἀρχ. Δελτ.*, II, *Παρ.* 24. *B.S.A.*, XXXIII, 85.

EAST CRETE

(a) *Excavated Sites*

PALAIKASTRO . . . Building . Perhaps the ancient Eleia. Small building at the N. end of the site. *B.S.A.*, VIII, 289. Hymn. Ibid., XV, 339.

PRAISOS . . . . City . . Architecture and other discoveries. Bosanquet, *B.S.A.*, VIII, 231 ff. Terracottas. Forster, ibid., XI, 243. Tombs. Marshall, ibid., XII, 63. Inscriptions. Bosanquet, ibid., XV, 281. Coins. Svoronos, 285. Head, 475.

(b) *Surface Finds*

AGIOS NIKOLAOS . . Ancient Lato pros Kamara. Spratt, I, 142. Sherds and walls seen by writer, 1934. *B.S.A.*, XXXIII, 94.

HIERAPYTNA . . . Spratt, I, 233. Some walls still extant. Coins. Head, 468.

ITANOS . . . . See Spratt, I, 194. Good walls. Cf. Halbherr, *A.J.A.*, 1896, 691. *Antiquary*, 1891, 202, 242. Coins. Svoronos, 200. Head, 469.

KALAMAFKA . . . Sherds on the E. and NE. slope of the Kastellos, seen by the writer, 1935.

MALLA . . . . Sherds at Agia Paraskeve, seen by the writer, 1935.

MILETOS . . . . Figurines from Dhrakona and Kountouro. Xanthoudides, ʼ *Ἀρχ. Δελτ.*, IV, *Παρ.* 10.

OLOUS . . . . Walls. Spratt, I, 134. Sherds seen by writer, 1932.

PSEIRA . . . . Sherds on S. and E. slopes. No buildings. Seager mentions a cemetery which he excavated, but it is not clear if it is Greek. Seager, *Pseira*, 7.

SITIA . . . . . Walls at Kharakia, seen by the writer, 1934. *B.S.A.*, XXXIII, 97.

TRAPEZOUS . . . Foundation of walls below Venetian castle. Mariani, *Mon. Ant.*, VI, 136.

TRYPETAIS . . . Walls seen by Evans, *Diary*, 1898.

V. THE HELLENISTIC PERIOD

(*See Maps 21 and 22*)

In discussing the distribution of sites during the Hellenistic Period, i.e. from *c*. 300 to 67, when the Roman conquest of the island took place, we must remember that much of the pottery is practically indistinguishable from Roman wares and that it is exceedingly difficult to place many of the sites with any certainty on one side or other of the dividing line. I have therefore added a series of ' Greco-Roman ' sites which can be taken with either period. In most cases they almost certainly antedate the Roman conquest, but it seems safer where doubt can arise to segregate them. The term, then, ' Greco-Roman ' is not a period but a confession of failure.

In spite of the wars which racked the island, the confusing changes of sides which remind one of the Wars of the Roses and the deliberate destruction of cities such as Lyttos, the population as a whole has increased, and more open sites are being chosen. Polybios, however, makes gloomy reading for this period.

Hellenistic Architecture

Of public buildings most traces have been swamped by the later Roman work. At Gortyna a pronaos was added on to the simple archaic cella and it is interesting to see that even at this date the columns of the façade are still divided into two groups by a wider central intercolumniation.

A very fine building was excavated on the slopes of the First Acropolis at Praisos (Fig. 53). Whether it was the residence of a rich man or a public guest-house is uncertain. The outer walls are of well-cut masonry built in uneven courses. The joints are very finely fitted though lime mortar has been used. The inner walls are of rubble and do not bond. Traces of cobble paving remained in parts but the usual flooring was the

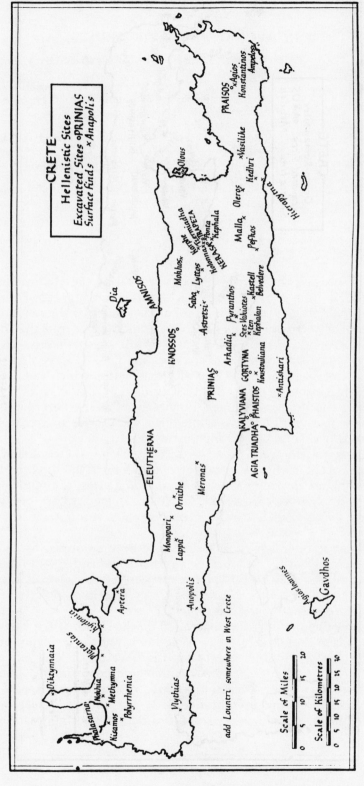

CRETE

Hellenistic Sites

Excavated Sites oPRINIAS
Surface finds ×Anapolis

MAP 21

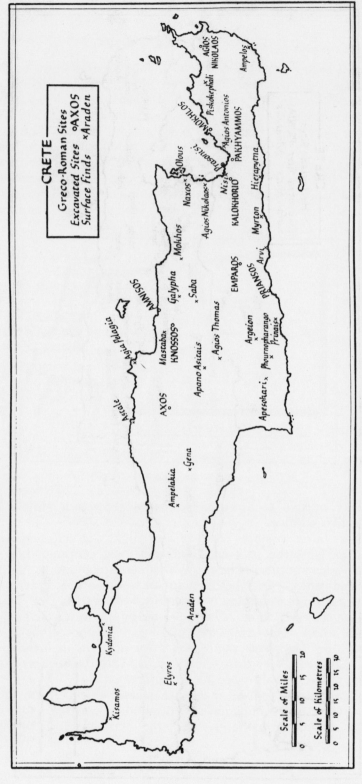

CRETE

Greco-Roman Sites
Excavated Sites oAXOS
Surface finds xAraden

Kisamos

Kydonia

Elyros

Araden

Ascale

Agia Pelagia

AMNISOS

Ampelakia

Gena

AXOS

Mastaba
KNOSSOS

Apano Asitais
Aguas Thomas

Galypha
Saba

Mokhlos

Naxos

Aguas Nikolaos

Solous

SINAKHLOS

Trasonisi

Aguas Antonios
PAKHYAMMOS

Piskokephali

AGIOS
NIKOLAOS

Ampelos

Argeion
Apeskhari
Phournopharango
Prinais

EMPAROS
PRIANSOS
Arvi

Nisi
KALOKHORIO
Myrton
Hierapytna

Scale of Miles

0   5   10   15   20

Scale of Kilometres

0   5   10   15   20

MAP 22

native rock or hard clay. The living quarters seem to have occupied the northern and eastern sides, while the South side was devoted to workrooms, one of which contained an impluvium in the middle and an olive press in one corner, while in the other were steps leading up to some room above. The house is built on a terrace, the southern wall being partly of the native rock and the northern wall being carried down as a retaining wall. Through the latter run water spouts which discharge into a rock-cut cellar below. The door jambs of massive stones and the thresholds are particularly well preserved and frag-

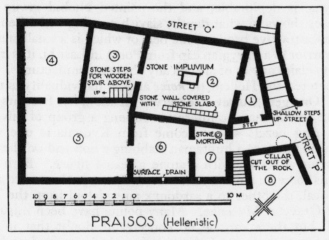

FIG. 53

ments of two stone window-frames showed a simple but effective cornice.

Hellenistic Tombs

The burial customs seem to vary slightly in different parts. In the West the rock-cut tombs are most common, but cist graves also occur. These two methods are found as far East as Pedhiadha. In Lasithi there are stories of cist graves, but the only tomb excavated was roughly built in three oval-shaped divisions, each about 2 metres long by 1½ wide, opening off each other. How they were covered it is impossible to say, since the uppermost metre had been removed in making the modern road. In East Crete old L.M.III tholoi are re-used and pithos burials were found at Praisos.

Hellenistic Pottery

The pottery follows the usual course of Hellenistic times, but interesting groups have been found at Knossos. One was from a cistern on the slopes of the Acropolis and contained what practically amounts to a complete corpus of shapes of the second century.[1] The other was found in a field on the Palace borders near the House of the Frescoes and appears to have been partly a votive deposit, partly the furniture of a shrine. The most striking shapes are the vases with high-swung looped handles decorated at the junction with the body with moulded faces, two or three over-ornate jugs decorated with vine leaves, sprays, and rosettes and human faces in relief, and objects not unlike candlesticks which may have served for the game of *kottabos* (Pl. XLII, 3).

Hellenistic Sculpture and Gems

The stone sculpture, as best exemplified by the finds at Gortyna, is deplorable, and the painted Niobid group from Priansos shows to what depths slavish copying had fallen. Of the few attractive bronzes, the best of which is a small statuette of a warrior in a Phrygian cap from Ponta in Lasithi, it is impossible to claim any as of specifically Cretan manufacture. Crete had entered the Hellenistic *koine* and its individuality is nearly lost. One gem, however, deserves mention, not from its artistic but for its historic interest. Among a group of silver-set ivory ring bezels said to come from Kydonia is one which shows on one face a huntsman stabbing a lion and on the other a warrior attacking with a stone a seated figure. Both these designs show an almost unbelievable likeness, the one to a gold bead seal, the other to a sardonyx amygdaloid from the Third Shaft Grave at Mycenae. Many points have been misunderstood, but there can be no conceivable doubt that in some strange way replicas of these designs had survived and were copied thirteen centuries after the originals had disappeared.[2]

Hellenistic Coins

In the coinage the Attic standard gradually replaces the Aeginetic. About 200 B.C. imitations of Athenian tetradrachms appear at Knossos, Kydonia, Gortyna, Hierapytna, Lappa, Polyrrhenia, and Priansos, each city inserting its own badge on the reverse. Coins symbolizing the alliance of Gortyna and Knossos were struck about 220, showing Europa on the bull : Labyrinth. Soon after occur specimens from Polyrrhenia, which show Philip V of Macedon : Seated female figure holding Nike.[3] The following cities coin for the first

---

[1] Shortly to be published by Miss B. Dunkley.

[2] For the undoubted genuineness of this ring bezel see Evans, *J.H.S.*, 1912, 294 f.

[3] The so-called alliance coins between Lyttos and Khersonesos are surely no more than a natural interchange of types between the capital and its harbour town.

time : Allaria (site unknown. Head of Athene : standing Herakles), Anopolis (young male head or horn of goat : palm branch), Apollonia (site unknown. Head of Apollo : stern of ship and *aplustre*), Arkadia (Head of Zeus Ammon : Athene), Arsinoe (site unknown. Head of Athene : Two dolphins), Lato pros Kamara (Head of Artemis : Hermes), Malla (Head of Zeus : Eagle). The following change their types : Axos (Head of Zeus or Artemis : Tripod or Thunderbolt), Khersonesos (Head of Athene : Eagle or prow of ship), Knossos (Head of Hera, Apollo or Athene : Labyrinth ; later—Head of Apollo or Zeus Ammon : circular or square labyrinth), Kydonia (Head of Diktynna, Apollo or Dionysos : Diktynna and hunting dog, bitch suckling Kydon or Nike), Gortyna (Europa in the tree and eagle : Bull standing or Europa on the bull ; later—Head of Zeus or Helios : Armed Athene and Nike, naked male figure or Europa on the bull), Hierapytna (Female head turreted : Palm tree and eagle), Lappa (Head of Poseidon or Artemis : Trident and dolphins, tripod, bull's head or lyre), Lyttos (Head of Zeus, Athene or Boar : Eagle or prow), Phaistos (Talos running : hound), Praisos (Zeus Diktaios enthroned : Bull, forepart of goat or Herakles), Priansos (Head of Artemis : Poseidon or palm tree between rudder and dolphin), and Rhaukos (Head of Poseidon or of horse : Trident or dolphins). Apart from the subjects which still remain typically Cretan, the coinage has no particularly local features.

To this period belong the boundary treaties between Olous *Hellenistic Inscriptions* and Lato and between Hierapytna and Itanos.[1] These are often of great interest as preserving names of streams, hills, marshes, &c., which are certainly not Greek, and which must have come down from Minoan times (see above, p. 269). They remind us of such modern jingles as the verses which give the boundaries between the communities of Gergeri and Anogeia.

Μαυροκορφὴ, Χηληδονιαὶς καὶ Καύκαλου Σπηλιάρα
καὶ Μαῦρος Κοῦμος καὶ ῎Ασπρο Ἁρμὶ καὶ τοῦ Σκινάκου ἡ Σκάλα.[2]

Boundaries are no less a subject of dispute to-day though endless litigation has taken the place of war.

[1] *C.I.G.*, II, 2554, 2561b. Can one of the so-called Eteocretan inscriptions from Praisos (*B.S.A.*, VIII, 125 ff.) be such a boundary treaty ? Cf. Walker, *Three Inscriptions from Crete*, 9 ff.

[2] The Black Peak, Celandine Hill, the Caves of Kafkalos and Black Summit and White Saddle, and the Ladder of Skinakos.

SITES WHERE HELLENISTIC REMAINS HAVE BEEN FOUND

WEST CRETE

(a) Excavated Site

ELEUTHERNA . . .   Walling, &c. Payne, *B.S.A.*, XXX, 266.

(b) Surface Finds

ANOPOLIS   . . .   Walls on summit. Pashley, II, 242, sherds seen by the writer, 1932. Coins. Svoronos, 5. Head, 458.

APTERA   . . . .   Some of the walls and the theatre. Pashley, I, 36. Proxeny decrees. Haussollier, *B.C.H.*, 1879, 418. Coins. Svoronos, 11. Head, 458.

DIKTYNNAIA . . .   Remains of city. Pashley, II, 29. Spratt, II, 196. Savignoni, *Mon. Ant.*, 1901, 285 (with plan). Sherds and architectural remains, seen by the writer, 1935.

KISAMOS . . . .   Vases in the local museum ; also cf. Savignoni, *Mon. Ant.*, 1901, 304.

KLAUDA . . . .   Modern Gavdhos. Sherds seen by Levi on Agios Ioannes Hill. *Art and Archaeology*, 1927, 176 ff.

KYDONIA   . . .   Cist graves. Xanthoudides, ᾿Αρχ. Δελτ., VI, Παρ. 164. *P. of M.*, III, Figs. 79, 80. Coins. Svoronos, 96. Head, 463.

LAPPA   . . . .   Tombs on the path from Zouridhi, seen by the writer, 1935. Coins. Svoronos, 209. Head, 470.

LOUNTRI . . . .   Figurine in the Candia Museum. *Catalogue*, 1583.

MERONAS   . . .   Sherds and lamps in the road-cutting at Sokhara, seen by the writer, 1935.

METHYMNA . . .   A few sherds seen by the writer, 1935.

MONOPARI   . . .   A few sherds and the base of some of the Venetian walls, seen by the writer, 1935. Cf. Spratt, II, 114.

NOKHIA . . . .   Sherds at Ompristaga, seen by the writer, 1935. Cf. previous period.

ORNITHE . . . .   A few sherds on the summit, seen by the writer, 1935.

PHALASARNA . . .   Cf. Spratt, II, 227. Many sherds on the surface. Tombs to SW. Savignoni, *Mon. Ant.*, 1901, 350.

PLATANIAS   . . .   Sherds and a stone trough at Riza, E. of the village, seen by the writer, 1935.

POLYRRHENIA   . .   Vases in the Khania Museum. Coins. Head, 474. Cf. Savignoni, *Mon. Ant.*, 1901, 315. Myres, *J.H.S.*, XVI, 181.

VLYTHIAS. . . . Walling described by Pashley, II, 120. Savignoni, *Mon. Ant.*, 1901, 387. Other forts near Anydhros. Thenon, *Rev. Arch.*, XVI, 114.

CENTRAL CRETE

(a) Excavated Sites

AMNISOS . . . . Deposit . Both in houses and cave. Marinatos, Πρακτικά, 1929, 95 ; 1933, 93.

KERASA . . . . Tomb . . Built tomb, excavated in 1937, by the writer.

KNOSSOS . . . . Deposit . Above little Palace. *B.S.A.*, XXXI, 92.

Tombs . . Near Fortezza. *J.H.S.*, LV, 166.

Town . . House near Fortezza. *Arch. Anz.*, 1932, 175.

TRAPEZA . . . . Cave . . A few sherds from the excavations of 1936.

(b) Surface Finds

ASTRETSI . . . . Sherds found by R. W. Hutchinson, 1937.

DIA . . . . . Sherd from hill W. of summit of the island, seen by the writer, 1935.

KARPHI . . . . Sherds at Τὰ Μνήματα, seen by the writer, 1935.

KEPHALA . . . . Silver and bronze coins seen by the writer, 1936.

KOLONNA. . . . Evans, *Diary*, 1896, saw tombs.

LYTTOS . . . . Walls and sherds. Coins. Head, 471.

MOKHOS . . . . Sherds and walls at Kalimniokhori, seen by the writer, 1935.

PONTA . . . . Sherds and a very fine bronze statuette, seen by the writer, 1936.

SABA . . . . . Sherds from a fort on the main road E. of the village, seen by the writer, 1934. *B.S.A.*, XXXIII, 80.

TZERMIADHA . . . A silver coin of Alexander from a field, seen by the writer, 1936.

SOUTH CRETE

(a) Excavated Sites

AGIA TRIADHA . . Sanctuary . To Zeus Velkhanos. Halbherr, *Rend. Linc.*, 1905, 380.

Tombs . . At Phalandra. *Rend. Linc.*, 1907, 298.

GORTYNA. . . . City . . Temple of Apollo. *Mon. Ant.*, I, 8 ; III, 1 ; XVIII, 181. Odeum, &c. *Annuario*, I, 373 ; II, 304 ; VIII, 25.

KALYVIANA . . . Tombs . . Poor burials here and at Kamara and Phalangari near by. *Mon. Ant.*, XIV, 654.

PHAISTOS. . . . City . . Temple, &c. *Mon. Ant.*, XII, 21 ; XIV, 350. *Arch. Anz.*, 1935, 244.

PRINIAS . . . . Town . . Main period of later occupation in earlier buildings. Repairs to fortifications. *Boll. d'Arte*, I, 28 ; II, 455.

Tombs . . Rock-cut tombs at Patella to the N. Taramelli, *Mon. Ant.*, XI, 328.

(b) Surface Finds

ANTISKARI . . . Silver coins of Gortyna, in the Candia Museum.

ARKADIA . . . . Walls on Kasteriotes. Vases and terracottas seen by the writer, 1934. *B.S.A.*, XXXIII, 84. Cf. Spratt, I, 310. Mariani, *Mon. Ant.*, VI, 182.

KASTELL BELVEDERE   Perhaps the ancient Stelai. *Arch. Anz.*, 1916, 156, mentions remains.

KOUSTOULIANA . . Vases from the pit at Gerolakkos, in the Gortyna Museum.

PYRANTHOS . . . Sherds from Τροχάλαις. Cf. Svoronos, 300. *B.S.A.*, XXXIII, 85.

STES VAKIOTES   Jug in the Candia Museum. *Catalogue*, 9214.
TEN KEPHALAN

EAST CRETE

(a) Excavated Site

PRAISOS . . . . City . . Architectural and other discoveries. Bosanquet, *B.S.A.*, VIII, 231 ff. Terracottas. Forster, ibid., XI, 243.

(b) Surface Finds

AGIOS KONSTANTINOS   Sherds seen by R. W. Hutchinson, 1936.

AMPELOS . . . . Brick stamps from Xerokampos. Halbherr, *Antiquary*, 1892, 154.

HIERAPYTNA . . . Spratt, I, 253. Coins. Head, 468. *C.I.G.*, 2555–6. Vases in local museum.

KEDHRI . . . . Figurine in the Candia Museum. *Catalogue*, 4642.

MALLA . . . . A few sherds seen by the writer, 1935, at Agia Parskeve.

OLOUS . . . . Treaty with Lato. *B.C.H.*, III, 290. Commercial treaty with Rhodes, seen by the writer, 1936.

OLEROS . . . . Sherds and walling at Kouri, seen by the writer, 1936.

PEFKOS . . . . A drachma of Gortyna and a stater of Rhaukos in the Candia Museum.

VASILIKE . . . . Sherds found by the writer, 1927.

SITES WHERE GRECO-ROMAN REMAINS HAVE BEEN FOUND

WEST CRETE

(b) Surface Finds

AMPELAKIA . . . Sherds in a field at Livadhos 20 min. S. of the village, seen by the writer, 1935.

ARADEN . . . . Tombs. Pashley, II, 256.

ASTALE . . . . Traces of large settlement on both sides of Bali Bay, seen by the writer, 1933. Cf. Taramelli, *Mon. Ant.*, IX, 317.

ELYROS . . . . Stelae, &c., from cemetery. Savignoni, *Mon. Ant.*, 1901, 427.

GENA . . . . . Sherds from building with good cut stones, recently destroyed in making the road, seen by the writer, 1933.

KISAMOS . . . . Architectural remains by the side of the main road, seen by the writer, 1935.

KYDONIA . . . Grave stelae. Mariani, *Mon. Ant.*, VI, 403.

CENTRAL CRETE

(a) Excavated Sites

AMNISOS . . . . Deposits . Both in houses and cave. Marinatos, Πρακτικά, 1929, 95 ; 1933, 93.

EMPAROS . . . . Deposits . At Agios Petros. Halbherr, *A.J.A.*, 1901, 281.

KNOSSOS . . . . Town and Many deposits and walls. *P. of* Acropolis *M.*, II, 432, 547, 550. *B.S.A.*, VI, 81.

(b) Surface Finds

AGIA PELAGIA . . Sherds and traces of walls on promontory, possibly site of ancient Dion. Taramelli, *Mon. Ant.*, IX, 318. Cf. Evans, *P. of M.*, I, 299.

APANO ASITAIS . . Gold necklace from a tomb, in the Candia Museum.

GALYPHA. . . . Vases in the Candia Museum. *Catalogue*, 22–7, 538.

MASTABA . . . . Sherds seen by Miss Money-Coutts and Miss Eccles, 1934. *B.S.A.*, XXXIII, 91.

MOKHOS . . . . Grave stelae and sherds at Mouri, seen by the writer, 1935.

OLOUS . . . . Sherds and walls at Kolokythia bay, seen by the writer, 1937.

SABA . . . . . Clay vases from Aspromouri, in the Candia Museum, *Catalogue*, 3797–803. Cf. Mariani, *Mon. Ant.*, VI, 89, for possible site of the cemetery.

SOUTH CRETE

(a) Excavated Site

PRIANSOS. . . . House . . Sculpture remains, &c. Marinatos, 'Aϱχ. Δελτ., 34/35, 1. Also a number of sherds seen by the writer, 1936.

(b) Surface Finds

AGIOS THOMAS . . Tombs and walls. Mariani, *Mon. Ant.*, VI, 184. Taramelli, ibid., 340.

APESOKARI . . . Large site at Ellenika. Sherds and cisterns seen by the writer, 1934. *B.S.A.*, XXXIII, 88.

ARGEION . . . . Sherds seen by the writer, 1934. *B.S.A.*, XXXIII, 86.

ARVI . . . . . Harbour town mentioned in *Arch. Anz.*, 1916, 156.

PHOURNOPHARANGO. Terracottas from fields, seen by the writer, 1934. *B.S.A.*, XXXIII, 86.

PRINIAS . . . . Considerable remains of settlement at Peze in Katokampos, seen by the writer, 1936.

EAST CRETE

(a) Excavated Sites

AGIOS   NIKOLAOS Building . Sherds. Tod., *B.S.A.*, IX, SITIAS 336.

KALOKHORIO . . Building At Tὸ ῾Ελληνικό. Hall, *Trans.* and tombs *Penn. Univ.*, I, 13.

MOKHLOS. . . . Town . . Houses and rock tombs on the Mainland opposite the island. Seager, *A.J.A.*, XIII, 274.

PAKHYAMMOS . . Building . At Ellenika, with aqueduct and cistern. Hall, *Trans. Penn. Univ.*, I, 13.

(b) Surface Finds

AGIOS ANTONIOS. . Lamps found in field near Kavousi. Boyd, *A.J.A.*, 1901, 156.

AGIOS   NIKOLAOS Some sherds and a late Doric capital seen by MIRABELLOU the writer, 1936.

AMPELOS . . . . Rock-cut tombs. Sherds all over Xerokampos, seen by the writer, 1934. *B.S.A.*, XXXIII, 99 f.

HIERAPYTNA . . . See previous periods.

MYRTON . . . . Grave seen by Evans, *Diary*, 4/4/94.

NAXOS . . . . Large walled settlement on Oxa hill. Cf.
Spratt, I, 126. Mariani, *Mon. Ant.*, VI,
249. Evans, *Diary*, 17/4/94. Sherds found
by the writer, 1935.

NISI . . . . . Extensive site, probably the ancient Istron.
Cf. *B.S.A.*, XXXIII, 95. Hall, *Vrokastro*,
79.

PISKOKEPHALI . . Grave stela in the Candia Museum. *Catalogue*, 122.

PRASONISI . . . Inscription on the S. face. Hall, *Trans. Penn.
Univ.*, I, 15. Cf. Halbherr, *Antiquary*,
1893, 13. (" Vrionisi ") and Chapoutier,
B.C.H., LIX, 376.

VI. THE ROMAN PERIOD

(Map 23, cf. Map 22 also)

With its absorption into the Roman Empire, brutally as it
was conquered [1] and at first repressed, Crete entered a period
of prosperity such as it had not known since the palmy days of
L.M.1. Sites such as Pharmakokephalo, Priniatikos Pyrgos,
Agia Photia, Pakhyammos, Mokhlos, and Tourloti are re-
settled for the first time since the Bronze Age. The population, if not the number of villages in the island, must have
exceeded that of the present century.

Most of the harbours available at that date (see above,
p. 3) are the site of at least warehouses, and such towns as
Syia, Diktynnaia, and Priansos show traces of elaborate aque-
ducts which brought down the water to these dry, sandy
settlements.

The absence of roads of certain Roman date is remarkable ;
but I should be very willing to believe that many of the paved
' *kalderims* ', which are loosely called Venetian or Turkish
roads, are really relics of the Roman occupation, while such
sites as that on Katharos, Stou Vasilikou near Agios Georgios,
at Kalamafka and Malla imply that the already existing Minoan
routes into Lasithi were in regular use. The eastern half of the
plain of Lasithi itself is divided up by deep cuttings into
rectangular patches of ground like a chessboard. These areas
are regular and usually about $\frac{1}{4}$ mile each way. The inhabitants say that these Λίνιαις, or cuttings, are Venetian, but in
Venetian times the plain was ' out of bounds ' on pain of death.

[1] The identification by Spratt (II, 91 f.) of the very breach by which
Metellus entered Eleutherna is unfortunately impossible, since Byzantine sherds occur throughout the walls of the tower in which the
present breach exists.

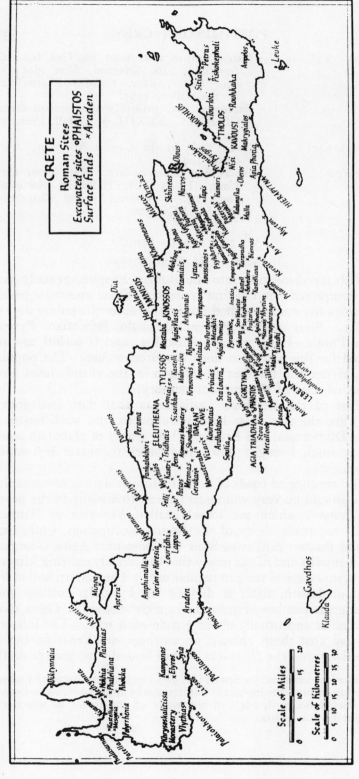

CRETE

Roman Sites

Excavated sites oPHAISTOS
Surface finds ×Araden

MAP 23

Scale of Miles
0   5   10   15   20

Scale of Kilometres
0   5   10   15   20   25   30

In spite of the fact that the level of the plain, thanks to the soil carried down from the surrounding hills, has risen many feet since Roman days, it is most probable that these Λίνιαις mark the site of Roman drainage works which may have enabled such a site as Megalos Potamos to be habitable.[1]

Caves are treated with renewed respect. Ida, Patsos, Amnisos, and the Diktaian cave at Psykhro all have deposits to show after a considerable gap. It looks very much as if the old Minoan stock was re-asserting itself racially now that there were conditions favourable to it. Crete was fortunate in having no history and in lying well away from the storm centres where emperors rose and fell. In the reign of Nero an earth-quake opened gaps in the ground at Knossos—no doubt in the area of the West Magazines of the Palace. Here were dis-covered in ' chests of tin ' (no doubt the decomposed lead lining of the ' kasellas ', or cists) documents written in an unknown script. These were forwarded to the emperor, who, believing them to be in the Phoenician alphabet, called in Semitic scholars who served him up with a remarkable history of the Trojan war purporting to be written by ' Diktys of Crete '.[2] Hadrian, though he never seems to have visited the island, was a great patron of the chief cities. Gortyna and Knossos in particular were embellished with public buildings and Aptera and Lyttos certainly came in for their fair share. Very few of the larger cities, indeed, do not show extensive Roman remains on the surface, a fact which has often deterred the prospective excavator of some promising city with a name famous in Greek times.

Of public buildings the Italian excavations at Gortyna have given us good examples. The chief temple, that of Pythian Apollo, had evidently retained its sanctity to such a degree that, in spite of the grandiose characters of such buildings as the so-called Praetorium, no more was done to it than the addition of an apse at the West end and the placing of four columns in the old cella. A circus, an amphitheatre, an Odeum, smaller temples such as that of Isis and Horus, public fountains and baths, all showed that the Romans were determined to place the stamp of their culture on the subject population. A

Roman Architecture

---

[1] The other name for this site is Vounos (the Hill), which must be a relic of the days when it stood on an eminence rising out of the marshy bottom. To-day it is on a level with the rest of the plain.

[2] *Scripta Minoa*, I, 109. For a knowledge of Minoan remains, cf. Mackail, *The Aeneid of Vergil*, 519 ff.

fashionable watering-place was founded in Imperial times at Lebena, which had hitherto been nothing more than a fishing village.

The best preserved of the private houses is the newly excavated Villa Dionysos at Knossos, whose mosaic pavements are fine examples of that art. Knossos, indeed, was little if at all inferior in wealth to Gortyna. The Basilica, as yet unexcavated, is a vast building, and the flat, open space to the East of it, which probably marks the site of the Forum or Agora, is also of considerable size.

Roman Tombs

How many of the rock-cut tombs were first hollowed out in Roman times one cannot say. It is to be noted that all those with niches or benches in them contained Roman sherds as well as any earlier ones there may be. At Lissos (Agios Kirkos) and Syia are large groups of barrel-vaulted tombs, freestanding and showing evidence of two stories (Pl. VIII, 2). The poorer burials were in rectangular cist graves often lined with heavy slabs of terracotta.

Roman Mosaic

The architecture, sculpture, and small arts differ little from those of other provincial centres, but at Syia there are remains of a mosaic pavement now sadly damaged, which represented a lion attacking a stag. The rock work and vegetation shown on it bear an extraordinary resemblance to the setting of a Minoan fresco, and we may well believe that in such out-of-the-way sites the old artistic feelings had been preserved and occasionally came to light in a new technique.

Roman Coins

Cistophoros coins were issued, probably at Gortyna, during the last years of the Republic. The Imperial mint continued to be situated at Gortyna, whose name is the only name of a city to be found. The types change, and, except for an inscription such as Zeus Kretagenes, Zeus Idaios, or Diktynna Sebaste, it would be difficult to assign them to Crete in particular. With the Emperor Domitian the inscription Koinon Kreton or K.K. appears, but with Marcus Aurelius or Caracalla appear the last coins which are certainly struck for Crete, though the great number of coins of Gordian seen in the hands of peasants implies some special connexion of that emperor with the island.

And so Crete went her prosperous undisturbed way until she recovered her importance as a key and a stepping-stone between the East and Europe. Then begin the weary wars of Saracens and Byzantines, of Genoese, Venetians, Turks, and Greeks. Eleven hundred years of trouble passed between the tranquil days of the Bronze Age and those of the Roman Empire. Eleven hundred years have passed since the Pax Romana was ended. We may hope that the full cycle has come round and that at long last this lovely island will again know peace.

SITES WHERE ROMAN REMAINS HAVE BEEN FOUND

WEST CRETE

(a) Excavated Site

ELEUTHERNA . . . City and   Walls, graves, and inscriptions.
Cemetery   Payne, *B.S.A.*, XXX, 266.

(b) Surface Finds

AMPHIMALLA . . Heavily walled building recently pulled down, seen by the writer, 1935.

APTERA . . . . Extensive remains seen by Pashley, I, 32. Spratt, II, 129.

ARADEN . . . . Remains seen by Pashley, II, 256.

ARDHAKTOS . . Sherds found by Emm. Akoumianos close to the village, 1935.

ASOMATOS   A small site on the opposite side of the road to
MONASTERY   the monastery, seen by the writer, 1935.

BENE . . . . . Cisterns and walls. Cf. Spratt, II, 105. Sherds seen by the writer at S. end, 1935.

DIKTYNNAIA . . . Extensive remains of city. Pashley, II, 29. Spratt, II, 196. Savignoni, *Mon. Ant.*, 1901, 285 (with plan).

ELYROS . . . . Extensive architectural remains. Pashley, II, 105. Thenon, *Rev. Arch.*, XIV, 396.

GERAKARI. . . . Sherds and remains found at Psarais, Agios Ioannes, and Palaioklisia, by the writer, 1935.

GONIAIS . . . . Roman imperial coins from Sklavokampos, seen by the writer, 1935.

HYDRAMON . . Inscription. Petroulakis, Ἐφ. Ἀρχ., 1915, 51.

IDAEAN CAVE. . . Sherds from outside entrance. Xanthoudides, Ἀρχ. Δελτ., 1918, Παρ. i, 15. Foundations of Houses. Fabricius, *Ath. Mitt.*, X, 62.

KAMPANOS . . . Coin from the village, tombs at Kamini and Kalogiannis, seen by the writer, 1935.

KASTELLIANA. . . Small site with mosaics at Ellenika, seen by the writer, 1935.

KASTRI . . . . Large settlement, walls, and sherds, seen by the writer, 1935.

KHRYSOSKALITISSA   Sherds between the monastery and Agios
MONASTERY   Panteleimon church, seen by the writer, 1935.

KISAMOS . . . . Fine Roman statue, glass vases, &c., in the local museum, architectural fragments in the fields.

KLAUDA . . . . Sherds seen on S. slopes by Levi, *Art and Archaeology*, 1927, 176 ff.

KORION *or* KORESIA . On Lake Kournas, an extensive site S. of Kavallos Metokhi, seen by the writer, 1935.

KOUROUTAIS . . . Sherds and lamp found by Emm. Akoumianos, 1935.

KYDONIA . . . Graves, *Ath. Mitt.*, 1900, 466. Many objects in the Khania Museum.

LAPPA . . . . Extensive remains of the city. Pashley, I, 83. Spratt, II, 117. Mosaics in the museum. At Ellenika on the opposite side of the river are remains seen by the writer, 1935.

LISSOS . . . . The modern Agios Kirkos. Extensive remains of city with many two-storied vaulted tombs. Pashley, II, 88. Savignoni, *Mon. Ant.*, 1901.

MERONAS . . . Sherds and coins at Tsokhoura, Makrydhiana, Moskhais, seen by the writer, 1935.

MESOGEIA . . . . Sherds and coins from a small site at Teresgona Ellenika, seen by the writer, 1935.

METHYMNA . . . Many walls and sherds seen by the writer, 1935. Cf. Pashley, II, 38. Spratt, II, 210.

MINOA . . . . Sherds both by the harbour and further up, seen by the writer, 1935. Cf. Spratt, II, 130.

MONASTERAKI . . Wall in the village, seen by the writer, 1933.

MONOPARI . . . Sherds seen by the writer, 1935. Cf. Spratt, II, 114.

MYRTHIOS . . . Sherds at Petrais and Agios Theodoros, seen by the writer, 1935.

NOKHIA . . . . Sherds at Ompristaga and Khalepa, seen by the writer, 1935.

ORNITHE . . . . Cisterns, walls, and sherds on the N. slope of the site, seen by the writer, 1935.

PALAIOKHORA . . Traces of a house at Trokhaloi. Savignoni, *Mon. Ant.*, 1901, 467.

PANKALOKHORI . Sherds and headless statue seen by the writer at *Τῆς Κίτρης τὸ μύλι.*, 1935.

PANORMOS . . . At Roumeli Kastelli. Cf. Spratt, II, 113. Considerable site.

PATELLA . . . . Small site near large rock-cutting S. of Phalasarna, seen by the writer, 1935.

PATSOS . . . . Site at Kephalia, sherds and walls seen by the writer, 1935. Inscription from Cave of Hermes Kranaios. Halbherr, *Mus. It. Ant. Clas.*, II, 913.

PERAMA . . . . Sites at *Τὰ Γρέββελα* and Palaioklisia, sherds and walls seen by the writer, 1935.

PHALASARNA . . . Besides remains on the main site are others at the S. end of the plain. *Στὸ Μετόχι*, cistern and walls. *Στῆς Παναγίας τὸ Λιβάδι*, cistern, aqueduct, and Doric capital. *Στὰ*

Λουσοθούρια and στὴν ᾿Αναλάβωσιν, graves,
seen by the writer, 1935.

PHALELIANA . . .	Fort at Tramontana, seen by the writer, 1935.
PHOINIX	Foundations of harbour town, built tomb, inscriptions, &c. Spratt, II, 250.
PLATANIAS . . .	Sherds at Amoutsa W. of the village, seen by the writer, 1935. Cf. Pashley, II, 23.
POIKILASSOS . . '.	Remains of town seen by Spratt at Trypete, II, 244. Altar in the church of Agios Antonios at Voukilasi (Svoronos, 141, 272) is built of Roman remains.
POLYRRHENIA . .	Many vases, &c., in the Khania Museum, traces of Roman work all over the site. Cf. previous references.
RHETHYMNOS . .	Sherds at Agrion to the S. Xanthoudides, ᾿Αρχ. Δελτ., IV, Παρ. i, 14.
RHOKKA	Many remains on the summit, Troulle. Cf. Spratt, II, 207. Also graves at Agios Georgios to the N., seen by the writer, 1935.
SELLI	Extensive settlement with good walling at Agromouloi, seen by the writer, 1935.
SISARKHA. . . .	Small fort at Santiri, seen by the writer, 1935.
SKOUPHIA . . .	Vaulted building seen by the writer, 1933.
SOULIA	Poor remains at Agia Galene. Halbherr, A.J.A., 1896, 593. Lamp in the Candia Museum. Catalogue, 2161.
SYIA	Extensive ruins of the city. Spratt, II, 241. Pashley, II, 102. Savignoni, Mon. Ant., 1901, 443. Elaborate rock-cut tomb at Phournos on the Elyros road, seen by the writer, 1935.
TZIDHAIS . . .	Small fort and cistern seen by the writer, 1933.
VIZARI	Sherds and loomweight from knoll S. of the village, seen by the writer, 1935.
VLYTHIAS. . . .	Considerable deposit near the fort, also graves on the other side of the river, seen by the writer, 1935.
ZOURIDHI. . . .	Remains at Agios Georgios and Agios Ioannes to the N. of the village and at Khristos to the S., seen by the writer, 1935.

CENTRAL CRETE

(a) Excavated Sites

AMNISOS	Deposits .	Both in shrine and cave. Marinatos, Πρακτικά, 1929, 95 ; 1933, 93.
KNOSSOS	City and acropolis	B.S.A., VI, 79, 81. Villa, J.H.S., LV, 164 ; LVI, 159. Foundations of Venetian aqueduct at Spelia.
	Tombs . .	P. of M., II, 433. B.S.A., VI, 82.

TYLISSOS . . . .   Deposit . Objects described. Hazzidakis,
T.V.M., 109.

(b) Surface Finds

AGIOS GEORGIOS . Sherds on the Kastellos, seen by the writer,
1935 ; and at Stou Vasilikou, seen by the
writer, 1937.

AGIOS VLASIS . . Tombs seen by the writer, 1933.

AGIOU GEORGIOU   Vases and coins from the S. slope, seen by the
PAPOURA   writer, 1936.

AGRIANA . . . . Built tombs at Agios Ioannes. Marinatos,
'Ἀρχ. Δελτ., IX, 13.

APANO ASITAIS . . Glass bottle in the Candia Museum. Catalogue, 136.

ARKHANAIS . . . Marble head in the Candia Museum. Catalogue, 217.

AVDHOU . . . . Silver ring from Tsape Metokhi in the Candia
Museum. Catalogue, 249. Sherds at Platia
Strata, seen by the writer, 1935.

DIA . . . . . Many sherds by Agia Pelagia bay and a very
extensive site all over the top of the island.

EMPAROS . . . . Extensive settlement. Halbherr, A.J.A., 1901,
281.

HERAKLEION . . . Considerable remains. Tombs. Xanthoudides, 'Ἀρχ. Δελτ., II, Παρ. 23. Remains
below the Museum. A.J.A., XL, 371 ff.

KAMINAKI . . . Tomb at τὰ Κοντσουνάρια settlement, walls,
sherds, aqueduct at Magatzedhais, seen by
the writer, 1935.

KARAVADHA . . . Boundary stone seen by the writer, 1936.

KASTELLI   Walls and sherds seen by Miss Money-Coutts
MALEVYZIOU   and Miss Eccles, 1934. B.S.A., XXXIII,
92.

KATHAROS . . . Sherds scattered over a large area by the spring
at the SE. corner of the plain, seen by the
writer, 1936.

KEPHALA . . . . Settlement and cemetery on the NW. side of
the hill, seen by the writer, 1936.

KERASA . . . . Coins and sherds from the fields, seen by the
writer, 1936.

KHERSONESOS . . Considerable remains of the public buildings
of the town. Cf. Spratt, I, 105. Xanthou-
dides,'Ἀρχ. Δελτ., IV, Παρ. i, 30. Marinatos,
Arch. Anz., 1935, 245.

KROUSONAS . . . Sherds on Κούπο, seen by Miss Money-
Coutts and Miss Eccles, 1934. B.S.A.,
XXXIII, 92.

LYTTOS . . . . Extensive remains of city. Spratt, I, 94.
Taramelli, Mon. Ant., IX, 387.

MASTABA . . . . Sherds and glass fragments seen by Miss
Money-Coutts and Miss Eccles, 1934.
B.S.A., XXXIII, 91.

MEGALOS POTAMOS or VOUNOS	Sherds seen by the writer, 1936. There are said to be walls below the surface.
MOKHOS	Tombs at Mouri, seen by the writer, 1935.
ORNIAS	Sherds seen by the writer, 1937.
STOU PARTHENI TO METOKHI	Sherds below the car road, seen by the writer, 1934. *B.S.A.*, XXXIII, 84.
POTAMIAIS . . .	Remains from Khalikias in the Candia Museum. *Catalogue*, 8990–2.
PSYKHRO . . .	Lamps in the upper grotto. Hogarth, *B.S.A.*, VI, 94. Sherds and walls at Skallia and στὸ Σταυρί, NW. of the village, seen by the writer, 1935–6.
RHAUKOS . . .	Many sherds to the NW. of the village, seen by Miss Money-Coutts and Miss Eccles, 1934. *B.S.A.*, XXXIII, 91.
ROUSSANOS . . .	The earliest sherds found in conjunction with walls which look earlier, seen by the writer, 1936. Cf. Evans, *Diary*, 1898.
SKHINEAS. . . .	Sherds on Koprana, seen by the writer, 1937.
THRAPSANOS . . .	Silver gilt ring in the Candia Museum. *Catalogue*, 442.

SOUTH CRETE

(a) Excavated Sites

AGIA TRIADHA . .	Villa. . .	*Rend. Linc.*, 1905, 378.
GORTYNA. . . .	City . .	General Topography : Spratt, II, 26. Thenon, *Rev. Arch.*, XVIII, 126. Taramelli, *A.J.A.*, 1902, 101. Excavations : Temple of Apollo, *Mon. Ant.*, I, 8 ; III, 1 ; XVIII, 181. Odeum, Praetorium, &c., *Annuario*, I, 373 ; II, 306 ; VIII, 35. *Boll.. d'Arte*, 1936, 360. Circus. Ibid., 364.
LEBENA	Temple, baths and fountain	Halbherr and Piginoni, *Rend. Linc.*, 1901, 291. Cf. Xanthoudides *Panathenaia*, 1911. Marinatos, *Ἀρχ. Δελτ.*, IX, Παρ. 13.
PHAISTOS. . . .	Deposit .	Above the palace. *Mon. Ant.*, XII, 21.

(b) Surface Finds

AGIA PHOTIA. . .	A number of large cisterns. Xanthoudides, *Ἀρχ. Δελτ.*, II, 24.
AGIO SIDHERO . .	Sherds and tradition of walls, seen by the writer, 1934. *B.S.A.*, XXXIII, 88.

AGIOS THOMAS . . Contents of a grave. Marinatos, *Arch. Anz.*, 1933, 314.

ANTISKARI . . . Bronze coin in the Candia Museum.

APESOKARI . . . Massive walls at Ellenika, seen by the writer, 1934. *B.S.A.*, XXXIII, 88.

ARVI . . . . . Sherds and bricks on knoll of Komitas, walls, sherds, and coins E. of the river, seen by the writer, 1935.

BIENNOS . . . . Lamps and sherds from the village of Vianos and just S. of it, seen by the writer, 1935.

GOULOPHARANGO GORGE Sherds and walls at Agios Savas, seen by the writer, 1934. *B.S.A.*, XXXIII, 87.

INATOS . . . . Aqueduct and other walls. Spratt, I, 304, 337. Pottery: Mariani, *Mon. Ant.*, VI, 177. Inscriptions: Halbherr, *A.J.A.*, 1896, 564.

KALYVIANA . . . Sherds in a well. *Rend. Linc.*, 1902, 318.

KASTELL BELVEDERE . Sherds and traces of walls in the SE. corner, seen by the writer, 1936.

KASTELLIANA. . . Grave stele. Mariani, *Mon. Ant.*, VI, 180, probably from Kastell Belvedere.

KERATOS . . . . Sherds on the summit, seen by R. W. Hutchinson, 1935.

STOU KOUSE . . . Sherds W. of the village, seen by the writer, 1934. *B.S.A.*, XXXIII, 90. Graves, *B.C.H.*, 1925, 473.

LASEIA . . . . Sherds and traces of walls. Causeway to Traphos island. Cf. Spratt, II, 7. Grave relief. *J.H.S.*, LII, 255.

STA LOUTRA . . . Cisterns and aqueduct. *Arch. Anz.*, 1916, 156.

MAKRY LIVADHI . Walls and sherds of small settlement. Xanthoudides, ᾿Αρχ. Δελτ., IV, Παρ. 10.

METALLON . . . Town site. Spratt, II, 21. Tombs. *Rend. Linc.*, 1907, 299.

PANAGIA . . . . Burial to the W. of the village and coins, seen by the writer, 1934. *B.S.A.*, XXXIII, 86.

PHOURNOPHARANGO. Coins seen by the writer, 1934. *B.S.A.*, XXXIII, 86.

PLATANOS . . . Sherds at Σιδηρογούρνα. Xanthoudides, ᾿Αρχ. Δελτ., II, Παρ. 25.

PRAITORIA . . . Pithos burials by the school NW. of the village, seen by the writer, 1934. *B.S.A.*, XXXIII, 85.

PRIANSOS. . . . Many walls both at the mouth and in the gorge. Cf. Spratt, I, 340. Also tombstone and glass from Larnaki promontory to the E., seen by the writer, 1936.

PRINIAS . . . . Graves and traces of walls at Peze in Katokampos, seen by the writer, 1936.

PYLOROS . . . . Sherds cover a considerable area at Lagarotopos and Ragavas, W. of Plora, seen by the writer, 1934. *B.S.A.*, XXXIII, 88.

PYRANTHOS	Sherds at Trokhalais, seen by the writer, 1934. *B.S.A.*, XXXIII, 86. Cf. Svoronos, 302, note. Inscription from Βλαχιανῶ, Xanthoudides, ᾿Αϱχ. Δελτ., II, Παϱ. 24.
RHYTION	Extensive surface deposit of sherds on the Kephala. Evans, *Diary*, 2/4/94. Cf. writer, *B.S.A.*, XXXIII, 86.
SOKARA	Grave. Marinatos, *Arch. Anz.*, 1933, 314.
STERNAIS	Cistern and aqueduct W. of the village. *Arch. Anz.*, 1916, 156.
VAGIONIA	Rectangular building and sherds at Ellenika, cisterns and wells at Niphadhi, seen by the writer, 1937.
STES VAKIOTES TEN KEPHALAN	Coins. Gold ring in the Candia Museum. *Catalogue* 586. Glass bottle, ibid., 149.
VASILIKE	A few sherds at Girokephala, base of a funeral stela from Rogalotopos, seen by the writer, 1934. *B.S.A.*, XXXIII, 87. Relief of Pan and Muses in the Candia Museum. *Catalogue* 206.
ZARO	Silver imperial coin in the Candia Museum.

EAST CRETE

(a) Excavated Sites

HIERAPYTNA	City	See previous periods. Grave and reliefs published by Marinatos. *J.H.S.*, 1932, 255. *Arch. Anz.*, 1933, 314.
KAVOUSI	Tomb	Walled tomb excavated by Marinatos. *A.J.A.*, XL, 371 ff.
MOKHLOS	Town	On the mainland. Seager, *A.J.A.*, XIII, 274.
	Fort	On the summit of the island. Seager, *Mochlos*.

(b) Surface Finds

AGIA PHOTIA	A site on the shore below the village, seen by the writer, 1934. *B.S.A.*, XXXIII, 100.
AMPELOS	Sherds on Pharmakokephalo, seen by the writer, 1934. *B.S.A.*, XXXIII, 100.
KALAMAFKA	Lamp and sherds at Sellia, seen by the writer, 1935.
KAMARI	Above Kritsa, coins and walls—also called Ellenika. *B.C.H.*, XXV, 282.
KAVOUSI	Graves at Khordhakia W. of the village. Hall, *Trans. Penn. Univ.*, I, 15. Lime kiln and cistern. Boyd, *A.J.A.*, 1901, 156. Houses at Kephalolimnos. Ibid.
LEUKE	Spratt, I, 241, saw remains of town at the NW end of Kouphonisi.

MAKRYGIALOS . . Large settlement seen by the writer, 1934. *B.S.A.*, XXXIII, 100.

MALLA . . . . Sherds and walls at Khlia, seen by the writer, 1935.

MILETOS . . . . The chief surface remains on the whole site. Cf. Spratt, I, 114. Tomb inscriptions from Armi. Xanthoudides, ᾿Αϱχ. Δελτ., IV, Παϱ. 10.

MYRTON . . . . Harbour town. *Arch. Anz.*, 1916, 150. Cf. Xanthoudides, ᾿Αϱχ. Δελτ., II, Παϱ. 25.

NAXOS . . . . Coins and sherds seen by the writer, 1935, on Oxa.

NISI . . . . . Large deposit of sherds all over the promontory. Hall, *Vrokastro*, 79.

OLEROS . . . . Sherds and walls at Myrtokoudhia, Stravolimni, and Kouri. Cf. Halbherr, quoted by Evans, *Diary*, 1896. *J.H.S.*, XIV, 277. Mariani, *Mon. Ant.*, VI, 207.

OLOUS . . . . Walls and aqueduct. Spratt, I, 134, re-used capital close to the isthmus, seen by the writer, 1936.

PATARAKI METOKHI . 1½ hr. above Kritsa. Sherds and inscription 1st cent. B.C. *B.C.H.*, XXV, 282.

PETRAS . . . . Vases from the Kephala. Xanthoudides, ᾿Αϱχ. Δελτ., IV, Παϱ. ii, 23.

PISKOKEPHALI . . Seal stones in the Candia Museum. *Catalogue*, 1447–8.

PRINIATIKOS PYRGOS Sherds. Hall, *Vrokastro*, 79.

ROUKKAKA . . . Good deposit of sherds in a field S. of the village, seen by the writer, 1934. *B.S.A.*, XXXIII, 95.

SITIA . . . . . Sherds on the beach to the E., seen by the writer, 1934. *B.S.A.*, XXXIII, 97.

TAPIS . . . . Burials at Kamarais, seen by the writer, 1936.

THOLOS . . . . Large building and graves. *A.J.A.*, 1901, 155.

TOURLOTI . . . Sherds from Khordhakia. Bosanquet, unpublished, seen by R. W. Hutchinson, 1936.

APPENDIX TO CHAPTER VI

SITES WITH REMAINS OF UNCERTAIN DATE

POST-MINOAN

(*See Map 24*)

AGIA EIRENE . . W. of the White Mountains. Spratt, II, 181, mentions traces of Cyclopean terracing of a road up to the Omalos Plain.

AGIOS IOANNES . NW. of Aradhena. Deffner, *'Εθνική Ζωή*, 13, 6, mentions a cistern.

ARADHO . . . W. of Bobia. Small fort, with no sherds, seen by the writer, 1934. *B.S.A.*, XXXIII, 90.

ELLENIKA . . . Between Agios Nikolaos and Elounta (Olous) at Kalos Lakkos, a spot mentioned in the Olous-Lato boundary treaty, a few architectural remains. Halbherr, *Mus. It.*, II, 177; III, 655. Mariani, *Mon. Ant.*, VI, 250, suggests it may be Erannos.

KALAMYDE . . . NE. of Palaiokhora. Pashley, II, 86, 124, saw city walls on the summit of a ridge near Vlythias.

KALERGI . . . N. of Kastelli Pedhiadhos. A small fort on the summit of Mt. Prophetes Elias, seen by the writer, 1934. *B.S.A.*, XXXIII, 81.

KALOI LIMENES . Between ' Fair Havens ' and Odhigitria Monastery, a beehive-shaped cave called Vrontospilio, with rock-cut steps and an artificial niche in front ; no sherds seen by the writer, 1932, 1936.

KAMPIA . . . Four kilometres E. of Aradhena. Deffner, *'Εθνική Ζωή* 13, 6, mentions remains.

KAROUMPAIS . . Between Zakros and Palaikastro. Spratt I, 234, saw ruins of what he took to be an Hellenic fort (cf., however, Minoan remains of uncertain date, p. 298). Halbherr, *Antiquary*, 1892, 153, identifies name with *Κάρυμαι*, a place in the territory of Itanos. Cf. Blass, 5060.

377

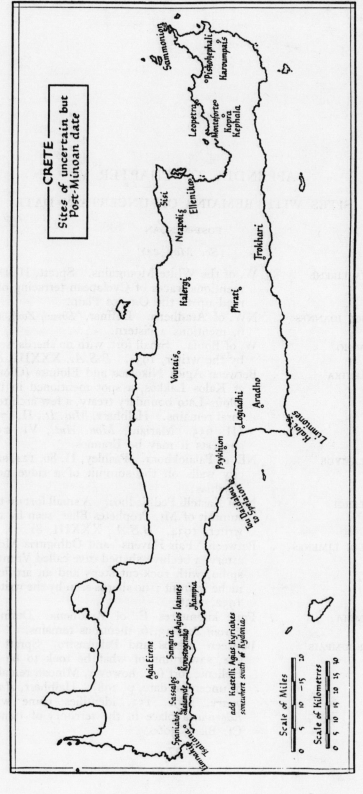

CRETE

Sites of uncertain but
Post-Minoan date

Sammonion
Piskohephali
Karoumpais

Leopetra
Montefortso
Kopra
Kephala

Sisi
Neapoiiġ
Ellenikạ

Kalergi

Phrari

Trokhari

Voutais

Aradho

Logiadhi

Kelos:
L'imunions

Psykhton

Tou Daidalou
to Spelaion

Kampia

Agios Ioannes
Koustogyrako
Samaria

Agia Eirene

Sassalọs
Halawide

Spaniakos

Halali...num...

Agios Kyriakes
Kastelli
somewhere south of Kydonia

add Kastelli Agias Kyriakes
somewhere south of Kydonia

Scale of Miles
0   5   10   -15   20

Scale of Kilometres
0   5   10   15   20   40

MAP 24

KASTELLI AGIAS KYRIAKES . SW. of Khania. The writer heard of ruins here, 1935.

KOPRA KEPHALA . W. of Praisos. Spratt, I, 167, saw cisterns and other remains, and thought it was the temple of Diktaian Zeus (see Palaikastro). He heard the natives call the surrounding hills Rikte. Bursian, II, 571, suggests the ruins are those of Dragmos. Cf. Halbherr, *Antiquary*, 1892, 213.

KROUSTOGERAKO . N. of Souia. The writer heard of remains on the Kastellos above in 1935.

LEOPETRA . . . On the coast W. of Sitia. Spratt, I, 158, describes insignificant ruins and suggests it was the ancient Asos.

LIMNAKI . . . W. of Palaiokhora. Spratt, II, 237, suggests it may have been Biennon. Savignoni, *Mon. Ant.*, 1901, 467, describes the remains.

LOGIADHI . . . W. of Liliana. *Rend. Linc.*, 1902, 318, mentions test-pits with a burnt layer suggesting cremation.

MONTEFORTE . . SW. of Sitia. Faulkner, *Mus. Class. Ant.*, II, 263, and Pashley on his map, place the ancient Allaria here.

NEAPOLIS . . . Vase in the Candia Museum, *Catalogue*, 3263, from Vagia or Pateteri (said to be from near Kainourio Khorio, presumably Neapolis).

PHRATI . . . Burial in coffin at Dryari. Levi, *Annuario*, X–XII, 388.

PISKOKEPHALI . . S. of Sitia. Bosanquet notes brick ruins at Ellenika on a hill opposite.

PSYKHION . . . Traditionally W. of Soulia, i.e. Agia Galene. Pashley, I, 304, heard of ruins at Kastri, S. of Melampais. A cave on Kavo Melissa is locally known as the Cave of Daidalos. It contains no ancient remains. There is a silver stater of Gortyna from here in the Candia Museum. The writer heard of ruins at Treis Petrais to the W.

SAMARIA . . . In the Agia Roumeli Gorge. Pashley, II, 85, 268, saw ancient city of 'Ellenais' an hour above the village. Rough walls and cisterns.

SAMMONION . . On Kavo Sidhero (Cape St. Isodore) ruins seen by Spratt, I, 189. Halbherr, *Antiquary*, 1891, 202. Mariani, *Mon. Ant.*, VI, 317, inscriptions at τὸ Βερνεγάδι.

SASSALOS . . . Near Agios Kirkos. The writer heard of remains here in 1935.

SPANIAKOS . . . Near Vlythias. Pashley, II, 119, mentions towers and a vaulted chamber. Cf. Savignoni, *Mon. Ant.*, 1901, 391.

SISI . . . . Traces of a small sanctuary at Kremasma to the E. Heads of clay animals. *B.C.H.*, 1929, 529.

TROKHARI . . . An hour below Keratos, near the sea. Stone whorl like Ionic volute, seen by the writer, 1935. Sherds said to be found in the fields.

TSALIANA . . . N. of Palaiokhora. .Pashley, II, 84, heard of remains on a hill a little to the SW.

VOUTAIS . . . SW. of Candia. Vases in the Candia Museum, *Catalogue*, 890, 3804–7, from Mesa Armi.

SELECT BIBLIOGRAPHY

I. PHYSICAL ASPECTS

V. Raulin, *Description Physique de l'Isle de Crète*, 1869
L. Khalikiopoulos, *Sitia*, 1903
T. A. B. Spratt, *Travels and Researches in Crete*, 1865
A. Trevor Battye, *Camping in Crete*, 1913
N. *Καλεμενόπουλος, Κρητικά*, 1894

II. TOPOGRAPHY

R. Pashley, *Travels in Crete*, 1837
T. A. B. Spratt, *Travels and Researches in Crete*, 1865
A. J. Evans, *Academy*, 1896 ; *B.S.A.*, II ; *Palace of Minos*, II, 1928
F. Halbherr, *Antiquary*, 1891, 1892 ; *A.J.A.*, 1896, 1897, 1901
L. Savignoni, *Mon. Ant.*, XI
A. Taramelli, *A.J.A.*, 1902 ; *Mon. Ant.*, IX
L. Mariani, *Mon. Ant.*, VI
E. Eccles, M. Money-Coutts, J. D. S. Pendlebury, *B.S.A.*, XXXIII
R. Thenon, *Rev. Arch.*, XIV–XVII

III. ANTHROPOLOGY

G. Sergi, *A.J.A.*, 1901
C. H. Hawes, *B.S.A.*, XI, XVI
W. L. H. Duckworth, *B.S.A.*, IX : *British Association Report*, 1903, 1910, 1912
W. Boyd Dawkins, *B.S.A.*, VII
Xanthoudides, *V.T.M.*

IV. MINOAN CRETE

1. General. *Cambridge Ancient History*, I and II, relevant chapters, 1923, 1931
   H. B. and C. H. Hawes, *Crete the Forerunner of Greece*, 1916
   D. Fimmen, *Die Kretisch-Mykenische Kultur*, 2nd ed., 1924
   G. Glotz, *Aegean Civilization*, 1925
   S. Marinatos, *ὁ Ἀρχαῖος Κρητικὸς Πολιτισμός*
   H. R. Hall, *Aegean Archaeology*, 1915 ; *The Civilization of Greece in the Bronze Age*, 1928
   N. Åberg. *Bronzezeitliche und Früheisenzeitliche Chronologie*, III and IV, 1933
   Sir Arthur Evans, *The Palace of Minos*, I–IV, and Index, 1922–37
   D. Mackenzie, *Aegean Palaces*, B.S.A., XI–XIV

2. Excavations. (a) English. A. J. Evans, *Palace of Minos*;
    Archaeologia, LIX, LXV. Hogarth, Dawkins, and others,
    B.S.A., VI–XII, XXVIII, XXX. J. D. S. Pendlebury
    and others, *The Stratigraphical Museum at Knossos*,
    1933–7
    (b) American. H. B. Hawes and others, *Gournia*, 1908.
    R. B. Seager, *Mochlos*, 1912. They and others, *A.J.A.*,
    1901, 1909; *Trans. Penn. Univ.*, I–II; *Anthropological
    Publications*, III and VII
    (c) French. Chapoutier and others, *Mallia*, I and II, 1928,
    1936
    (d) Italian. Halbherr, Pernier, and others, *Festòs*, I, 1935;
    Mon. Ant., IX, XII, XIII, XIV, XIX; *A.J.A.*, 1897;
    Rend. Linc., 1903/5/7; *Annuario*, VIII, XIII, XIV;
    Mem. Ist Lomb., XXI
    (e) Greek. Xanthoudides, Hazzidakis, Marinatos and others,
    Ἐφ. Ἀρχ., 1900/3/4/6/12/22; *Ἀρχ. Δελτ.*, I, III, XII;
    Πρακτικά, 1922–9; *B.S.A.*, XIX; *Tylissos Villas Min-
    oennes*, 1931; *Vaulted Tombs of Mesará*, 1929
3. Art. G. A. S. Snijder, *Kretische Kunst*, 1936
    E. J. Forsdyke, *Minoan Art*, 1929
    A. J. Evans, *Palace of Minos, passim*
4. Pottery. D. Mackenzie, *J.H.S.*, 1903, 1906
    A. J. Evans, *Palace of Minos, passim*
    E. Hall, *Trans. Penn. Univ.*, II
    E. J. Forsdyke, *Catalogue of Vases in the British Museum*, I, i,
    1927
    H. W. Pendlebury, *B.S.A.*, XXXI
    H. Frankfort, *Studies*, II, 1927
5. Architecture. A. J. Evans, *Palace of Minos, passim*
    I. Noack, *Ovalhaus und Palast*
    D. Mackenzie, *B.S.A.*, XI–XIV
    Cf. also A. J. B. Wace and others, *B.S.A.*, XXIV, XXV
6. Seals. A. J. Evans, *Cretan Pictographs* (*J.H.S.*, 1894); *Further
    Discoveries* (*J.H.S.*, 1897); *Palace of Minos, passim*
    Matz, *Frühkretische Siegel*, 1928
    Levi, *Annuario*, VIII
    Xanthoudides, *Ἐφ. Ἀρχ.*, 1907 and 1913
7. Script. A. J. Evans, *Scripta Minoa*, I, 1909; *Palace of Minos,
    passim*
    F. Chapoutier, *Mallia, Ecritures*, 1930
8. Religion. A. J. Evans, *Mycenaean Tree and Pillar Worship*, 1901;
    *The Earlier Religion of Greece in the Light of Cretan Dis-
    coveries*, 1931; *The Ring of Nestor*, 1925; *Palace of
    Minos, passim*
    M. Nilsson, *Minoan-Mycenaean Religion*, 1927
9. Foreign Relations. A. J. Evans, *Palace of Minos, passim*
    H. R. Hall, *J.H.S.*, XXV; *B.S.A.*, VIII, XVI
    J. D. S. Pendlebury, *Aegyptiaca*, 1930; *J.E.A.*, XVI
    H. Frankfort, in *The Mural Painting of el-Amarneh*, 1929
    G. D. Wainwright, *Liv. Ann.*, VI; *J.E.A.*, XVII; *J.H.S.*, LI
    D. Fimmen, *Die Kretisch-Mykenische Kultur*, 1924

V. POST-MINOAN CRETE

1. Excavations. (*a*) English. Bosanquet and others in *B.S.A.*, VI, VIII, X, XVI, XXIX

   (*b*) French. Demargne and others in *B.C.H.*, XXV, XXVII, XLIX, LI

   (*c*) Italian. Halbherr and others, *A.J.A.*, 1897, 1902, 1934; *Mon. Ant.*, I, III, XII, XVIII; *Annuario*, I, II, VIII, X–XII; *Boll. d'Art.*, I, II, 1936; *Rend. Linc.*, 1901, 1907

   (*d*) Greek. Marinatos in *B.C.H.*, LX

   (*e*) American. *A.J.A.*, 1901, 1909; *Trans. Penn. Univ.*, III

2. Art. (*a*) Pottery. H. G. G. Payne in *B.S.A.*, XXIX; J. P. Droop, *B.S.A.*, XII; M. Hartley, *B.S.A.*, XXXI; S Xanthoudides, *B.S.A.*, XII; D. Levi, *Annuario*, X–XII

   (*b*) Architecture. L. Pernier, *A.J.A.*, 1934; S. Marinatos, *B.C.H.*, LX

   (*c*) Bronzes. E. Kunze, *Kretische Bronzereliefs*, 1934

   (*d*) Sculpture and terracottas. S. Benton, *J.H.S.*, 1937; L. Pernier, *Annuario*, II; R. J. H. Jenkins, *Dedalica*, 1937; F. Halbherr, *A.J.A.*, 1901; E. Dohan, *Metropolitan Museum Studies*, III, 2; E. Kunze, *Ath. Mitt.*, 60/61

   (*e*) Numismatics. J. Svoronos, *Numismatique de la Crète Ancienne*, 1890; W. Wroth, *British Museum Catalogue of Coins, Crete and the Aegean Islands*, 1886; B. Head, *Historia Nummorum*, 2nd ed., 1911

   (*f*) Inscriptions. M. Guarducci, *Inscriptiones Creticae*, I, 1935

ADDENDA

WEST CRETE

AGIA GALENE . . Bronzes found in the sea ; Roman. *Κρητικὲς Σϑλίδες*, II.

ASPROUKIA . . . In Apokorona. Cave ; L.M.III—Roman. Ibid.

KANTANOS . . . By modern town. Praetorium (?) ; Roman. Ibid.

KYDONIA . . . . Mosaic floor ; Hellenistic. Ibid.

LAPPA . . . . Statuette of a woman ; Classical. *J.H.S.*, LVII, 139

SELI KISAMOU . . Hypaethral shrine ; L.M.III. House ; Hellenic. *Κρητ. Σελ.*, II.

CENTRAL CRETE

AMNISOS . . . . Deposit. Minoan. Head with inlaid eyes ; Archaic. Temple ; Greek. *J.H.S.*, LVII, 138.

DREROS . . . . Architectural and other finds ; Archaic–Roman. *B.C.H.*, LXI, 5. *J.H.S.*, LVII, 140.

KASTELLI PEDHIADHOS Tombs ; Roman. *Κρητ. Σελ.*, II.

KNOSSOS . . . . Stratum ; E.M. Pavement with Causeways, W. of Palace ; M.M.I Deposit. Protogeometric and Roman. Walls ; M.M.III–Archaic. Late red figure, Hellenistic, Roman. Kiln ; Classical. Cistern ; Hellenistic. *J.H.S.*, LVII, 137. Well ; Hellenistic. Walling of aqueduct ; Roman. Vases from near Teke ; Geometric.

KOMAIS . . . . Deposit ; Greco-Roman. *Κρητ. Σελ.*, II.

KOUNAVOI . . . Terra-cotta plaques from Skenderi. Greco-Roman. Ibid.

MALLIA . . . . Gold-hilted sword with figure of acrobat ; M.M.IIIb–L.M.Ia. Large stone with hieroglyphs. Ibid., 140.

MESA LAKONIA . . Stone axe ; Neolithic. Seen by writer 1938.

MESA LASITHI . . At Armi ; Protogeometric sherds. At Agioi Apostoloi, good site ; M.M.III, little Archaic. Katellos, traces of walls. Panagin Kroustallenia, pithos burials ; Archaic. Vigla, fort ; M.M.III. Patellais, pithoi and walls ; Archaic. Seen by the writer, 1938.

OLOUS . . . . Papoura, larnax burials ; L.M.III. Trakhili, ditto. Agia Triadha and Lagou, foundations ; L.M.III—Protogeometric. Exo Poros, remains of uncertain date. Ellenika, temple ; Geometric–Classical. *Κρητ. Σελ.*, II.

PHANEROMENE . . Cave near Avdhou ; L.M.III–Roman. Ibid. (Cf. *J.H.S.*, LVII., 139.)

PHOIN'KIA . . . Stou Steriakou to Metokhi, chamber tombs ; L.M.III. Ibid.

PINAKIANO . . . Kardhamoutsa, bronze double axe ; M.M.III. Walls and sherds ; Archaic. Seen by writer 1938.

TZERMIADHA . . Kastellos, Karphi, Papoura, Kerasa, &c. Neolithic–Hellenistic. Cf. *J.H.S.*, LVII, 140.

VATHEIA . . . . Circular tomb ; Geometric. *Κρητ. Σελ.*, II.

ZAGOURIANOI . . Walls ; Roman. Ibid.

EAST CRETE

AGIOS IOANNES . . Between here and Skhinokapsala. Traces of road seen by writer 1938 ; Roman.

ITANOS . . . . Inscribed dolphin in Fitzwilliam Museum ; Archaic.

KASTRI . . . . Between Oreino and Stavrokhori, large site seen by writer 1938 ; Protogeometric.

KHAMETOULO . . Sto Dokhi. Sherds and walls seen by writer 1938 ; M.M.III, L.M.I, L.M.III, Roman.

LASTROS . . . . At Kynegospilios. Site seen by writer 1938 ; Archaic.

LEOPETRO . . . Foundations and sherds seen by writer 1938 ; Classical–Roman.

OREINO . . . . Apano Ellenika, foundations and sherds seen by writer 1938 ; Protogeometric. ' The Dragon's Gate ', between here and Stavrokhori, fort seen by writer 1938 ; L.M.

SITANOS . . . . Sta Katalemata, foundations seen by writer 1938 ; L.M.

SITIA . . . . . Pyxis of green schist (?) ; E.M.III. *J.H.S.*, LVII, 139.

ZAKROS . . . . At Skinarais Metokhi, fort seen by the writer 1938 ; L.M. Wall across mouth of second gorge north of Katsounaki. ? date.

Index

Note.—Sites only occurring in the lists after each period or in the lists of routes (page 20 ff.) are not given. The letter *R.* denotes that a site is mentioned only in connexion with a route

PLATE I

2. THE LADHA CLIFFS, WEST OF SPHAKIA

1. THE AGIA ROUMELI GORGE

PLATE II

1. THE WHITE MOUNTAINS, XYLOSKALA

PLATE II

2. MOUNT IDA FROM PHAISTOS

3. APHENDES KAVOUSI FROM PAKHYAMMOS

PLATE III

1. MOUNT DIKTE AND THE PLAIN OF LASITHI

2. NIDHA PLAIN FROM THE IDAEAN CAVE

PLATE III

3. THE PLAIN OF ANOPOLIS AND THE WHITE MOUNTAINS

4. THE GORGE OF PATSOS

PLATE IV

1. EAST COAST AT EREMOPOLIS (ITANOS)

2. KAVALLOI ISLANDS

PLATE IV

3. GULF OF MIRABELLO FROM KAVOUSI

4. PSEIRA ISLAND

PLATE V

1. TRAPEZA : NEOLITHIC CAVE

2. PLATANOS : EARLY MINOAN

PLATE V

3. MOKHLOS : EARLY TO LATE MINOAN

4. GOURNIA : LATE MINOAN

PLATE VI

2. ELLENIKA ZAKROU

1. KAVOUSI

PROTOGEOMETRIC AND GEOMETRIC SITES

PLATE VI

3. KOURTAIS. PROTOGEOMETRIC

PLATE VII

1. THE CITADEL OF LATO

2. KASTELL BELVEDERE (STELAI ?)
ARCHAIC AND CLASSICAL SITES

PLATE VII

3. PRAISOS

4. SYBRITA

ARCHAIC AND CLASSICAL SITES

PLATE VIII

1. WALLS OF KASTERIOTES (ARKADIA). CLASSICAL

2. AGIOS KIRKOS (LISSOS). ROMAN

PLATE VIII

3. TES VAKIOTES E KEPHALA

4. XEROKAMPOS (AMPELOS)

CLASSICAL TO ROMAN SITES

PLATE IX

1. EARLY MINOAN I INCISED WARE

2. EARLY MINOAN I PAINTED WARE

PLATE X

1. EARLY MINOAN II PAINTED AND MONOCHROME WARE

2. EARLY MINOAN II PAINTED AND MOTTLED WARE

3. EARLY MINOAN II AND III AND MIDDLE MINOAN I STONE VASES

PLATE XI

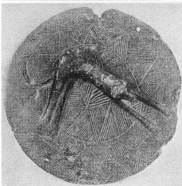

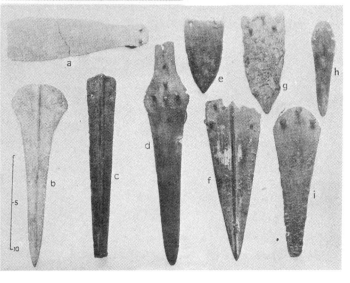

1. EARLY MINOAN II AND
   III STONE VASES

2. EARLY MINOAN II
   STONE LID

3. EARLY MINOAN II AND
   III AND MIDDLE MINOAN
   I DAGGERS

PLATE XII

1. EARLY MINOAN II AND III FIGURINES

3. EARLY MINOAN II VASE

2. EARLY MINOAN II AND III FIGURINES

PLATE XIII

2. EARLY MINOAN III SEAL AND FOREIGN HEAD

1. EARLY MINOAN II GOLD WORK

3. EARLY MINOAN III POTTERY

4. EARLY MINOAN III POTTERY

PLATE XIV

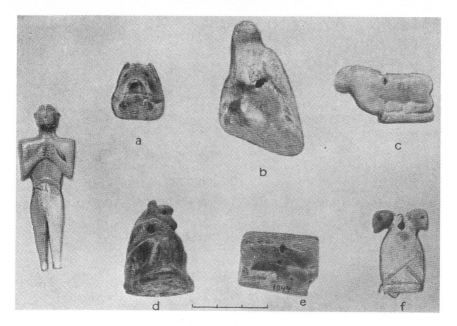

1. EARLY MINOAN III SEALS. MIDDLE MINOAN I STATUETTE

2. MIDDLE MINOAN Ia POTTERY FROM KNOSSOS

PLATE XV

1. EARLY MINOAN II HOUSE, VASILIKE   2. MIDDLE MINOAN Ia BASEMENT, KNOSSOS
3. WEST FACADE OF PALACE, MALLIA   4. WEST COURT, PHAISTOS

PLATE XVI

MIDDLE MINOAN I*a* BASEMENT, KNOSSOS   2.   MIDDLE MINOAN II PILLAR,
KNOSSOS

3.   WEST COURT, KNOSSOS

PLATE XVII

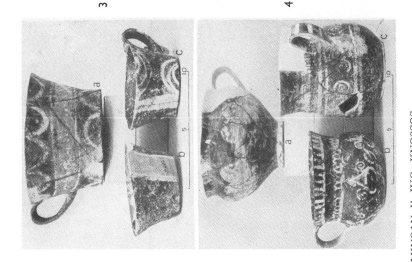

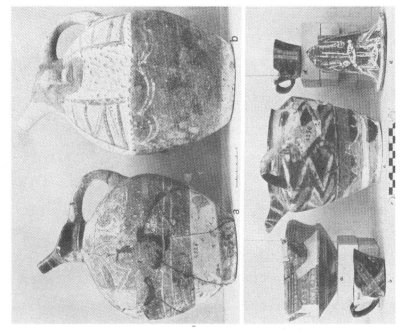

1. a, MIDDLE MINOAN Iɑ JUG; b, MIDDLE MINOAN Ib JUG, KNOSSOS
2-4. MIDDLE MINOAN Ib POTTERY, KNOSSOS

PLATE XVIII

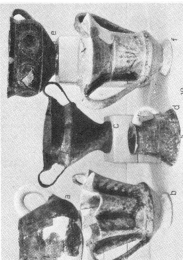

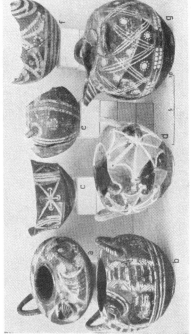

MIDDLE MINOAN I POTTERY

1. AGIA TRIADHA   2. KOUMASA AND PLATANOS

3. KAMARAIS CAVE   4. AGIA PHOTIA AND GOURNIA

PLATE XIX

MIDDLE MINOAN I POTTERY

1. PALAIKASTRO
2. PALAIKASTRO
3. VASILIKE AND GOURNAIS
4. PSEIRA, VASILIKE, MOKHLOS

PLATE XX

1. MIDDLE MINOAN I CLAY
FIGURINES FROM KHAMAIZI

2. MIDDLE MINOAN I CLAY
FIGURINES FROM PETSOPHAS

3. MESOPOTAMIAN STONE HEAD
FROM KNOSSOS

4. EGYPTIAN STATUE, XIITH
DYNASTY, FROM KNOSSOS

PLATE XXI

1. FAIENCE PLAQUES IN SHAPE OF HOUSES FROM THE 'TOWN MOSAIC,' KNOS-SOS. MIDDLE MINOAN II

2. TOMB GROUP FROM ABYDOS, XIITH DYNASTY, CONTAINING MIDDLE MINOAN II VASE

PLATE XXII

1. PORTI AND PALAIKASTRO

3. KAMARAIS, PHAISTOS AND KNOSSOS

4. PHAISTOS

2. PHAISTOS

MIDDLE MINOAN II POTTERY

PLATE XXIII

1. THEATRAL AREA, ETC., KNOSSOS

2. GRAND STAIRWAY, KNOSSOS

PLATE XXIV

1. NORTH LUSTRAL AREA, KNOSSO

2. NORTH ENTRANCE, KNOSSOS   3. WEST MAGAZINES, KNOSSOS

PLATE XXV

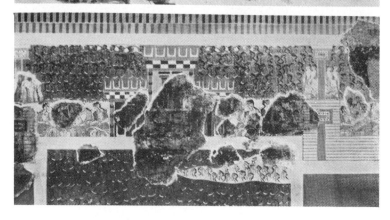

1. 'SAFFRON GATHERER' FRESCO, KNOSSOS
2. DOLPHIN FRESCO, KNOSSOS
3. MINIATURE FRESCO, KNOSSOS

PLATE XXVI

1

2

3

MIDDLE MINOAN III POTTERY FROM KNOSSOS

PLATE XXVII

2. *a*, MIDDLE MINOAN III*b*–LATE
MINOAN I*a* VASE, PAKHY-
AMMOS

b, MIDDLE MINOAN I VASE, PAK-
HYAMMOS

1. MIDDLE MINOAN III*b* PITHOS,
KNOSSOS

3. MIDDLE MINOAN III
STONE VASES, KNOSSOS

4. CYCLADIC VASE FROM KNOSSOS

PLATE XXVIII

1. MIDDLE MINOAN III VASES FROM
KNOSSOS
a, FAIENCE
b, CLAY. INSCRIBED INSIDE
c, CLAY. PAINTED TO IMITATE
STONE

2. FAIENCE FIGURE OF
GODDESS, KNOSSOS.
MIDDLE MINOAN III

3. MIDDLE MINOAN III FAIENCE
PLAQUES, KNOSSOS

4. INSCRIBED CLAY DISC, PHAISTOS

PLATE XXIX

1. CARAVANSERAI AND VIADUCT, KNOSSOS

2. SOUTH PROPYLAEUM, KNOSSOS

PLATE XXX

1. THRONE ROOM, KNOSSOS

2. HARBOUR TOWN PSEIRA

PLATE XXXI

1. LITTLE PALACE, KNOSSOS

2. TEMPLE TOMB KNOSSOS

PLATE XXXII

1. PAINTED RELIEF OF THE PRIEST KING, KNOSSOS

2. FRESCO FROM AGIA TRIADHA

PLATE XXXIII

1. LATE MINOAN I*a* VASE, AGIA TRIADHA

2. LATE MINOAN I*a* POLYCHROME VASE ISOPATA

3. LATE MINOAN I*a* JAR, PSEIRA

4. LATE MINOAN I*a* JAR, KNOSSOS

PLATE XXXIV

1. GOURNIA

2. PALAIKASTRO   3. PALAIKASTRO

LATE MINOAN I*b* POTTERY

PLATE XXXV

LATE MINOAN II POTTERY FROM KNOSSOS

PLATE XXXVI

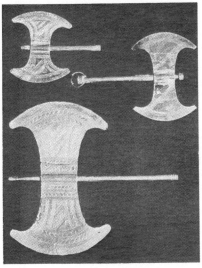

1. LATE MINOAN I AND II SWORDS, ZAPHER PAPOURA
2. LATE MINOAN I BRONZE VASES, KNOSSOS
3. GOLD VOTIVE AXES. LATE MINOAN I–II, ARKALOKHORI
4. LATE MINOAN Ia JEWELLERY KNOSSOS

PLATE XXXVII

1. BOXER VASE   2. CHIEFTAIN VASE

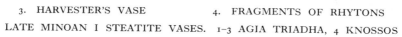

3. HARVESTER'S VASE   4. FRAGMENTS OF RHYTONS

LATE MINOAN I STEATITE VASES. 1-3 AGIA TRIADHA, 4 KNOSSOS

PLATE XXXVIII

1. STONE VASES FROM KNOSSOS. LATE MINOAN I

2. STONE LAMPS FROM PSEIRA.
LATE MINOAN I

3. STONE LAMP, KNOSSOS. LATE
MINOAN I

PLATE XXXIX

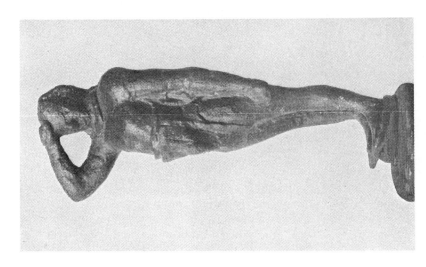

2. BRONZE STATUETTE FROM TYLISSOS.
LATE MINOAN I ($\frac{1}{2}$)

1. IVORY STATUETTE, KNOSSOS. LATE
MINOAN I ($\frac{1}{2}$)

PLATE XL

1 *and* 2. LATE MINOAN I*b* VASES FROM EGYPT
3. LATE MINOAN III VASES FROM KNOSSOS
4. LATE MINOAN III SARCOPHAGUS FROM GOURNIA

PLATE XLI

I   2

PROTOGEOMETRIC STATUETTES IN CLAY. KARPHI

3. PROTOGEOMETRIC CLAY
HEAD, KALOKHORIO

4. GEOMETRIC CLAY
HEAD, VROKASTRO

PLATE XLII

1. VASE FROM PROTOGEOMETRIC
TOMB, KNOSSOS

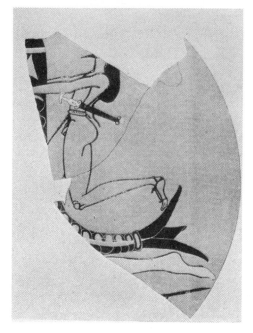

2. ARCHAIC PINAX FROM PRAISOS

3. HELLENISTIC VASES FROM KNOSSOS

PLATE XLIII

1. ARCHAIC TERRACOTTA SIMA FROM PALAIKASTRO

2. ARCHAIC STATUE FROM ELEUTHERNA

3. FIFTH CENTURY GRAVE STELA FROM AGIA PELAGIA